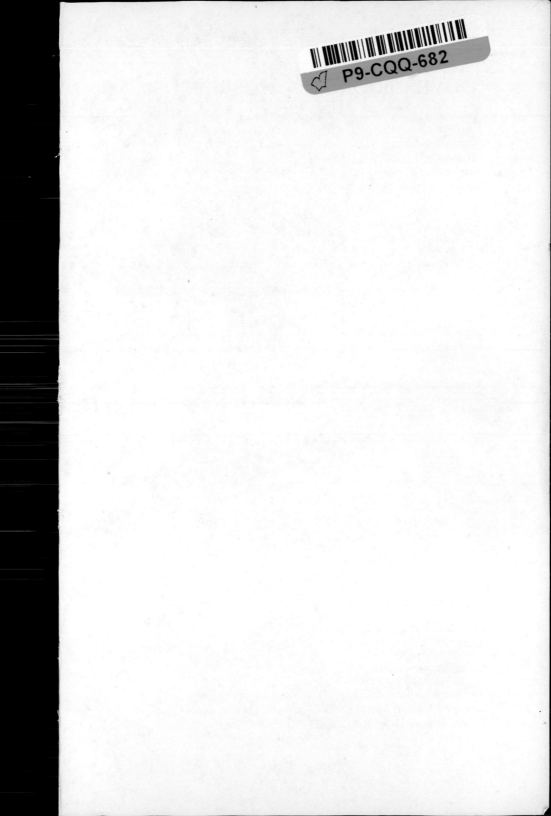

J. S. BACH

ALBERT SCHWEITZER

ENGLISH TRANSLATION BY
ERNEST NEWMAN

In Two Volumes
VOLUME II

Dover Publications, Inc., New York

This Dover edtion, first published in 1966, is an unabridged and unaltered republication of the work originally published by Breitkopf and Härtel in 1911.

International Standard Book Number: 0-486-21632-2
Library of Congress Catalog Card Number: 66-20414

Manufactured in the United States of America
Dover Publications, Inc.
180 Varick Street
New York, N. Y. 10014

CONTENTS.

Volume II.

CHAPTER XIX.

BACH AND AESTHETICS.

We argue about absolute music, tone-painting, programme music and tone-language as about actual fundamental problems, and think it a matter for historians only that tendencies towards tone-painting, programme music, or avowed musical "narration" were noticeable in Italian, German and French music as early as the seventeenth and eighteenth centuries. However primitive the pictorial and poetic music of the two or three generations before Bach may have been, in respect of their means and possibilities of expression, we can see in it the same instincts and pretensions as in the most modern and most subtilised programme music of a Liszt or a Strauss.

This old art, however, was not wholly primitive. It may be possible to regard Froberger, Kuhnau and the composers of the Italian and French character-pieces as simply naïve painters in music, who overstepped the bounds of pure music without realising all the bearings of what they were doing. But the composers for the Hamburg theatre knew what they wanted. Music, in their eyes, was a representation of actions, scenes, and ideas. They thought themselves capable of expressing everything in tone. Mattheson even gives recipes for the clear and correct expression of the emotions in music. In a cantata of 1744 for the eighth Sunday after Trinity, Telemann represents the false prophets in sheeps' clothing by a complete circle of fifths through all the twelve major scales*. Here the

* Jacob Adlung, *Anleitung zur musikalischen Gelahrtheit*, 2nd ed. 1783, p. 395.

symbolism is rather metaphysical. But there are many other passages in Telemann that are admirable in their pictorial purpose and achievement.

The music among which Bach grew up, whose full unfolding he was able to witness, and whose consummation he is, took for itself by preference the title of "expressive" (affektvoll) in distinction from all others, meaning to indicate thereby that its purpose was graphic characterisation and realism. Although our musical æstheticians must have known this — for the histories of music testify sufficiently to it — they made no attempt to examine the music of that epoch thoroughly and to enquire what light it might throw on the nature of the art, but took the line of sweeping aside these phenomena as merely transitory pathological perversions of pure muisc.

Bach proves himself an exponent of the "affektvoll" music of his epoch by the Capriccio — the programme-sonata on the departure of his brother. Instead of asking themselves, however, whether the same spirit cannot be detected in his later music, the æstheticians chose to regard the Capriccio as an interesting indiscretion of his youth, with which he paid his tribute to his epoch, and which we can forgive him in consideration of the "pure music" of the preludes and fugues. But they omitted to analyse the music he wrote in conjunction with poetry in the chorales, cantatas and passions, and to ask whether the pictorial tendencies of contemporary music may not be found in Bach also.

Only one of the musical æstheticians, Mosewius, had tried to comprehend Bach's art as the art of characteristic musical representation*. He had, however, no successor. His book *Johann Sebastian Bach in seinen Kirchenkantaten* (1845), although it is cited here and there, did not exercise the slightest influence on Bach research.

From the second half of the nineteenth century on-

* See ante, p. 246 ff.

wards, when the struggle over modern music began, men's views upon Bach were not so unprejudiced as those of Mosewius. It was admitted, of course, that there were some curious things in his works. Now and then it had to be admitted that the imitative or pictorial purpose was quite obvious: for instance, in the chorale "Durch Adams Fall ist ganz verderbt" (V, No. 13), where the fall of Adam is suggested by falling sevenths in the bass, or in an aria in *Hercules am Scheidewege*, where the music depicts the serpents mentioned in the text, and where there are other striking examples of the same kind. If anyone noticed such a case, he thought it his duty to represent it as quite without significance, so as not to injure the reputation Bach had achieved as a classical composer, and to save him from the suspicion of having done anything to pervert pure music into representative music. Spitta took care that no one should be misled by this or that piece of characterisation into doubting for a moment that Bach was a priest of absolute music, or should fail to get the "right conception of his art".

When he came to what seemed to him a particularly dangerous place in a cantata, he thought it as well to protect humanity, as it were, by putting a fence round it. "Ready as Bach was," he says at one point, "to sprinkle his works with picturesque figures, he did not do so as a result of fundamental principles based on a sense of the graphic power of music. Those figures are transient flashes, and their presence or absence cannot alter the value or intelligibility of the composition in its integrity. In studying Bach, when we meet with some conspicuously melodious line or some strikingly harmonious tune, that happens to coincide with an emphatic or emotional word, we are too ready to attribute to them a much closer and deeper connection than can ever have dwelt in the purpose of the composer."* This citation is typical of Spitta's

* Spitta II, 575, 576.

point of view. His analyses, — in other respects so wonderful and penetrating — fail just at the point where he should look for the inmost connection between the poetic thought and Bach's musical expression. The many striking instances of tone-painting do not impel him to enquire whether other characteristic themes and figures are not also prompted by the pictures and ideas suggested in the text, and whether Bach's *Stimmung* is not so much a generalised emotional state as one woven out of concrete musical ideas. He could not see the possibility of the text being reflected in the music as in clear running water. He wishes to guard against it being thought too characteristic. So Spitta regards the coincidence of strikingly expressive themes or figures with "characteristic or expressive words" as mostly accidental, and warns us against "attributing to them a much closer and deeper connection than can ever have dwelt in the purpose of the composer." Thus in order to prove that Bach's music was not materialistic, the most remarkable feature of his work has to be explained as a kind of musical accident. It reminds us of the famous Dutch philosopher Geulinx, whose dread of philosophical materialism was so great that he would not admit any influence of the thought and the will upon the movements of the limbs, and held that God had regulated the body and the soul like two absolutely parallel pieces of clock-work, so that the same thing would always happen at precisely the same time in the corporeal sphere and in the spiritual. Thus what seemed explicable, from the external standpoint, only by a direct connection of the two, was really the coincidence, predestined from eternity, of a mental idea and a bodily movement. In the same way Spitta's dread of musical materialism absolved him from the necessity of a careful enquiry into the connection of word and tone in Bach by a few authoritative dicta upon "the true nature of the art". With his "la question ne sera pas posée" he tries to scare off any one who would like further information as to Bach's attitude towards his texts, — a question of interest for the understanding not only of Bach's work but of the nature of music in general.

We can partly comprehend this point of view, for the architectonic and contrapuntal perfection of his works gives such deep and pure satisfaction to the mind that appreciates these purely musical qualities of them, that almost everything else that could be found in them must seem of secondary importance. In Spitta, too, there was the instinctive fear that Bach might be pressed into the service of a certain kind of modern pictorial music that was anathema to him and his adherents. He was partly influenced also by a justifiable dislike for the kind of superficial modernisation of the old music that sometimes takes the place of thorough research, and prides itself on bringing the old masters nearer to our own time.

Thus Bach's cantatas were issued, year after year, just at the time when Wagner and Berlioz were setting musicians by the ears, and no one perceived what treasures in the way of dramatic and pictorial music were hidden in the big grey volumes, and what vistas they opened out to musical æsthetics. Today it is still a reproach to our æstheticians, even the best of them, that they know nothing of the two hundred Bach cantatas and but a few of the organ chorales. The extraordinarily expressive and pictorial conception of music that these works reveal have exercised no influence whatever on the ordinarily accepted or debated theories of the nature of music.

One would have thought that the most pressing duty of æsthetics was to study these latest discoveries, searching in them for light on the basic problem of all music, — the question of the nature of thematic invention. The attraction was truly great enough, for one had only to read through five or six volumes of the cantatas to be struck, more than happens in the case of any other music, by certain recurring singularities, inner affinities, variants of the same theme, and some inexplicable bizarreries. What an enigma is offered us by the themes of the *St. Matthew Passion* alone! Think of the joyous writing in Judah's air of contrition, "Gebt mir meinen Jesum wieder", ("Give me my dear Lord beloved"); of the wild two-part flute accompaniment in the bass arioso "Ja freilich will in uns das Fleisch und Blut zum Kreuz gezwungen sein", ("Aye, surely now can flesh and blood atone"); of the shapelessness — so senseless from the musical point of view — of the theme of the aria "Können Tränen meiner Wangen nichts erlangen", ("Though in vain be all my wailing"); of the remarkable affinity between certain ariosos and the arias that follow them, — in short, of all the things that surprise the musician the more he studies the work, that become, to his sorrow, more and more inexplicable to him, and which he does not know how to perform, for the meaning of them is unknown to him, until he guesses that this music is not self-existent, but has sprung from some strong external force, that will not obey the laws of harmonious thematic structure.

Aesthetics, however, lost this chance of being, for once, directly helpful to practical art; it passed by almost unregardingly the singular problem presented by the motives of the Passions, the cantatas, and the chorale preludes, and had no perception that this classical master probably had something like a definite musical language of his own, in which ideas struggled for concrete expression. On the other hand the artists, who worked at the cantatas, had an intuition of where the key to this music was to be sought. Their practical experiences brought them many a surprising discovery. But they failed to correlate their knowledge, of which they spoke in vague terms and mostly among themselves, their chief concern being to let the works speak for themselves by bringing out correct editions of them.

We thus have a musical æsthetic in which Bach has not had his say. Statistics of the number of times his name appears in works dealing with the nature of music would leave us very disappointed. Even in so thorough a treatise as Combarieu's *Les rapports de la musique et de la poésie** Bach plays hardly any part. The French author has this excuse, that he had not a sufficiently intimate knowledge of German to enable him to fathom the Bach of the cantatas. The German æstheticians, however, go no more thoroughly into his works. This is due not only to the fact that Bach is as yet really very little known, but to the whole character of our investigations into the nature of music. Our æstheticians do not set out from the works of art themselves. They usually stop just where music begins. Schopenhauer, Lotze and Helmholtz occupy a much larger place in their studies than Bach, Mozart, Schubert, Beethoven, Berlioz and Wagner. In the æsthetic treatises that deal with painting we find a much more thorough æsthetic of the art-works than in those devoted to music. Therefore we need not wonder that musical æsthetic stands perplexed before the problems that actual music presents to it. At the end, when all the theories derived from definitions and from the physiology of sound have been properly dealt with, the real problems of music — tone-painting, descriptive music, programme music, the coöperation of music with the other arts — are polished off in a few supplementary words.

CHAPTER XX.

POETIC MUSIC AND PICTORIAL MUSIC.

The immediate impression Bach's works make upon us is of a dual kind. Their message is quite modern; but at the same time we feel that they have no kinship whatever with post-Beethovenian art. Bach's music seems to us modern in so far as it makes a strong effort to get beyond

---

* Paris, Alcan, 1894.

the natural indefiniteness of musical sound, and aims at the most thorough musical expression possible of the poem with which it is associated. Its object is pictorial, representative. It differs from modern art, however, in its manner of reproducing the poem, and the means by which it does so. There lies between Bach and Wagner not only a century and a half of time, but a whole world. The former represents a wholly different species of representative music from that of his Bayreuth champion. It is thus necessary first of all to get clear ideas as to the nature of representative music and the several varieties of it.

The problem is part of the general one of the coöperation of the arts. This is always wrongly regarded from the standpoint of one art alone. In reality it is a universal problem, and one that lies at the root of our thinking upon art in general. But we must first of all get away from the conventional verbal formulæ that here, as elsewhere, stand in the way of better knowledge.

We classify the arts according to the material they use in order to express the world around them. One who expresses himself in tones is called a musician; one who employs colours, a painter; one who uses words, a poet. This, however, is a purely external division. In reality, the material in which the artist expresses himself is a secondary matter. He is not only a painter, or only a poet, or only a musician, but all in one. Various artists have their habitation in his soul. His work is the product of their coöperation; all have a part in each one of his ideas. The distinction consists only in this, that one idea is dominated by one of these artists, another by another of them, and they always choose the language that suits them best.

It may happen that the "other artist" and the possibilities of the "other language" assume so prominent a place in their consciousness that they are at variance with themselves, not knowing which art they really ought to cultivate. It was so with Goethe, who, on his return from Wetzlar, did not know whether he should devote himself to painting or to poetry. "I wandered," he tells in his *Dichtung und Wahrheit*, "down the Lahn, free of will but fettered by my feelings, in one of those frames of mind in which the presence of dumb nature is so grateful to us. My eye, practised in detecting the pictorial and super-pictorial beauties of the landscape, revelled in the view of the tufted rocks, the sunny summits, the moist ground, the towering castles and the blue hills smiling in the distance. I wandered on the right bank of the stream that flowed along in the sunlight at some distance below me, partly hidden by thick willows. The old desire sprang up in me to be able to paint these things worthily. I chanced to have a fine pocket-knife in my left hand; all at once I heard an imperious command from the depths of my soul to throw the knife into the stream. If it fell into the water, my desire to be an artist would be satisfied; if its immersion were hidden from me by the overhanging willows, I should renounce the desire. The whim was carried out as quickly as it was conceived. Without any regard for the usefulness of the knife, which was of a composite kind, I threw it as far as I could into the stream with my left hand. But I experienced that deceptive ambiguity of oracles about which the ancients used to complain so bitterly. The furthest willows prevented my seeing my knife fall into the stream, but the water leaped up like a fountain and was perfectly visible to me. I did not interpret the phenomenon in my favour, and the doubt it awoke in me had the unfortunate consequence that I henceforth pursued my studies in painting more negligently and intermittently, thereby fulfilling the judgment of the oracle myself."

For all that he remained a painter. His designs indeed are amateurish, and his understanding of the masterpieces of painting is not so complete as he himself thought it was. But he sees and depicts everything like a painter. He is always congratulating himself on the gift of seeing the world with the eye of a painter, whose pictures were always before him. Venice appeared to him as a succession of pictures by the Venetian school. The unfathomable mystery of his style is the way in which a couple of sentences, without any real attempt at description on his part, will bring the whole scene as it appeared to him before the eye of the reader, suggesting to him all kinds of things he neither sees nor hears, but which he can no more forget than if they had been actually part of his own experience. In *Faust* we have a succession not so much of scenes as of vivid pictures. Goethe paints his own portrait at different periods of his life, against an idyllic, naïve, tragic, burlesque, fantastic or allegorical background. His landscapes are not merely built up out of words; like the painter, he has really seen them all, and he employs words like resonant spots of colour, in such a way that they conjure up the living scene before the reader's eye.

Many other authors since Goethe's time have passed from painting to verbal description and remained pictorial in essence, though choosing the material in which they could best depict the world as they saw it. Taine is certainly a painter. We can only understand rightly the loose and yet wonderfully clear structure of Gottfried Keller's stories when we realise that it is not the poet but the dramatic painter who guides the pen. In Michelangelo, again, who is the greater, — the poet or the painter? We call Heine our greatest lyrist. Should we not call him, from the standpoint of "the universal art", the most inspired painter among the lyric poets? Böcklin is a poet who has got among the painters. It is the poetic imagination that has led him to the fictions of his wonderful but in the last resort unreal landscapes. His visions master him to such an extent that impossibilities in the composition, even errors of drawing that are at first sight disconcerting, are matters of indifference to him. He had recourse to pencil and palette because he thought he could thus reproduce most vividly his poems of the elemental forces. His paintings are in the last resort symbols of poems that were inexpressible in words. It is thus quite natural that the reaction against him comes from the French painters, who, with their objective realism, have no sympathy with such a relation of poetry and painting, and combat an art showing tendencies of this kind from the standpoint of absolute painting, just as the partisans of absolute music make war on the music that bases itself on poetry. The painter cannot do otherwise than criticise with almost unjust harshness Böcklin's picture of the plague, in the Basel Museum. But if we let the picture — that almost seems like the drawing of a child of genius — appeal to us as poetry, we see at once its real greatness.

The essential distinction between German and French painting comes from this attitude towards poetry. Anyone who comes in contact with artists of both countries, and analyses the first impressions of German artists in Paris and the impressions of French artists at the sight of German works, and tries to see to the root of the unjust judgments on both sides, will soon observe that the difference in their views has its origin in the difference of their attitudes towards poetry. The German painter is more of a poet than the French. Therefore French painting reproaches German painting with a lack of real, objective feeling for nature. German painting, on the other hand, in spite of its admiration for the splendid technique of the French, feels somewhat chilled by a kind of deliberate poverty of imagination that it detects in it. In literature these contrasted ways of looking at nature have given Germany a splendid lyrical poetry that the French have never been able to achieve.

Painting, then, is suffused with poetry, and poetry with painting. The quality of either of the arts at a given moment depends on the strength or the weakness of this inter-coloration. As regards their means of expression each of them passes into the other by imperceptible gradations.

It is the same with music and poetry. We reckon Schiller among the poets. He himself held that he was really a musician. On the 25th May 1792 he writes to Körner: "When I sit down to express an idea, I am more often possessed by the musical essence of it than by a clear conception of its contents, as to which I frequently can hardly make up my mind*." Behind his words, indeed, there is not pure intuition, as with Goethe, but sound and rhythm. His description is sonorous, but pictorially unreal, presenting no living scene to the reader's eye. His landscapes are really all theatre decorations. Lamartine, again, is a musician, because he suggests rather than paints. Nietzsche's experience with music was like Goethe's with painting. He thought it a duty he owed to his talents to experiment in composition. His musical works, however, are of even less importance than Goethe's drawings. How can these awkward creations entitle him to the name of musician? Yet a musician he was. His works are symphonies. The musician does not read them; he hears them, as if he were going through an orchestral score. What he sees are not words and letters, but themes developing and interlacing. In *Jenseits von Gut und Böse* he even finds those little fugued intermezzi into which Beethoven often diverges. Wherein does this quality exist? Who can analyse it? In any case Nietzsche himself had a full consciousness of the musical essence of his poetic creations. This is why he used to get so angry with the modern man who "leaves his ears in a drawer", and merely skims the pages of a book with this eyes. Moreover, it is evident from the clear connection of the ideas, through all their apparent incoherence and disconnection, that the poet of *Also sprach Zarathustra* worked out his ideas not in word-logic but in tone-logic, as musical motives. After having brought an idea to its definite conclusion and apparently finished with it, he will suddenly bring it in once more without the least warning, just as the musician picks up a theme again.

---

* See Schiller's *Briefwechsel mit Körner* (Veit, Leipzig, 2nd ed. 1894) I, 453.

Wagner is one of the musical poets, only that he is master not only of word-speech but of tone-speech. Nietzsche's well-known formula for the artistic complexity of the man whom he revered and hated as no one else did runs thus: "As a musician Wagner's place is among the painters, as a poet his place is among the musicians, as artist in general his place is among the actors*." For Wagner, again, certain painters were musicians. The great masters of the Italian Renaissance, he says in one place, "were almost all musicians, and it is the spirit of music that makes us forget, when we are lost in contemplation of their saints and martyrs, that we are actually seeing with our eyes."**

Every artistic idea is complex in quality until the moment when it finds definite expression. Neither in painting, nor in music, nor in poetry is there such a thing as an absolute art that can be regarded as the norm, enabling us to brand all others as false, for in every artist there dwells another, who wishes to have his own say in the matter, the difference being that in one his activity is obtrusive, and in another hardly noticeable. Herein resides the whole distinction. Art in itself is neither painting nor poetry nor music, but an act of creation in which all three coöperate.

The close and tense relation in which the arts stand among each other gives each of them a desire for expansion, that allows the art no peace until it has attained its utmost possible limit. Then it is further impelled to appropriate a portion of the territory of another art. Not only does music try to paint and narrate like the two other arts; they in their turn do likewise. Poetry tries to paint pictures that really need to be taken in by the eye, and painting tries to seize not only the visible scene but the poetic feeling underlying it. Music, however, working in a medium so little fitted to depict concrete ideas, soon reaches its

* *Jenseits von Gut und Böse*, p. 256.

** *Beethoven*, (*Gesammelte Schriften*, IX, 146)

limits of clear representation of poetic and pictorial ideas. For this reason pictorial and poetic tendencies have in all epochs exercised a pernicious influence upon music, and have given birth to a false art, that imagined it could express objects and ideas which it is far beyond the powers of music to render. This false music lives by pretensions and self-deception. Its arrogant view of itself as the only perfect music has always brought it into discredit.

It thus becomes comprehensible how some people could look with suspicion upon poetic and pictorial intentions in music, and in times of danger adopt the motto of "absolute music", this being the banner of pure art they hoisted over the works of Bach and Beethoven, — erroneously and inappropriately as it happens.

But not only is the creative art complex; our reception of it is not less so. In every true artistic perception there come into action all the feelings and ideas of which a man is capable. The process is multiform, though it is only in the rarest cases that the subject has any inkling of what is going on in his imagination, and what mental overtones complicate the ground tone which, as it seems to him, exclusively occupies his attention.

Many a man erroneously thinks he sees a picture whereas he really hears it, his artistic emotions arising from the music — perhaps silent — that he perceives in the scene represented on the canvas. Anyone who does not hear the bees in Didier-Pouget's picture of the flowery heath does not see it with the eye of the artist. Again, anyone who is not fascinated by the most ordinary painting of a pine wood — hearing the infinite distant symphonies of the wind sweeping over the tree-tops, — sees only as half a man, i. e. not as an artist.

So again in music. Musical sensibility is to some extent a capacity for tone-visions, of whatever kind it may be, — whether it deals with lines, ideas, forms, or events. Associations of ideas are always going on where we would not suspect them.

Let us ask the audience of a performance of a work by Palestrina to account for the solemn effect it has made on them. The majority would confess that they had felt themselves transported into the vast nave of a church, and saw the sunlight streaming through the windows of the choir into the twilight of the building. We all poetise more than we are apt to imagine. This can be shewn by a simple experiment. Try to look but not hear, and to hear but not let any visual associations step over the threshold of consciousness, and the other artist in us, whom we imagined to be uninterested, will at once spring up and demand his rights.

Every artistic feeling is really an act. Artistic creation is only a special case of the artistic attitude towards the world. Some men have the faculty of reproducing in speech, colours, tones, or words the artistic impression made on them and many others by what goes on in the world around them. It is not so much that these are more fundamentally artists than the others, but only that they can speak and the others are dumb. When we see the passionate effect made by art on men who are only "receptive", and how much their mute imagination can add to the works of others, it no longer seems a paradox that it is only by accident that some of the great ones have received the gift of speech.

Art is the translation of æsthetic associations of ideas. The more complexly and intensely the conscious and unconscious concepts and ideas of the artist communicate themselves to us through his art-work, the deeper is the impression. It is then that he succeeds in stimulating others to that vivacity of imaginative feeling which we call art, in contradistinction to what we hear and see and experience in our ordinary moments.

The part of a work of art that is perceptible by the senses is in reality only the intermediator between two active efforts of the imagination. All art speaks in signs and symbols. No one can explain how it happens that the artist can waken to life in us the existence that he has seen and lived through. No artistic speech is the adequate expression of what it represents; its vital force comes from what is unspoken in it.

In poetry and painting this is less noticeable, since the language of each of these arts is also the language of daily life. We need, however, only read a poem by Goethe, and test the words of which it consists by the wealth of suggestions that they arouse in us, to see at once that words in art become suggestive symbols, by means of which the imaginations of two artists hold converse together. "In truth", says Wagner, "the greatness of the poet can be best measured by what he refrains from saying, in order to let the inexpressible itself speak to us in secrecy."*

In painting, the inadequacy of the thing said is still more striking. We cannot estimate how much the spectator must add of his own before a coloured canvas can become a landscape. An etching, indeed, makes extraordinary demands on the imagination, for the representation in black and white is only a symbol of the landscape, and has no more reality than a symbol. And yet this symbolical delineation is, for anyone who can interpret it, perhaps the most potent means of conjuring up the faculty of complete vision.

In this way there comes into painting, in the place of the naïve "This is", the noteworthy "This signifies" of artistic speech. It will be learned and assimilated by familiarity. It even happens at times that the speech fails, the symbols not being clear to the spectator, and appearing merely as agglomerations of lines and colours, — either because the artist has put more into them than they can express, or because the spectator has not caught the secret of his speech.

In music the expression is wholly symbolical. The translation of even the most general feelings and ideas

---

* *Zukunftsmusik*, in his *Gesammelte Schriften*, VII, 172.

into tone is a mystery. The latest researches into the physiology of musical sensation do not help us in the least; they merely conquer for musical æsthetic a wonderful colonial territory, which, however, to the end of time will yield it nothing. "The thing that is most important is, and will remain, unexplained," says Hanslick, — "the nervous process by which the sensation of tone becomes converted into feeling, a mental mood."*

The more ambitious the musical expression is, the more noticeable is the symbolical element in it. Before long it addresses to the imagination of the hearer pretensions which, with the best will in the world, cannot be admitted, and comes violently into collision with the more suggestive element in artistic speech. It is wrong, however, to imagine that so-called pure music speaks a language that is not symbolical, and that it expresses something of which the meaning is unequivocal. It too appeals to the hearer's power of imagination, only that it is concerned more with abstract feeling and abstract beauty of line than with concrete expression. Only in this way does it become possible for the poetic imagination to make itself intelligible, so far as it can, to the musical imagination.

As a rule we employ the criterion of immediate intelligibility, and, from the standpoint of absolute music, will only allow that art to be valid that appeals immediately to the unprepossessed and unprepared hearer. This would make perfect tone-speech an impossibility. It is like refusing to recognise a foreign language as a language unless it is immediately intelligible to every one at a first hearing. Every language subsists only by a convention, in virtue of which a certain sensation or idea is regarded as corresponding to a certain aggregation of sounds. It is the same in music. Anyone who understands the language of a composition, and knows the significance of certain combinations of tone, perceives ideas in the music

* *Vom Musikalisch-Schönen*, 1st ed. 1857; 10th ed. 1902.

that do not speak directly to the uninitiated, though they are there all the time. Few composers, however, have been great enough to fashion a language for themselves in which they could express intelligibly the concrete part of their ideas. The others, whenever they venture outside the limits of the generally accepted moods, begin to wander in their speech, though they still think themselves intelligible. Finally they add a programme to their music, that hangs out of its mouth like the strips on which the primitive painters used to indicate what their characters were saying. This naïve descriptive music is to be found not only in the past. The average modern and even the most up-to-date symphonic poem is just as naïve, no matter how great may be its inventive and technical power, since here also a concreteness of expression is claimed that in reality has not been long attained, and is, in general, unattainable by music.

This is, in fact, the tragedy of music, that it can only express with limited intelligibility the concrete image from which it has sprung. From the indefiniteness of the tone-picture itself, however, we must not conclude a corresponding indefiniteness of the fancy that prompted it, and claim that music of this kind is absolute music. We have a warning example in Weber's *Konzertstück*. In 1821, on the morning of the day of the first performance of *Der Freischütz*, Weber brought his wife the *Konzertstück* which he had just completed, and played it to her and his favourite pupil Benedict, telling them at the same time what the music was meant to represent:

"*Larghetto*. On the terrace of the castle stands the châtelaine, looking sadly into the distance. Her husband is with the Crusaders in the Holy Land. She has no news of him. Is he dead? Will she see him again?

"*Allegro appassionato*. Horror! She sees him lying on the battlefield, abandoned, wounded. The blood flows from his wounds . . . . . . and she cannot hasten to his side!

"*Adagio e tempo di marcia*. Tumult and the glittering

of weapons in the distance, coming from the wood. They draw nearer. They are knights carrying the cross. The banners wave, the people break out into cries of joy, and . . . . . . he is there!

"*Più mosso, presto assai.* She runs to meet him. He embraces her. Wood and field add their jubilant cries to the hymn of faithful love."

The pupil immediately wrote out the "explanation", but Weber would not allow it to be published with the music*. Had it not been preserved by accident, no one would have imagined the events depicted in the *Konzertstück*, and it would naturally be regarded as a piece of pure music.

Beethoven's works were also written under the impression of definite scenes, in spite of the fact that they are claimed to be pure music. When asked for an explanation of the D minor sonata, he replied, "Read Shakespeare's *Tempest.*" In the adagio of the F major quartet (op. 18, No. 1) he had in his mind the grave-scene from *Romeo and Juliet.* The E major sonata (op 81) even bears an authentic inscription; it depicts a farewell, a separation and a return. More particularly in his latest chamber music we have a strong feeling that the musical sequence of ideas is determined by a poetic mood of some kind; we have however, no hints by which we can definitely reconstruct from the music the situation the composer had in his mind.

Liszt improvised best when his imagination had been set working by the perusal of poetry.

Hanslick, in his *Vom Musikalisch-Schönen*, does indeed recognise facts of this kind, but considers this kind of composing "in leading strings" to poetry, as distinct from "pure" musical invention, to be merely exceptional. The knowledge of the concrete ideas from which the music arose is of no consequence for our understanding of it.

---

* See Johannes Weber's interesting *Les illusions musicales et la vérité sur l'expression*, 2nd ed., Paris, 1900.

"It is æsthetically a matter of indifference," he says, "if Beethoven worked upon definite subjects in every one of his compositions; we do not know these subjects; therefore, so far as the work is concerned, they do not exist. It is the work alone that lies before us, without any commentary; and just as the jurist ignores everything that is not embodied in acts and deeds, so nothing exists for the æsthetic judgment that lies outside the work of art."*

This is untrue. Certainly only the pure music lies before us. But this is only the hieroglyph, in which are recorded the emotional qualities of the visions of the concrete imagination. This hieroglyph appeals perpetually to the fancy of the hearer, requiring it to translate the drama of the emotions back again into concrete events, and to find a path along which he can see, as well as he can, the line that has been taken by the creative imagination of the composer. Notable musicians have confessed that they could not grasp the latest works of Beethoven. This derogates neither from them nor from Beethoven; it only implies that their imagination had no point of contact with his.

The ordinary hearer is easily satisfied. The poorest little anecdote is enough to put him "in the mood of the work", and to find everything in it that he is expected to find. It is not so long since that the attempt was made to popularise Beethoven's sonatas and Mendelssohn's *Lieder ohne Worte* by giving them suggestive titles. We have become more unfeeling now, and will not tolerate attempts of this kind to place the creative fancy on its legs. We care for nothing that has not come from our knowledge of the tongue the composer speaks, or from our own poetic intuition, and that has this mark of truth in it, that it is inexpressible and so cannot be made intelligible to anyone else. Only the greatest artists have the right to show others the path their own imagination followed when listening to a piece of music.

---

* *Op. cit.* p. 98 ff.

Wagner daringly interprets Beethoven's great C sharp minor quartet as "an actual day of Beethoven's life". In the introductory adagio we have an expression of melancholy on wakening at dawn. This is overcome. In the presto Beethoven turns his "unspeakably cheerful glance" on the outer world. He gazes reflectively upon life. After the short adagio, — "a sombre meditation" — he awakes, and in the final allegro "strikes the strings to a dance that the world had never heard before."* Perhaps Beethoven would have expressed the contents of his music in quite other words and images. Nevertheless Wagner's interpretation is not a "commentary" to be made merry over like the ordinary musical interpretation. Here it is a case of "the poet speaks".

Just as there are painters and musicians among the poets, so there are poets and painters among the musicians. They become clearly distinguished from each other in proportion as the "other artist" is able to assert himself in their conceptions. Poetic music deals more with ideas, pictorial music with pictures; the one appeals more to the feeling, the other to our faculty of representation. The incoherency of the discussion upon tone-painting, programme music and representative music has been due in great part to the fact that no account has been taken of the two main currents in music that now flow parallel to each other, now cross each other, — it being assumed that every sin against pure music was of the same order.

Beethoven and Wagner belong more to the poets, Bach, Schubert and Berlioz more to the painters.

Beethoven is often called a poet by Wagner, who thinks that the awakening of "the other artist" in him was the crucial point of his career. The first period of free and careless musical invention was followed by another, in which Beethoven speaks a language that often seems arbitrary and capricious, the ideas being held together

---

* Wagner, *Beethoven* (in *Ges. Schriften*, IX, 118).

only by a poetic purpose, which, however, could not be expressed with poetic clearness in music. Then comes the period in which the deeply sensitive man suffered acutely, when he could no longer make himself intelligible to his hearers, who regarded him simply as a mad genius*. The successive symphonies relate the longing of music to transcend its own element and become universal art, until at last, in the ninth symphony, it seized upon speech, worked out its own salvation, and united the severed arts in one.

We may look at the introduction of the chorus at the end of the ninth symphony in another light, — regarding it as an error, the end of the symphony rather than the beginning of the genuine music-drama: but this does not affect the justice of Wagner's view of Beethoven's musical development.

Perhaps Wagner has interpreted Beethoven too much in terms of himself. In reality Beethoven's fancy is much more pictorial than Wagner's. Compare their ways of expressing themselves verbally, which is always a clue to the process of formation of a man's ideas. Wagner has nothing of Beethoven's abrupt, drastic style. He hardly ever uses pictures, — differing here, again, from Berlioz, whose mind is crowded with them. For a musician, Wagner's writing, as a rule, is unusually rational. The pictorial bias usually predominates among musicians, as their conversation shows. When they wish to explain anything, they have recourse to pictures, heap one comparison upon another, mix the appropriate and inappropriate together, employ the strangest expressions, and then think they have made what is inexpressible in the idea comprehensible. Those who, like Wagner, aim only at expressing the emotional quintessence of the idea, are rather exceptional. Even Schumann expresses himself more pictorially than Wagner. The latter is never purely realistic, either in his prose or his music. He will not even allow that the

---

* Wagner, *Oper und Drama* (*Ges. Schriften*, III, 344).

representation of the purely characteristic is the province of painting itself, which, he holds, should express ideas. He maintains that the ideal creative quality of Renaissance painting decayed in proportion as it got out of touch with religion. He seriously maintains that since that period it has continuously declined.

He wishes his own pictorial music to appeal not to the imagination but to the emotions. Even when the music expresses something visual, the pictorialism is not an end in itself but symbolical of an idea. He would prefer to dispense altogether with the plastic imagination, and set bodily before the spectator's eye the action that is being emotionally represented in music. The best and most exalted tone-painting, he says in one place, is that in which the tone-painter addresses himself to the feeling instead of to the imagination,* that is to say, when the external object of the musical picture is simultaneously made visible to the hearer. According to him, the true tone-picture is the music of the drama. So that Wagner is opposed to what is generally looked upon as tone painting, since this does not aim at the simultaneous bewitching of the senses by the music and the visible presentation of the object that the music describes. "All we can express in music," he says, "are feelings and sentiments."

His themes are harmonic in quality. They get their characteristic quality from a basic chord that mounts up out of the ocean of harmony as the idea emerges from the depths of feeling. His modulations are not simply musical, but have a poetic significance. In the true sense they are only necessary when they correspond to something that happens in the domain of feeling.

The art of a Schubert or a Berlioz is much more materialistic. Of course they express emotions; but when they become wholly characteristic they hold to the picture for its own sake. Their painting appeals to our faculty of

---

* *Oper und Drama* (*Ges. Schriften*, IV, 234).

representation, and to a certain extent becomes an aim in itself, which is never the case in Wagner. In the accompaniments to Schubert's songs there is more realistic tone-painting than in all Wagner's music dramas.

Berlioz's pictorialism is even more apparent. His art has nothing whatever in common with Wagner's; it follows quite a different path. For Berlioz the perfection of tone-painting is not the pure expression of feeling, but extravagant delineation. His music is directed to the externalities of the event. Even when he is writing for the stage he aims at the obtrusive clearness of programme music. We see the thing simultaneously in a double form — on the stage and in the music; Wagner gives it to us only once, but complete, the music not reproducing the visible action itself, but expressing the emotional correlative of the event, which would otherwise remain unexpressed.

It was this attachment to the external that made Wagner unable to understand Berlioz's music. In the moving love-scene in the *Romeo and Juliet* symphony, he tells us, he was at first enchanted by the development of the main themes. During the course of the movement the enchantment evaporated, till he experienced absolute discomfort. "It is true that the motives", he says, "were present in the famous balcony-scene of Shakespeare; the great mistake of the composer lay in retaining faithfully the dramatist's disposition of them."*

See, again, what Berlioz has selected from Goethe's *Faust* — a series of scenes for musical painting, taken arbitrarily, without much regard to the drama itself.

The themes of Schubert and Berlioz are not so harmonic in essence as those of Wagner. They are not, like these, founded on a certain basic harmony. They have their origin in the pictorial imagination; they are like the characteristic lines of a draughtsman. The distinction is

---

* *Über Franz Liszts Symphonische Dichtungen* (*Ges. Schr.* V, 250).

hard to define in detail, though it is clear enough to the imagination. None the less it reveals the essential difference in nature between the two kinds of music.

The pictorial element in Schubert and Berlioz is not always sufficiently distinctive for us to contrast them decisively with Wagner. In spite of all the difference between them, they have this in common with him, and with post-Beethovenian music in general, that they express in tones a poetic sequence of ideas, whether in the form of a song or in that of a programme, and do not confine themselves, as in essentially pictorial music, to seizing a feeling or an event in one pregnant moment and painting it from its picturesque side, without any concern for the moment before or the moment after. They undertake to follow in detail the adventures of a poem, and are consequently poetic musicians. Bach does not do this. He is the most consistent representative of pictorial music,— the direct antipodes of Wagner. These two are the poles between which all "characteristic" music resolves.

CHAPTER XXI.

WORD AND TONE IN BACH.

The relation of Bach's music to its text is the most intimate that can be imagined*. This is evident even in externalities. The structure of his musical phrase does not merely fit more or less the structure of the poetic phrase, but is identical with it. In this respect we may contrast Bach with Handel. In the latter, the musical

* See also Arnold Schering's interesting essay *Bachs Textbehandlung* (Kahnt, Leipzig, 1900), — in which the poetic element in Bach's music is described for the first time, and very finely and searchingly, — and André Pirro's monumental study *L'Esthétique de J. S. Bach* (Fischbacher, Paris, 1907), which confirms and completes, in the most gratifying way, the conclusions arrived at in the present volume.

period of a long verbal passage consists of separate fragments joined together in the most masterly way, the verbal phrase, however, having to surrender something of its own natural form in order to accommodate itself to that of the music. There always results a certain antagonism between the rhythm of the two factors. We get the impression that if we were to let a Handelian theme fall to the ground, the tone-melody and the word-melody would separate under the shock; whereas a Bach phrase would remain unbroken and inseparable, his musical phrase being only the verbal phrase re-cast in tone. His music is indeed not so much melodic as declamatory. He is what Guido Adler maintains Wagner is, a product of the great music of the Renaissance.

The melodic impression his phrases make on us is due to his clear and consummate sense of form. Though he thought declamatorily, he could not help writing melodically. A vocal theme of Bach's is a declamatorily conceived phrase, that by accident, as if by a marvel perpetually repeated, assumes melodic form, whether it be a recitative, an arioso, an aria, or a chorus. His texts, regarded from the standpoint of form, were as unapt for music as any that could be imagined. A Biblical verse does not fall into any musical period, not even a verbal one, for it has its origin not in a rhythmical feeling but in the necessities of translation. It was no better with the original texts given him by his librettists. These again have no inner unity, being painfully pieced together out of reminiscences of the Bible and the hymn-books. But when we read the same sentences in Bach's music, they all at once fall into definite musical phrases.

The declamatory unity of tone and word in Bach reminds us of Wagner. While, however, it is self-evident in the latter, the verbal phrase itself being musically conceived, so that the music only adds the intervals, as it were, in Bach the phenomenon is more wonderful — the music seems to confer a higher vital power on the words, divests them of their lowly associations, and shows them in their true form. This marvel is so perpetually repeated in the cantatas and Passions that we come to regard it as a matter of course. But the more deeply we penetrate into Bach, the more we are filled with the ever-renewed and ever-increasing astonishment that the thoughtful soul feels in presence of those daily occurrences of nature that are at the same time the greatest marvels.

If we have once absorbed a Biblical verse in Bach's setting of it, we can never again conceive it in any other rhythm. It is impossible for anyone who knows the *St. Matthew Passion* to run over in his mind the sacramental words of the evening Communion without consciously or unconsciously giving the words the accents and duration that they have in Bach's declamation. No one who knows the cantata *Nun komm der Heiden Heiland* (No. 61) can ever again think of the "Siehe! Ich stehe vor der Tür und klopfe an" ("Behold, I stand at the door and knock")* apart from Bach's phrasing of it. Even if he has forgotten the actual intervals, the musical ground-plan of the passage has become, after several hearings, so much the plan of the passage itself, that it is impossible to think of the one without the other.

It would be incorrect to suppose that in every good musical setting the music has the same power of persistence. It is not found in the same degree in anyone but Wagner — not even in Schubert. The extraordinary thing is that in Bach's music the reminiscence depends less on the intervals than on the accents and quantities of the declamation itself; although, of course, his themes are so characteristic and drastic in their intervals that they are memorable from this side as well.

One of the most remarkable examples of his declamation is the arioso-like opening recitative of the cantata *Gleichwie der Regen und Schnee vom Himmel fällt* (No. 18)**. The nearly equal divisions of the original passage are gathered

* Rev. III, 20.

** Isaiah LV, 10 and 11.

up by the music into one great unified phrase that resolves and obliterates, as if by magic, all the rigidities of the verbal passage, giving us the impression that the poetic thought has waited for centuries for this music in order to reveal itself in its true plastic outline.

Even when Bach's music is more aria-like in structure, it still retains this purely declamatory quality. Recite, for example, the first aria of the cantata *Selig ist der Mann* (No. 57)*, strictly according to the quantities and the accents of the music, without for a moment considering the intervals, and you will get an idea of how veracious Bach's musical declamation is.

If the verse he is setting has rhyme and a regular length of line, he passes over these and fastens upon the inner form of the passage. His musical phrase is never dominated by the recurrence of the rhyme. In the text of the aria in the *St. Matthew Passion*:

"Gerne will ich mich bequemen
Kreuz und Becher anzunehmen
Trink ich doch dem Heiland nach",

it seems almost impossible for music to rise superior to the rhyme. Bach succeeds, however, by his distribution of the accents and the intervals, in so diverting our attention from it that we are unconscious of it when it is properly sung. The first "ich" must be accented as the music indicates, and as its relation to the previous arioso, "Der Heiland fällt", obviously demands.

The phrase goes thus:

* James I, 12.

It is not Bach's fault if many of our singers bring out here the poet's line-divisions and rhymes instead of Bach's musical phrase.

Any one who goes through the separate voices of *Nun ist das Heil und die Kraft* (No. 50)* will discover that Bach phrases declamatorily even when he seems to be merely writing fugal parts.

Effective as his method is, it does not always seem natural at first sight. Often, indeed, Bach's way of turning a passage into music seems quite unnatural; rhythm, structure, accents, syllabic values, — all give at first the impression of being wrong. The syllable that would ordinarily receive the main accent is, if possible, merged and lost in the shadow of the unaccented part of the bar; another one, of no value at all, is thrown into high relief by some striking interval; we find no pause just where we would expect one. Thus every stroke that Bach makes in order to bring out the musical form of the phrase is, considered by itself, incomprehensible. Nor would it be difficult to show that in some of his recitatives or arias Bach has sinned here and there against the natural accent. When, however, we look at the piece as a whole, singing the notes with freedom and at the same time with the quantities Bach has allotted to them, we see it in relief, — as it were in a kind of acoustical perspective, — of which detailed analysis could convey no idea. This art defies narrow scrutiny. It rests on an intuitive appreciation of the coöperation of the details, the total effect of which is seen by the composer at a glance. It follows that there is no surer way of destroying Bach's effect than the false artistic freedom which many singers, perplexed by the many strangenesses of the music, permit themselves in order to remedy the "chance" quality of the notes that Bach has written**.

---

* Rev. XII, 10.

** See, on this point, Alfred Heuss's article *Bachs Rezitativbehandlung mit besonderer Berücksichtigung der Passionen*, in the *Bach-Jahrbuch* for 1904, pp. 82 ff. The discussion that followed

Bach converts into tone not only the body but the soul of the verbal passage. This is clearly seen in his harmonisations of the chorales. The greatest masters of the chorale-piece, Eccard, Praetorius and others, harmonised the melody; Bach harmonised the words. For him the chorale-melody by itself is indefinite in character; it only acquires a personality when allied with a definite text, the nature of which he will express in his harmonies.

Weber long ago saw that the chorale-movements of the cantatas and Passions are not purely musical. Bach's son Philipp Emmanuel had published them without the corresponding texts. He had no perception of his father's poetic intentions. His idea was simply to give the world a collection of examples of the chorale-movement at its best*. At the beginning of the nineteenth century, when Abt Vogler's mathematical-æsthetic system of harmony was exciting general admiration, Weber, his pupil, thought he owed it to the honour of his teacher to show that he had also surpassed old Bach in the chorale-movement, going more systematically to work than the cantor, — the astonishing thing being that the latter, without knowing Vogler's system, should have written such rich harmonies. With this end in view he compares twelve of Bach's harmonisations with twelve corresponding ones by Vogler, and demonstrates that the old master is inferior to the new one, many of his strange harmonic progressions having no *raison d'être***.

---

the article, especially the contribution of Moritz Wirth, was also interesting, though at the same time it showed how little the question has hitherto been studied.

* *Johann Sebastian Bachs vierstimmige Choralgesänge, gesammelt von Philipp Emmanuel Bach.* Part I, 1765, Part II, 1769. See B. G. XXXIX, pp. 177 ff.

** Weber's *Ausgewählte Schriften,* ed. Reclam, pp. 89—97: *Zwölf Choräle von Seb. Bach, umgearbeitet von Vogler, zergliedert von Karl Maria von Weber.* Georg Joseph Vogler was born at Würzburg in 1749, studied music and theology in Italy, became a priest in Rome, and settled in 1775 in Mannheim, where he founded a school of music. Later he lived in Paris, Stockholm,

To put this down to Weber's lack of judgment would be wrong, as his views were quite just. From the standpoint of pure music Bach's harmonisations are wholly enigmatic, for he does not work upon a tonal succession that in itself forms an æsthetic whole, but follows the lead of the poetry and the verbal expression. How far he lets these take him from the natural principles of pure composition may be seen from his harmonisation of "Solls ja so sein, dass Straf und Pein"*, in the cantata *Ich elender Mensch, wer wird mich erlösen* (No. 48), which as pure music is indeed intolerable, Bach's purpose being to express all the wild grief for sin that is suggested in the words.

The fault lay with Philipp Emmanuel, who published the chorale-movements without their texts, thereby showing that he did not understand the nature of his father's art. A great service was therefore done to Bach by the Berlin choral conductor Ludwig Erk (1807—1883) when he published the preludes with the verses to which the composer had set the melodies**.

If we take Erk's collection and examine the successive arrangement of the same melody, we see that they assume all kinds of characters according to the poetic harmonisation. A broad, victorious melody in the major is pursuing its course, when suddenly a theme of mourning enters and dominates it. What majesty the Passion melody "Herzliebster Jesu, was hast du verbrochen", assumes in the *St. Matthew Passion*, when it expresses the words "Ach, grosser König, gross zu allen Zeiten"! The quaver sequence

---

and London. In 1807 he became Hofkapellmeister at Darmstadt, where he founded a music school that was attended by Weber and Meyerbeer. He died in 1814.

* The melody is that of "Ach Gott und Herr".

** Ludwig Erk, *Johann Sebastian Bachs Choralgesänge und geistliche Arien*; Leipzig, Peters: Part I, 1850, Part II, 1865. The work has been frequently reprinted. The chorales have lately been translated into French, with fine understanding, by Albert Mahaut, and published with an enthusiastic preface by Vincent d'Indy (Breitkopf and Härtel, 1905/6).

in the bass, which is inexplicable from the standpoint of pure music, is the triumphal chariot that carries it. We may say that in Bach's chorales every line, every word is painted, and thrown into a kind of embossed relief.

Wagner once remarked of one of his modulations, that at first sight seemed too daring and abrupt, that in reality it was not so, since it originated in the meeting of two motives that had already been heard frequently; and that the ear, knowing these, would take in the almost extravagant harmony as something quite natural. Bach, in his chorales, works on a similar principle. The melody is familiar; he can therefore permit himself the most audacious harmony, the ear being in no danger of missing the continuity of the melody.

The poetic significance of Bach's chorale-pieces, however, is only fully seen when the choir sings not the melody but the text, emphasising not the melodic accents but the words that Bach has so strongly — sometimes even too strongly, — underlined in his harmonies. The more we examine these chorales, the more we become conscious of the suppressed passion of expression there is in them, to which there is no parallel anywhere in literature.

Only a few of Bach's chorale-pieces for the organ have come down to us*; but those we have suffice to show us his method of working. When the Arnstadt consistory

* Breitkopf's catalogue of 1764 mentions a *Vollständiges Choralbuch mit in Noten aufgesetzten Generalbasse von 240 in Leipzig gewöhnlichen Melodien* by Johann Sebastian Bach, priced at 10 thalers. ("Complete Chorale-Book of 240 familiar Leipzig melodies, with the thorough-bass written out in notes"). This book of chorales is lost. In Schemelli's *Gesangbuch* of 1736 some of Bach's figured basses are given; they may have been taken from his Leipzig chorale-book. See Spitta III, 109 ff. We further possess some harmonisations that have been preserved in copies made by Bach's pupils. They are included in the Peters edition of the chorale-preludes. (Peters ed. of Bach's Organ Works, V, pp. 39, 57, 102 No. 1, 103 No. 2, 106, 107; VI, No. 26. See also B. G. XL, pp. 60 ff.; and the harmonisations of the chorale-partitas in Peters V, pp. 60, 68, 102, 103.)

remonstrated with him for exceeding his leave of absence, the opportunity was at the same time taken to rebuke him for his too temperamental chorale-accompaniments. "Point out to him", so the report runs, "that in the chorales he has made many curious *Variationes*, and mingled many strange tones with them, so that the congregation was confused thereby."* We can understand this censure when we look at the harmonisation of "In dulci Jubilo" (Peters V, No. 103), that was intended to accompany the congregational singing. It mattered nothing that Bach filled the breath-pauses between the lines of the melody with passage-work: that was the common practice of the time. But when the melody enters again it disappears in the harmonic flood. We must of course remember that as the congregational singing was led by the choir, Bach could permit himself a little freedom.

In this *Sturm und Drang* the poetic tendency is already revealed. In the chorale "Vom Himmel hoch, da komm ich her" (Peters V, 106), that Krebs has preserved for us, the interlacing and surrounding of the melody by joyous scale-passages is explained by the fact that Bach was depicting the angels of heaven referred to in the poetry. A characteristic feature of the chorale-movements of this youthful period is the piled-up masses of chords, with their comparative disregard of any strict leading of the voices.

His style of accompaniment in his mature period may be seen in "Herr Gott! dich loben wir", (Peters VI, pp. 65—69)**, where every verse is treated independently. The harmonies are clarified and the writing contrapuntal, but, compared with modern chorale-accompaniment, unusually animated throughout and over-rich in passing notes. The poetic intention is perfectly evident. Anything characteristic in the text is immediately depicted

* See Spitta I, 315, 316.

** *Te deum laudamus.* In the old hymn-book it is referred to as *Hymnus S. Ambrosii et Augustini.*

in the music. Observe the majestic crotchet-motion in all the voices from the moment when the words "Dein göttlich Macht und Herrlichkeit" enter (p. 66, bar 8 ff.), and the chromatic motive of grief that enters with the words "Nun hilf uns, Herr" (p. 67, bar 19 ff.), the reference being to the death-agonies of Jesus*. The line "Hilf deinem Volk" p. 67, bars 39 ff.) is illustrated by means of a rhythm which, in the cantatas and chorale-preludes, expresses peace, — simply because the word "segnen" occurs here**. Immediately afterwards we have the Bach motive of joy (p. 68, bar 6 ff.), as the text refers to celestial delight***. Later (p. 69, bar 13 ff.), the sorrowful, yearning prayer "Zeig' uns deine Barmherzigkeit" ("Show us Thy compassion") is expressed in trembling chromatics. Finally, at the words "Auf dich hoffen wir, lieber Herr" ("In Thee, dear Lord, is our hope") (p. 69, bars 23 ff.), the rhythm of peace returns that was employed in the lines "Hilf deinem Volk, Herr Jesu Christ, and segne was dein Erbteil ist". Anyone who has the least acquaintance with the intentions of Bach's methods of expression will find that he has reproduced in his music, with speaking fidelity, the salient points of the text. A study of the text along with the chorale harmonisations will shew how closely interdependent tone and word are in Bach. The full influence of the poetry upon the music, however, can be seen only in the chorale-preludes and the cantatas, where the musical painting is more self-dependent.

It goes without saying that Bach seizes the poetic mood

---

* "Nun hilf uns, Herr, den Dienern dein,
Die mit deinem teuren Blut erlöset sein."
("Help now thy servants, oh Lord, who are redeemed by Thy precious blood".)

** "Hilf deinem Volk, Herr Jesu Christ,
Und segne was dein Erbteil ist."
("Help Thy people, and bless Thine inheritance.")

*** "Wart und pfleg ihr zu aller Zeit
Und heb sie hoch in Ewigkeit."
("Tend and cherish them to all eternity.")

in its finest nuances. We can fully apply to it Wagner's remark that music should express the inexpressible, the very root of the poetic idea, the expression of which is beyond the power of verbal speech, that is too intellectual for the purpose.

His conception of the Bible words is not always the customary one; it comes from a profound and very personal emotion. The music he has given to the sacramental words of the Last Supper in the *St. Matthew Passion* is astounding. There is not a trace of grief. The music breathes peace and majesty; the nearer it draws to the end, the more stately becomes the quaver-movement in the basses. Bach sees Jesus standing before the disciples with radiant face, prophesying of the day when He will again drink from the cup at the heavenly supper with them in His father's kingdom. Bach has thus emancipated himself from the conventional idea of the scene, and, by means of his artistic intuition, has attained a juster sense of it than theology has ever done.

The commencement of the recitative of the Passion, "Aber am ersten Tage der süssen Brote", ("Now the first day of the feast of unleavened bread") is notably bright, — almost joyous; so is the chorus of disciples, "Wo willst du, dass wir dir bereiten das Osterlamm zu essen". ("Where wilt Thou that we prepare for Thee to eat the Passion"). Bach continues in this ingenuous and somewhat joyous mood until Jesus utters the "Wahrlich, ich sage euch, einer unter euch wird mich verraten" ("Verily I say unto you that one of you shall betray Me"). The "Wahrlich! du bist auch einer von denen, denn deine Sprache verrät dich", ("Surely thou also art one of them, for thy speech bewrayeth thee") in the Second Part of the work, is very briefly treated, without a suspicion of passion. It is simply a passing remark of the soldiers, — again a fine stroke of the imagination.

Everywhere, in fact, there is the same profound view and the same characteristic expression of the emotions and actions. Moreover, Bach now and then heightens the sentiment of his text in the most striking way; he turns contentment into exultant joy, and grief into violent despair. Not that he neglects the nuances of feeling even in thus intensifying it; his music expresses many degrees of joy and of sorrow. But all of them are surcharged with emotion. When he translates a feeling into tone, he voices it in its extreme form.

In the first chorus of the cantata *Ach, lieben Christen seid getrost* (No. 114), he expresses the "getrost" in terms of such overflowing joy that the music goes far beyond the text. There is the same joyous excitement in the resignation expressed in the first chorus of the cantata *Was mein Gott will, das g'scheh allzeit* (No. 111).

It is the same with the organ chorales. What the chorale-preludes "Mit Fried und Freud fahr ich dahin" (Peters V, No. 41) and "Wer nur den lieben Gott lässt walten" (Peters V, 54) express is joy of an animated kind, not the peaceful confidence of which the text speaks.

Bach is thus bent on making the music characteristically expressive at any cost. Before he decides simply to write beautiful music to a text, he searches the words through and through to find an emotion which, after it has been intensified, is suitable for musical representation. He remodels his text to suit the way he means to express it in music. The words are finally no more than a shadow-picture of the music. Bach's relation to his text is active, not passive; it does not inspire him so much as he inspires it. His music lifts the words to a higher power, bringing out in transfigured form what seems struggling for expression in the mediocrity or, — as often enough happens — the banality of the poem.

For this reason there are hardly any tasteless Bach texts for anyone who reads through his works. He even becomes a little impatient at the constant complaints about the cantata poems, for he hears them with all the poetry

Bach has added to them, — a poetry beside which that of the original poet is only a clumsy reflection*.

We are appalled at the triteness of such words as those of the alto aria in the cantata *Ach lieben Christen seid getrost* (No. 114): "Du machst, o Tod, mir nun nicht ferner bange, wenn ich durch dich die Freiheit nur erlange, es muss ja so einmal gestorben sein". When, however, we hear them with the music, they express most eloquently the blissful joy of the redeemed soul, in which the painful word "gestorben" (dead) only appears in order to be triumphed over. The addition of "es muss ja so einmal gestorben sein" has given Bach a pretext for transforming the text into a poem of death and transfiguration.

Hundreds of examples of the same kind could be given. We get the impression that the composer is even indifferent to the actual words of his text and their banalities, not merely because they have the same savour for him as for his contemporaries, but because he is conscious how little really remains of the words when he has poured his own poetic power upon them. It was a similar consciousness of strength that made him burden himself with the contemporary Italian form of the *da capo* aria; he was secretly aware that his musical declamation could vivify even a mere pattern of this kind.

There is a great difference between the respective attitudes of Bach and Mozart towards a poor text. Both of them make us forget it by their music, but for quite different reasons. Mozart's object is to distract our minds

* It is, of course, not denied that a re-modelling of the text is imperatively called for now and then. To give without alteration the recitative "O Sünder trage mit Geduld", from the cantata *Ach lieben Christen seid getrost* (No. 114), which contains a dissertation on the "dropsy of sin", would be doing Bach a disservice. Translations into foreign languages should be quite free, aiming only at giving the text that Bach has expressed in his music, — i. e. the ideal text. This principle has been followed in the French versions published by Breitkopf and Härtel. Gustave Bret's translation of *Sie werden aus Saba alle kommen* is a masterpiece of this kind.

from the text by means of music that is beautiful in itself. Bach gives it a new profundity and a new form in his music.

How does he handle his music when the poem presents a series of points for expression? To what extent does he attempt to reproduce these successions of ideas in tone?

He does not try to do so. Many cases can indeed be pointed to in his works where the music scrupulously follows every verbal detail of the poem. In the cantata *Nun komm' der Heiden Heiland* (No. 61), for example, the line "Das sich wundert alle Welt" has an animation that makes it stand out sharply from the remainder. But in all these cases it is not so much a matter of an independent musical reproduction of the changing ideas of the text, as of underlining isolated and salient lines and words. Bach does not follow his text line by line, no matter how tempting the episodes it presents; he expresses the characteristic emotional content, the word that seems to him vital for the mood of the whole, in an eloquent melodic motive. He is sure that in so doing he has expressed the poem itself. Whether we are reading a chorale-prelude from the *Orgelbüchlein* or a large chorus from one of the cantatas, it is all the same; almost invariably the motive that appears in the first bar is maintained to the last, as if the composer were indifferent to the details of the text.

If the orchestra, for example, has broken into an exuberant motive of joy, it will not give it up, even though the poem should afterwards express feelings of another kind. If there comes some specially characteristic word, it is thrown into harmonic relief. The first chorus of the cantata *Mache dich, mein Geist, bereit, wache, fleh und bete* (No. 115) is dominated, like that of *Wachet auf* (No. 140), by a soaring, animated motive that symbolises the "wachen" (waking); the music will not be turned from its course by the concept of "beten" (to pray); all Bach does is to bring this home to us by a striking modulation. In the chorale-fantasias, again, the shadows of certain words seem to pass occasionally over the music.

On the whole we can say that Bach only takes into account in his music the most salient episodes of the text, confining himself mainly to expressing the basic mood of it. Often this seems to him to reside in some contrast, which he will suggest by a conflict of two characteristic motives. The classical example of this is the introductory chorus of the cantata *Ihr werdet weinen und heulen, aber die Welt wird sich freuen* (No. 103). His fondness for sharp contrasts makes him particularly delight in texts of this kind. Even when the antithesis suggested in the poem is purely incidental, he will fasten upon it and make it the fundamental idea of his music.

In the Capriccio on the departure of his brother, Bach entered upon the path that leads to programme music. It was not, however, the naïve programme music of a Kuhnau, who undertook to tell whole histories in music, but an art fully conscious of the limits of what can be intelligibly expressed in tone, and confining itself to a sequence of a few plastic scenes, admirably characterised in the music. Bach's experience in this youthful experiment led him afterwards to aim at expression on other lines. His artistic greatness is shown in the fact that in an epoch of confident and pretentious programme music he rises superior to it from the beginning, and never aims at trying to express in music what music is incapable of expressing.

The naïve programme musicians of the past and the present are like the Biblical painters who, relying on the fact that every detail of certain of the sacred stories is known, deluded themselves that they had really represented these scenes when they had accumulated the various objects and persons concerned on their canvas, while all the time they had failed to make the real thing, the event itself, comprehensible. A man with a knife; a boy bound to a pile of wood; a ram's head in a bush; a bearded face looking down from the clouds, — this, they thought, was the sacrifice of Isaac. A man and a woman at a well; in the background a town; on the road leading to it twelve men scattered about here and there in pairs — this was supposed to tell the story of Jesus and the woman of Samaria. The real action is added by the spectator, out of the convention that resolves the simultaneous grouping of the figures on the canvas into a succession in time. As a rule very few of the Biblical stories are really "paintable", in the true sense of the word, for the event does not present a single pregnant situation which contains and elucidates the whole action. Thus the majority of Biblical painters, by having to presuppose so much knowledge of the subject on the spectator's part, have given us not pictures but illustrations, that exceed the limits of true painting to the same extent that descriptive programme music exceeds those of true music.

Bach, however, did not let the general knowledge of the chorales and Biblical texts mislead him into an attempt to depict in his music all the details and salient episodes of his text. He keeps within the real possibilities of musical expression, even in cases where another man would think it safe to rely on the general knowledge of the words to carry off his strokes of pictorialism.

He thus makes no effort to represent all the episodes and evolutions of the text. He expresses the essential elements in the idea, not its vicissitudes. He underlines, indeed, any characteristic detail, brings out contrasts, employs the most powerful nuances; but the vicissitudes of the idea, its struggles, its combats, its despair, its entry into peace, all that Beethoven's music and that of the post-Beethoven epoch try to express — of this there is nothing in Bach. Nevertheless his emotional expression is not less perfect than Beethoven's. It is simply another kind of perfection. His emotional utterance has a power and an impressiveness such as we rarely meet with in other music. His capacity for characterising the various nuances of an emotion is quite unique.

Thus Bach's music is also emotional music in the truest

and deepest sense, though he pursues a path far remote from that of Wagner. Both composers aim at realising poetic ideas in music; both avoid programme music, i.e., a naïve translation of the poem into sound; both remain strictly within the real possibilities of musical expression. But they are different in this respect, that Bach depicts the idea in its static, Wagner in its dynamic life. There is no art to which Wagner's definition of the nature of music is less applicable than that of Bach. According to Wagner, the harmonic changes must be inevitable in the sense that they are motived by the poetry, and express an emotion that demands the intensifying power of music. This is not the case with Bach's modulations. Generally speaking they are of a purely musical nature. They too are "inevitable", but in the sense that they are a logical unfolding of what was latent in the theme from the beginning. So far those are right who meet all modernisations of Bach, good and bad, with the objection that his art is "pure music". In this way they express, even if obscurely, the truth that, unlike Beethoven and Wagner, he does not represent an emotion as a series of dramatic incidents. The perception of this distinction is of the first importance for the performance of Bach's music. It makes us realise the error of imposing upon Bach the Beethovenian and Wagnerian dynamics, the purpose of which is to heighten the harmonic expression of the various poetic incidents. Bach's music is of a different order.

Beethoven and Wagner poetise in music; Bach paints. And Bach is a dramatist, but just in the sense that the painter is. He does not paint successive events, but seizes upon the pregnant moment that contains the whole event for him, and depicts this in music. That is why the opera had so little attraction for him. He knew the Hamburg stage from his youth; he was intimate with the leading people at the Dresden theatre. If nevertheless he never wrote an opera, it was not because the external circumstances were unfavourable, but because, unlike Wagner, he did not conceive action and music in one. The musical drama is for him a succession of dramatic pictures; he realises it in his Passions and cantatas.

In Bach the poetic idea is embedded in the theme. This is not, as in Wagner, a melodic determination of a certain harmony welling up out of the depths of the ocean of tone; it is more akin in origin to the thematic invention of Berlioz. It resembles the latter's themes in its emotional vehemence and a certain pictorial tendency, for it is the product of the same kind of plastic imagination. Bach's view of tone-painting is different from Wagner's. For the latter, self-existent tone-painting is only a makeshift. His ideal is that music shall address itself, as in drama, to feeling rather than imagination. Bach, on the other hand, appeals to the conceptual imagination. Tone-painting is an end in itself with him. The ideal before him is not the self-expression of this pictorialism, but the carrying of it to the extremest limits of realism.

The first thing he looks for in a text is the image or idea that gives an opportunity for a definitely plastic musical expression. This image may lie at the very root of the thought, or it may be a mere incident in the text; in either case it is for Bach the essential element in the words, and he works it out without troubling whether, by so doing, he is really expressing or not the emotional content of the poem.

His idea of a good poet is one who gives the maximum of images that are translateable into sound. We sometimes wonder that he did not weary of the doggrel of Picander, his chief librettist. When, however, we consider the plastic variety of these libretti, we can see at once what attracted Bach to them time after time. Nor does he object to his librettist giving him the same pictures again and again; on the contrary, he reproduces them in tone with ever new delight. We really get the impression that he demanded pictorial opportunities of this kind. He even forgives his librettist when he adds extraneous pictures of his own to the classical text of a chorale-strophe*. In the *St. John Passion* he cannot dispense with the rending of the curtain and the earthquake at the death of Jesus; he inserts these events in his text, although they do not occur in the fourth Gospel.

The difference between Wagner and Bach becomes most evident in their conceptions of natural events. Wagner conceives nature through his emotions; Bach, — in this respect like Berlioz — through his imagination. Bach is not satisfied until he is sure that the hearer actually sees the dust of the whirlwind, the clouds scudding across the sky, the falling leaves, the raging waves. When his poets came to the end of their tether, all they had to do was to bring nature on the scene; they could be sure of satisfying him in this way. This is the explanation of the fact that the secular cantatas are veritable nature-poems**.

The great thing, however, is that this nature-painting is always musical. Abt Vogler, the other great master whom Weber placed by the side of Bach, also aimed at tone-painting, but found that though it was very successful with the people, the musicians looked askance at him for it. "They complained," he says***, "that I tried to represent on the all-powerful instrument, the organ, natural phenomena such as thunder, earthquakes, collapsing walls, &c." — and he tells us how he succeeded, in the village church at Upsala, not only with crying children and howling dogs, but in making a deaf mute "feel" the thunder. Bach certainly could not cite such testimonies for *his* painting. However realistic it is, it always keeps within the limits of musical symbolism. Here again the whole expression lies in the theme; it is this that stimulates the conceptual imagination of the hearer.

---

* See, for example, the second verse of the chorale cantata *Ich hab' in Gottes Herz und Sinn* (No. 92).

** In the French translation the secular cantata *Weichet nur, betrübte Schatten* has been justly called the "Spring Cantata".

*** *Choralsystem* (1800), p. 102.

His tone-painting is never obtrusive. It lasts as long as the occasion that called it forth, but not a moment longer. This perfect moderation, in spite of the great vivacity of the tone-painting, becomes all the more astonishing when we examine his recitative accompaniments. In the *St. Matthew Passion* he gives the most drastic musical expression to every characteristic word in the account of the Passion. But it never delays the story for a moment. The tone-painting merely heightens the plastic impression of the words.

A typical example of Bach's method may be seen in the first aria of the cantata *Siehe, ich will viel Fischer aussenden* (No. 88). The words are taken from Jeremiah XVI, 16: "Behold, I will send for many fishers, saith the Lord, and they shall fish them; and after will I send for many hunters, and they shall hunt them." In the first part the strings paint the rolling waves of a lake; the second part is filled with clashing fanfares in the wind instruments.

At times Bach will paint, in a single passage, several characteristic words in succession.

It is an interesting psychological observation that in the Bach family the gift for painting went along with that for music. Samuel Anton Bach, who came of the Meiningen stock, and who studied with Johann Sebastian at the beginning of the thirties, was not only a capable organist but an eminent portrait painter in pastel; and his double gift was inherited by his descendants*. Johann Sebastian's grandchild, the son of Philipp Emmanuel, gave up music and, to his father's horror, became a painter.

The idea that prompted Bach to paint a musical picture is not always equally clear to us. It often takes us some time to discover how he has realised his text in music. But when once we have grasped the sense of the music, it seems unthinkable that the poem could be depicted from any other standpoint. Daring as his painting often

* For further information about these pastel painters of the Meiningen branch of the family, see Wolfrum, *J. S. Bach*, pp. 13, 14.

is, the final and enduring impression is one of absolute satisfaction; and this is the fundamental proof of the veracity of his art.

Not only the avowed picture but every characteristic movement is regarded pictorially by Bach. Expressions like *erwachen* (awake), *auffahren* (ascend), *auferstehen* (arise), *steigen* (mount), *emporschwingen* (soar), *eilen* (hasten), *straucheln* (stumble), *wanken* (stagger), *sinken* (fall), wherever they occur, furnish the germ-idea of the theme. It is noteworthy, however, that Bach's imagination also conceives motion when it is not actually expressed in the text but only implied. A number of the most striking themes and motives, that otherwise would be quite incomprehensible, are explained in this way.

What is the meaning, for example, of the accompaniment of the arioso of the *St. Matthew Passion*, "Ja! freilich will in uns das Fleisch und Blut zum Kreuz gezwungen sein" ("Aye, surely now can flesh and blood atone, if the Cross hold them bound"), with its curious flickering flute accompaniment, and its abstruse conclusion? —

The preceding recitative has told us that Simon of Cyrene had been given the cross of Jesus to carry. Bach sees Jesus labouring under the cross, stumbling along, sinking on His knees, and breaking down; he paints this picture of Him in the accompaniment, while the arioso comments upon the scene.

The conductor who has grasped the meaning of this recitative will not let his flutists group their three notes in the usual sentimental *diminuendo*, but will make them give a heavy emphasis each time to the third note, and preserve this accentuation to the end, without a *rallentando* or *diminuendo*. In this way the simple motive, without the necessity for any further explanation, will conjure up before the imagination of the hearer the picture of Christ staggering under the burden of the cross.

Another example of Bach's representation of movement is to be seen in the first chorus of the cantata *Brich dem Hungrigen dein Brot* (No. 39). The text* runs thus: — "Is it not to deal thy bread to the hungry, and that thou bring the poor that are cast out to thy house? When thou seest the naked, that thou cover him, and that thou hide not thyself from thine own flesh?" The music seems at first curiously disjointed. Spitta** surmises that it is prompted by the conception of the breaking of bread. He feels bound, indeed, to add a saving clause; "how far", he says, "Bach is from mere triviality is seen in the sequel, where the same accompaniment continues to quite other words. It simply gives the passage a peculiarly delicate and pliant character; it was this that Bach was chiefly aiming at."

Here both the explanation of the tone-painting and the excuse for it are wrong, — the excuse, because we could not reproach Bach with anything worse than retaining a picture in his music after the necessity for it in the text had gone by; the explanation, because no one who listens to the music can take it to be a picture of the breaking of bread. What then is the meaning of it? The monotonous instrumental accompaniment, with the regular crotchets in the bass, has more the character of a march. A certain unrest enters with the vocal parts; it is as if we heard uncertain, tottering steps defiling past us. One of the chief themes runs thus: —

* Isaiah LVIII, 7.

** *J. S. Bach*, III, 82.

The music thus depicts the wretched ones who are being supported and led into the house. As soon as the words "führe in das Haus" have been uttered, the picture ceases in the accompaniment, which is now constructed of other themes.

In the cantata *Es ist ein trotzig und verzagtes Ding* (No. 176) Spitta* is horror-struck at the gavotte-like character of the first aria. "As a piece of music", he says, "it is perfectly charming, but it does not agree at all with the text, which speaks of the timidity of the Christian before Jesus, the God-possessed and wonder-working." If the condition of the autograph did not forbid it, the worthy biographer of Bach would like to believe that the music has been taken from some other cantata, and has nothing whatever in common with this text. "All we can do", he concludes, "is simply to point out the discrepancy."

The discord between the text and the music disappears as soon as we realise that Bach had the idea of movement here. The words run thus: "When I enquire after the Master thy (i. e. the sun's) beloved light shall be clouded, for I am afraid by day." The situation is explained by the preceding recitative, in which Nicodemus waits for the sun to set in order to go to Jesus. In the aria he is on his way to Him; in the following recitative he is with Him. The aria thus represents him soliloquising as he walks delicately and circumspectly but joyously in the twilight. The rhythm that runs through the movement — ♩ ♩ | 𝅗𝅥 ♩ ♩ | 𝅗𝅥 ♩ ♩ | 𝅗𝅥 ♩ ♩ | 𝅗𝅥 is really the only characteristic thing in the text that music can fasten upon. Here the music in no way aims at expressing pure "feeling".

Examples of this kind show that when we are studying Bach, the seemingly shortest and most direct way from the text to the music is not always the right one. To discover his real thought we must very often follow him along the by-paths that surround his idea, which is strongly

---

* *J. S. Bach,* III, 81.

pictorial in essence. His music is very often a picture of a situation.

Allied with this pictorial instinct is the plastic symbolism which Bach's music confers on abstract thoughts. In the first chorus of the cantata *Du sollst Gott deinen Herrn lieben von ganzem Herzen* (No. 77), he ventures to elucidate the saying of Jesus that the whole law is contained in the commandment of love. He builds up the chorus on the *cantus firmus* of the chorale "Dies sind die heil'gen zehn Gebot", bringing it in in the basses in augmentation, and in the trumpets in diminution. Further, in order to add to the great and small commandments the very smallest, the "tittles" of the law, of which Jesus speaks in the sermon on the mount, the chorus and orchestra have in addition a motive derived from the first notes of the melody. This movement is typical of very many other pieces of symbolism in his work, equally daring, and yet fundamentally musical in conception.

He does not even shrink from finding a musical symbol for the abstract idea of "time". In the cantata on the chorale —

> "Wer weiss, wie nahe mir mein Ende,
> Hin geht die Zeit, her kommt der Tod."

(No. 27) the flight of time is suggested in the orchestra by a mysterious pendulum stroke, that never ceases throughout the opening chorus. There is a similar representation in the first chorus of the cantata *Alles nur nach Gottes Willen* (No. 72).

Bach's music is thus pictorial to the extent that wherever possible his themes and motives are conditioned by a pictorial association of ideas, whether this can be found directly or indirectly in the text, and whether it is a salient feature of it or not. There are motives the pictorial origin of which we should not recognise at first sight, if the key to them were not afforded by others of the same kind. If we arrange the themes and the motives of the chorale fantasias, cantatas, and Passions according to their formal affinities and their congruence with the text, we see that whenever Bach has to find music for analogous ideas, a whole group of pictorial associations of ideas comes forward as if in obedience to an inner law.

At the same time we discover that certain feelings are expressed in the same formulae as the pictorial ideas to which they correspond. Motives that proceed by sure, strong steps symbolise strength, authority, confident faith; those that stride along boldly symbolise pride and defiance; others, that are uncertain in their gait, symbolise vacillation or the lassitude of death. In view of this regular return of definite musical formulae in Bach's works we cannot but attribute to him a complete tonal language.

Wagner maintained that Beethoven had a language of this kind. "In long, connected stretches of sound," he says, "as in larger, smaller, or even the smallest fragments, it (i. e. instrumental music) became, in the poetic hands of Beethoven, vowels, syllables, words and phrases of a language in which something hitherto unheard, unspeakable and never yet spoken, could find voice. Every letter of this language was an infinitely soulful element, and the measure of the joining of these elements was unlimited freedom of judgment, (*und das Mass der Fügung dieser Elemente unbegrenzt freies Ermessen*), as is possible only to the tone-poet who longs for immeasurable expression of the most unfathomable longing."*

Speaking of himself Wagner says, with reference to the time when he was writing *The Flying Dutchman*: "I had had to acquire the capacity for musical expression in the same way as one learns a language .... But now I had thoroughly learned the language of music; I was at home in it now, as in a veritable mother-tongue; when I had anything to say I had no longer to trouble about the formal side of expression; it was at my command just as

---

* *Das Kunstwerk der Zukunft*, (*Ges. Schriften* III, 110).

I had need of it, to communicate a definite impression or feeling according to my inner impulse."*

On the other hand he will not admit that Bach has a developed language. In *Das Judenthum in der Musik* he almost makes it a reproach against Mendelssohn that he is influenced by Bach. "Bach's musical language", he says, "was formed in a period of our musical history in which the general musical language was striving after the faculty of surer individual expression; it was still so hampered by formalism and pedantry that its purely human expression only managed to find utterance in Bach by reason of the abnormal strength of his genius. Bach's language bears the same relation to that of Mozart and that of Beethoven as the Egyptian Sphinx to the Greek statues of human beings: as the Sphinx with its human face strives to come out of the body of the animal, so Bach's noble human head strives to come out of the periwig."**

At the time when he pronounced this judgment (1852) Wagner could not have known many of Bach's works. But even later, when he had looked into the cantatas, he clung to his opinion. From his standpoint he could not admit Bach's musical language to be of equal value with that of Beethoven and his own, since it does not represent the play of successive emotional episodes but only a definite emotion. Its strong bias towards the pictorial only strengthened his view that Bach could not free himself of the naïve materialistic conception of music.

If, however, we recognise poetic music and pictorial music as two equally legitimate basic styles of the art, we must not regard Bach's simple language of feelings and pictures as a primitive form that was surpassed by Beethoven and Wagner, but as the utterance of one particular kind of musical imagination. The nearest affinity to the musical language of Bach's cantatas is that of the

---

* *Eine Mitteilung an meine Freunde*, (*Ges. Schriften* IV, 387).

** *Ges. Schriften* V, 101, 102.

accompaniments to Schubert's songs; these also make large use of pictorial associations.

The unique thing in Bach is the clearness and completeness of the language. Its elements, being mostly of the pictorial order, can be much more exactly shown than those of Beethoven and Wagner. We can really speak of the roots and derivations of his language. Almost all the characteristic expressions that impress us by their regular recurrence in the cantatas and Passions resolve themselves into about twenty to twenty-five root-themes, mostly pictorial in origin. These well-defined groups comprise, for example, the already mentioned "step"-motives for the expression of firmness, indecision, or tottering; the syncopated themes of lassitude; the theme that depicts tumult; the graceful wavy lines that depict peaceful rest; the serpentine lines that contort themselves at the mention of the word Satan; the charming, flowing motives that enter when angels are mentioned; the motives of rapturous, naïve, or passionate joy; the motives of distressful or noble grief. No attempt is here made to give a schematic catalogue of Bach's themes. It is only intended to point out, — what any musician can easily verify for himself — that the wealth of Bach's musical language does not consist in any special multiplicity of themes and motives, but in the manifold shadings by means of which a few general formulae are made to express characteristic ideas and feelings. If it were not for this interesting variety in the individual forms and formulæ, Bach's tone-language might almost be called monotonous.

The establishment of a musical language in Bach is not a mere pastime for the æsthetician, but a necessity for the practical musician. It is often impossible to play a work of his in the right tempo, and with the right accent and the right phrasing, unless we know the meaning of the motive. The simple "feeling" does not always suffice. The serious errors that even judicious commentators can commit when, without taking into consideration Bach's musical language as a whole, they try to explain pieces that call for elucidation, may be seen from Spitta's remarks, cited above, upon the cantatas *Brich dem Hungrigen* (No. 39) and *Es ist ein trotzig und verzagt Ding* (No. 176). There is only one way to avoid falling into the fantastic, — a comparative study of all the cantatas. They explain each other. No one can conduct one cantata properly unless he knows them all.

Short explanations may be given to an audience if they are confined to simple hints as to Bach's method of musical characterisation. They are objectionable when they are meant to induce the audience to regard the cantata in question as "modern music". Unintelligent modernisation of Bach is the greatest hindrance to the true understanding of his works.

To the plain man, indeed, many explanations will seem fantastic that are not really so. This however is due to Bach himself, whose music is frequently extraordinarily audacious. Apart from that, there are certain movements in his works the riddle of which will never be fully solved, and the elucidation of which will always be somewhat arbitrary. Very often, however, a musical picture that has been regarded as undecipherable is suddenly explained by an analogous picture that we have come across by hazard in another cantata.

The understanding of Bach's musical language is also valuable for the interpretation of the purely instrumental works. Many pieces in the *Well-tempered Clavichord*, in the violin sonatas, or in the Brandenburg concertos speak quite definitely to us, as it were, when the meaning of their themes is explained by the text that accompanies similar themes in the cantatas.

Two objections may be raised to the assumption of a complete musical language in Bach — that he occasionally parodied his own works in a really thoughtless way, and that so far as we know he never said anything, either to his pupils or to his sons, with reference to his pictorial purposes. Both objections are unanswerable from the historical standpoint. On the other hand they cannot invalidate the facts as revealed to us in the scores. They only make us ask to what degree Bach was conscious of his musical language being a means of expression peculiar to himself, and the result of profound artistic reflection. But to this question, again, no definite answer is possible, for it is even more difficult to fix upon the border-line between the conscious and the unconscious in the case of Bach than in that of any other genius. His musical language is so clear, and makes so deep an impression, that we cannot but regard it as deliberate. Unlike Wagner, Bach never felt the necessity of explaining his own mental processes either to himself or to others. A psychological common denominator between the two cases will probably never be found.

Nor can much be said upon the origin and development of Bach's musical language. In the chorale-partitas of the Arnstadt and Mühlhausen period certain poetic ideas are already thrown into high relief in the music. This is especially the case with the last strophes of *O Gott, du frommer Gott* (Peters V, 68 ff.). The seventh verse speaks of death and burial. A wonderful melodic line, similar to one found in the cantata *Ich steh' mit einem Fuss im Grabe* (No. 156) and elsewhere, depicts the descent into the kingdom of the dead: —

The eighth verse speaks of the sleeping souls' expectation of the resurrection. Bach conceives it as a painful longing, and so writes a number of variations upon the chromatic motive which he had already employed in the "Lamento" of the *Capriccio*, and which is so often met with afterwards in his music —

In the final variation the risen souls break out into a jubilant song of praise of the Trinity. In the course of it we have one of Bach's most characteristic rhythms — that of tranquil happiness —

In other works of his youthful period we find poetic ideas expressed in a more or less definite way. In the first part of a chorale prelude upon *Jesus meine Freude* (Peters VI, No. 29), we first of all get a picture of the feverish unrest of the world, that leads the anxious soul to seek out Jesus; at the words *Gottes Lamm, mein Bräutigam*, it has found Him; a wonderful *dolce* in $^3/_8$ time depicts its rapture.

A fantasia on the Easter chorale *Christ lag in Todesbanden* (VI, No. 15) begins with heavy descending semiquavers, that seem to fetter the melody and draw it down into the depths —

At the words *Des sollen wir fröhlich sein* ("Let us be joyful") the music brightens, flowing along in a delightful triplet movement (Peters VI, p. 41), and ending in an impetuous song of triumph.

These experiments, however, are not pursued tentatively for any long period. The musical language appears complete and perfect at once. Its first document is the chorales of the *Orgelbüchlein* (Peters V)*. This collection contains such improvisations of the Weimar period as he thought worth preserving. The title that Bach gave this work, (of which he afterwards made a clean copy at Cöthen), is sufficient to show the treasures of musical poetry that it contains. The works themselves confirm this impression. They represent a particular type of chorale prelude; they originate in the simple melody itself, which is supported by a motive treated in thorough contrapuntal style. This motive contains the idea of the poem; it is, in a manner, the poetic illustration of the melody. And here we can detect the motives Bach uses in order to express pictures and emotions in music. These forty-five chorales are the dictionary of his musical language, the key to the understanding of his music as a whole.

When Bach planned this collection he would be about thirty years old. From this time until his death he does not swerve in the slightest degree either from his poetic conception of music or from the musical language in which he had found expression for his ideas. The language of the cantatas is the same as that of the *Orgelbüchlein*.

One change is indeed noticeable — as time goes on, the pictorial quality of his thinking becomes more and more evident. In the earlier works it is still kept under to some extent by the melodic interest. Later on it asserts itself irresistibly. In the end Bach writes themes that are strikingly characteristic in themselves but are not quite grateful to the ear. The great chorale fantasias *Jesus Christus unser Heiland* (Peters VI, No. 30) and *Christ unser Herr zum Jordan kam* (Peters VI, No. 17), for example, almost overpass the border-line of music that is meant to appeal to the ear. Again, in the affecting cantata *Ich glaube, lieber Herr, hilf meinem Unglauben* (No. 109), in which Bach depicts wavering faith, we have the impression that the pictorial bias is too prominent in the music.

---

* See p. 281 ff.

Here we are bound to think Bach wrong. He has ventured beyond the natural limits of music. His mistake, however, has nothing in common with that of the naïve practitioners of tone-painting. They fail because they mistake the nature of music; he fails because he cultivates to its final consequences the language in which he expresses himself so consummately, with the result that, for the ordinary intelligence, the melodic and the beautiful are almost wholly lost in the plastic. It is an error of which only genius is capable.

CHAPTER XXII.

THE MUSICAL LANGUAGE OF THE CHORALES.

PICTORIAL AND SYMBOLICAL REPRESENTATION.

Where a chorale text offers him a picture, however external it may be, Bach takes this as the basis of his music. The fall of Adam in *Durch Adams Fall ist ganz verderbt* ("Through Adam's fall mankind fell too") (V, No. 13) is depicted by the following *basso ostinato* —

In the Easter hymn *Erstanden ist der heilige Christ* ("Christ is arisen") (V, No. 14), the bass has this motive —

while in the other part we find progressions like this —

The appearance of the angels in the chorales *Vom Himmel hoch* (V, No. 49) and *Vom Himmel kam* (V, No. 50) is represented by a charming maze of ascending and descending scales. Bach attempts similar pictures in the first canonic variation on *Vom Himmel hoch, da komm ich her* (V, p. 92), in a fughetta on the same chorale (VII, No. 54), and in a simple harmonisation of it (V, p. 106).

When he is arranging the melody *Allein Gott in der Höh' sei Ehr'* ("To God alone on high be praise") he never forgets that the melody is supposed to be the angels' song, and so he sets it in the form of light duets or trios of ravishing charm (VI, Nos. 3—11); in two of these fantasias (VI, Nos. 5 and 10), the upward and downward motion is almost too realistically painted; the ascension and disappearance of the angels are represented by ascending cadences (VI, Nos. 8, 10 and 11).

The hymn *Ach wie flüchtig, ach wie nichtig* (V, No. 1), compares the transitoriness of life to the cloud "that soon arises and soon has passed away". Bach reproduces this image by an ingenious scale-passage. About twenty years later he writes, upon the same chorale, a chorus (cantata No. 26), that is simply an amplification of this little picture. The same design, only in rather more energetic strokes, is seen in the first chorus of the secular cantata *Der zufriedengestellte Aeolus*, in which Bach represents the play of the unchained winds, driving the clouds over the sky in all directions. The three examples, showing the unchangeable nature of Bach's musical language, are here shewn together:

Chorale prelude: "Ach wie flüchtig, ach wie nichtig (V, No. 1).

Chorale cantata: "Ach wie flüchtig, ach wie nichtig" (No. 26.)

"Der zufriedengestellte Aeolus" (*Dramma per musica*).

The fantasia upon *Christ unser Herr zum Jordan kam* ("Christ our Lord to Jordan came") (VI, No. 17), and the orchestral accompaniment to the first chorus of the cantata (No. 7) on the same melody, represent the motion of waves. The quick semiquavers rustle along in beautiful wavy lines over the melody in the bass. A small fantasia on the same chorale (VI, No. 18) is indeed one of the most interesting miniatures to be found anywhere in music. It is based on four motives. — (1) the first line of the melody, (2) its inversion, (3) the melody in an accelerated form, (4) the inversion of this:

First line: Inversion of this:

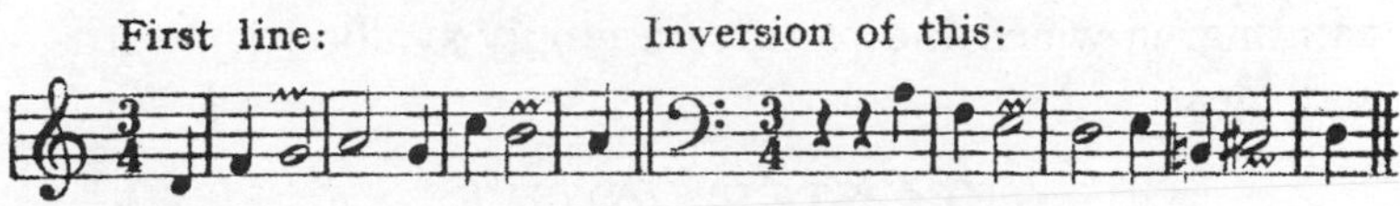

The first line in accelerated form:

Inversion of this:

These four motives are worked into an extremely realistic picture of great and small waves rising and falling and overwhelming each other. It is a picture for the eye, however, rather than the ear.

The symbolism of the chorale *Dies sind die heiligen zehn Gebot'* ("These are the Ten Commandments") (V, No. 12) is rather primitive. It consists in the tenfold recurrence in the pedal of the first melodic period. In a little fughetta upon the same chorale (VI, No. 20) the theme of the first notes of the melody again appears ten times. The symbolism of the great chorale prelude on this "catechism-hymn" (VI, No. 19) is more profound. It aims at reproducing the dogma of the text. In a lengthy fantasia each of the separate parts goes its own way, without rhythm, without plan, without theme, without regard for the others. This musical disorder depicts the moral state of the world before the law. Then the law is revealed. It is represented by a majestic canon upon the melody of the chorale, running through the whole movement. The idea in itself is grand; but the effect of the chorale prelude does not come up to expectation. The abstract representation of the antithesis between order and disorder is not really a matter for music.

The examples of this more external order of tone-painting are relatively few in number. The true greatness of Bach is not revealed in these, but in a kind of spiritualised tone-painting, in which the pictures are only symbols for words and ideas.

THE "STEP" MOTIVES.

Tranquil and even melodic lines represent the idea of strength and confidence; uncertain and wavering steps indicate lassitude and weakness.

The text of the last Christmas chorale but one in the *Orgelbüchlein, — Wir Christenleut' han jetzund Freud'* ("Now are we Christians joyful") (V, No. 55) speaks of firm belief in the Christmas tidings*. This is symbolised by the continual repetition of the following widely-spaced figure in the bass—

This interpretation of it might be thought too daring if Bach had not similarly expressed the idea of confident faith in other chorales.

The great prelude upon *Wir glauben all' an einen Gott* (VII, No. 60) is particularly interesting in this connection. It consists of a gentle, almost dreamy fantasia upon the motive of the first line of the chorale text. In order to understand to what extent this music reproduced the *Credo* for Bach, we must bear in mind the definition of faith in Luther's catechism, according to which its essence consists in child-like love and trust in the Father. The conception of faith as "absolute confidence" is expressed in the "step" motive of the bass —

In the chorale prelude upon the Communion hymn, *Jesus Christus unser Heiland* (VI, No. 30), (in the collec-

---

* "Wir Christenleut' han jetzund Freud,
Weil uns zum Trost ist Christus Mensch geboren,
Hat uns erlöst, wer sich dess tröst
Und *glaubet fest,* soll nicht werden verloren."

tion of chorales on the catechism hymns), Bach wishes to illustrate the Lutheran dogma of the communion. We know that Luther was opposed to the rationalism of Zwingli, who regarded the sacramental words as symbolical and the whole celebration as a simple ceremony of remembrance. To Luther, the essence of the doctrine of the sacrament was faith in a real change in the elements, in virtue of which the communion gives remission of sins. This *credo quia absurdum* suggests to Bach a theme of extraordinarily wide spacing. It is as if some one were standing on a rolling ship and planting his feet wide apart in order to keep a firm footing —

This theme is characteristic rather than musical, and Bach develops it at too great length; the *cantus firmus* of the melody, that should hold the whole together, is split up into fragments, with long interludes between them. The total effect of the work is thus not organic.

This may also be said in general of almost all the larger arrangements of the catechism hymns in the third Part of the *Klavierübung*. They are constructed on the same plan as the chorales of the *Orgelbüchlein*, the sentiment of the words finding expression in a characteristic motive that plays round the *cantus firmus*. In the *Orgelbüchlein* the effect is excellent, because the movements are short, and are held together by the melody that runs uninterruptedly through them. As soon, however, as the characteristic motive, instead of merely accompanying the melody contrapuntally, becomes an independent picture, in which the lines of the *cantus firmus* follow one another at long intervals, we get a piece of music that is neither intellectually nor formally satisfactory, — not intellectually, because the characteristic motive now aims at being something more than the poetical illustration of the melody;

and not formally, because the work necessarily becomes formless. The chorales of the *Orgelbüchlein* were Dürer engravings in music; the long chorale preludes in the *Klavierübung* are like etchings done on the scale of big canvases.

Wavering steps symbolise lassitude. In the chorale *Herr Gott, nun schleuss den Himmel auf* (V, No. 24) the text speaks of a man who has finished his course and now goes with weary steps to the gate of eternity*. In the rhythm of the bass we hear the uncertain steps of the pilgrim —

Again in the chorale *Hilf Gott, dass mir's gelinge* (V, No. 29), the text of which expresses the same idea as *Herr Gott, nun schleuss den Himmel auf*, the bass staggers wearily along.

In the chorale *Da Jesus an dem Kreuze stund* (V, No. 9) the drooping of the exhausted body of Jesus on the cross is expressed in the following rhythm —

Pictorial ideas are thus chiefly expressed by means of themes in the bass. Böhm's *basso ostinato* plays a great part in Bach's chorales. In the *Puer natus in Bethlehem* (V, No. 46), the text of which describes the adoration of the wise men from the East, the bass depicts a constant succession of deep obeisances —

* "Herr Gott, nun schleuss den Himmel auf, mein'Zeit zu End sich neiget.
Ich hab vollendet meinen Lauf, dess sich mein' Seel' sehr freuet;
Hab g'nug gelitten, mich müd' gestritten,
Schick' mich fein zu, zur ew'gen Ruh',
Lass fahren was auf Erden: will lieber selig werden."

The *basso ostinato* of the Easter chorale *Heut' triumphieret Gottes Sohn* (V, No. 28) is only intelligible when we remember that in the Old Testament the victory of the Messiah is described under the image of the treading of the wine-press. It is in this conception that the haughty steps of the bass in Bach's prelude have originated —

That this interpretation is correct is proved by the aria *Er ist's, er ist's,* from the cantata *Gott fahret auf* (No. 43), the text of which refers to this Old Testament image. Here again Bach's music suggests a haughty stamping movement; he does not hesitate to use even intervals like these —

In the Easter chorale *Christ lag in Todesbanden* (V, No. 5) the bonds of death are symbolised by heavy basses that draw the melody down into the depths —

THE MOTIVES OF BEATIFIC PEACE.

When Bach wishes to express a certain kind of intimate gladness or blissful adoration, he often employs a rhythmical motive that may be seen in its typical form in the chorale *Herr Gott, nun sei gepreiset* (V, No. 22)* —

* "Herr Gott, nun sei gepreiset, wir sagen frohen Dank,
Dass du uns Gnad' erwiesen, gegeben Speis' und Trank,
Dein mildes Herz zu merken, den Glauben uns zu stärken,
Dass du seist unser Gott."

It is seen again in the ninth variation upon *O Gott, du frommer Gott* (V, pp. 74 ff.), where it illustrates the words in which the Father and the Son are praised —

"Gott Vater, dir sei Preis, hier und im Himmel oben,
Gott Sohn, Herr Jesu Christ, dich will ich allzeit loben."

We find the same rhythm in the chorales *Gelobet seist du Jesus Christ* (V, No. 17) and *Vater unser im Himmelreich* (V, No. 48). It seems a little strange, at first sight, that it should also dominate the hymn *Alle Menschen müssen sterben* (V, No. 2). Bach's music takes its character from the end of the first verse, that speaks of death as the "Genesen zu der grossen Herrlichkeit, die den Frommen ist bereit" ("the recovery to the great glory that is prepared for those who love God"). The melody of the hymn that speaks of the inevitability of death is thus enveloped in a motive that is lit up by the coming glory.

The rhythm often appears so veiled and disguised that we are hardly conscious of it at first. In these cases it represents this particular emotion in its deepest and most intimate form. It is by means of a rhythm of this kind that Bach expresses, for example, the mystic adoration in the chorale *Jesu meine Freude* (V, No. 31) —

In the bass figure of the Christmas chorale *Lob sei dem allerhöchsten Gott* (V, No. 38), it assumes a still more indefinite form.

THE MOTIVES OF GRIEF.

Bach has a dual expression for grief. To depict lamentation of a noble kind he employs a sequence of notes tied in pairs; torturing grief is represented by a chromatic motive of five or six notes.

The typical form of the motive of noble lamentation is seen in the small chorale upon *O Lamm Gottes* (V, No.44)

The second of the two tied notes must always be lightly breathed, making the motive seem like a series of sighs from the depth of the soul.

The chromatic motive for grief is something of this kind—

It appears even in the youthful works, e. g. the "Lamento" from the *Capriccio*. It will be seen again in the eighth variation upon *O Gott, du frommer Gott* (V, p. 73), where Bach wishes to depict the painful longing with which the dead in their graves await the resurrection. In the chorales of the *Orgelbüchlein* the chromatic motive frequently appears. It runs through the melancholy musical meditation upon *Das alte Jahr vergangen ist* (V, No. 10), and determines the affecting harmonisation of the Passion chorale *Christus, der uns selig macht* (V, No. 8). Towards the end of the chorale prelude *O Mensch, bewein' dein' Sünde gross* (V, No. 45) it is used to paint the agonies of Jesus on the cross.

THE MOTIVES OF JOY.

For joy, again, Bach had two formulae of expression. At times he represents it by a long and animated series of quaver or semiquaver scale passages; at others by the rhythm

The first formula, that represents more particularly direct and naïve joy, is seen in the chorales *Erstanden ist der heil'ge Christ* (V, No. 14), *Es ist das Heil uns kommen her* (V, No. 16), *Gottes Sohn ist kommen* (V, No. 19), *In dir ist Freude* (V, No. 34), *In dulci jubilo* (V, No. 35),

Lobt Gott, ihr Christen, allzugleich (V, No. 40), and *Puer natus in Bethlehem* (V, No. 46).

The second motive is used to express the joy of the aged Simeon in the chorale *Mit Fried' und Freud' ich fahr dahin* (V, No. 41) —

It expresses both lively and radiant joy. In the chorale *Wer nur den lieben Gott lässt walten* (V, No. 54), Bach even employs it to express the joyful feeling of confidence in God's goodness. The significance of it always changes according to the rhythmical variations it assumes. The more lively the joy to be expressed, the more lively is the motive. Examples may be seen in the two Easter chorales *Der Tag, der ist so freudenreich* (V, No. 11) and *Erschienen ist der herrlich' Tag* (V, No. 15); it is seen in a more drastic form in the chorales *In dich hab' ich gehoffet, Herr* (V, No. 33), *Von Gott will ich nicht lassen* (VII, No. 56), and the Passion hymn *Wir danken dir, Herr Jesu Christ* (V, No. 56).

Bach is very fond of this motive of joy, because the multiplicity of which the rhythm of it is capable allows him to depict joy in all possible nuances — the quiet and mystical as well as the most unrestrained. One of the most animated themes of rejoicing in the chorale preludes is the *basso ostinato* of *In dir ist Freude* (V, No. 34) —

For joyous ecstacy Bach does not employ a motive, but an exuberant musical arabesque, coursing above placid harmonies. For this kind of expression there is naturally much more scope in the cantatas than in the chorales, for Bach knew that the flexibility and variety of modulation that passages of this kind require, and that only a solo instrument can give, are hardly possible with the finest organ registration. Runs like those of the violin solo in the *Laudamus te* of the B minor Mass cannot be attempted upon the organ. On the other hand, the simple arabesque that entwines the melody of the Christmas chorale *Christum wir sollen loben schon* (Adagio, V, No. 6) is consummately effective. It embraces a whole world of unutterable joy. In the great arrangement of *Vater unser im Himmelreich* (VII, No. 52), again, where he aims at reproducing the wonderful exegesis of the Lord's Prayer in the Lutheran catechism, Bach employs a free and flexible melodic line. Unfortunately this noble work, like most of the other large versions of the chorales in the *Klavierübung*, is worked out at such excessive length that as a whole it does not produce the anticipated impression*.

THE "SPEAKING" MOTIVES.

Bach's predecessors had employed in their chorales the motives derived from the lines of the melody wherever they seemed to be musically effective; but they had given no thought to the poetic significance of the repeated chorale-motive. Bach, however, saw that the motive should bring the corresponding words to mind. In the *Orgelbüchlein*, therefore, the motive derived from the chorale is employed only where there is a meaning in the repetition of the words.

In the chorale *Dies sind die heil'gen zehn Gebot* (V, No. 12) he introduces the motive of the commencement of the melody ten times, as if the "Dies sind die heil'gen zehn Gebot" ("These are the ten commandments") were being announced ten times. In the prelude upon *Helft mir Gottes Güte preisen* ("Help me to praise God's goodness") (V, No. 21) the voices reiterate this invitation to each other in the melodic notes belonging to it. In the same

* This, however, does not apply to the three *Kyries* and the chorale *Aus tiefer Not schrei ich zu dir* (VI, No. 13) in this collection. These are worked out less as free fantasias than in the style of the Pachelbel chorales. Their tonal effect is magnificent.

way, in the chorale *Herr Jesu Christ, dich zu uns wend'* (V, No. 25) Bach brings out the "Herr Jesu Christ" in his music, and in *Wenn wir in höchsten Nöten sind* (V, No. 51) the voices repeat the "Wenn wir in höchsten Nöten sind" ("In our hour of deepest need"). The chorales upon *Allein Gott in der Höh' sei Ehr'* (VI, Nos. 3—11), all make use of the motive formed from the opening notes of the melody; the chorale upon the *Kyrie* (VII, No. 39a, b, c) are based on the same procedure. In the great chorale upon *Vater unser im Himmelreich* (VII, No. 52), it is the word "Father" that keeps recurring in the music; in the prelude upon *Wir glauben all* (VI, No. 60) the voices repeat this *credo*. The frequent employment of canon in the chorales of the *Orgelbüchlein** has no poetic significance.

THE "EXPRESSIVE" CHORALES.

By the term "expressive" chorales is here meant those in which the succession of words, phrases, or ideas is duplicated in the music. Bach employs this method of reproducing the text with much reluctance; he only does so when the texts are quite short and extremely characteristic.

As a rule he is content to lay particular stress on this or that word; the striking major cadence, for example, to the profoundly sorrowful arrangement of *Das alte Jahr vergangen ist* (V, No. 10) is occasioned by the consolatory conclusion of the first verse and of the poem in general**.

---

* V, Nos. 3, 8, 15, 19, 35, 37, 44.

** 1st Verse: "Das alte Jahr vergangen ist;
Wir danken dir, Herr Jesu Christ,
Dass du in Not und in Gefahr,
So treu geführt uns dieses Jahr."

("The old year is dead; we thank thee, Lord Jesus Christ, for having led us safely through it.")

5th Verse: "Hilf uns in jeder Erdennot;
Bring uns einst selig über'n Tod,
Dass wir mit Freuden auferstehn
Und mit dir in den Himmel gehn."

(Help us in all our need; and after a happy death may we rise again in joy to dwell with Thee in heaven.")

The trills towards the end of *In dir ist Freude* (V, No. 34) correspond to the "alleluia" of the text. In the mystical chorale upon *Komm heil'ger Geist* (VII, No. 37) the alleluia is expressed by a joyous sequence of semiquavers. The ascending final cadence of *Valet will ich dir geben* (VII, No. 50) is explained by the text, —

"Valet will ich dir geben, du arge falsche Welt;
Dein sündlich böses Leben durchaus mir nicht gefällt.
Im Himmel ist gut wohnen; hinauf steht mein Begier;
Da wird Gott ewig lohnen dem, der ihm dient allhier."

("Farewell, thou false and wicked world; thy sinful life pleases me not. I long for the better life of heaven; there will he who has served God win his eternal reward").

Towards the end of the chorale *O Mensch, bewein' dein' Sünde gross* (V, No. 45), several of the poetic ideas are brought out clearly in the music. The chromatic motive in bars 19 and 20 emphasises the words "dass er für uns geopfert würd" ("that He was sacrificed for us"); the ascending semiquaver sequence, that is like a series of sighs and groans —

corresponds to the line "Trug uns'rer Sünde schwere Bürd" ("He bore the heavy burden of our sins"); the *adagiosissimo* of the final bar is motived by the words "Wohl an dem Kreuze lange" ("long He hung on the cross"). At the commencement of this chorale prelude Bach has not attempted to bring out any particular words in the music, since the text offered him none that seemed striking enough for the purpose*.

A long and tender *adagio* at the end of a chorale prelude upon *Allein Gott in der Höh' sei Ehr'* (VI, No. 8) is meant to express the "Nun ist gross Fried' ohn' Unterlass, all' Fehd' hat nun ein Ende" ("now is there great and endless peace, now all strife is over"), with which the first verse of the hymn concludes.

Towards the end of the powerful fugal chorale *Aus tiefer Not schrei' ich zu dir* (VI, No. 13) the "joy" rhythm ♫♩♫♩♫♩ enters and finally carries everything triumphantly before it. There is apparently nothing in the

---

* The first two strophes of the hymn run thus: —

"O Mensch bewein dein Sünde gross,
Darum Christus sein's Vaters Schoss
Äussert und kam auf Erden;
Von einer Jungfrau rein und zart
Für uns er hier geboren ward;
Er wollt der Mittler werden.

Den Toten er das Leben gab
Und legt dabei all' Krankheit ab,
Bis sich die Zeit herdränge,
Dass er für uns geopfert würd,
Trug unsrer Sünden schwere Bürd
Wohl an dem Kreuze lange."

(The following English version is that of Mr. Claude Aveling, in Breitkopf and Härtel's edition of the *St. Matthew Passion*: —

"O man, for thy transgression moan.
For thee Christ left His Father's throne,
Came down on earth from heaven;
Of Virgin born, He was made man,
Thy soul to free from sorrow's ban,
Has His dear life been given.

He turned darkness into light,
He healed the sick, to blind gave sight,
Until that hour of anguish
When He, whose ransom made thee free,
Bowed down with sin long borne for thee,
Upon the Cross did languish.")

The poem, as it goes on, treats of the whole of the sorrows of the Passion at some length.

text to justify this. Bach, however, is trying to represent the Lutheran doctrine of repentance, according to which all true repentance leads of itself to the joyful certainty of salvation; and so the motive of joy, that struggles against the gloom of the music and eventually gains the upper hand, has a profound significance. It represents the same idea as the splendid major cadence previously mentioned.

Bach frequently expresses the idea of a poem by two or more simultaneous motives. In the Easter chorale *Erstanden ist der heil'ge Christ* (V, No. 14) the bass gives out the motive of resurrection, while the quavers in the middle part express joy. In the *Puer natus in Bethlehem* (V, No. 46) the middle parts give voice to the joy of the wise men from the East, while the bass depicts their obeisances.

In the little chorale prelude on *Wenn wir in höchsten Nöten sind* (V, No. 51) the text is translated into music in a particularly intimate way. The motive derived from the commencement of the melody is of such a kind that the three lower voices repeat continually the words "Wenn wir in höchsten Nöten sind" ("when we are in our greatest need"). Over this lament the melody flows along in semiquavers like a divine song of consolation, and in a wonderful final cadence seems to silence and compose the other parts.

Only in two chorale preludes has Bach reproduced all the changing details of the text, — in the third verse of *O Lamm Gottes* (VII, No. 48) and in an arrangement of *Jesus Christus unser Heiland* (VII, No. 31).

The chorale *O Lamm Gottes*, as is well known, consists of three similar strophes, that are only distinguished from each other by the fact that the first two end with "Erbarm dich unser, o Jesu" ("Have compassion on us, Jesu"), and the third with "Gib uns deinen Frieden, o Jesu" ("Give us thy peace, oh Jesu"). Bach, in his fantasia, reproduces only the ground-mood of the first two verses. In the third also he begins quite simply, keeping up a tranquil quaver motion over the *cantus firmus*, which is in the bass. But at the words "All' Sünd hast du getragen" ("Thou hast borne all our sins") it suddenly appears as if the full depth of this confession of guilt had all at once become manifest to the voices. They take possession of the motive —

and repeat along with it, time after time, "All' Sünd hast du getragen . . . . . . All' Sünd' hast du getragen". At the words "Sonst müssten wir verzagen" ("Or else must we despair") the chromatic motive expresses their desperation. After a passionate outcry the harmonies descend deeper and deeper, as if a sense of dread were creeping over the voices, and they dared no more than whisper the horror they feel —

But as soon as we come to the line "Gib uns deinen Frieden, o Jesu", all anxiety is banished. An expressible felicity wells forth from the rising and falling quaver-sequences. One is inclined to think that this motion, as in certain of the Christmas chorales, represents the heavenly host calling out its "Peace on earth" from the clouds to mankind below. Like some preludes upon the angelic song "Allein Gott in der Höh' sei Ehr" ("Glory to God in the highest"), the last verse of *O Lamm Gottes* concludes with an ascending cadence, as if the heavenly messengers, after bringing the prayed-for peace, were returning to their own kingdom —

In the *Klavierübung* Bach had treated the melody *Jesus Christus unser Heiland* as a communion chorale. Without troubling further about the text belonging to it, he had worked it into a fantasia, in which steadfast faith in the remission of sins in the sacrament was represented by a characteristic "step" motive. In a prelude on the chorale, probably written at a later date (VI, No. 31), Bach illustrates in his music the four lines of the first verse —

"Jesus Christus unser Heiland,
Der von uns den Zorn Gottes wand;
Durch das bitter Leiden sein,
Half er uns aus der Höllenpein".

("Jesus Christ our Saviour, Who turned from us the wrath of God, and by His bitter sorrow rescued us from the pains of hell.")

The fantasia on the first line is wonderfully fervent, as if penetrated by the magic of the word "Heiland" ("Redeemer"). It is followed immediately by a representation of the strokes of God's wrath, in a motive that resembles somewhat in its rhythm the accompaniment of the arioso "Erbarm' es Gott", that is sung in the *St. Matthew Passion* when Christ is being scourged —

In the third section Bach depicts the "bittere Leiden" ("bitter pain") by means of a fantasia based on the chromatic motive of grief in similar and contrary motion, and ending thus —

The last line, "Half er uns aus der Höllenpein" ("He saved us from the pains of hell') is reproduced by the short but expressive motive of resurrection —

We fancy we can see in this affecting ending the strong arm of the Saviour drawing mankind upward to rescue it from hell. The motive is overpowering even at its first enunciation —

In the cadence the triumphant ascension is depicted in a melodic line extending over three bars. We do not know which to admire most, — the simplicity of this musical language or the clarity of it.

CHAPTER XXIII.

THE MUSICAL LANGUAGE OF THE CANTATAS.

PICTORIAL THEMES.

Bach was particularly fond of representing in music the motion of waves. His librettist Picander knew this, so in the secular cantata in honour of the royal house he brings in all the rivers of Saxony and Poland and makes them sing the praises of the sovereigns. The best piece of painting of this kind is perhaps the delightful one of the waves in the cantata *Schleicht, spielende Wellen* (B. G. XX[2]), written for the birthday of Augustus III. The resemblance between the chief theme of the first chorus of this work and the accompaniment to Schubert's well-known *Barcarolle* is very interesting —

In the church cantata *Jesus schläft, was soll ich hoffen* (No. 81), the subject of which is the stilling of the storm (Mark IV, 35—41), Bach first of all paints the restless heaving of the waves and then the bursting of the storm. The orchestral accompaniment of the first chorus of *Christ unser Herr zum Jordan kam* (No. 7) is a representation of the waves of the Jordan. It is worth noticing in what very different ways he depicts the motion of flowing water and the glassy surface of a lake.

Very often a single word suffices to conjure up the "wave" motive in his music. "Mein Wandel auf der Welt ist einer Schiffahrt gleich" ("My course through the world is like a voyage"), sings the bass in an arioso in the cantata *Ich will den Kreuzstab gerne tragen* (No. 56). Bach finds in this a sufficient pretext for giving the cellos the following figure throughout the whole movement —

The bass figure of the aria "Sich üben im Lieben", in the cantata *Weichet nur, betrübte Schatten* (B. G. XI[2]) —

is explained by the fact of the occurrence in the text of the words "Hier quellen die Wellen" ("Here flow the waters").

A recitative in *Preise dein Glücke, gesegnetes Sachsen* (B. G. XXXIV) is accompanied by the wave-like motion —

merely because the word" Ostsee" ("Eastern sea") occurs in it.

In the cantata *Siehe, ich will viel Fischer aussenden* (No. 88) Bach sees before him the Lake of Gennesareth, on the banks of which Jesus, in fulfilment of a certain passage in the Old Testament, calls His disciples to be fishers of men. This vision prompts the use of the wave motive —

In an aria in the cantata *Von der Vergnügsamkeit* (B. G. XI²), a similar motion is evoked by the incidental occurrence of the word "Weltmeer" ("ocean"). In the cantata *Meine Seel' erhebt den Herren* (No. 10) a recitative speaks of God's promise to make the posterity of Abraham as numerous as the sand on the sea-shore. Bach at once feels bound to transport the hearer to the shore by means of this accompaniment —

He is equally fond of describing the motion of the clouds. He generally does this by means of scale figures merging into each other in similar and contrary motion. Typical examples may be seen in the chorus "Ach wie flüchtig, ach wie nichtig" (No. 26), the great piece of tone-painting at the beginning of the cantata *Der zufriedengestellte Aeolus*

(B. G. XI²)*, and the bass aria "Die Welt ist wie ein Rauch und Schatten" in the cantata *Was frag' ich nach der Welt* (No. 94).

At the opening of the Spring cantata, *Weichet nur, betrübte Schatten* (B. G. XI²), vaporous arpeggios floating upward symbolise the rising mist. The dark clouds of our sins, to which reference is made in an aria of the cantata *Mein liebster Jesu ist verloren* (No. 154), are represented by a precipitant and uneasy motive —

We often hear the pealing of the funeral bells in Bach's music. It does not even need any definite word to call up a musical picture of this kind; the mere mention of death and the end of things is enough. Sometimes it is only bells sounding vaguely from afar, that we hear in the *pizzicati* of the strings; very frequently, however, the peal is close and loud, Bach employing the whole of his instrumental forces. Among the most interesting orchestral passages of this kind are the symphonic accompaniments to the first movement of the cantata *Liebster Gott, wann werd' ich sterben* (No. 8) and to the recitative "Der Glocken bebendes Getön", from the *Trauerode* (B. G. XIII³)**. Bach, in these pictures, aims at an extraordinary realism of sound and rhythm. In the aria "Schlage doch bald, sel'ge Stunde", from the cantata *Christus der ist mein Leben* (No. 95) the bass runs thus —

* Cited on p. 58.

** See also the cantatas *Komm, du süsse Todesstunde* (No. 161), *Meinen Jesum lass ich nicht* (No. 124), *Herr Jesu Christ, wahr'r Mensch und Gott* (No. 127), *Herr, gehe nicht ins Gericht* (No. 105).

In the recitative "Siehe, ich stehe vor der Tür und klopfe an", from the cantata *Nun komm der Heiden Heiland* (No. 61; first version), Bach writes an accompaniment descriptive of the knocking of the Lord —

He is fond, again, of representing laughter in music, as we may see in the first chorus of the cantata *Unser Mund sei voll Lachens* (No. 110), and the aria "Wie will ich lustig lachen!" in the cantata *Der zufriedengestellte Aeolus* (B. G. XI³). Note also the *basso ostinato* of the recitative "Jedoch dein heilsames Wort macht, dass mir das Herze lacht", from the cantata *Herr Jesu Christ, du höchstes Gut* (No. 113). In the cantata *Wo gehest du hin* (No. 166) the theme of the aria "Man nehme sich in acht, wenn das Glücke lacht" ("Let us beware when fortune laughs") runs thus —

The devil appeals strongly to the musician in Bach. As he is represented in the opening chapters of the Bible as a serpent, Bach always delineates him by means of a contorted motive. According to his theology, Satan is identical with the devil; therefore whenever the "evil one" is spoken of as Satan he introduces the twistings of the serpent.

In the first chorus of the Michaelmas cantata *Es erhub sich ein Streit* (No. 19), and in the verse "Und wenn die Welt voll Teufel wär" from the cantata *Ein' feste Burg* (No. 80), Bach launches a whole army of devils against the divine power. A very characteristic Satan motive is found in the cantata *Dazu ist erschienen der Sohn Gottes* (No. 40). The text of the bass aria runs thus, — "Höllische Schlange! wird dir nicht bange? Der dir den Kopf als ein Sieger zerknickt, ist nun geboren" ("Hellish serpent, are thou not afraid? The victor who shall crush thy head is born"). In the music we not only see the contortions of the serpent, but hear the angry stamping of the heel which, according to the old prophecy, is to crush its head —

At the words "Der dir den Kopf als ein Sieger zerknickt" the serpent motive touches its lowest point in the bass. The next recitative of the cantata speaks of the serpent in paradise. It is represented by a gently rocking phrase —

Bach visualises it hanging down from the tree before the woman, and deluding her with its crafty speech. Therefore the accompaniment too is suspended in the air; only here and there does a supporting bass note enter.

In the cantata *O heil'ges Geist- und Wasserbad* (No. 165) the librettist speaks of Jesus as the "Heilschlänglein" ("little serpent of healing"), referring to the passage in St. John's Gospel where the crucifixion of Jesus is compared to the raising of the brazen serpent by Moses in the wilderness*. Any other composer would have passed over this tasteless word; Bach, however, is grateful for

* John III, 14 and 15. "And as Moses lifted up the serpent in the wilderness, even so must the Son of man be lifted up; that whosoever believeth in him should not perish, but have eternal life."

it, since it gives him the opportunity to depict the movements of the "little serpent of healing" —

To the angels also Bach gives a motive. It is founded on the light, floating rhythm that is given out by the strings and flutes in the sinfonia of the *Christmas Oratorio*, while the oboes represent the music of the shepherds —

The same motive recurs in the bass and in the interludes of the chorale "Wir singen dir in deinem Heer" at the end of this part of the *Christmas Oratorio*, this hymn — as the previous recitative attests, — being sung by the men who join in with the music of the angels.

The music of the aria "Bleibt, ihr Engel, bleibt bei mir", from the cantata *Es erhub sich ein Streit* (No. 19) might have been copied from the sinfonia of the *Christmas Oratorio*, but for the fact that it dates from at least ten years earlier —

The same motive appears in the trio "O wohl uns!" from the cantata *Das neugeborene Kindelein* (No. 122) —

As there is no mention of angels in the text, it may be thought that the resemblance of this bass figure to the angel motive is purely accidental. If, however, we refer to the previous recitative, it at once becomes clear why Bach introduces the angel motive here. It runs thus: "Die Engel, welche sich zuvor vor euch, als vor Verfluchten scheuten, erfüllen nun die Luft im höhern Chor" ("The angels, which formerly avoided you, as though you were accursed, now fill the air in a lofty choir"). Thus here, as in the chorale in the *Christmas Oratorio*, Bach imagines angels and men singing together.

Everything that suggests a motion that can be reproduced in a musical line is represented by Bach in music. He never allows words like "ascend" and "uplift" to escape him. Every one knows how he expresses the "Et exspecto resurrectionem" (in the B minor Mass) in the first trumpet—

The accompaniment to the duet "Ich lebe mein Herze", from the Easter cantata *So du mit deinem Munde bekennest* (No. 145), is based on a similar ascending figure —

The aria "Mein Jesus ist erstanden", from the cantata *Halt im Gedächtnis Jesum Christ* (No. 67), is dominated by the following motive —

It appears again in the great choruses of the cantatas *Wachet auf, ruft uns die Stimme* (No. 140) and *Mache dich mein Geist bereit, wache fleh' und bete* (No. 115), where it represents the act of rising to which the text refers.

There is a very characteristic theme in the cantata *Schwingt freudig euch empor* (No. 96), resembling the beating of wings —

We have the same oscillations in the accompaniment to the aria "Der Glaube schafft der Seele Flügel", from the cantata *Wer da glaubet und getauft wird* (No. 37).

The recitative "Auf sperren sie den Rachen weit" ("They open wide their mouths"), from the cantata *Wo der Herr nicht bei uns hält* (No. 178) is illustrated in music in this way —

An inverse motion symbolises, in the *St. Matthew Passion*, the passage "Der Heiland fällt vor seinem Vater nieder" ("The Saviour sinks before His Father"); and in the cantata *Ich hab' in Gottes Herz und Sinn* (No. 92) the words "Seht, wie bricht, wie reisst, wie fällt!" ("See, how breaks, how bursts, how falls!"); it appears again at the words "Wenn alles bricht, wenn alles fällt" ("When all things break, when all things fall"), in the opening aria of the cantata *Ich habe meine Zuversicht* (No. 188).

A "fall" motive, again, accompanies the chorale "Es woll' uns Gott genädig sein" ("God be gracious to us"), in the cantata *Die Himmel erzählen die Ehre Gottes* (No. 76). Its intervals of the seventh remind us of the bass figure in the chorale prelude *Durch Adams Fall* (V, No. 13). It runs thus —

The text of the chorale gives no pretext for this motive, but the previous recitative does. This ends with the words "Drum sei dir dies Gebet demütigst zugeschickt" ("Be this prayer most humbly sent to Thee"). The accompaniment is thus meant to indicate the chorale as the humble prayer, and to evoke the vision of it being sung by a great kneeling host.

Bach does not even shrink from a complicated representation of motion, if he thinks this will enable him to suggest it more realistically. In the aria "Stürze zu Boden, schwülstige Stolze" ("Fall to the ground, thou swollen pride"), from the cantata *Erhalt' uns Herr bei deinem Wort* (No. 126), he is not content merely to depict the fall, but shows us repeated efforts to rise again, until there comes the final plunge —

The fall and the effort to rise again are depicted also in the aria "Wir waren schon zu tief gesunken" ("We had fallen too low"), from the cantata *Es ist das Heil uns kommen her* (No. 9) —

Most musicians know how Bach, in the first chorus of the cantata *Wer sich selbst erhöhet* (No. 47), expresses the words of Jesus, "Wer sich selbst erhöhet, der soll erniedrigt werden, und wer sich selbst erniedriget, der soll erhöhet werden" ("Whoever shall exalt himself shall be abased, and whoever shall abase himself shall be exalted") —

Bach's consistency in the representation of movement may be seen from a recitative in the cantata *Gott fähret auf mit Jauchzen* (No. 43), in which he renders the word "zerstreuen" ("scatter") in exactly the same way as in the accompaniment to Jesus' words in the *St. Matthew Passion,* "Ich werde den Hirten schlagen, und die Schafe werden sich zerstreuen" ("I will smite the shepherds, and the sheep shall be scattered") —

In the alto aria of the cantata *Ach Gott vom Himmel sieh darein* (No. 2) he expresses the words "Tilg o Gott die Lehren, die dein Wort verkehren" ("Blot out, oh Lord, those who pervert Thy word") by a picture of musical perversity of such a kind that throughout the movement we have the impression that the voice and the accompaniment are not together. This movement is very like the little chorale prelude upon the angels' song *Allein Gott in der Höh' sei Ehr* (VI, No. 5) in which Bach tries to depict the charming disorder of the heavenly host in the clouds.

He also represents in his music attempts at movement. A characteristic example is the theme of the aria "Herz, zerreiss des Mammons Ketten" ("Burst the bonds of Mammon, oh heart"), in the cantata *Tue Rechnung, Donnerwort* (No. 168), which is a veritable Laokoon-design in music —

How far he will venture to go in music is shewn in the Christmas cantata *Christum wir sollen loben schon* (No. 121). The text of the aria "Johannis freudenvolles Springen erkannte dich mein Jesu schon" ("John leaped for joy in the womb when he recognised Jesus") refers to the passage from the Gospel of St. Luke, "And it came to pass that when Elisabeth heard the salutation of Mary, the babe leaped in the womb". Bach's music is simply a long series of violent convulsions —

THE "STEP" MOTIVES.

Bach never lets slip words that express running or walking. In the opening arioso of the cantata *Sehet wir gehen hinauf nach Jerusalem* (No. 159) he seems to paint Jesus going before the disciples, then turning round to them, and standing still to repeat once more the sorrowful words that they cannot comprehend —

In the cantata *Es ist euch gut, dass ich hingehe* (No. 108), in the verse "Es ist euch gut, dass ich hingehe; denn so ich nicht hingehe, so kommt der Tröster nicht zu euch" ("It is expedient for you that I go away. For if I go not away, the Comforter will not come unto you")*, Bach gives to the basses the "walking" motive, while the noble arabesque of the oboe above it expresses sublime consolation —

In the cantata *Wo gehest du hin* ("Where goest thou") (No. 166), the "walking" motive is again used to illustrate the text. Another characteristic example is the theme of the fugal prelude to the cantata *Tritt auf die Glaubensbahn* ("Tread the path of faith") (No. 152) —

In the recitative "Geh' Welt! behalte nur das Deine" ("Go, world! keep thou thine own alone"), from the cantata *Sehet welch eine Liebe* (No. 64), Bach represents the words "Geh Welt", by the same bass figure that he uses, in the *St. Matthew Passion*, to depict the setting-out of Jesus and the disciples towards Gethsemane —

In the cantata *Ach Herr, mich armen Sünder* (No. 135) the music that companies the word "Weicht all', ihr Übeltäter, weicht" ("Away, all ye evil-doers") suggests a hurrying away in terror —

* John XVI, 7.

The act of hastening away is charmingly suggested again in the bass of the aria *Wir eilen mit schwachen, doch emsigen Schritten* ("We hasten with weak, yet diligent steps"), in the cantata *Jesu, der du meine Seele* (No. 78) —

In the cantata *Erfreute Zeit im neuen Bunde* (No. 83), the words "Eile, Herz, voll Freudigkeit" ("Hasten, heart, full of joyfulness") are expressed by a similar movement. Bach has marked all these quaver passages that represent movement *staccato*, — of course a heavy *staccato*.

He symbolises someone hurrying after or by the side of another by imitative passages for the voices, often almost in canon*.

The wide range of symbolism that he makes the "step" motive cover cannot be correctly estimated from the chorale preludes. Measured, tranquil steps indicate resolution and confident faith, — as, for example, in the bass accompaniment to the *Credo* in the B minor Mass —

* The following examples may be cited among many: the duet with chorus "Kommt, eilet und laufet" from the Easter oratorio, the arias "Ich folge dir gleichfalls" and "Eilt, ihr angefochtnen Seelen" from the *St. John Passion*, the aria "Entziehe dich eilends, mein Herze, der Welt", from the cantata *Meinen Jesum lass ich nicht* (No. 124), and the aria "So schnell ein rauschend Wasser schiesset, so eilen unsres Lebens Tage", from the cantata *Ach wie nichtig* (No. 26).

There is the same tranquil motion in the basses in the *Confiteor*.

When the intervals are more widely-spread they symbolise strength, pride, and defiance. Typical examples are the themes of the chorus "Herr, wenn die stolzen Feinde toben" ("Lord, when the proud enemy rages") in the *Christmas Oratorio* —

This pictorial idea is carried to still further lengths in the themes of the cantata *Nun ist das Heil und die Kraft* (No. 50) —

From the same root is derived the *Fecit potentiam* of the Magnificat —

and the theme of the basses in the *Deposuit potentes*, especially the end of it —

This represents the word potentes" ("the mighty"), while the violins render the idea of "deposuit" ("He hath cast down") —

In the aria "Gewaltige stösst Gott vom Stuhl hinunter" ("God hath cast down the mighty from his seat"), in the cantata *Meine Seel' erhebt den Herren* (No. 10), — the German Magnificat, — the two motives are united in one theme —

These motives illuminate for us the gigantic idea that Bach wished to express in the theme of the organ fugue in E minor —

THE "TUMULT" MOTIVE.

Bach employs a particular group among these "stamping" motives wherever he has to represent the tumult of combat, as if he desired to suggest to the hearer the hoof-beats of the horses and the rumbling of the marching columns.

The typical example of these motives is to be seen in the cantata *Ein' feste Burg* (No. 80), where Bach forms from it the music that accompanies the second verse, "Mit unsrer Macht ist nichts getan . . . es streit für uns der rechte Mann", ("With our own might we can do nothing . . . there fights for us the right one") —

The "tumult" motive appears in a slightly different form in the aria "Streite, siege, starker Held" ("Strive and conquer, hardy hero"), in the cantata *Nun komm der Heiden Heiland* (No. 62; second composition) —

In still another form it accompanies, in the cantata *Gott der Herr ist Sonn' und Schild* (No. 79) the supplication of the believer, "Gott, ach Gott, verlass die Deinen nimmermehr .... obgleich sehr wider uns die Feinde toben" ("God, oh God, forsake not Thine own ..... though the enemy rage against us") —

The "tumult" motive appears again in the final aria of the cantata *Wachet, betet* (No. 70) —

where it represents the uproar at the end of all things. In the concluding aria of the cantata for Low Sunday, *Halt im Gedächtnis* (No. 67) Bach employs it for the great tone-picture in which he portrays the appearance of Jesus to the eleven disciples. The music paints the turmoil made by the world round these terrified men; at the sight of Jesus they sing "Wohl uns, Jesus hilft uns kämpfen" ("Oh joy, Jesus helps us in the fight"); and as soon as the Saviour utters his "Friede sei mit euch" ("Peace be unto you") the "tumult" motive is silenced.

In the aria "Gute Nacht, du Weltgetümmel", ("Good night, oh tumult of the world"), in the cantata *Wer weiss, wie nahe mir mein Ende* (No. 27) there is another motive of the same kind.

The clear-cut quality of Bach's musical language may be seen from the fact that in the *St. John Passion* the words of Jesus "Wäre mein Reich von dieser Welt, meine Diener würden darum kämpfen, dass ich den Juden nicht überantwortet würde" ("If my kingdom were of this world, then would my servants fight, that I should not be delivered to the Jews") are accompanied by a figure —

derived from the "tumult" motive.

THE MOTIVES OF EXHAUSTION.

Bach expresses exhaustion and weakness by means of syncopated "step" motives.

A weary, dragging walk is depicted in the cantata *Ich steh mit einem Fuss im Grabe* (No. 156), where Bach lays the earthly pilgrim in the grave, at the end of his pilgrimage, in this fashion —

In the cantata *Mit Fried' und Freud' ich fahr dahin* (No. 125) the weary motion is represented more as a kind of falling forward —

The first part of the opening chorus of the cantata *Brich dem Hungrigen dein Brot* (No. 39) is dominated by a similar representation of a man wearily dragging himself along, for Bach, fastening on the words "Und die so im Elend sind, führe ins Haus" ("And those who are in misery, take them into thy house"), paints a procession of tottering figures being conducted under the sheltering roof*.

In the cantata *In allen meinen Taten* (No. 97) occurs this passage:

"Leg ich mich späte nieder,
Erwache früh' ich wieder,
Lieg oder ziehe fort,
In Schwachheit und in Banden ....."

("If I go to rest late, awake early, lie down or go forth, in weakness and in bonds"). The theme with which Bach expresses the lying down and rising again is almost too characteristic —

Jaded and uncertain steps also represent vacillating faith. Elaborate pictures of this kind are found in the cantata *Ich glaube, lieber Herr, hilf meinem Unglauben* (No. 109). The theme of the aria "Wie zweifelhaftig ist mein Hoffen" ("How uncertain is my hope") may be especially mentioned**—

* On the problem of this chorus see p. 46.

** See also the aria "Bald zur Rechten, bald zur Linken lenkt sich mein verirrter Schritt" ("My wandering steps go now to the right, now to the left") from the cantata *Herr Christ, der ein'ge Gottessohn* (No. 96), and the aria "Wir zittern und wanken" ("We tremble and reel") from the cantata *Herr, gehe nicht ins Gericht* (No. 105).

Syncopated "step" motives, in an idealised form, express the weariness that has found rest in Christ. Of this order are the themes of the beautiful sacred lullabies in which Bach describes the blissful weariness of death. Thus in the first chorus of the cantata *Christus, der ist mein Leben, Sterben ist mein Gewinn* (No. 95), the orchestra works out the motive —

A well-known example is the noble theme of the aria "Schlummert ein, ihr matten Augen" ("Close in sleep, ye weary eyes"), from the cantata *Ich habe genug* (No. 82) —

THE RHYTHM

The rhythm is mostly associated by musical people with the idea of dignity or solemnity. It is used in the *grave* section of the old French overture with the same signification as in the Graal scene in *Parsifal*. The E flat prelude for organ at the beginning of the collection of the greater catechism chorales illustrating the Lutheran doctrine is worked out in this rhythm, as it needs to be unusually majestic. Bach employs it again in the Easter cantata *Christ lag in Todesbanden* (No. 4), to express the sixth verse, "So feiern wir das hohe Fest" ("So we celebrate the high feast"). In the cantata for Palm Sunday, *Himmelskönig, sei willkommen* (No. 182) it is prompted by the word "Himmelskönig" ("King of heaven") —

Grave. Violino concertante.

The same rhythm occurs in several arias in which mention is made of the godhood of Jesus. In the Christmas cantata *Gelobet seist du, Jesus Christ* (No. 91), it elucidates the text "Die Armut, so Gott auf sich nimmt" ("God takes poverty upon Himself") —

It is found again in the first chorus of the cantata *Herr Jesu Christ, wahr' Mensch und Gott* (No. 127). Even the phrase "Fürst des Lebens" ("Prince of life") in an aria in the cantata *Der Himmel lacht, die Erde jubilieret* (No. 31) is enough to make Bach feel justified in introducing the rhythm of majesty —

This solemn rhythm must not be confused with another, that resembles it externally in that it also divides each bar-beat into two notes, one of which has the value of three quarters, the other of a quarter only. This latter is mainly distinguished from the other motive by the fact that it almost invariably appears in animated triple time, while the rhythm of solemnity is used in slow $^4/_4$ time; moreover it generally begins on the up-beat, and is interspersed with notes of other values or with pauses, while the rhythm of solemnity begins with the down-beat and continues without interruption.

This other rhythm, which may be represented by a formula of this kind —

expresses violent passions, sometimes of a joyful, but generally of a grievous kind. Bach especially employs it to represent terror, horror and despair.

Its typical form may be seen in Peter's aria of remorse. "Ach mein Sinn" in the *St. John Passion.* Another example occurs in the opening duet of the cantata *Ach Gott, wie manches Herzeleid* ("O God, what grief of heart") (No. 58) —

Bach also expresses in this way the words "Mein letztes Lager will mich schrecken" ("My last state will dismay me"), in the cantata *O Ewigkeit, du Donnerwort* (No 60) —

The rhythm is also employed whenever he wishes to suggest slow and heavy movement, as in the aria "Komm, süsses Kreuz" ("Come! dear Cross") in the *St. Matthew Passion,* where the music accompanies the steps of Joseph of Arimathaea as he carries the cross. It can also represent the falling of the scourge — as in the arioso "Erbarm es Gott" ("Thy mercy show, oh God") in the *St. Matthew Passion* — or the convulsive movements of the head of an angry serpent, as in the aria "Geduld, wenn mich falsche Zungen stechen" ("Patience, though false tongues should sting me").

The ambiguity of this rhythm comes from the fact that there are a number of cases of the representation of movement that may be interpreted in more than one way. Still it is never doubtful what Bach means to express in this or that case by the rhythm. By means of the metre and the build of the phrase he can give it each time so individual a character that its bearing on the text is clear without further explanation.

A common feature of all the forms of the rhythm so far cited is that the short note is not to be accented lightly, but heavily, so that it has the effect not of a final aspiration of the previous note, but of a preliminary tone and accent to the note that follows it. Written out exactly, the rhythm of solemnity and that of passion would appear thus —

This opinion is not refuted by the fact that Bach, where he marks ties in these rhythms, always groups the notes belonging to the same beat under a tie, in this manner —

By this he only means to indicate that the passage as a whole is to be played *legato*. The solution of the question does not turn upon the ties that Bach has marked, but on whether the short note is to be played heavily or lightly. If heavily, then the ear necessarily accepts it in each case as the fore-accent to the succeeding note. The opening duet in *Ach Gott, wie manches Herzeleid* (No. 58) may be cited in proof of this. In spite of the fact that Bach has marked the tempo *adagio*, and written the ties thus the movement is dominated by the "passion" rhythm. It does not make its proper effect until we play the short notes not lightly, but with a certain degree of heaviness. Observe the inward unrest that makes itself felt in this music, and in that of the aria "Mein letztes Lager will mich schrecken", in *O Ewigkeit, du Donnerwort* (No. 60). It comes from the sequence of violent intervals that Bach uses.

These two arias present the problem in such an interesting form because the texts allow of both a passionate and a peaceful interpretation. Both are in dialogue form. The lament "Ach Gott, wie manches Herzeleid begegnet mir zu dieser Zeit" ("Ah God! what grief of heart is mine") is answered by the other voice with "Geduld! Geduld" ("Patience! Patience"); to the terrified cry "Mein letztes Lager will mich schrecken", the other rejoins "Mich wird des Heilands Hand bedecken" ("The hand of the Lord will cover me"). The right way of rendering the music therefore depends upon our knowing which of the two feelings Bach is expressing. If the passionate rhythm were not otherwise vouched for, we might conceive the music in both these arias as expressing the quiet consolation of the text. Nor must we forget the general observation that, where a text gives Bach the choice between two feelings, he very often decides for the more passionate one, without considering whether in this way he best reproduces the sense of the text as a whole.

As a matter of fact, he also employs a ♩.♪ ♩.♪ ♩.♪ rhythm in which the short note must be regarded as supplemental to the previous one, and is to be as lightly breathed as possible. Precisely noted, it would run thus —

This rhythm belongs to the large category of those that represent light and charming movement, and express symbolical ideas like peace and happiness. Its affinity with the rhythm of solemnity and passion exists only on paper and for the eye; in performance, and for the ear, it has nothing whatever in common with the other. Externally it is distinguished from the "solemnity" rhythm by the fact that it is usually met with only in triple time, and from the "passionate" rhythm by the fact that it never begins on the up-beat*.

The question of the various rhythms in Bach is of the greatest practical importance. The average conductor is not clear about the matter, and so renders them all in the same way, thus negating the characterisation that Bach intended them to have. The occurrence, meaning, and proper way of rendering this rhythm in Bach should be made the object of a special and searching enquiry.

THE RHYTHMS OF FELICITY.

Motives constructed on the rhythm express, both in the cantatas and the chorales, the feeling of charm and happiness. In the cantata *Erschallet, ihr Lieder* (No. 172), the duet "Komm, lass mich nicht länger warten, komm, du sanfter Himmelswind" ("Come, thou gentle breeze from heaven, keep me not waiting longer"), is accompanied by the following progression in the bass —

This rhythm, however, for the most part does not appear in its pure form, but in sundry variants. In the accompaniment to the aria "Sei getreu . . . . . . nach dem Regen blüht der Segen" ("Be faithful . . . . . . after the rain will come the blessing"), in the cantata *Weinen, Klagen* (No. 12), it assumes the following shape —

It is suggested also in the duet "Beruft Gott selbst, so muss der Segen auf allem unsern Tun im Übermasse ruh'n"

* The classical example of this rhythm of charm is quoted on p. 103.

("Call upon God Himself, and blessing will rest in abundance upon all our doings"), in the cantata *Siehe, ich will viel Fischer aussenden* (No. 88). In the cantata *Auf Christi Himmelfahrt allein* (No. 128), it appears in combination with the "joy" motive —

It sometimes receives further animation from the addition of semiquaver runs, when it takes the form in which we meet with it, for example, in the cantata *Lobe den Herrn meine Seele* (No. 143) —

Even in the accompaniment figure of the recitative "Ach, Herr Gott, durch die Treue dein, wird unser Land in Fried' und Ruhe sein" ("Ah, Lord God, by Thy faithfulness our land shall find peace and quiet"), in the cantata *Nimm von uns, Herr, du treuer Gott* (No. 101) we may detect the essential movement of the "felicity" rhythm —

It is recognisable, again, in the music to the words "Ein geheiligtes Gemüte sieht und schmecket Gottes Güte" ("A sanctified soul sees and tastes the goodness of the Lord"), in the cantata *Erhöhtes Fleisch und Blut* (No. 173)—

Another motive of felicity is prompted by the idea of quiet, gently-flowing waves. In a recitative in the cantata *Ihr Menschen, rühmet Gottes Liebe* (No. 167), the following accompaniment appears in the bass at the words "Mit Gnad' und Liebe zu erfreuen" ("To rejoice with the grace and love of God") —

The recitative in the *Trauerode,* that speaks of the happy death of the princess, has the following bass to it —

Compare with this the accompaniment to the aria "Vergieb, o Vater, vergieb unsre Schuld" ("Forgive, oh Father, forgive our sin"), in the cantata *Bisher habt ihr nichts gebeten* (No. 87) —

The theme of the aria "Sanfte soll mein Todeskummer" ("My death shall be sweet") in the Easter oratorio runs thus —

In the middle section of the first chorus of the cantata *Es ist nichts Gesundes an meinem Leibe* (No. 25) the motive of calmly-moving water is used to express the words "peace" —

In all these cases the motion of the waves is meant to convey a spiritual symbolism, as is seen when we compare with them the bass accompaniment to the recitative "Die stille Pleisse spielt mit ihren kleinen Wellen" ("The tranquil Pleisse plays with its little waves"), in the secular cantata *Auf schmetternde Töne* —

Bach expresses a warmer tinge of peaceful joy by a motive in this rhythm , usually in $^{12}/_{8}$ and $^{9}/_{8}$, but occasionally also in $^{6}/_{8}$ and $^{3}/_{4}$ time. Rhythms of this kind are not often met with in other composers. Bach, however, is very fond of them, forming out of them the loveliest and most flexible of his great phrases. The affinity of these themes with the angel motives is obvious. Both are meant to represent graceful motion of an almost superterrestial kind, by means of which Bach wishes to express the transfigured joy that has vanquished grief.

One of the finest themes of this order is that of the aria "Ich will leiden, ich will schweigen" ("I will suffer, I will be silent") in the cantata *Bisher habt ihr nichts gebeten* (No. 87) —

We may cite also the theme of the aria "Gedenk' an uns mit deiner Liebe, schleuss uns in dein Erbarmen ein" ("Think of us with Thy love, and enfold us in Thy pity") in the cantata *Wir danken dir Gott* (No. 29) —

In the first chorus of the cantata *Also hat Gott die Welt geliebt* (No. 68), a similar theme expresses the idea of the eternal, compassionate love of God —

From this rhythm, again, is derived a heavier form, in which the third quaver must be played with a certain amount of accent. Bach employs it for the representation of sorrowful pathos. Typical examples of it are the Siciliano of the fourth sonata for violin and clavier, and the violin accompaniment to the aria "Erbarme dich" in the *St. Matthew Passion.*

Besides these three main forms of expression for the emotions signified by such words as "peace" and "happiness", there is a fourth motive, that externally resembles the "solemnity" rhythm*. An example may be cited from the theme of "Friede sei mit euch!" ("Peace be unto you") in the final aria of the cantata *Halt im Gedächtnis Jesum Christ* (No. 67) —

THE MOTIVE OF TERROR.

To express terror, Bach employs a series of reiterated quavers or semiquavers on the same note; he represents it, that is, as trembling or shuddering. The method in itself is rather primitive, but Bach achieves great effects with it, as we can see from the first movement of the cantata *O Ewigkeit, du Donnerwort* (No. 60), through which there

* See p. 99.

runs an unbroken series of shudders. Another example may be seen in the recitative with chorus "O Schmerz! Hier zittert das gequälte Herz" ("Oh grief! His tortured heart at last doth quail") in the *St. Matthew Passion.*

The phrase "Erschrecket! ihr verstockten Sünder ("Terror seize you, unrepentant sinners"), in the cantata *Wachet, betet* (No. 70), is accompanied by whole chords in reiterated semiquavers —

In the recitative "Ach, soll nicht dieser grosse Tag" ("Ah! shall not this great day"), in the same cantata, Bach employs a trembling bass in order to depict the terror at the Last Judgment; and in a recitative in the cantata *Schauet doch und sehet* (No. 46), where reference is again made to the end of the world, the horror of the trembling bass is intensified by the addition of the chromatic motive—

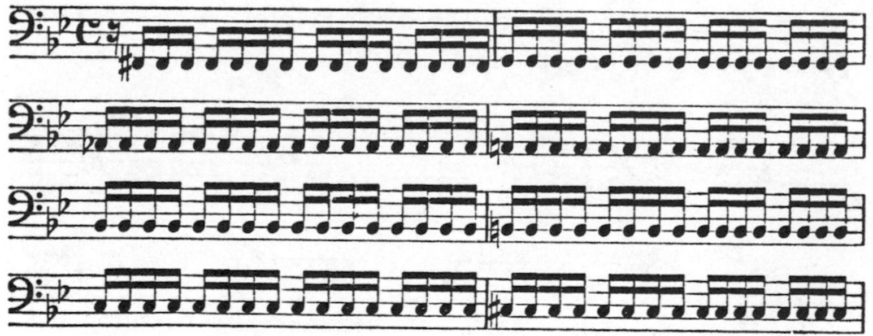

To paint the anxiety of the disciples after the death of Christ, in the cantata *Am Abend aber desselbigen Sabbats* (No. 42), Bach gives out in recitative, after the prelude, the following verse from St. John's Gospel, "Then the same day at evening, being the first day of the week, when the doors were shut where the disciples were assembled, for fear of the Jews, came Jesus and stood in the midst", with the trembling bass as sole accompaniment —

THE MOTIVES OF GRIEF.

To express grief, Bach employs the two motives that have already appeared in the *Orgelbüchlein* — a chromatic progression of five or six notes, typifying torturing grief, and a uniform sequence of notes in pairs, that is like a series of sighs.

The chromatic motive is frequently used to throw a particular word into high relief — for example in the final chorus of the Christmas cantata *Christen, ätzet diesen Tag* (No. 63), at the words "Aber niemals lass geschehen, dass uns Satan möge quälen" ("But never let Satan molest us") —

In a recitative in the cantata *Gelobet seist du Jesu Christ* (No. 91), the word "Jammertal" ("Valley of distress") is brought out in the same way.

He often uses the chromatic progression as a *basso ostinato*. The first chorus of the cantata *Jesu, der du meine Seele hast durch deinen bittern Tod* (No. 78) is founded on the following bass —

The *basso ostinato* of the first chorus of the cantata on Hans Sachs's song, *Warum betrübst du dich, mein Herz* (No. 138), runs thus —

A well-known example is the bass figure, repeated thirteen times, of the *Crucifixus* in the B minor Mass —

The sighing motive appears in two forms — one realistic, the other more idealistic. The former is meant to represent actual sighs; in the latter the sighing is more spiritual, and the motive serves for the expression of noble lamentation.

The words "Ächzen und erbärmlich Weinen" ("Sighs and piteous weeping"), in the cantata *Meine Seufzer, meine Tränen* (No. 13), are rendered in music that suggests veritable sobbing —

In the first chorus of *Schauet doch und sehet, ob irgend ein Schmerz sei wie mein Schmerz* ("Behold and see if there be any sorrow like unto my sorrow") (No. 46) the violas never cease their sighing —

The words "Seufzer, Tränen, Kummer, Not" ("Sighs, Tears, Grief, Distress"), in the cantata *Ich hatte viel Bekümmernis* (No. 21) are translated into music in this way—

It cannot be denied that in many cases Bach has greatly intensified the sorrowful mood of the words, simply in order that his orchestra may have a pretext for lamentation. But never do we become satiated with his painting of clamorous grief, although he is always making use of the same motives. This is due not only to the fine quality of his art and to the perpetually new forms in which the motive appears, but also to the fact that the method of representation he adopts is wholly natural. It is this constant naturalness that makes Bach's musical language so consummate.

The motive of noble grief is chiefly distinguished from the other by its closer intervals and smoother motion, the harmony thus transfiguring the grief.

In a recitative in the *Trauerode* this "grief" motive appears in the following form —

A typical example may be seen in the melodic line of the accompaniment to the great chorale chorus "O Mensch, bewein' dein' Sünde gross" ("Oh man, bewail thy grievous sin") at the end of the first part of the *St. Matthew Passion* —

That Bach was fully conscious of the meaning this motive had for him may be seen from the fact that for the opening chorus of the cantata *Wir müssen durch viel Trübsal in das Reich Gottes eingehen* (No. 146) he makes use of a clavier concerto *andante* that is based on the rhythm of two tied notes, simply adding the chorale parts to it. The movement is the well-known one commencing thus —

Here the periodic interruption of the natural motion by wider intervals is very interesting. The same peculiarity characterises a large number of Bach's themes of grief. It is seen in its most striking form in the accompaniment to the words "Ich wünschte mir den Tod, wenn du, mein Jesus, mich nicht liebtest" ("I would desire to die, if thou, my Jesus, didst not love me"), in the cantata *Selig ist der Mann* (No. 57) —

Further examples of Bach's way of depicting elevated grief may be seen in the opening of the cantata *Ich will den Kreuzstab gerne tragen* (No. 56), and the sinfonia of the cantata for the third Sunday after Easter — *Weinen, Klagen* (No. 12). In the cantata *Himmelskönig, sei willkommen* (No. 182), with its wonderful Passion atmosphere, the bass of the aria "Jesu, lass durch Wohl und Weh' mich auch mit dir ziehen" ("Jesus, let me follow Thee through weal and woe") runs thus —

The mourning chorale "Der Gott, der mir hat versprochen" ("The God who has promised me") in the cantata *Meine Seufzer, meine Tränen* (No. 13) is also accompanied by the rhythm of noble grief.

Bach employs it, again, whenever he wishes to express melancholy longing, as in the accompaniment to the first aria of the cantata *Ach ich sehe, jetzt da ich zur Hochzeit gehe* (No. 162), and in the first aria of *Liebster Jesu, mein Verlangen* (No. 32).

The motive of noble grief, in an idealised form, depicts the longing for death. The death-lullaby, "Letzte Stunde brich herein, mir die Augen zuzudrücken" ("Come, oh last hour, and close my eyes"), in the cantata *Der Himmel lacht, die Erde jubilieret* (No. 31), begins thus —

THE MOTIVES OF JOY.

To express joy, Bach uses in the cantatas the same two motives that he had employed in the chorales. The first consists of a succession of rapid notes, and expresses joy of a more direct and naïve kind; the other is based on the rhythm , or on this , and more particularly typifies joyous agitation.

An example of the first kind may be seen in the runs of the solo violin in the opening aria of the cantata *Erfreute Zeit im neuen Bunde* (No. 83) —

It is more especially the joyous mood of Christmas that Bach expresses in this way, as is shewn by a number of choruses for that season, — for instance the cantata for the third day of Christmas, *Ich freue mich in dir* (No. 133). The final chorale "Sei Lob und Preis" ("Glory and Praise") in the cantata *Ihr Menschen rühmet Gottes Liebe* (No. 167) is accompanied in this way —

The second of these two motives is the one most frequently used in the cantatas, as it is in the chorales. It can assume manifold shapes, and so can express many varieties and shades of joy. In Bach's works there are at least two hundred motives constructed upon this rhythm of joy, while it is scarcely met with in Handel and Beethoven. It is seen in its typical form in the violin solo of the *Laudamus te* in the B minor Mass, —

The bass in the opening chorus of the German Magnificat, — the cantata *Meine Seel' erhebt den Herren* (No. 10) — moves about in this way —

The bass in the first chorus of the cantata *Herr Gott, dich loben wir* (No. 16) has the same motion —

The main motive of the orchestral accompaniment to the first chorus of the cantata *Nun komm' der Heiden Heiland* (No. 62; second composition) belongs to the same category —

The chorus "Jauchzet, ihr erfreuten Stimmen" ("Rejoice, ye gladsome voices") in the cantata *Gott man lobt dich in der Stille* (No. 120), is also wholly dominated by the motive of joy.

An example of the employment of this rhythm in the accompaniment of recitatives may be seen in *Preise dein Glücke, gesegnetes Sachsen* (B. G. XXXIV), where Bach uses it to express in music the fidelity and love of the subjects who joyfully throw themselves at the feet of their sovereign.

Bach is particularly fond of constructing bass figures out of this motive of joy. Three typical examples may be cited from among many: —

The duet "Er kennt die rechten Freudenstunden" ("He knows the hours of real joy"), from the cantata *Wer nur den lieben Gott lässt walten* (No. 93) —

The opening chorus of the cantata *Lobe den Herrn, meine Seele* (No. 69; first composition) —

The aria "Wohl mir, Jesus ist gefunden, nun bin ich nicht mehr betrübt" ("Oh joy, Jesus is found again; now am I no more sorrowful") in the cantata *Mein liebster Jesu ist verloren* (No. 154) —

These motives symbolise a joy that is still to some extent restrained. The more audacious the theme, the more unfettered is the joy.

When Jesus took Peter away from his nets, bade him have no fear, and promised to make him a fisher of men, the disciples, judging from the motive with which Bach accompanies these words, must have been transported with joy —

But even this motive seems temperate in comparison with the more exuberant ones. One of these is the bass of the aria "Erholet euch, betrübte Stimmen . . . Mein Jesus lässt sich wiedersehn, o Freude der nichts gleichen kann!" ("Recover yourselves, oh afflicted voices . . . My Jesus returns; oh joy without compare") in the cantata for the third Sunday after Easter, *Ihr werdet weinen und heulen* (No. 103) —

The most extravagant of all the extravagant motives of joy is seen in the bass figures in the aria "Gelobet sei der Herr" ("Praised be the Lord") in the chorale cantata *Gelobet sei der Herr, mein Gott* (No. 129) —

Ecstatic joy is not expressed by a definite motive, but by dreamy arabesques in a solo instrument. An example may be seen in the violin accompaniment to the duet "Wann kommst du mein Heil" ("When comest thou, my salvation"), in *Wachet auf* (No. 140). In the first aria of the cantata *Weichet nur, betrübte Schatten*, the oboe sings a Spring Song of extraordinary loveliness, while the arpeggios in the strings depict the mists floating upward —

Rapturous joy is expressed again in the accompaniment to the aria "Ich will doch wohl Rosen brechen, wenn mich gleich die Dornen stechen" ("Yet I will gather roses, even though the thorns prick me"), in the cantata *Wahrlich ich sage euch* (No. 86) —

Other examples may be seen in the violin solo in the aria "Ich traue seiner Güte" ("I trust in His goodness") in the chorale cantata *In allen meinen Taten* (No. 97); the flute solo in the soprano aria in the chorale cantata *Was Gott tut, das ist wohlgetan* (No. 100); the oboe soli in the two cantatas that express the longing for death, — *Liebster Jesu, mein Verlangen* (No. 32), and *Ich habe genug* (No. 82).

In the aria "Die Seele ruht in Jesu Händen" ("The soul is at rest in Jesus' hands"), in the cantata *Herr Jesu Christ, wahr'r Mensch und Gott* (No. 127), the oboe weaves celestial garlands of sound round the tolling of the funeral bells.

THE CO-OPERATION OF THE MOTIVES.

Since so many of Bach's motives have their definite meanings, we can understand him sometimes using two or more together or in succession in order to give full expression to his text. A cursory perusal of any volume of the cantatas will afford examples of this. In the *Christmas Oratorio* Herod is terrified when the mages tell him of the birth of the Messiah; but he reflects "Warum wollt ihr erschrecken? . . . O solltet ihr euch nicht vielmehr darüber freuen?" ("Why should you fear? Should you not rather rejoice?"), and Bach underlines this thought by giving us the motive of terror and that of joy in succession —

In the first chorus of the cantata *Ihr werdet weinen und heulen, aber die Welt wird sich freuen* (No. 103) the motive of joy and the chromatic motive of sorrow are used antithetically.

In the opening chorus of *Jesu, der du meine Seele* (No. 78), the thought of Christ's suffering and that of joy in the salvation it brings are expressed by opposing the motive of joy to that of grief —

In the arias "Friede sei mit euch" ("Peace be unto you") from *Halt im Gedächtnis Jesum Christ* (No. 67), and "Gute Nacht, du Weltgetümmel" ("Farewell, thou turmoil of the world"), from *Wer weiss wie nahe mir mein Ende* (No. 27), the motive of joy and that of tumult are played off against each other.

In the cantata *Ihr Menschen, rühmet Gottes Liebe* (No.167) occur the words "Gottes Wort, das trüget nicht; es geschieht, was er verspricht. Was er im Paradies den Vätern schon verhiess, haben wir, Gott lob, erfahren" ("God's word does not deceive; it has happened as He promised. What he promised in Paradise to our forefathers, has, God be praised, now come to pass"). This is expressed in the bass by a "step" motive that symbolises the steadfastness of God's pledge, and by a "joy" motive that answers to the "God be praised" for the fulfilling of the promise —

This interpretation is confirmed by the Easter cantata *So du mit deinem Munde bekennest* (No. 145). The words of the opening chorus, "So du mit deinem Munde bekennest Jesum, dass er der Herr sei, und glaubest in deinem Herzen, dass ihn Gott von den Toten auferweckt hat, so wirst du selig" ("If with thy mouth thou dost acknowledge that Jesus is God, and dost believe in thy heart that God hath raised Him from the dead, thou shalt be blest"), are expressed in two themes, corresponding respectively to the words "glauben" ("believe") and "selig" ("blest") —

In the first chorus of the cantata *Ach lieben Christen, seid getrost* (No. 114) we have the trembling motive of fear and the ascending motive of joy side by side —

When the picture painted in the text requires it, Bach will even employ three themes together. In the cantata *Wohl dem, der sich auf seinen Gott* (No. 139) he has to express the words "Das Unglück schlägt auf allen Seiten um mich ein zentnerschweres Band; doch plötzlich erscheinet die helfende Hand; mir scheint des Trostes Licht von weitem" ("Misfortune overwhelms me on every side as with heavy bonds; but suddenly appears the helping hand, and the light of comfort shines on me from afar"). In the music we have three themes. The first symbolises the "overwhelming with heavy bonds" by means of a characteristic motive expressive of twining—

A mounting theme depicts the rescuing hand, rising up out of the ruin; the third paints a flickering light, in a style made familiar to us in many other cantatas.

In an aria in the cantata *Herr, wie du willst* (No. 73) Bach first of all represents sighing, then the swoon of death, then the tolling of the funeral bells. The accompaniment to the first chorus of the cantata *Was soll ich aus dir machen, Ephraim* (No. 89) is made up of three themes, one expressing God's anger, the second the sorrowful question, and the third, sighs and lamentation.

Frequently the same idea is represented by several related motives. In the great choruses of the *Christmas Oratorio* we usually find two or three different motives of joy; similarly in the expression of grief we find various kinds of sighing motives.

Bach goes a step further. He not only places motives of different signification in conjunction or in succession, but tries to express composite feelings by welding two motives into one theme. Here we see how fully conscious he was of his own musical language, and how daring it is; examples of combined themes of this kind can hardly be found in other composers.

A typical specimen is the theme of *Nun ist das Heil und die Kraft* (No. 50), which consists of a combination of the motive of strength and the motive of joy —

In this way Bach expresses thematically the whole substance of the text, the subject of which is the triumph of God and the rejoicing over Satan's fall (Rev. XII, 10).

In the cantata *Meine Seufzer, meine Tränen* (No. 13) the words of an aria run thus — "Ächzen und erbärmlich Weinen hilft der Sorgen Krankheit nicht; aber wer gen Himmel schauet . . . dem kann leicht ein Freudenlicht in der Trauerbrust erscheinen" ("Our sighs and tears cannot help us in our sickness and sorrow; but he who looks towards heaven will find his mourning lit up by a ray of joy"). Bach's theme is the sighing motive dissolving into the motive of joy —

In the *St. Matthew Passion* we have a large number of themes composed of two motives*. That of the aria and chorus at the beginning of the Second Part expresses at the same time the hurried steps and the laments of the Daughter of Zion, seeking her friend in the garden of Gethsemane. In the aria "Sehet, Jesus hat die Hand uns zu fassen ausgespannt" ("See, Jesus has stretched out His hand to grasp us"), we hear the pealing of the bells of salvation, and see the movement with which the Lord lifts up redeemed humanity to Him on the cross. In the setting of the text "Geduld, Geduld, wenn mich falsche Zungen stechen" ("Patience, patience, when false tongues wound me") we first of all have the word "Geduld" expressed in quiet quavers, and then the stinging of the false tongues is depicted in a precipitate motion to and fro —

The theme of the aria "Können Tränen meiner Wangen nichts erlangen, o so nehmt mein Herz hinein" ("Though in vain be all my wailing, naught availing, oh receive this heart of mine") runs thus —

* See the chapter on the *St. Matthew Passion*.

We are supposed to be witnessing the scourging of Jesus. In the first two bars are depicted the blows falling on His back; this motive is derived from the accompaniment to the previous arioso, "Erbarm' es Gott". What follows is only a musical form of the cry —

with which the Daughter of Zion, who is looking on, breaks in upon the torture.

CONCLUSION.

This enumeration of the principal sources of Bach's tonal language, and the chief uses to which he puts it, cannot possibly give a complete idea of his method of musical expression. It is meant only to stimulate reflection and research, and to show that the key to the performance of many of Bach's works is to be looked for in the significance that the composer attaches to certain definite motives.

It goes without saying that the foregoing analysis indicates only the meanings the themes most commonly bear. In the "Kreuzige" of the *St. John Passion*, for example, the rhythm has nothing to do with the motive of joy, but serves here, as in other cases, only to make the motion more animated. Bach employs it for the same purpose in the aria "So löschet im Eifer der rächende Richter", in the cantata *Es reifet euch ein schrecklich Ende* (No. 90). It would be equally false to see the "sighing motive" in every theme composed of successions of two tied notes. Bach's musical language is simply based on the fact that for the representation of certain feelings he prefers certain definite rhythms, and that this association is so natural that it at once tells its own story to anyone with a musical mind. This does not at all exclude the employment of these rhythms in other ways, especially when the object is the representation of motion of some kind. Nor must we forget that many rhythms that look the same on paper were conceived by Bach in wholly different ways. His works are peculiarly fitted to convince us of the imperfection of our methods of noting music, so far as the reproduction of the organic life of the tones is concerned. We can therefore maintain with some confidence that the same rhythm in Bach's music does not represent two distinct feelings, and that the expressive elements of his tonal language are more clearly cut than those of any other composer. It would hardly be possible to show so many verbal symbols in anyone else's work. It has been said that in music the rhythms correspond roughly to the consonants, and the intervals and harmonies to the vowels, since they give sonority to the rhythms. If this comparison is broadly correct, it tallies very closely with what we find in Bach's musical language. The tonal tissue that the intervals give to the rhythm defines the quality of the emotion. Bach's intervals have also a special significance of their own, though the discovery of general formulæ is incomparably more difficult here than in the case of the rhythms. We can say with certainty, however, that skips of sixths are generally plentiful when he has to express joy, while uneasiness and something like loathing are often expressed by means of the diminished third. Strange and widely-separated dissonances are employed to represent pain and horror.

The more we study the cantatas, the more it becomes evident that only the coarsest elements of Bach's tonal language can be reduced to formulæ. At the same time, however, we become conscious how little of what can be observed has really been noted thus far, and how much is still to be revealed by comparative research into the whole of Bach's work, until the individuality and the perfection of the expression in his music are made clear enough to executants to influence their performances of the works.

CHAPTER XXIV.

THE ARNSTADT, MÜHLHAUSEN, WEIMAR, AND CÖTHEN CANTATAS.

Forkel maintains that in Bach's earliest compositions the marks of genius are indeed evident, but that "they also contain so much that is unnecessary, so much that is immature, extravagant, and tasteless, that they are not worth preserving, at any rate for the general public." * Only in his thirty-fifth year, — i. e. 1720, — did Bach, according to his first biographer, attain perfect mastery of polyphony **.

This is purely fantastic. Only the three or four very earliest of Bach's cantatas have the air of being experiments; in those that follow, the style is already sure and finished. If ever a composer's period of probation was short, it was his.

The Easter cantata *Denn du wirst meine Seele nicht in der Hölle lassen* (No. 15), belongs to the Arnstadt epoch. Bach appears to have performed it also at some later date. Like the cantatas of the Northern composers, it is pompously orchestrated. The final chorale "Weil du vom Tod erstanden bist", with its fanfare-like interludes in the wind, is very impressive. Bach would be eighteen or nineteen years old when this cantata was written.

---

* Forkel, p. 49.
** Forkel, pp. 23—25.

The cantata *Gott ist mein König* (No. 71) was produced at Mühlhausen on 4th February 1708, on the occasion of the election of a new Town Council. On that day in each year one third of the Council of forty-eight undertook the conduct of the business of the town until the same date in the following year. The election began with a ceremony in the church. The cantata performed on the occasion was generally printed. This was the case with Bach's cantata; it was the only one issued during his lifetime. The printing, however, was regarded not as a publication for the benefit of Bach, but as an act in honour of the Mühlhausen Council*.

For this festive occasion there was a brilliant orchestra — three trumpets, two flutes, two oboes, bassoon, first and second violins, viola, "violonc", kettle-drum and organ. Each instrument has an obbligato part, not separately, however, but as part of a particular orchestral and choral ensemble. There are three of these, — the first formed by the trumpets, the second by the flutes, oboes, and bassoon, and the third by the strings. The chorale portions are divided between a *tutti*, which Bach calls *coro pleno*, and a smaller group, that only sings when *senza ripieni* is indicated. The charm of the work comes from the co-operation and contrast of the three instrumental and two choral masses. The setting for choir and orchestra of the prayer from the 74th Psalm — "Du wollest dem Feinde nicht geben die Seele deiner Turteltaube" — is full of feeling**.

* The parts alone were printed, not the score. In the textbook the cantata is called a *Glückwünschende Kirchen-Motette* ("Congratulatory Church-Motet"). The two officiating burgomasters were Adolf Strecker and Georg Adam Steinbach. Both the autograph score and the autograph parts have survived.

** Spitta found a fragment of a Bach cantata belonging to the Mühlhausen epoch in the cantor's house at the village of Langula (Spitta I, 343). The Wedding Cantata *Der Herr denket an uns* (B. G. XIII, 75 ff) must also belong to this time. It was probably composed for the second marriage of the pastor Stauber (Spitta I, 370 ff.). Bach was compelled to write the orchestral part for strings alone.

The score of the cantata *Aus der Tiefe rufe ich* (No. 131; Psalm 130) has at the end the note "Auff Begehren Tit. Herrn. D. Georg. Christ. Eilmar's in die Musik gebracht von Joh. Seb. Bach, Org. Molhusino" ("Set to music by Joh. Seb. Bach, organist at Mühlhausen, by request of Herr D. G. G. Eilmar"). Eilmar, — *Pastor primarius* at the church of the Blessed Virgin — was a great admirer of church music, and a personal friend of Bach's.

The only instruments employed in this cantata are strings, oboe and bassoon. On every page we can see that Bach is beginning to emancipate himself from the Northern composers. The orchestral interruptions are not so lengthy as in the two previous cantatas. The young man still follows Buxtehude, however, in the employment of the chorale. In the arioso "So du willst, Herr, Sünde zurechnen" the soprano sings "Erbarm dich mein" to the melody of "Herr Jesu Christ du höchstes Gut"; and the same melody is used in the arioso "Meine Seele wartet". The whole work is so deeply felt and so natural in effect that the modern hearer enjoys it as much as the Mühlhausen audience of 1707.

From the first years of the Weimar period we have two cantatas — *Nach dir, Herr, verlanget mich* (No. 150), and *Gottes Zeit ist die allerbeste Zeit* (the *Actus tragicus*, No. 106).

The first of these gives a characteristic example of Bach's method of expressing grief and joy. In order to express the anguish of the cry "Nach dir, Herr, verlanget mich" ("For thee, oh Lord, I long") he employs the chromatic sequence so often met with in the later cantatas —

In the aria "Doch bin und bleibe ich vergnügt" ("Yet I am and shall be content"), the bass is dominated by the motive of joy —

The conclusion, however, is in the form of a chaconne upon a *basso ostinato*, in which we have an anticipation of the master of the *Crucifixus* in the B minor Mass.

We do not know for whose death the mourning cantata *Gottes Zeit ist die allerbeste Zeit* (No. 106) was written. Spitta's researches shew that there was no death in the ducal family at that time. It seems to have been an old man, to whom the "Mit Fried' und Freud' fahr ich dahin" (from Simeon's song of praise) would be appropriate.

The text is as perfect as the music. It is composed of verses from the Bible, in which the antithesis is worked out between the Old Testament fear of death and the New Testament joy in death. "Put thy house in order, for thou must die" says the prophet Isaiah, whereupon the chorus joins in with "It is the old decree". But at once a soprano strikes in, as if hastening hither from another world, with the final call of the Apocalypse, "Yes, come Lord Jesu, come", to which the orchestra adds the chorale "Ich hab' mein Sach' Gott heimgestellt" ("I have cast my care on God"). We can see the Cross on Golgotha. The soul repeats the words of Jesus, "Into Thy hands I commend my spirit", and is answered with the words spoken to the thief, "This day shalt thou be with me in paradise". The comforted soul sings "In joy and peace I pass away". Finally the chorale "Glorie, Lob, Ehr' und Herrlichkeit" ("Glory, Praise, Honour, and Joy") is sung to the melody "In dich hab' ich gehoffet, Herr" ("In thee, oh Lord, is my hope"). The last line, "Through Jesus Christ, Amen", widens out into a brilliant fantasia, which terminates with the theme in augmentation in the orchestra.

Bach probably compiled the text of this cantata himself. It was certainly not done by any Weimar poet, for none of the poets of that time would have been so self-denying as to have refrained from introducing verses of his own. In any case it is one of the most perfect texts, from the musical point of view, to be found anywhere.

The work commences with a sonatina for two flutes, two gambas, continuo and organ. It is based on a motive in E flat, expressive of transfigured grief; this runs through the whole work. To grasp these harmonies is to be transported far from all earthly pain; the words from the Apocalypse come into one's mind that Bach probably had in his — "And God shall wipe away all tears from their eyes, and there shall be no more death, neither sorrow, nor crying, neither shall there be anymore pain; for the former things are passed away."

No other instruments are used in the cantata besides the two flutes and the two gambas. Their veiled *timbre* belongs to the very essence of the music. We seem to see an autumn landscape with blue mists floating across it.

The dramatic life and the intimate union of words and music in the *Actus tragicus* specially endeared it to the early admirers of Bach, among them Zelter. The cantata was first publicly revived by the Cecilia Society of Frankfort-on-the-Main, under Schelble, in May 1833*. It had to be repeated in December. It was still called for, and was given again in each of the two following years. It was first published in 1830, by Simrock. If it was the *St. Matthew Passion* that rescued Bach's music from its Babylonian captivity, it was the *Actus tragicus* that prepared the path for its return and levelled the ground for it. Even when we know all the cantatas we always go back with pleasure to this work, written by Bach at the end of his twentieth year. The *Actus tragicus* was the favourite cantata of Julius Stockhausen.

On the whole it is hard to tear ourselves away from these early works, which are the only ones that Bach wrote in the pure form of the old cantata. When he began to supply the regulation cantata for the church service at

---

* See p. 246.

the Weimar Court, he decided in favour of the new style, and wrote his music to the free texts supplied him by Salomo Franck and Erdmann Neumeister. Franck lived at Weimar; Neumeister at that time was at Sorau, which town he left for Hamburg shortly afterwards, in 1715. Bach's conversion to the modern cantata may be dated about 1712*. When he was made Konzertmeister, in 1714, it became his duty to supply each year a definite number of compositions for the church. In place of dramatic texts, compiled from Biblical verses and stanzas from hymns, we now get wretched poems, that are always cut out to the same pattern. The arioso is supplanted by the *da capo* aria and the *secco* recitative. The plan is still further impoverished by the fact that the choir now recedes wholly into the background; it figures only at the beginning and at the end. There is none of the animated alternation between solo and chorus that we find in the *Actus tragicus* and the cantata *Aus der Tiefe*. Nor does the composer now try to cast the whole work into one mould; the cantata henceforth divides into separate numbers.

How was it possible for Bach to renounce in a moment all the artistic riches that he had been able to use with such masterly effect in his first cantatas? How can we account for the fact that henceforth he never returned, even in one exceptional case, to the form of the old cantata? As we read the Bible we regret more than anything that he, a Bible student, should have refrained from setting so many splendid passages that would certainly have been attractive to him as a musician, merely because there were no continuous Biblical passages in the cantata-form that he had adopted. There is hardly an admirer of his who has not felt that he would give the two hundred church cantatas for one hundred works in the style of the *Actus tragicus***.

---

* On the subject of the old and new cantata see p. 80 ff.

** It is a curious fact that one of the Bach pioneers, Moritz Hauptmann, though admiring the *Actus tragicus*, thought its musical structure "a monstrosity of movements that jostle and hang on

The chronology of these earliest cantatas presents no difficulties, for the whole style of the works shows that they must have been composed before any of the others. Moreover, in the case of *Gott ist mein König* the date of the first performance is noted on the score, and in the case of *Aus der Tiefe* a note of Bach's own indicates that it was written in Mühlhausen.

The chronological arrangement of the majority of the succeeding cantatas is not so easy to determine. Only a few of them have the year noted on the cover; the approximate dates of the others have to be deduced from external and internal evidence. Spitta and Rust undertook this task independently, and the results obtained by each agree in the main with those of the other*. The external evidences are those of the handwriting, the style of the notes, and the paper. Bach's writing changed with the years, as may be seen from the specimens given in volume XLIV of the Bachgesellschaft edition. Cantatas, therefore, in the same handwriting belong to the same period. Much more exact clues, however, are given by certain characteristics of the notation. Bach first adopted the double cross in 1732. It is therefore practically certain that cantatas in which this sign is used belong to a later date than that. There is further the evidence afforded by his way of writing the oboe d'amore part. This instru-

---

to each other". See Hauptmann's letters to Otto Jahn and Hauser, in Spitta I, 466. Spitta explains Bach's adoption of the *da capo* aria in this way: "When Bach had made himself familiar with the Italian *da capo* aria, he became conscious of a waste of power, since in this form he could say many things in a simpler and therefore better way, without foregoing any of his originality." (I, 465.) It is hard to see what "waste of power" there is in composition in the style of the *Actus tragicus*; nor is it any easier to understand how anything can be better or more simply expressed in the *da capo* aria than in the old arioso. Spitta is trying to explain the inexplicable, without falling back on the only possible solution — that Bach followed the fashion.

* See Spitta's remarks and Rust's prefaces. The following chapters are based on Spitta's chronology, the value of which only the professional historian can fully appreciate.

ment, — which, according to Walther's *Musiklexikon*, was invented in 1720 — stood a third lower than the ordinary oboe. Bach first uses it in the score of the cantata *Die Himmel erzählen die Ehre Gottes* (No. 76), which bears the date 1723. The new instrument naturally offered some difficulties in the way of notation. Bach experiments. In the B minor Mass (1733) he writes for it in a new way; in the secular cantatas *Angenehmes Wiederau* and *Schleicht, spielende Wellen*, that certainly belong to 1737, he adopts another method. These facts enable us to decide whether a cantata was written between 1723 and 1733, between 1733 and 1737, or after 1737. But the most weighty evidence is afforded by the water-marks on the paper he used. The manuscripts exhibit about half-a-dozen distinct marks, showing that Bach bought large quantities at a time. Cantatas written on paper with the same water-mark thus belong to the same period. If we can decide the date of one cantata, it often enables us to settle the chronology of more than a dozen others.

Sometimes a valuable clue is given by the writing of those who helped to copy out the parts. If it is that of Emmanuel or Friedemann, we know the latest year in which the cantata could have been composed, for we know when these two sons left the paternal house. Interesting data, again, are supplied by the use of the material of secular cantatas for sacred works. In almost every case we know the date of origin of the former; and as we may suppose that the rearrangement was usually made not long after the original, we can fix the date of the new version with some certainty.

The problem would be very simple so far as the Leipzig cantatas are concerned if we had the printed version of the texts that were given out for the church music on Sundays and Feast days. We possess, however, only three of these, — one for the Easter Feast days and the two following Sundays of the year 1731, one for the Whitsuntide Feast days and the Feast of the Trinity of the same year, and one for the Christmas of 1734 (the *Christmas Oratorio*)*.

To some extent we are compensated for the absence of these programmes by the published poems of Picander, who wrote most of the texts for the Leipzig cantatas. Bach composed his cantatas for immediate use. The date of the publication of the text thus gives us also the year when the music was written.

Besides these external evidences there are the internal ones. Bach usually produced within a short space of time a series of works having an inner relationship to each other, as if he wished to embody simultaneously, in several examples, a certain type that engrossed him for the moment. Thus it frequently happens that four or five cantatas that follow each other according to the order of the ecclesiastical year exhibit a striking similarity among themselves, which is most noticeable, as a rule, in the structure of the opening choruses. These works, of course, belong to the same period.

The problem is therefore not to settle the chronology of isolated cantatas, but that of definite groups that are clearly distinguishable from each other by certain external and internal characteristics, and that can be assigned to a definite period by means of one or two of the works, the date of which can be proved in other ways. Perhaps Spitta has occasionally drawn too sweeping conclusions from external evidences such as that of the cantatas being written on the same paper. This, however, does not affect the general result of his acute inquiry into the chronology of the works.

Questions of detail have in this case little practical interest. What does it signify if we cannot be sure whether a given cantata was written a year earlier or a year later? There is no such consistent artistic evolution observable in the succession of Bach's cantatas as there is, for ex-

* See B. G. XLV[1] (1895), preface, p. 76 ff.

ample, in that of Beethoven's symphonies. The distance that Beethoven travels between two symphonies is greater almost than that which Bach traversed in a hundred cantatas*. He is one of those rare personalities that do not become, but always are. We could almost say that his cantatas form a closed circle. The last resemble the first,—if by the first we understand those in which he adopts the new style of cantata.

In his Weimar period he set about a dozen of Franck's texts to music. He was fond of this poet, being attracted by his mysticism and his deep feeling for nature. He may also have liked Franck for his habit of making more use of verses from the Bible than Neumeister and the others did; he was, on the whole, the most conservative of the new school.

One of the best known of the Bach cantatas to a text by Franck has always been *Ich hatte viel Bekümmernis* (No. 21). The cover of the score is inscribed: "Per ogni Tempo. Concerto a 13: 3 Trombe, Tamburi, 1 Oboe, 2 Violini e Viola, Fagotto and Violoncello, 4 Voci con Continuo di J. S. Bach. Den 3ten post Trinitas 1714." Diligent research has failed to discover the part for the drums; a knowledge of Bach's style, however, makes it easy to supply it. In any case it is absolutely essential in performance.

The cantata is in two parts; the first was given before the sermon, the second after it. One result of this division is that the work has no real culminating point; it is not quite clear at which moment grief gives way to consolation.

Like the *Actus tragicus*, which it resembles also in many other ways, this cantata is prefaced by a sinfonia, founded on an affecting dialogue between the oboe and the first violins, the other instruments supplying the harmonies. In the choruses the alternation between the voice parts

---

* This, of course, applies only to the cantatas of his period of maturity. In the few youthful cantatas that we possess we can see a very rapid development.

and the instrumental *ensemble* ceases; the orchestra strives to be independent, though with only occasional success; very frequently it merely doubles the vocal parts, or ceases altogether.

The theme of the first chorus runs thus —

It is identical with that of an organ fugue, with the exception that the latter is in the major (Peters II, p. 7). The chorus "Sei nun wieder zufrieden", — with which are inwoven two verses of the chorale "Wer nur den lieben Gott läßt walten" — is extraordinarily sonorous.

The plaintive theme of the aria "Seufzer, Tränen, Kummer, Not", woven, as it were, out of sighs —

is very characteristic.

The painting of the storm at the words "Sturm und Wellen", in the aria "Bäche von gesalznen Tränen" is precise and expressive; we do not know how it could be improved upon. The declamation is not faultless, as Mattheson pointed out with a certain malicious joy*. We must agree with him that the fourfold repetition of the word "Ich" at the commencement of the first chorus is somewhat ill-considered. We have here a reminiscence of the old motet-style. Mattheson's censure of the declamation in the duet "Komm, Herr Jesu, und erquicke" is, however, unjustifiable.

Even Bach's great biographer Spitta does not find this duet to his liking. "The duet", he says, "is what church music should never be — dramatic . . . Bach's delight in polyphonic working has made him, — uninten-

---

* See p. 178.

tionally, no doubt, — accentuate the dramatic element to an almost painful point when the voices bandy to and fro incessantly the words 'Ach nein! ach ja! du hassest mich! ich liebe dich!' ... The only mitigating circumstance is that the soprano part would be sung in those days by a boy, which would partly prevent the duet from having the appearance of a charming love-duet, as it always has now."*

His fears were groundless. Anyone who is free from prudery in matters of church music must delight in this ardent dramatic piece, and be deeply affected by the dialogue of the soul with its Comforter. If anything can be objected to, it is the *da capo* form in which Bach has cast the duet, with the result that the entreaty "Komm, mein Jesu, und erquicke mich" is repeated at the end, after the Saviour, in the middle section, "Ach Jesu, durchsüße mir Seele und Herze", has banished care and sorrow. But the mystical love-glow that finds such eloquent expression in Bach's works cannot be objected to from any standpoint of church music. So long as the Song of Solomon remains in the Bible, its allegorical language cannot be forbidden in religious music. Bach, a Lutheran and a mystic, delights in the Song of Solomon, as does his librettist Franck.

This can be seen in the two cantatas *Komm, du süsse Todesstunde* (No. 161)** and *Ach ich sehe, jetzt da ich zur Hochzeit gehe* (No. 162)***, in which the ideas of the Song of Solomon and the Apocalypse are blended. There is ardent longing in the song of the two flutes that accompanies the words:

"Komm du süsse Todesstunde,
Da mein Geist Honig speist,
Aus des Löwen Munde.
Mache meinen Abschied süsse,
Säume nicht, letztes Licht,
Dass ich meinen Heiland küsse!"

* Spitta I, 537, 538.
** For the sixteenth Sunday after Trinity, 1715.
*** For the twentieth Sunday after Trinity, 1715.

("Come, thou sweet hour of death, when my soul shall be fed with honey from the mouth of the lion. Make my farewell sweet; delay not, oh my last light, the moment when I shall kiss my Saviour").

The organ accompanies this with the chorale "Herzlich tut mich verlangen".

The aria "Mein Verlangen ist, den Heiland zu umfangen" grows out of the sigh of yearning —

In the recitative the soul pictures death to itself as a "soft sleep"; and at once the instruments sink downwards in blissful lassitude —

At the idea of the resurrection, joy breaks forth and continues in clear tones, while the alto sings "So schlage doch, du letzter Stundenschlag!" ("Strike then, last hour!"). The chorus concludes with the chorale strophe —

> "Wenn es meines Gottes Wille,
> Wünsch' ich, dass des Leibes Last
> Heute noch die Erde fülle".

("If it is the Lord's will, let the earth take today the burden of my body"). This funeral song is surrounded by the orchestra with exultant demisemiquavers.

The cantata *Ach, ich sehe, jetzt da ich zur Hochzeit gehe* (No. 162) is, as a rule, of a severer beauty. In the aria "In meinem Gott bin ich erfreut" ("I rejoice in my God") the bass leaps joyously in a veritable dance. The chorus contributes only the final chorale.

The cantata *Mein Gott, wie lang', ach lange* (No. 155)* is also without an opening chorus. It begins with a twelve-bar repetition of the same note in quavers, creating an effect of anxiety**. Then the soprano sings —

> "Mein Gott, wie lang', ach lange?
> Des Jammers ist zu viel,
> Ich sehe gar kein Ziel
> Der Schmerzen und der Sorgen . . . ."

("My God, how long, oh, how long? Too great is my distress. No end do I see to sorrow and care.") "Du must glauben, du mußt hoffen" ("Thou must believe, thou must hope"), say the alto and tenor consolingly, while the bassoon and the cello maintain uninterruptedly one of those curiously extended figures with which Bach symbolises steadfast faith. A motive in demisemiquavers, that forms the middle part of the theme, then enters at the words "Jesus weiß die rechte Stunde, dich mit Hilfe zu erfreuen" ("Jesus knows the right hour at which to gladden thee with His help"), and its meaning becomes apparent. The theme in which Bach symbolises the combination of firm faith and joyful hope runs thus —

The soprano aria "Wirf mein Herze, wirf dich noch in des Höchsten Liebesarme" ("Throw thyself, my heart, into the loving arms of the Most High") breathes a quite sensuous passion. The wild rhythm of the strings —

* For the second Sunday after Epiphany, 1716.
** See p. 103 ff.

merges sharply into a long chord, which however, does not express rest, but trembling and shuddering, while the bass now takes over the passionate theme. This procedure is repeated five times. The picture given in the text could not be represented more realistically in music.

The solo cantata for bass, *Der Friede sei mit dir* (No. 158) is simple and unassuming. As the title of the copy that has come down to us shows, Bach used it twice, — for the Purification of Mary and for Easter Tuesday. The text is probably by Franck. In this work Bach employs no orchestra, but merely contrabass, organ and solo violin.

The Spring sunshine fills the two works that Bach wrote for Palm Sunday and Easter of the year 1715. For the first of them, *Himmelskönig sei willkommen* (No. 182), he had to make shift with the limited orchestra that was all that was permitted during the period of the Passion. He employs only one flute and the strings. None the less is he able to represent musically the word "Himmelskönig" ("King of Heaven") in the orchestral introduction, by means of the rhythm of solemnity*. With the declamation of the words "Himmelskönig sei willkommen" even Mattheson would not have been able to find fault. The arrangement of the voices, which Bach repeats twice in the same form, is very interesting; all four voices, from the soprano to the bass, repeat the "Willkommen" in turns. In the further course of the cantata the Passion mood becomes more and more prominent. The tenor aria "Jesu, lass durch Wohl und Weh" is accompanied by the "grief" motive —

* The theme is quoted on p. 94.

This is followed by a chorale chorus, in the style of Pachelbel, on "Jesu, deine Passion ist mir lauter Freude". The final chorus, "So lasset uns gehen in Salem der Freuden", has a striking resemblance, both thematically and structurally, to the opening chorus of the cantata *Sie werden aus Saba alle kommen* (No. 65).

This is one of the most impressive illustrations of the fact that Bach's greatness consists not in the capacity for manifold expression, but in the fact that he always tries to express the same idea perfectly in the same vein. It is therefore impossible for him to write two different pieces of music to depict a procession at once joyous and solemn.

The Easter cantata *Der Himmel lacht, die Erde jubilieret* (No. 31) requires an orchestra that in those days would have been thought quite monstrous — three trumpets, kettledrum, three oboes, *taille* (tenor), first and second violins, first and second violas, bassoon, first and second violoncellos, and *continuo*. Words can give no idea of the splendid way in which, in the orchestral introduction — a separate movement worked out on large lines — Bach makes the heavens laugh and the earth rejoice. The opening chorus is gigantic. The bass aria "Fürst des Lebens, starker Streiter, hochgelobter Gottessohn" ("Prince of life, puissant Fighter, blessed Son of God"), is naturally dominated by the motive of solemnity —

To prevent anyone spoiling the grave effect by too fast a tempo, Bach expressly marks the movement *molto adagio.*

At the end, poet and musician unite in mystic reveries upon death:

"Letzte Stunde brich herein, mir die Augen zuzudrücken,
Lass mich Jesu Freudenschein und sein helles Licht erblicken."

("Come, last hour, and close my eyes, that Jesus may show me the light of His joy"), sings Franck. To this Bach writes a glorified cradle song —

Over the final chorale, again, there hovers a "glorified voice", in the violins and trumpet *unisono.*

We do not know why, in the other Easter cantata written at Weimar, *Ich weiss, dass mein Erlöser lebt* (No. 160; text by Neumeister), Bach employed only violins and the *continuo,* the latter strengthened by the bassoon. External considerations may have imposed these drastic limitations upon him. In any case, this cantata is one or two years older than *Der Himmel lacht, die Erde jubilieret.*

Of the Whitsuntide cantatas belonging to the Weimar period we have only one, *Wer mich liebet, der wird mein Wort halten* (No. 59; text by Neumeister), and that only in a later arrangement. The instrumentation of the opening duet is curious — two trumpets, kettledrum and strings. In the final aria we meet with one of Bach's most extravagant "joy" figures —

The text runs — "Die Welt mit allen Königreichen ... kann dieser Herrlichkeit nicht gleichen, womit uns unser Gott erfreut" ("The world with all its kingdoms cannot compare with this glory wherewith God rejoices us"). The final chorale has not come down to us.

The Weimar period was very rich in Advent and Christmas cantatas. *Nun komm' der Heiden Heiland* (No. 61; text by Neumeister) was written for the first Sunday in Advent in 1714*. In the first chorus Bach undertakes to build up the old Advent hymn into a French overture; he actually gives it the title of "Overture". During the solemn first part (*grave*) the voices sing in succession the supplicatory line of the chorale, "Nun komm' der Heiden Heiland"; then all together they sing "Der Jungfrauen Kind erkannt". The *allegro* section, which Bach has marked *gai*, begins with "Des wundert sich alle Welt"; at the words "Gott solch Geburt ihm bestellt" the *grave* returns. Think what we will of the experiment of uniting a French overture and a mediæval chorale, the tonal effect of the chorus is wonderful. So also with the final Amen, that takes the form of a chorale fantasia upon the melody "Wie schön leuchtet der Morgenstern". The whole work seems to be filled with a sweet and magical youthfulness, that even lends a charm to the primitive harmonic structure.

The aria "Öffne dich mein ganzes Herze, Jesus kommt und ziehet ein" is thematically interesting; it is developed from the motive —

This aria is introduced by the recitative "Siehe, ich stehe vor der Tür und klopfe an" (Rev. III, 20), in which Bach

* This was the first version. There is a second cantata (No. 62) founded on the old Advent hymn.

gives a declamatory watchman's-call to the bass, and accompanies it by rigid *pizzicati* chords, representing the knocking of the expected One*. For the sake of this recitative the cantata should be one of the first to be performed with the object of making Bach popular.

On the cover of *Nun komm' der Heiden Heiland*, as is well known, Bach has written a note upon the "Order of the morning service in Leipzig on the first Sunday in Advent". As it bears also the date 1714, Spitta concluded that Bach had been invited by Kuhnau, on the first Sunday in Advent in that year, to perform one of his cantatas in Leipzig. A later theory is more probable — that Bach produced the cantata at St. Thomas's at a later date, perhaps during the vacation, on the first Sunday in Advent 1722, after he had applied for the Leipzig cantorate**.

The fine solo cantata for tenor, *Meine Seele rühmt und preist* (No. 189; for the fourth Sunday after Easter), probably belongs to the later Weimar period. It consists of two exquisitely beautiful arias; the accompaniment is for flute, oboe and violin.

The beauty of the solo cantata *Barmherziges Herze der ewigen Liebe* (No. 185, for soprano, alto, tenor and bass; for the fourth Sunday after Trinity) is somewhat impaired by the dry, didactic text.

The cantata *Wachet, betet, seid bereit allezeit* (No. 70; text by Franck), was written in 1716, two years after *Nun komm' der Heiden Heiland*. A comparison of the two will show the progress Bach had made in this short time; he has now acquired a means of expression and suggestion so perfect that though in after years he may indeed vary it, he never surpasses it. In *Wachet, betet* he does not merely set the text to music, but paints a picture of the Last Judgment. In the opening chorus the trumpet gives its dire summons to humanity to justify itself —

---

* See p. 78.

** On this question see Richter, *Bachjahrbuch*, 1905, p. 57 ff.

In the recitative "Erschrecket, ihr verstockten Sünder" he depicts the trembling of the dammed who are conscious of their guilt; this immediately ceases when mention is made of the saved whom the Redeemer takes home with Him to bliss. The recitative "Ach soll nicht dieser grosse Tag", with its animated bass, reminds us of the beginning of the cantata *O Ewigkeit, du Donnerwort* (No. 60); in the following aria, at the words "Schalle, knalle, letzter Schlag", Bach paints a picture of the end of the world, in which he employs his familiar "tumult" motive —

In striking contrast to this pictorial music are the passages that voice the mystic longing of the elect for the end of things. In the aria

"Lass der Spötter Zungen schmähen,
Es wird doch und muss geschehen,
Dass wir Jesum werden sehen
Auf den Wolken in den Höhen".

("Though the tongues of mockers revile us, we shall yet see Jesus in the skies"), the first violin part reminds us strongly of the *Laudamus te* in the B minor Mass. Could Bach have had in his mind the passage from the first Epistle of Peter (I, 7—8), "Jesus Christ, whom having not seen ye love; in whom, though now ye see Him not, yet believing, ye rejoice with joy unspeakable and full of glory?" Even more superterrestrial is the music of the *adagio* that begins and ends the last aria, "Seligster Erquickungstag . . . Jesus führet mich zur Stille . . ."*

* According to Spitta (I, 571, 643, II, 362) the cantata in its present form is a Leipzig revision of 1723. This may also be the case with the cantata *Der Himmel lacht, die Erde jubilieret* (No. 31).

The cantatas *Bereitet die Wege, bereitet die Bahn* (No. 132) and *Herz und Mund und Tat und Leben* (No. 147) were intended for the fourth Sunday in Advent. Both texts are derived from Franck's poems.

Bereitet die Wege was written in 1715. The passage from the fortieth chapter of Isaiah ("In the wilderness prepare ye the way of the Lord") is given out in the bright and joyous tones of a boy soprano, the orchestra playing round it as if with rays of sunlight. In the aria "Ach bedenket was geschenket", exuberant arabesques in the violin entwine round the vocal part. The text is founded on a verse in the Apocalypse, "These ... have washed their robes and made them white in the blood of the Lamb". Bach takes it in a mystical sense. The final chorale that appears in Franck's poem is omitted. When Bach produced the work in Leipzig he probably substituted for this another chorale, which would be distributed to the choir on detached sheets, and so has been lost. In St. Thomas's, figurate music was only given on the first of the Sundays in Advent. If Bach desired to perform his Weimar Advent cantatas there, he would have to alter them slightly so as to adapt them for other Sundays. In this case he did it by cutting out the final chorale and substituting another. He produced the other cantata for the fourth Sunday in Advent, *Herz und Mund und Tat und Leben* (No. 147), in Leipzig on the Feast of the Visitation of the Virgin Mary, altering the title on the cover accordingly. He probably revised the music also, as appears from the division of it into a *prima* and a *seconda parte*, for during the early Leipzig years he mostly adopted the two-part cantata form. In the opening chorus and in the aria "Ich will von Jesu Wunden singen" the trumpet is used with magnificent effect. The other numbers are notably delicate and intimate in treatment; they are carried through in flowing triplet rhythms, that are especially effective in the two chorale fantasias for chorus and orchestra, "Wohl mir, dass ich Jesum habe" and "Jesus bleibet meine Freude".

We are involuntarily reminded of the opening chorus of the cantata *Liebster Immanuel* (No. 123), which follows the same procedure.

In spite, however, of the intimacy of his mood here, Bach never lets pass any opportunity for tone-painting that Franck's text may offer him. The alto recitative "Der höchsten Allmacht Wunderhand" speaks of the "skipping and springing" of the child in Elisabeth's womb at the greeting of Mary. Bach illustrates this in his music by a sequence of convulsive movements, repeated throughout the whole number by the oboes in short disconnected groups —

He troubles little about the musical sense of the other words of the number. Again in the aria "Johannis freudenvolles Springen erkannte dich mein Heiland schon", in the cantata *Christum wir sollen loben schon* (No. 121), he depicts the quivering of the body of the mother who is about to bear the Baptist, only here the painting is still more realistic*.

The whole character of the Christmas cantata *Uns ist ein Kind geboren* (No. 142; text by Neumeister), seems to indicate that it was written three or four years before the two cantatas for the fourth Sunday in Advent. It perhaps dates from between 1712 and 1714. This is probable, among other things, from the somewhat dry declamation and the undeveloped form of the chorale fantasia that forms the final number.

* See p. 86.

The cantata *Tritt auf die Glaubensbahn*, again, (No. 152; for the Sunday after Christmas), has a succession of declamatory passages that are not free from faults, which is rather surprising, as it belongs, according to Spitta, to the year 1715. Bach's determination to be characteristic makes him give the following passage to the bass at the words "In Israel zum Fall" —

The inharmoniousness and rhythmic emptiness of Franck's text are answerable for the defects of the music. That Bach was embarrassed by them is evident from the improvements he tried to make in the text. He turns "seinen Glaubensbau gründet" into "seinen Glaubensgrund leget"; "in dieser Zeit" into "zu aller Zeit"; "nach Leiden und Schmach" into "nach Trübsal und Schmach". But he assuredly forgave his poet everything in consideration of the dialogue between Jesus and the soul at the end: "Wie soll ich dich, Liebster der Seelen, umfassen ..." "Du musst dich verleugnen und alles verlassen ..." ("How shall I comprehend thee, Beloved of souls? ..." "Thou must deny thyself and forsake everything"). Jesus takes the soul with Him to the strains of a wondrous gigue —

Here Bach's music begins to reveal itself as the art of "charm" that he afterwards claims it to be in *Phoebus and Pan*. Spitta, indeed, protests again here that the colour of the duet is contrary to the true church style*.

The cantata opens with a delightful instrumental prelude founded on the "step" motive —

---

* Spitta I, 560—562.

out of which Bach afterwards made an organ fugue*. The choir is not used.

The declamatory effects that Bach employed even at that time when the text permitted them may be seen in the cantata *Gleichwie der Regen und Schnee vom Himmel fällt* (No. 18), which dates from 1713 or 1714. The recitative upon the long opening passage from Isaiah LV, 10 is an incomparable masterpiece. The declamation is astoundingly effective, again, in the litany "Herr Gott, hier wird mein Herze sein", in which the choir joins four times with "Erhör' uns, lieber Herr Gott". It is a pity that Neumeister, who had a better sense of verbal rhythm than Franck, is so often banal in his ideas.

The aria "Mein Seelenschatz ist Gottes Wort" is accompanied throughout by a delightful "wave" motion, that impressed even Spitta. There seems no justification for it in the text, unless we assume that the oft-repeated word "net" aroused in Bach one of those musical visions that some quite subordinate association would evoke in him when the text he was setting was rather dry and empty.

For prelude the cantata has a powerful Sinfonia in chaconne form, built upon the theme —

If we remember that in the cantata *Tritt auf die Glaubensbahn* (No. 152) the instrumental introduction is inspired by the opening words of the text, and that the theme of the Sinfonia of the cantata for Sexagesima Sunday shows the same structure as the motives Bach employs to express steadfast and confident faith, it will not seem an improbable

* See I, 275.

assumption that here he is symbolising the steadfastness and inviolability of the word of God that is uttered later.

He probably did not compose music with any particular joy to Franck's text for the twenty-third Sunday after Trinity, *Nur jedem das Seine* (No. 163). It contains neither poetic ideas nor pictorial images. This, to be sure, is less the fault of the poet than of the Gospel for the day (Matthew XXII, 15—22), that deals with the subject of the tribute money. The religious valuation of tax-paying is not a grateful theme for a cantata text. Bach, evidently in despair, sets the final aria "Nimm mich mir und gib mich dir" in dialogue form, so as at least to work in a duet. The orchestra gives out at the same time the melody "Meinen Jesum lass ich nicht". The final chorale, taken from Heermann's hymn "Wo soll ich fliehen hin?" has only a figured bass*.

In Cöthen there was no church music, the Court having adopted the Reformed faith. From 1717 to 1723, i. e., from his thirty-second to his thirty-eighth year, Bach wrote cantatas, if at all, only occasionally and for special purposes. The only two that can be attributed to this period are *Wer sich selbst erhöhet, der soll erniedriget werden* (No.47) and *Das ist je gewisslich wahr* (No. 141). Their texts are found in a yearly cycle of cantata poems issued by the State Secretary Helbig in 1720.

The two themes by which Bach expresses the idea of the fallen being exalted and the exalted falling have already been cited as typical of his method of representation**. The pictorial purpose is visible also in the orchestral introduction; see, for example, the fall in the basses in the fifth to the seventh bars. The wonderful feature of this chorus,

* The cantata for the third Sunday in Lent, 1716, *Alles was von Gott geboren*, also belongs to the Weimar period. We do not possess it now, however, as an independent work, Bach having at a later date incorporated it almost wholly in the cantata *Ein' feste Burg*.

** See pp. 83, 84

however, is not its pictorial effects, but Bach's success in making such natural and agreeable music of them.

This pictorialism is continued in the two arias. In the first, "Wer ein wahrer Christ will heissen, muss der Demut sich befleissen", the first violin gives the picture of the necessary exercises in *Demut* (humility), — the figures being persistently forced downwards in spite of their efforts to ascend —

The theme of the oboe and violin in the aria "Jesu beuge doch mein Herze" is founded on the same idea. We seem to see the wavy lines of a twig which some one is testing by bending it.

Spitta believes that Bach wrote this work for Hamburg. In that year, 1720, the seventeenth Sunday after Trinity — the Gospel for which day is embodied in the cantata — fell on the 22nd September. Bach, however, did not go to Hamburg until November, his journey having been delayed by the death of his wife. It is thus doubtful whether he produced the cantata then. It is one of the few that he has carefully supplied with phrasing and expression marks. In the B. G. edition the solo instrument in the first aria is wrongly given as *Organo obbligato*; it should be the violin. If the cantata is to be performed nowadays, the text of the recitative "Der Mensch ist Kot, Staub, Asch' und Erde" will certainly have to be altered.

The cantata *Das ist je gewisslich wahr* (No. 141), for the third Sunday in Advent, is a little obscure. In the first chorus one is tempted to assume that the declamation is deliberately naïve, Bach's object being to express by the uniform length of the notes the child-like quality of the confession that is being made. It is extremely effective. The succeeding arias, however, rather rouse the suspicion that Bach has adapted Helbig's text to some music already existing. It is incredible that he should have deliberately declaimed the words "Jesu, Trost der geistlich Armen" in the way he does. Spitta thinks that the opening chorus is an arrangement of some earlier duet.

Indirectly associated with the Cöthen period is the cantata for the third day of Easter, *Ein Herz, das seinen Jesum lebend weiss* (No. 134). It is founded on a Cöthen "Gratulation" cantata, the title of which we do not know, the cover of the first sheet of the score being lost. We needs must lament that such beautiful music should have been made impossible by the poor text with which it is associated; a typical case is afforded by the commencement of the first aria —

Auf, auf, auf, auf Gläu-bi-ge!

In later years Bach twice took up this cantata with a view to improving it, as may be seen from the various parts that are extant. He could not, however, alter the chief numbers.

Altogether, then, there are about twenty-five cantatas that we can attribute with certainty to the pre-Leipzig period.

CHAPTER XXV.

THE LEIPZIG CANTATAS OF 1723 AND 1724.

According to the Necrology, Bach wrote five complete yearly series of church cantatas. In Leipzig this kind of church music was performed on fifty-nine Sundays and Feast days*; so that Bach must have written two hundred

* See I, 126 ff.

and ninety-five cantatas. A hundred and ninety of these have survived; of these about a hundred and sixty-five belong to the Leipzig period. Bach was cantor at St. Thomas's for twenty-seven years. This gives six cantatas per annum — not a large figure when we think, for example, of the productivity of a Telemann.

The works, however, were spread unequally over all these years. In the later Leipzig period Bach did not write much church music; so that in the earlier years he must sometimes have written as many as twenty cantatas per annum.

The first cantata of his to be performed in Leipzig is thus referred to in Joh. Seb. Riemer's *Jahrbuch*: "On the 7th February *Dom. Estomihi* Herr Sebastian Bach, Kapellmeister in Cöthen, underwent his probation for the post of cantor, rendered vacant by the death of Herr Kuhnau" *. The title of the cantata is not given; it was *Jesus nahm zu sich die Zwölfe* (No. 22).

The unknown poet has taken from the Gospel for this last Sunday before the Passion (Luke XVIII, 31—43) only the first and fourth verses — Christ's announcement to the disciples of His coming Passion; he unfortunately passes over the expressive series of pictures in the second and third verses. Following tradition, the bass gives out the words of Jesus in an arioso; the orchestra — strings and oboes — adds a symphonic accompaniment that is wonderfully expressive of the sorrow of Jesus and His inner firmness. The whole movement has a somewhat march-like character. The succeeding chorus, "Sie aber vernahmen der keines", reproduces very effectively the mutual questionings of the disciples.

The charming syncopated theme of the aria "Mein Jesu, ziehe mich nach dir" ("Jesus, draw me near to thee") paints the picture suggested in the words —

---

* See Richter, *Die Wahl J. S. Bachs zum Kantor der Thomasschule*, in the *Bachjahrbuch* for 1905, p. 58. The year referred to is 1723.

The aria "Mein alles in allem, mein ewiges Gut" ("My all in all, my endless treasure), which is based on the "joy" motive, is overpowering in the energy of its flight. The final chorale has a ravishing orchestral accompaniment.

We do not know whether this cantata pleased the Leipzigers or not. It sounds enchantingly throughout. Spitta thinks that Bach laid it out so simply in order not to depart too far from the style of Kuhnau.

On the 30th May 1723, the first Sunday after Trinity, the new cantor introduced himself to the Leipzigers with the cantata *Die Elenden sollen essen* (No. 75); we learn from the *Acta Lipsiensium academica* that it was received "with good *applausu*"*. It is in two parts, but is otherwise as simply constructed as the probation cantata. The first chorus, as in *Nun komm' der Heiden Heiland* (No. 61), is cast in the French overture form. The stately *grave* section comprises the words "Die Elenden sollen essen, dass sie satt werden, und die nach dem Herrn fragen, werden ihn preisen", and the *allegro* the words "Euer Herz soll ewiglich leben". Here again the chorale, "Was Gott tut, das ist wohl getan", has a charming orchestral accompaniment, that is developed out of the first motive of the melody. The "sinfonia" that opens the second part is a fantasia on the same melody. This is the only occasion on which Bach has treated a chorale in purely orchestral style. Of the solos the most striking is the bass aria "Mein Herze glaubt und liebt", with its wonderful trumpet accompaniment —

* See Spitta II, 355 ff.

Another trumpet cantata *par excellence* is the one performed on the second Sunday after Trinity, *Die Himmel erzählen die Ehre Gottes* (No. 76). No one who has once heard them can forget the marvellous theme to which Bach has set the two verses from the Psalms that compose the opening chorus. The movement is one of the most effective of his inventions; it is literally intoxicating.

Even if Bach had not noted on the cover of this cantata that he wrote it for the second Sunday after Trinity, 1723, we would be sure that it originated at the same time as the one last mentioned. In its bipartite form, in the symphonic introduction to the *Seconda Parte,* in the instrumental accompaniment to the chorale, in the use of the same melody to end the first and second part, in the character of the solos, it is plainly the twin-sister of the other.

The falling bass figure —

in the accompaniment to the chorale "Es woll' uns Gott genädig sein" is motived by the conclusion of the previous arioso, "Drum sei dir dies Gebet *demütigst* zugeschickt" ("Be this prayer most *humbly* offered to Thee"). We can see a crowd of people kneeling and bowing their heads.

In the tenor aria, the haughty and defiant motive —

symbolises the words "Hasse nur, hasse mich recht, feindlich's Geschlecht" ("Hate me well, oh my enemies"). In the middle section, where mention is made of "embracing Jesus by faith", the nestling melodic line of the voice suggests the persecuted soul seeking refuge in its Redeemer. The aria "Hört ihr Völker Gottes Stimme", in which the soprano voice addresses its alluring cry to all the world, is generally taken so slowly that the brightness and charm of it are lost. In the arioso-like recitative "So lässt sich Gott nicht unbezeugt" the orchestra depicts most expressively the words "the heavens are stirred, and the soul and body are moved".

In these first months in Leipzig Bach did not keep to the same poet. He did not collaborate with Picander until 1724. We can rarely discover the names of his previous librettists. Sometimes he harked back to Franck and Neumeister. From the latter he took the text of the cantata *Ein ungefärbt Gemüte* (No. 24), which he produced on the fourth Sunday after Trinity. This also ends with a chorale with a bewitching orchestral accompaniment. In the chorus "Alles nun, das ihr wollet, dass euch die Menschen tun", Christ's words are given out rather too disconnectedly. At the commencement "Alles" is repeated four times and "Alles nun" twice; the *allegro* before the *fugato* breaks off with the words "Alles nun, das ihr wollet". It was fortunate that Mattheson did not see this cantata.

The declamation is more expressive in the opening chorus of the cantata for the seventh Sunday after Trinity, *Ärgre dich, o Seele nicht* (No. 186; text by Franck), the cover of which bears the date 1723. Here the final chorale of the first part, with its orchestral accompaniment, almost becomes a chorale fantasia; it was probably repeated after the second part. In the tenor aria "Mein Heiland lässt sich merken in seinen Gnadenwerken" the oboe gives out the "joy" motive. In the soprano aria "Die Armen will der Herr umarmen" the bass and the violin figures that twine round the melody are of transcendent tenderness; and the final duet in gigue-form, "Lass, Seele, kein Leiden von Jesu dich scheiden" (for soprano and alto) exhales a Dionysiac joy.

The score is one of the most perfect of Bach's clean copies; perhaps it represents a drastic revision and expansion of a Weimar cantata. The happy improvements made in Franck's text may be the work of Bach's librettist of that time. On the other hand, the score of the solo cantata for the thirteenth Sunday after Trinity, *Ihr, die ihr euch von Christo nennet* (No. 164) has been so hastily written that it is hardly decipherable. Bach has tried his best to compose warm music to Franck's remarkably dry effusions on the subject of Christian love. In the final duet, "Händen, die sich nicht verschliessen, wird der Himmel aufgetan" ("To hands that are not closed will Heaven be opened") he cannot refrain from representing in his music the antithetical motions described in the words, — the unison theme of the flutes, oboes and violins is given out in inversion by the orchestral basses.

For the first Sunday in Advent he probably performed one of his Weimar cantatas; and as in the Leipzig churches there was no music given on the following Sundays, he had ample time to prepare for the three Christmas Feast Days. On the first of these he produced *Christen, ätzet diesen Tag* (No. 63), — a noble and animated piece of festival music. In the opening and final chorus the orchestra includes, besides the strings, four trumpets, three oboes and bassoon, — and of course kettledrums. In the first chorus a charming effect is made at the words "Kommt und eilt mit mir zur Krippen" ("Hasten with me to the manger"), the soprano always being three beats ahead of the other voices. In the final chorus we have the chromatic "grief" motive at the words "dass uns Satan möge quälen" ("that Satan may torment us"). Anyone who thinks that Bach cannot write in an agreeable popular style should read the duet "Ruft und fleht den Himmel an, kommt ihr Christen, kommt zum Reihen".

In the cantata for the second day, *Dazu ist erschienen der Sohn Gottes* (No. 40) the music is of the "characteristic" order. In the first chorus the words "dass er die Werke des Teufels zerstöre" ("that he may destroy the works of the devil") are always scanned thus ♪ ♪ ♪ | ♪ 𝅘𝅥𝅯 𝅘𝅥𝅯 ♪

𝅘𝅥𝅯 𝅘𝅥𝅯 𝅘𝅥𝅮 𝅘𝅥𝅮, giving the effect of something monstrous and horrid. In the bass aria "Höllische Schlange! wird dir nicht bange? Der dir den Kopf als ein Sieger zerknickt, ist nun geboren" ("Hellish serpent, are you not in fear? He who shall bruise thy head is now born"), the first violins have the twisting "serpent" motive, while the rhythm of in the remainder of the orchestra represents the heavy trampling of the conqueror. At the words "der dir den Kopf als ein Sieger zerknickt" the "serpent" theme descends to the bass. The recitative "Die Schlange, so im Paradies" ("The serpent, as in Paradise") is accompanied by rocking figures, suggestive of the seductive reptile swaying to and fro on the tree before the eyes of Eve*.

It is inconceivable how Zelter could arrange the first chorus to the words "Ihr seid Gottes Kinder, und wisset es nicht" ("Ye are God's children, but know it not"). We cannot blame him very severely, however, for Bach himself treated this chorus badly, using it for the *Cum sancto spiritu* in the F major Mass.

The cantata *Sehet, welch' eine Liebe hat uns der Vater erzeiget* (No. 64) was probably intended for the third day of Christmas. The first chorus consists of a splendid strict fugue, the instruments not having an independent part, but merely reinforcing the voices. It is like an idealised old motet, and makes us regret that Bach did not write more choruses of this kind.

The recitative "Geh', Welt" ("Go, world") is accompanied by the "hastening" motive in the bass —

From this there afterwards grows the motive with which the violin, in the aria "Was die Welt in sich hält" ("What the world contains"), suggests that the things of this world

* For these motives see p. 79.

are equally transitory. Only two soloists — soprano and alto — are needed in the cantata if the short and unessential bass recitative be sacrificed. The three chorales are extraordinarily impressive.

Thus from May to December 1723 Bach wrote at least eight cantatas. For the other Sundays he made use either of his Weimar cantatas or of the works of other composers,— though he could not have adopted the latter procedure often in the early part of his Leipzig period, since every cantor made it a point of honour to produce as much church music as possible. Bach probably gave few of Kuhnau's cantatas, the heirs of the former cantor having left the shelves at St. Thomas's as empty as Bach's own heirs were to do at his death.

The cantata *Singet dem Herrn ein neues Lied* (No. 190), probably written for the New Year 1724, is unfortunately in such an imperfect state that no performance of it is possible. Of the first chorus we have only the parts for the voices and the first and second violins. The parts of the cantata were probably separated owing to Bach having re-set the music to the text "Lobe Zion deinen Gott" for the jubilee celebration of the delivery of the Augsburg Confession, on 25th June 1730. The portions we have are merely those not used for this purpose. The solemn final chorale, however, is complete, and is admirably suited, even as regards the text, to musical festivities at the New Year. The text of the cantata is perhaps by Picander, for we find the new version of 1730 in his works.

On the Sunday after New Year, Bach probably performed the cantata *Schau, lieber Gott, wie meine Feind'* (No. 153). Here he gives the choir only chorales to sing, probably because it was impossible to prepare so much figurate music at once with the St. Thomas scholars, especially as they were wanted for the New Year singing in the streets. The musical characterisation in the tenor aria "Stürmt nur, ihr Trübsalswetter" is very fine. The alto aria "Soll ich meinen Lebenslauf unter Kreuz und

Trübsal führen" is one of Bach's most beautiful lyrical pieces. This cantata also is one that would become popular in the churches.

At Epiphany — the day of Jesus's baptism — the revelation of the glory of the Saviour to the whole world is celebrated. The cantata (No. 65) written for Epiphany in 1724 accordingly opens with the prophecy of Isaiah LX, 6, "Sie werden aus Saba alle kommen" ("All they from Sheba shall come"). As we listen to this chorus we see a procession of the Wise Men from the East and their followers, of the kind the early Italian artists used to paint. The horns, flutes and oboes give out a stately processional music. The harmonic sequences are intentionally of striking simplicity; even the *unisono* is used to obtain the effect of naïveté*.

The procession halts, and to the accompaniment of flutes and oboes we hear the mediæval chorale —

"Die Kön'ge aus Saba kamen dar,
Gold, Weihrauch und Myrrhen brachten sie dar.
Alleluja, Alleluja."

("The kings came from Sheba, bringing gold, frankincense, and myrrh"). The poetic situation requires that it should be sung by the fresh voices of children, not by the mixed choir, and above all not with sentimental nuances. It is a pity that the two upper parts of the chorales are everywhere sung by women's voices, that have not the right *timbre* and ingenuousness for chorale singing.

The two arias are meditations upon the picture. In the first, "Gold und Ophir ist zu schlecht . . . Jesus will das Herze haben" ("Gold and Ophir are too poor . . . Jesus desires the heart"), Bach employs the same motive of intimacy —

* For a counterpart to this chorus see p. 137.

upon which the chorale prelude *In dich hab' ich gehoffet, Herr*, (Peters V, No. 33) is built. On the other hand the following "Nimm mich dir zu eigen hin, nimm mein Herze zu Geschenke" ("Take me for thy own, take my heart as a gift") glows with passion. The movement reminds us of the painting of the "Wiedersehen" in Beethoven's well-known sonata, so full is it of tears and cries of joy. The theme, which is most effectively orchestrated, runs thus* —

Other cantatas in which "effect" predominates are the two remaining ones written for the Epiphany of 1724, — *Mein liebster Jesus ist verloren* (No. 154) and *Jesus schläft, was soll ich hoffen* (No. 81), for the first and fourth Sundays after Epiphany respectively. Both have dramatic texts, and the choir sings nothing but chorales.

In the former, the expression of grief and longing in the tenor aria, at the words "Mein Jesus ist verloren, o Wort, das mir Verzweiflung bringt!" ("My Jesus have I lost; oh word that brings me to despair") is most touching. At the word "Donnerwort" ("word of thunder") the instruments break out into a *tremolando* in semiquavers, as in the cantata *O Ewigkeit, du Donnerwort!* (No. 60). In its rhythm the passage reminds us of the aria expressive of Peter's despair, "Ach mein Sinn", in the *St. John Passion.*

In the alto aria *Jesu, lass dich finden* ("Jesus, let me find Thee") we hear this delightful and alluring cry —

* This is one of the cantatas with which the Paris Bach Society achieved its victory.

over a monotonous but uneasy bass, which is repeated higher up by the violins and violas —

These figures symbolise the dark clouds of sin, which, according to the text, conceal the soul of the Redeemer. The duet "Wohl mir, Jesus ist gefunden" ("Happy am I; Jesus is found") is the positive of the foregoing negative, inasmuch as its two joyous motives are simply transformations of those already quoted —

The answer of the boy Jesus, "Wisset ihr nicht, dass ich sein muss, in dem das meines Vaters ist" ("Wist ye not that I must be about my Father's business"), being a quotation from the Bible, is set in arioso form; only alto, tenor and bass are employed.

The cantata *Jesus schläft, was soll ich hoffen* (No. 81) deals with the episode of the stilling of the tempest (Matthew VIII, 23—28). The accompaniment to the first aria paints the preliminary motion of the waves, that heralds the coming storm —

Owing to the lame way in which the aria is usually performed, the hearer is seldom made conscious of the meaning of this accompaniment. Any conductor who wants to render it properly will have a hard struggle with his strings before he gets them to give the needful emphasis to the second of the tied quavers, in order to bring out the counter-rhythm in the second and fourth beats, by means of which Bach suggests restlessness.

The approach of the storm is painted in the tenor aria "Die schäumenden Wellen" ("the foaming waves"). It is not yet the big waves that we see, but the white crests, suggested in the demisemiquaver gallop of the violins. Jesus then rises. "O ye of little faith, why are ye so afraid", He says in a beautiful arioso. The storm is now let loose. The mounting octaves in the strings show the waves piling up one on the other, and then collapsing—

In the midst of all this we hear the cry of Jesus, "Peace, troubled sea". It is characteristic of Bach's habit of seizing upon only one moment for his tone-painting that he does not depict the stilling of the waters.

It is not known who provided him with the text for these sister cantatas, but he was a true poet. It is a pity Bach did not keep to him. No one has arranged the Gospel stories so simply and delicately as he.

In this latter cantata, again, only alto, tenor and bass are employed. Perhaps Bach at that time had no capable soprano, or the boy's voice may have been spoiled by the New Year singing. We may almost believe that Bach's experience of the choir in the Festival cantatas had so undeceived him that he did not expect much from it. This seems indicated by the fact that the cantata for the Purification of the Virgin, *Erfreute Zeit im neuen Bunde* (No. 83) is also written as a solo cantata for alto, tenor and bass. Midway comes the intonation of "Lord, now lettest thou thy servant depart in peace" (*Nunc dimittis*, Luke II, 29—31), which is interrupted by meditative recitatives. The text is perhaps by Picander. The joyous opening aria for alto and the final aria for tenor, "Eile, Herz, voll

Freudigkeit", contain some fine passages for a solo violin.

The text of the cantata for Quinquagesima Sunday, *Du wahrer Gott und Davids Sohn* (No. 23), is from the hand of the poet who had so happy a gift for casting the Gospel stories into concise pictures. The two blind men sit by the roadside near Jericho and supplicate expectantly the coming prophet*. The oboes voice their lament. The bass imports into the duet a peculiar march-like rhythm; it is as if the blind men heard in the distance the Easter caravan that is bringing Jesus. Then comes the contemplative recitative "Ach gehe nicht vorüber, du aller Menschen Heil!" ("Ah, pass not by, thou healer of all mankind"), to which the violins and oboes add the principal chorale of the cantata „"Christe, du Lamm Gottes" ("Christ, thou Lamb of God").

The following chorus, "Aller Augen warten, Herr, du allmächtiger Gott, auf dich" ("All eyes wait upon Thee, Almighty God"), gives the impression of a crowd moving about with hurried and unrhythmic steps —

Jesus is not yet there. Then come a funeral march and the chorale "Christ, du Lamm Gottes". It is He! The funeral march dies away. The two healed men follow the procession, singing again, as they go, the "Christ, du Lamm Gottes".

If these cantatas are to make the deep impression they should, no pauses between the numbers must be allowed to break up the unity of the picture. Spitta thinks they were written in Cöthen, and that Bach originally wanted to perform them at Leipzig as probation works instead of *Jesus nahm zu sich die Zwölfe* (No. 22). If this be so,

* The poet does not base his work on the prescibed Gospel passage (Luke XVIII, 31—34), but on the version in Matthew XX 29—34, which alone speaks of the two blind men.

the sympathetic poet must be sought in Cöthen. It is not improbable; and it would explain why Bach did not continue to work with him.

For Easter Bach wrote the chorale cantata *Christ lag in Todesbanden* (No. 4), the consummate expressiveness of which has always been marvelled at. Each verse is as if chiselled in music. The words "Zwingen" ("force") and "Gewalt" ("power") in the second strophe are represented by a proud bass figure that runs through it all —

Exuberant joy is expressed by the semiquavers with which the violins accompany the verse "Jesus Christus, Gottes Sohn, an unsrer Statt ist kommen" ("Jesus Christ, the Son of God, is come in our stead"). In the chorus "Es war ein wunderbarer Krieg, da Tod und Leben rungen" ("It was a marvellous struggle between life and death") we seem to see a knot of bodies in conflict, as in a picture of Michelangelo. The bass in the sixth verse, "So feiern wir das hohe Fest" ("So we celebrate the high feast") is founded on the rhythm of solemnity —

These cantatas are among the most powerful but at the same time the most difficult of all. A choir not used to Bach should postpone the performance of them for some years; they need not weeks, but months of study.

The first chorus of the cantata for the third Sunday after Easter, *Weinen, Klagen, Sorgen, Zagen* (No. 12; text by Franck), is a sketch for the Crucifixus of the B minor Mass, with which it has the chromatic *basso ostinato* in common —

The aria "Sei getreu" ("Be faithful") is accompanied by the chorale melody "Jesu meine Freude".

If the Whitsuntide cantata *Erschallet ihr Lieder* (No. 172) belongs to the year 1724, Bach has probably altered it somewhat for a later performance. The voice parts, written on large paper, can indeed only date from after 1727, as they bear the water-mark M A. The employment of the obbligato organ in the duet points to a still later date; Bach does not use the organ in this way until after 1730. The text is certainly by Franck.

The opening chorus with the three trumpets is splendid in its flow. In the aria to the Holy Trinity only the three trumpets and kettledrum are used. The violin figure in the aria "O Seelenparadies, das Gottes Geist durchweht" ("O paradise of the soul, filled by the spirit of God") is easily explained; it symbolises the mysterious motion of the wind of heaven. Anyone who has heard the song of fir-woods rustling in the distance will recognise it again here.

In the instrumental bass of the duet "Komm, du sanfter Himmelswind" ("Come thou gentle wind of heaven") we hear the same motive of transfigured bliss as in the chorale prelude upon *Alle Menschen müssen sterben* (Peters V, No. 2) —

The luxuriant arabesques in the organ bring with them the fragrance of the Whitsun melody "Komm, heil'ger Geist, Herre Gott" ("Come, Holy Ghost, Lord God"). It is better, however, to substitute the oboe for the organ.

The parts of the Whit Tuesday cantata *Erwünschtes Freudenlicht* (No. 184) have the water-mark I M K. Bach used this paper between 1724 and 1727. It is most probable that the cantata was composed for the year 1724. It begins with the recitative —

"Erwünschtes Freudenlicht,
Das mit dem neuen Bund anbricht!
Wir, die wir sonst in Todestälern irrten,
Empfinden reichlich nun,
Wie Gott zu uns den längstersehnten Hirten sendet . . ."

("O longed-for light of joy that breaks forth with the new covenant! We who had wandered in the valley of the shadow of death now know that God has sent the long-desired shepherd to us.") Bach would not have been himself had he not given us, during this recitative, the flute-call of the shepherd. It is sounded brokenly, as if the shepherd were walking on distant heights, and his melody floated down only in fragments —

Another pastoral melody in the flutes dominates the charming duet, wonderfully accompanied by the orchestra, "Gesegnete Christen, glückselige Herde", of the length of which even the ordinary hearer is unconscious. The flutes have another delightful and alluring melody in the final chorus, "Guter Hirt" ("Good Shepherd") —

Hardly any other cantata is so suitable as this for becoming acquainted with the lyrical side of Bach*.

In the Trinity cantata *O heiliges Geist- und Wasserbad* (No. 165) the first aria is in fugal form**. In this way

---

* Spitta wrongly holds that the cheerful character of this cantata shews it to be an arrangement of a secular cantata. See Spitta, II. 399 ff.

** It is a solo cantata for soprano, alto, tenor and bass. The text — not a specially grateful one — is by Franck.

the dogmatist Bach means to express the surety of grace by baptism. The aria "Jesu, meines Todes Tod" ("Jesus, death of my death") is based on the striking theme that depicts the contortions of the "Heilschlänglein" ("little serpent of healing") referred to in the text*.

The cantata for the eleventh Sunday after Trinity, *Siehe zu, dass deine Gottesfurcht nicht Heuchelei sei* (No. 179) also begins with a fugue, this time for chorus. The music is clever and interesting, — which is as much as even a Bach could do with such a text.

On the following Sunday he probably gave the cantata *Lobe den Herrn, meine Seele* (No. 69; first composition), with its monumental opening chorus. For the accompaniment he uses the Festival orchestra — strings, three trumpets, three oboes, and bassoon.

We do not know what the Christmas cantatas were in the year 1724.

Altogether we have more than twenty Sunday cantatas written by Bach during his first eighteen months in Leipzig. In addition there are two sacred occasional cantatas.

On the 24th August each year, St. Bartholomew's day, the new Council was elected. The church ceremony that preceded the entry into office took place on one of the following week-days, usually the Monday or the Friday. In 1723 it was on Monday, the 30th August**. Bach had composed for the occasion the cantata *Preise, Jerusalem, den Herrn* (No. 119), the text of which is probably by Picander. The pompous work consists of the two choruses "Preise, Jerusalem" and "Der Herr hat Guts an uns getan". The first is in the French overture form; the voice parts do not enter until the *allegro*. The *grave* section is a positively overwhelming picture of solemnity. The score is written for strings, three oboes, two flutes, four trumpets and kettledrum. The trumpets, however, are only used for

---

* The theme is quoted on p. 80.

** Spitta, II, 362.

fanfare-like interludes, — a method of employment that increases their effect. The recitative "So herrlich stehst du, liebe Stadt" ("So splendid art thou, beloved town") is introduced and ended by the following signal in the wind—

In the aria "Wohl dir, du Volk der Linden" we hear the rhythm of solemnity. The soli, — the words are rather poor dithyrambs upon magistracy in general and the Leipzig magistracy in particular — are naturally somewhat overweighted by the choruses.

The first performance of the cantata after Bach's death was given in the Gewandhaus at Leipzig under Mendelssohn on the 23rd April 1843, on the occasion of the unveiling of the Bach monument at the St. Thomas school.

The other sacred occasional cantata, *Höchst erwünschtes Freudenfest* (B. G. XXIX) was composed for the dedication of the organ at Störmthal, near Leipzig. It was given there on Tuesday, the 2nd November 1723, under Bach himself*. It is especially interesting from the fact that it is cast in the form of an orchestral suite. The first chorus exhibits the tripartite scheme of the overture; the second aria, "Hilf Gott, dass es uns gelingt", is a gavotte; the third, "Des Höchsten Gegenwart allein", is a gigue; the last, "O wie wohl ist uns geschehen", is a minuet. The declamation in the gavotte aria and in the minuet aria, however, is so strange and imperfect that one is inclined to think Bach must have taken these movements from an orchestral suite or a secular cantata**.

---

* The date has been discovered from the church ordinances. The new organ was built by Zacharias Hildebrand, a pupil of Silbermann. See Spitta II, 365.

** The banal declamation did not strike Spitta. If the hypothesis of borrowing be correct, all his reflections upon the fact that Bach has here employed the form of the orchestral suite for a cantata fall to the ground.

CHAPTER XXVI.

THE MAGNIFICAT AND THE *ST. JOHN PASSION.*

B. G. XI[1]. Magnificat.
B. G. XII[1]. The St. John Passion.

On the great Feast days the Magnificat was given in figurate music at the evening service in Leipzig. It followed the sermon.

Bach twice set this poem (Luke I, 46—55). One of these compositions, for solo soprano, has been lost. Rust, in the preface to B. G. XI[1], says he saw the score in Dehn's possession about 1855; so that a work of Bach's has been lost before the very eyes of the editors of the great Bachgesellschaft edition. Of the other Magnificat we have two scores, an older one in E flat major, and a later one in D major, representing the definitive form of the work. The first edition, published by Simrock in 1811, was based on the E flat score, Pölchau, the editor, not becoming acquainted with the other until a later date. The clean copy of the D major score, which was made about 1730, surpasses in beauty even the autographs of the *St. Matthew Passion* and the *Christmas Oratorio.*

Bach probably wrote the Magnificat for the evening service of Christmas 1723, — so at least we may assume from several movements, not forming part of the text, which, according to the older of the two scores, were inserted between the verses of the Magnificat. After the *Et exultavit,* "Vom Himmel hoch, da komm ich her" was sung; after the *Quia fecit* came "Freut euch und jubilieret"; after the *Fecit potentiam* came the *Gloria in excelsis*; after the *Esurientes implevit* came the hymn *Virga Jesse floruit.* These hymns were not rendered by the choir that stood beside the great organ, but by some choristers in the small gallery opposite, accompanied by a smaller organ. It seems that these hymns were part of the Leipzig evening service. Kuhnau had written a cantata upon them. Spitta conjectures that in Bach's time the mediæval rocking of the child was still customary at St. Thomas's, although the council, as early as 1702, had insisted upon the abrogation of the old custom*. Bach's Magnificat, according to this view, would really be stage music accompanying the representation of the scene in the manger at Bethlehem.

If the Magnificat were sung on other Feast days the extraneous numbers would naturally be omitted, which accounts for Bach not including them in the D major score. This became the property of Emmanuel; we know from a text-book that has survived that he gave the work in this form in Hamburg in 1779.

As the time allotted to the Magnificat in the evening service was fairly short, Bach had to adjust his music accordingly. It has not suffered by this; its admirable concision exhibits the beauty of the music under the best possible circumstances.

The first chorus is dominated by the "joy" motive in uninterrupted semiquavers. Although three trumpets are used here, the instrumentation is not at all thick, for Bach employs the wind with extreme care. This holds good also of the *Fecit potentiam* and the *Gloria*. Perhaps in the *Gloria* the vocal triplets ascending and massing above each other are too orchestral in style for them to give the effect we anticipate.

---

* See Rust's preface to B. G. XI[1], and Spitta II, 372. The texts of these additional movements were taken by Bach direct from Kuhnau, whom he follows in using in the *Gloria*, instead of the accepted but wrong Vulgate version — "et in terra pax hominibus bonae voluntatis" — the more correct translation of the Greek original — "et in terra pax, hominibus bona voluntas". Instead, however, of declaiming the last three words together, as the sense demands, he makes nonsense of them by separating "bona voluntas" from "hominibus". The added movements will be found in B. G. XI, p. 101 ff.

The fugue upon *Sicut locutus est* was one of the pieces in which Zelter found many things to censure. He would have liked the *Comes* "more uniform in shape, and the fifth voice more correctly introduced". Although this chorus is marked *a capella* by Emmanuel, it must be accompanied by the harmonies of the organ. Even in the tender trio *Suscepit Israel* Bach would not have dispensed with the organ accompaniment. The silence of the contrabass and bassoon only signifies that the instrumental bass is to be given out by soft eight-feet stops. It is advisable to have four or five voices to a part in this movement, so as to get the right fulness without doing any violence to the *cantus firmus* of "meine Seel' erhebt den Herren" in the oboes. Perhaps Bach's organist assisted in this melody with some light registers.

In the bass and in the cadences to the soprano air *Et exsultavit* we hear the characteristic Bach motive of joy, as though a blinding ray of sunlight suddenly vibrated through the gentle Advent twilight —

This motive is usually not heard by the audience, — it disappears in the excessive *diminuendo* that is usually foisted on the cadence. The bass that accompanies the additional chorale "Freuet euch und jubilieret" (added in the Christmas performance), is merely a rhythmical transformation of this motive —

In the soprano aria *Quia respexit humilitatem* the "lowliness" of the chosen maiden is expressed by figures descending and bowing, as it were, that give rise to an accompaniment of indescribable charm,— a veritable musical picture of the Madonna —

Even in the *Ecce enim ex hoc beatam*, where the voice sings the fame of her who shall be called blessed to all time, the accompaniment retains this motive of humility.

The *Et misericordia*, in which the muted strings and the flutes give out *ritornelli* that seem to come from a superterrestrial world, should be sung, wherever practicable, not by one but by three or four voices.

The chorus *Fecit potentiam* is built upon a broad theme that proceeds by haughty intervals, symbolising the word "strength" —

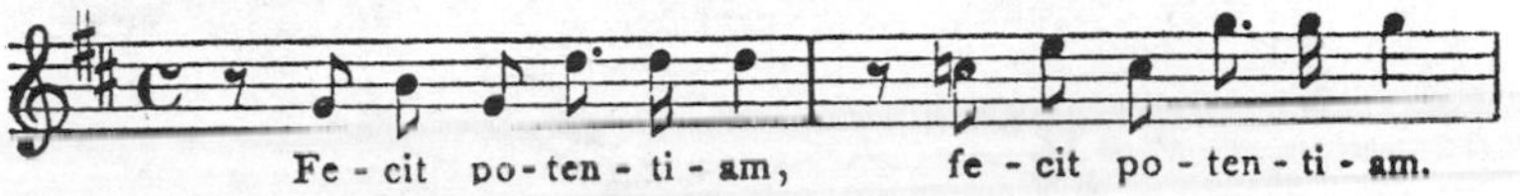
Fe - cit po - ten - ti - am, fe - cit po - ten - ti - am.

In the accompaniment to the tenor aria *Deposuit potentes de sede, et exaltavit humiles* Bach employs three motives. One in descending motion represents the words "He hath put down . . . from their seats".

Another, — one of the powerful "step" motives, that appears in various forms now in the bass, now in the violins, — indicates that it is "the mighty" who are thus treated —

A third motive, that ascends gently, expresses the words, "and exalted them of low degree" —

The meaning of the motives is confirmed by the fact that they reflect the declamation of the various sentences. It must be borne in mind that the fine ascending line of the theme of *exaltavit humiles* only makes its proper effect when the violins phrase it not thus —

but thus —

The accompaniment to the *Esurientes* is made out of two motives. The first, a species of the "joy" motive, is like a sunny smile —

It belongs to the words "He hath filled the hungry with good things". The other is a softened version of the motive of the *Deposuit* —

It symbolises the motion in terms of which Bach conceives the words "the rich he hath sent empty away".

In performance, of course, the two motives must stand out clearly from each other. The "joy" motive must be played *piano*; the other must enter *forte*, and the tempo must quicken slightly.* If the two motives are thus contrasted throughout the movement the hearer will at once recognise their meaning.

We unfortunately do not possess the figured *continuo* part to the Magnificat, so that the difficult task is thrown on the organist of selecting the harmonies from the mass of the voices and completing them according to his own feeling. In many of the solo numbers, especially in the *Quia fecit mihi magna*, where there are no instruments playing, very few will succeed in rendering the part to their own satisfaction and that of the hearers.

The *St. John Passion* was probably the first that Bach wrote. If the *St. Luke Passion* be really his, this would be the first. Spitta, however, scarcely makes out his case for its authenticity**. It is indisputable that the score is in Bach's writing; but as soon as we try to date the work we run against insurmountable difficulties. Spitta attributes it to the first Weimar years. This is inadmissible, for the cantatas of that period are incomparably more mature than this Passion. Nor does the autograph belong to this epoch; it dates from the middle Leipzig period, and so would force us to suppose that Bach, in the years of his greatest mastery, made a fresh copy of an unimportant work of his youth, just as it stood. This is impossible. He never took up an earlier composition without fundamentally improving it. We know, on the other hand,

---

* The more spiritedly and heavily these semiquaver sequences are played the better. They must give the impression of lively resentment. In the cadence of the prelude, — bar 7 — there is a transition to the "joy" motive —

This bar must of course be played in a *piano subito*. One is almost tempted to add the strings each time to the flutes in the spirited semiquaver passages.

** Spitta II, 508—518, 708.

that he applied a much lower critical standard to the works of other men.

The most natural supposition therefore is that he copied some one else's Passion about 1730 with a view to performing it. Perhaps in doing so he touched it up here and there, which would account for the fact that there are occasional traces of his own genius in the insignificant work. No importance is to be attached to the inclusion of this Passion in Breitkopf's catalogue of 1761. For that uncritical time, everything found among Bach's papers in his handwriting was his own work.

To the practical musician it is a matter of pure indifference whether the *St. Luke Passion* is proved to be authentic or not, since he will hardly ever be tempted to perform it.

As Agricola and Emmanuel, in the Necrology, give the number of the Passions as five, — without detailing them — it is quite possible that they too regarded the *St. Luke Passion* as an original work. How summary their enumeration is may be estimated from the fact that in the preceding rubric they lump together "many oratorios, Masses, Magnificat . . . ."

There were really, then, only four Bach Passions. Of these only two have come down to us*. The two lost ones came after the *St. John Passion*, — one of them probably a year or two after this. In 1725 Picander published his *Erbauliche Gedanken auf den Grünen Donnerstag und Charfreitag über den leidenden Jesum, in einem Oratorio entworfen*. As it was for Bach that he wrote almost all his remaining church texts, it is practically certain that the composer commissioned this Passion oratorio from him and set it to music.

The text is as wretched as it well could be**. For the Gospel version Picander substitutes a short versified

* On the subject of the five Passions see Spitta II, 504 ff.

** It is given in Spitta II, 873 (German edition).

narrative of the Passion. In the aria he attains the climax of tastelessness, as the following examples will shew:

Evangelist. Und endlich kam die Mörder-Schaar
Mit Spießen und mit Stangen,
Und Judas, der ihr Führer war,
Gab Jesum, nach gemachtem Schluß.
Der Feinde Raserei gefangen.
Da wollt es Petrus wagen,
Mit seinem Schwerdte drein zu schlagen.

Peter: Aria. Verdammter Verräther, wo hast du dein Hertze?
Haben es Löwen und Tiger verwahrt!
Ich will es zerfleischen, Ich will es zerhauen,
Daß Ottern und Nattern die Stücke zerkauen,
Denn du bist von verfluchter Art.

In the third part of Picander's poems is the text of a "Passions-Musik nach dem Evangelisten Marco am Charfreitag 1731". Bach not only commissioned this poem, but even prescribed the form of the verses. Being unwilling that the music of the *Trauerode* he had written in 1727 at the death of Queen Christiane Eberhardine should lie unused, he wanted to convert it into a Passion. Picander did his work satisfactorily; Bach had simply to write the text of the opening and final choruses and three arias of the new poem under the old music*. Thus we probably possess the finest parts of the *St. Mark Passion*. We need no longer look for any new discoveries in connection with Bach's Passions, as was at one time hoped.

When Spitta undertook to date the *St. John Passion* he did not take into consideration the possibility that Bach might have produced it in Leipzig in 1723, some weeks before his appointment to the cantorship. He took it for granted that it was composed in Cöthen, on the ground of the paper on which some of the parts are written; he also

* Rust was the first to point out the relation of the *Trauerode* to the lost Passion of 1731, — in his famous essay on Bach's frequent employment of the same music for new purposes (B. G. XX², p. 9 ff.).

assumed that the text was compiled and the music composed in some haste. He afterwards shows, however, that the haste was to no purpose, Bach not being nominated until after Easter. But it is hardly probable that the Council would allow the Passion music, which in 1723 it was the turn of St. Thomas's to give, to be suspended on account of the vacancy in the cantorship*. It would be more likely to look out for a substitute, as in the case of the cantatas. We know that though there was no cantor at the New Church in 1729 the Passion music was not omitted, but was undertaken by one of the candidates. We may assume the same procedure to bave been adopted during the vacancy at St. Thomas's. Of all the candidates Bach lived nearest; he could easily come at that time, as there was no church music in Cöthen; we know that after the New Year he began to work at a Passion and wrote out the parts; it is therefore practically certain that the Council had commissioned him to undertake the Passion music for 1723, and that he complied by producing the *St. John Passion.*

This was the third Passion music in the "modern" style that the Leipzigers had heard at the Good Friday evening service. In 1721 Kuhnau had been compelled to write a Passion in the operatic style he hated so cordially**.

The text of the *St. John Passion* is founded on the celebrated poem of the Hamburg councillor Brockes, — a poem which Mattheson, Handel, and Keiser had set to music***. Bach, however, makes use of it only for certain arias. For the bombastic versified narrative of the Passion, which the other composers thought such a fine poetical achievement, he substitutes the text of the fourth Gospel.

From Brockes' arias he only takes isolated ideas, which

---

* The following argument is based on the acute observations of B. F. Richter in the *Bachjahrbuch* for 1905, p. 63 ff.

** On the subject of the old and the new Passion see I, 80ff.; on Kuhnau's position in the struggle see I, 90.

*** On the quality and the significance of Brockes' Passion see I, 93ff.

he then works up freely in his own way*. Here he must have had the assistance of some one with a sensitive poetic faculty. The new version is noticeably better than the original. It avoids the insipidities of this, and turns its dramatic ideas to better purpose. Compare, for example, these two extracts: —

Brockes.

"Bei Jesu Tod und Leiden leidet
Des Himmels Kreis, die ganze Welt;
Der Mond, der sich in Trauer kleidet,
Gibt Zeugnis, daß sein Schöpfer fällt;
Es scheint, als lösch' in Jesu Blut
Das Feuer, der Sonne Strahl und Glut.
Man spaltet ihm die Brust — die kalten Felsen spalten,
Zum Zeichen, daß auch sie den Schöpfer sehn erkalten.
Was tust denn du, mein Herz?
Ersticke Gott zu Ehren,
In einer Sündflut bittrer Zähren!"

Bach.

"Mein Herz, in dem die ganze Welt
Bei Jesu Leiden gleichfalls leidet,
Die Sonne sich in Trauer kleidet,
Der Vorhang reißt, der Fels zerfällt,
Die Erde bebt, die Gräber spalten,
Weil sie den Schöpfer sehn erkalten:
Was willst du deines Ortes tun?

Soprano.

Zerfließe, mein Herze, in Fluten der Zähren,
Dem Höchsten zu Ehren,
Erzähle der Welt und dem Himmel die Not,
Dein Jesus ist tot."

We are tempted to assume that the delicate unknown poet who assisted in the *St. John Passion* was the same who supplied the text of the cantatas *Sie werden aus Saba alle kommen* (No. 65), *Mein liebster Jesu ist verloren* (No. 154), and *Du wahrer Gott und Davidssohn* (No. 23)**.

At its first performance the *St. John Passion* had not its present form. It began with the chorale chorus "O Mensch bewein' dein' Sünde gross", which now comes at the end of the first Part of the *St. Matthew Passion.* It contained three arias — "Himmel reisse, Welt erbebe!", "Zer-

* The following derive from Brockes' text:
1. Alto aria: "Von den Stricken meiner Sünden";
2. Bass arioso: "Betrachte meine Seel";
3. Tenor aria: "Erwäge wie sein blutgefärbter Rücken";
4. Bass aria: "Eilt, ihr angefochtnen Seelen";
5. Tenor arioso: "Mein Herz, in dem die ganze Welt";
6. Soprano aria: "Zerfliesse, mein Herze";
7. Final chorus: "Ruhet wohl".

** See p. 159 ff.

schmettert mich, ihr Felsen und ihr Hügel", and "Windet euch nicht so, geplagte Seelen" — which Bach replaced by others at some later performance of the work. It ended with the chorale "Christe, du Lamm Gottes", which was afterwards transferred to the cantata *Du wahrer Gott und Davidssohn* (No. 23). These alterations were probably made for a new performance of the *St. John Passion* in 1727. In place of the deleted numbers Bach wrote the great introductory chorus "Herr, unser Herrscher", the arias "Ach mein Sinn" and "Erwäge wie sein blutgefärbter Rücken", the arioso "Betrachte meine Seel", and the final chorale "Ach Herr, lass dein lieb Engelein".

For a still later performance he went through the parts and improved certain details*. To this revision belongs, for example, the instruction that in certain parts of the first chorus only the violoncellos and bassoons are to take the quavers, while the contrabass and the organ take each time the second crotchet. At the same time he marked the phrasing and the dynamic indications in the parts. These successive redactions are deducible from the state of the various parts.

The score of the *St. John Passion* is not autograph throughout, but Bach has given the whole a most careful supervision. Here again the original *continuo* part is lost. Fortunately it lay before Hering when he made a copy of the Passion at the request of Emmanuel, and he inserted it in the copy. The figuring in the B. G. edition is based on this.

The musical character of the *St. John Passion* is conditioned by the nature of the Passion narrative in the fourth Gospel. This lacks the simplicity and naturalness of the story in St. Matthew. The latter gives a series of short scenes, to which lyrical meditations can be attached; in St. John the events are more spun out and dramatic

* Altogether we can deduce from the parts four performances of the *St. John Passion* under Bach himself.

in form, so that the text has no points of repose. The arias had to be inserted almost by force.

The St. John text is also poorer in musical quality than that of St. Matthew. It lacks the institution of the communion, Gethsemane, the episodes of the arrest, — everything that fills out the first Part of the *St. Matthew Passion* — and many other animated strokes. Bach himself was conscious of this, so he supplemented the narrative of the fourth Gospel by several episodes from St. Matthew, — the weeping of Peter, the rending of the curtain, and the earthquake at the death of Jesus.

St. John's version of the Passion is in the main only a picture of the great scenes of the trials before the high priest and Pilate. It has an air of excitement and passion. Bach was aware of this characteristic, and he reproduces it in his music. He carries on the action by means of the choruses of the priests and the people.

It is remarkable that apart from the "Crucify him" he has employed three choruses each twice, and one three times*. We may explain this identity by the supposition that he hoped to make the wild cry of the people more impressive by setting it to several small themes and repeating these frequently. It is doubtful, indeed, what prompted him to render the dignified setting of the scribes' words "Write not the king of the Jews" in the light, mocking music of the song of the soldiers, "We greet thee, King of the Jews". Perhaps the accidental similarity of the verse-structure of certain stanzas of the Passion narrative had more influence on Bach's resolve to give them the same musical setting than modern commentators would care to admit.

In these choruses of the people Bach does not try to intensify the dramatic element. He depicts the crowd

* "Wäre dieser nicht ein Übeltäter" = "Wir dürfen niemand töten". "Sei gegrüsset, lieber Judenkönig" = "Schreibe nicht: der Judenkönig". "Wir haben ein Gesetz" = "Lässest du diesen los". "Jesum von Nazareth" = "Nicht diesen, sondern Barrabam" = "Wir haben keinen König".

as uniformly fanatical. When he comes to the passages "This was no evildoer" and "We ought to put no man to death", — which, considered by themselves, should be set more calmly and reflectively — he gives them an extended chromatic theme that is unsurpassably dreadful in its effect —

Wä - re die - ser nicht ein Ü - bel - tä - - - ter.

And in the "Crucify him" the idea of the long-drawn howls of an excited crowd has certainly determined the character of the theme —

Kreu - - zi - ge! Kreu - - zi - ge!

At intervals the "Crucify him" is repeated in furious ascending semiquavers, as if the maddened crowd were raising a thousand arms towards heaven.

Even in the theme of "Wir haben ein Gesetz" ("We have a law") and "Lässest du diesen los" ("If thou lettest this man go") there is something wild, in spite of the attempt to slow the movement down; the passage is dominated by the dreadful intervals of a fourth that are characteristic of the "Crucify him" —

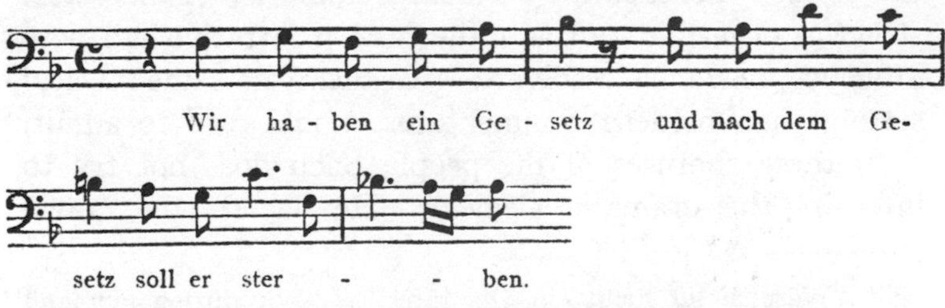
Wir ha - ben ein Ge - setz und nach dem Ge-
setz soll er ster - - ben.

In the theme of "Sei gegrüsset" ("Hail, King of the Jews") we have a representation of the mocking genuflexions of the soldiers —

Sei ge - grü - ßet lie - ber Ju - den - kö - nig.

accompanied by obtrusive repetitions of a motive of obeisance in semiquavers in the flutes and oboes —

The modern hearer has little perception of the nature of this accompaniment, as the flutes and oboes are generally inaudible. If the choir is at all large, it is advisable to strengthen the instruments with a piccolo in the higher octave. The same doubling of the wood wind in a higher octave is equally necessary in certain parts of the "Crucify him"; and the furious semiquavers that accompany the "Nicht diesen, sondern Barrabam" ("Not this man, but Barrabas") and the "Wir dürfen niemand töten" ("We should put no man to death") can hardly be given out too strongly. On the whole the orchestra in the *St. John Passion* cannot be too large if it is to do justice to the demoniacal quality of the music.

In the chorus "Lasset uns den nicht zerteilen" ("Let us not divide it") it is very difficult to bring out properly the semiquaver phrases in the instrumental basses that are meant to depict the rattling of the dice in the bowl. It is as well not to employ the full chorus here, but only three or four voices to each part, — which, indeed, is more in keeping with the scene. The organist can greatly assist in making the semiquavers effective by playing them with appropriately clear eight or four-feet stops. If he does this skilfully, no one will know that he is playing; every one will be pleased with what he takes to be the fulness of the tone of the violoncellos.

In the *St. John Passion* the accompaniment of the recitatives falls to the organ alone; the string quartet is not used, as in the *St. Matthew Passion*, to throw the words of Jesus into higher relief. Bach, however, has prescribed to the organist a particular tone-colour for these passages.

In the recitatives, again, Bach has preserved in the most admirable way the special tint of the narrative as it is in St. John. His setting of the words of Jesus reproduces the superterrestrial, almost abstract elevation that characterises the Christ of the fourth Gospel from the beginning. The Jesus of St. Matthew is much more human. The greatest mistake that can be made in the rendering of the part of Jesus in the *St. John Passion* is to infuse even the slightest trace of sentimentality into it. It must be sung with simple, elevated pathos.

The pictures of the rending of the curtain and of the earthquake are like sketches for the corresponding episodes in the *St. Matthew Passion*. In the accompaniment to the words "Da nahm Pilatus Jesum und geisselte ihn" ("Then Pilate took Jesus and scourged Him") we have, in the bass, the same rhythm, suggestive of the falling of the blows, that we have in the arioso "Erbarm es Gott, hier steht der Heiland angebunden! O Geisselung!" ("Have mercy, God! Lo, hand and foot their chains have bound Him") in the *St. Matthew Passion*. A *stringendo* to the end is effective here. The melisma at "and wept bitterly" is much more extended here than in the *St. Matthew Passion*, where it is continued in the aria "Erbarme dich".

The arias exhibit all the extraordinary youthful freshness that constitutes the charm of the solo movements in the cantatas of the first Leipzig period. The sense of hastening in the soprano aria "Ich folge dir gleichfalls mit freudigen Schritten" ("I follow thee also with joyous steps") and the bass aria "Eilt, ihr angefochtnen Seelen" ("Hasten, ye troubled souls") is conveyed in Bach's usual manner — by quick passages in imitation. In the latter aria the interjections of the chorus "Wohin? Wohin?" ("Whither?") must be given without any *rallentando* or *diminuendo.* The answers "Nach Golgatha" ("To Golgotha") and "Zum Kreuzeshügel" ("To the hill of the Cross") should be given out *pianissimo* and in a tranquil tempo, and be separated by as long a pause as possible from the last "Wohin?" It is interesting to compare this movement with the opening duet of the Easter oratorio *Kommt, eilet und laufet* (B. G. XXI[3]), that is laid out on the same large lines, but expresses a more tranquil hastening. If the direction *Basso in ripieno tacet* were not expressly given, we should be tempted to try the effect in this movement of the *St. John Passion* of giving the bass part to three or four voices, since the single voice, owing to its low position, cannot come through the orchestra properly.

It is hard to render the bass aria with chorale, "Mein teurer Heiland", in such a way that it shall answer to the ideal one has formed of it in reading it. For the chorale, two or three voices to a part are enough.

An indescribable felicity breathes from the arioso "Betrachte meine Seele" and the succeeding aria "Erwäge doch". The harmonies fluctuate between major and minor; and the veiled *timbre* of the two viole d'amore is very appropriate. It is like a smile through tears; we seem to be transported to the fields where the "Himmelsschlüsselblumen" ("primroses of heaven") bloom. In the lovely arching curves of the instrumental melodic lines of the aria we seem to see the rainbow of which the text speaks, stretching over the world redeemed—

The movement should pass before the hearer like a vision. As a rule, however, the singer drags it out too much and makes it too heavy. It is a pity that the part for the viola d'amore has usually to be played on the muted violas, which do not take the upper parts of it easily. It is an open question, too, whether, in the arioso, the lute part is best rendered by the *pizzicati* of the strings. The cembalo would make the best effect here. It is also an unsettled question whether we should employ the piano or the harp.

The sombre beauty of the alto aria "Von den Stricken meiner Sünden mich zu entbinden, wird mein Heil gebunden" is seldom made apparent, owing to the way the tempo is dragged. The expressive syncopated theme —

and that in the bass, that seems to strive upwards with difficulty —

should co-operate to suggest Jesus writhing in His bonds. If the movement be taken twice too slowly, and overdone with *rallentandi*, it loses its meaning and merely gives the feeling of wearisome protraction.

The theme of the aria "Zerfliesse, mein Herze, in Fluten der Zähren" ("Let my heart dissolve in floods of tears") is woven out of spiritualised sighs, while the bass of the motive of terrified trembling in the preceding arioso, "Mein Herz, in dem die ganze Welt bei Jesu Leiden gleichfalls leidet" ("My heart, in which the whole world suffers with Jesus") is retained. If the hearer is to perceive the significance of the sighing motive, the wind instruments should not accent the strong beat of the bar, but the last note of the slur, — which Bach has here written out in full — in this way —

In the aria "Ach mein Sinn, wo willst du endlich hin" Bach depicts wild and passionate grief. We seem to see a man rushing hither and thither in despair. At the finish Bach does not repeat the *ritornello*, but breaks off in a sudden shriek. He expressly marks these last two bars *forte*; but in spite of this conductors sometimes play them with a *rallentando* and *diminuendo*.

The aria "Es ist vollbracht" ("It is finished") is developed out of the falling sequence in which Jesus, as His head sinks in death, breathes forth His last words —

In the *vivace* interlude "Der Held aus Juda siegt mit Macht" it is advisable to employ a few bright children's voices instead of the solo alto.

The final chorus is also based on a descending motive —

In accordance with the previous passage of the text, "There laid they Jesus therefore, because of the Jews' preparation day; for the sepulchre was nigh at hand", Bach of course depicts the interment of Christ. Motives such as these —

must be played with particular care, without, however, doing any violence to the tenderness that fills the whole movement.

We may suppose that Bach was not satisfied with the chorus "O Mensch, bewein dein' Sünde gross" ("O man, bewail thy grevious sin") as an introduction to the *St. John Passion,* because the words of the chorale did not seem to him sufficiently characteristic of the fourth Gospel; the quality of this is exactly expressed by the words "Herr unser Herrscher, dessen Ruhm in allen Landen herrlich ist! Zeig uns durch deine Passion, dass du, der wahre Gottessohn, zu aller Zeit, auch in der grössten Niedrigkeit, verherrlicht worden bist" ("Lord our Redeemer, whose name in all the world is glorious, show us by Thy Passion that Thou, the true Son of God for evermore, art glorified even in the deepest humiliation"). The music tries to convey this dual idea of suffering and glory. The flutes and oboes express the thoughts connected with the Passion; throughout the movement they sigh and wail incessantly —

Bach's figured bass indicates that the organ is to accompany, in a higher octave, the sustained dissonances of the flutes and oboes. This gives the music a curiously bitter and gloomy character, which at first distresses the hearer, as he cannot reconcile it with the words "Lord our Redeemer, whose name in all the world is glorious".

The strings, in grave and tranquil semiquavers, symbolise the majesty of the glorified Son of God —

The lofty expression of this is reinforced by the soft organ-point, repeated in quavers, in the bass —

It is in this way that Bach's music, like the narrative in the fourth Gospel, conveys simultaneously the ideas of majesty and suffering. The abasement of the Saviour is symbolised by the passage of the grave semiquaver sequence from the violins to the bass. This happens at the second return of the words "Lord our Redeemer" and at the second repetition of the words "Show us by Thy Passion". Note also the descent of the voices at the words "even in the deepest humiliation", and the upward striving of the semiquaver figure at "art glorified".

Verbal explanation necessarily gives a certain disfiguring coarseness to this musical symbolism. But even Spitta admitted that this chorus needs interpretation, and that from the purely musical standpoint it is incomprehensible.

Large dynamic outlines are hardly possible in this movement if we are not to diminish the effect of the *piano* that Bach has marked for the words "even in the greatest humiliation". Repeated experiences will show us how wrong it is to introduce the *piano* in the chorus at the words "Show us by Thy Passion", however desirable this *piano* — which is prescribed for the whole orchestra, except the basses — may seem to be. On the other hand the declamation of the chorus can hardly be too full of dynamic light and shade. It rests with the organist to assist in the rendering of the semiquaver figure, where it occurs three times in the bass, in such a way that it is clear to every hearer without being at all obtrusive.

CHAPTER XXVII.

THE CANTATAS OF THE YEARS 1725—1727.

The cantatas of 1725, 1726 and 1727 are mostly recognisable from the fact that the paper on which they are written bears the water mark I M K. For the *Trauerode,* composed in September 1727 on the death of Queen Christiane Eberhardine, Bach used a paper with the water mark M. A.; this paper he then continued to use for several years.

At the death of the Queen, public mourning was commanded for four months. From September 1727 to January 1728, therefore, no cantatas were given; even the organ was silenced. Bach thus had a period of rest. This could not have been wholly agreeable to him, since the national mourning meant a considerable diminution of the musicians' perquisites.

The majority of the cantata texts of this period are by Picander. His first cycle of cantata poems extended from the first Sunday in Advent 1724 to the corresponding Sunday in 1725. Bach may have gone to him because he wrote rapidly and with facility, and, as he himself boasts, he had some musical knowledge. The bad points in his work, however, far outweigh the good. He has no idea of working up poetically the situation given him in a Gospel. For the most part he writes at random, drifting along in commonplace. His texts are usually so little characteristic that with very slight alterations they could be adopted to the Gospel for any other Sunday. Here is a typical specimen of his banality, — a recitative from the cantata *Siehe du, dass deine Gottesfurcht nicht Heuchelei sei* (No. 179):

"Das heut'ge Christentum ist leider schlecht bestellt:
Die meisten Christen in der Welt sind laulichte Laodicäer
Und aufgeblas'ne Pharisäer, die sich von außen fromm bezeigen,
Und wie ein Schilf den Kopf zur Erde beugen.
Im Herzen aber steht ein stolzer Eigenruhm;
Sie gehen zwar ins Gotteshaus und tun daselbst die äußerlichen Pflichten,
Macht aber dies wohl einen Christen aus?
Nein! Heuchler könnens auch verrichten!"

Among the cantatas of this period are some that have so many similar internal characteristics that we may regard them as intimately allied, — e. g. the two solo cantatas *Wo gehest du hin* (No. 166; for the fourth Sunday after Easter) and *Wahrlich, ich sage euch* (No. 86; for the fifth Sunday after Easter). As these two Sundays come together, the works must have originated at the same time.

In the opening aria of *Wo gehest du hin* the accompaniment aims at depicting the supernaturally elastic steps of Jesus after His resurrection —

The same means are employed, in the *St. Matthew Passion*, to illustrate Christ's prophecy that after His resurrection he would go before them into Galilee. The quavers are of course not to be played legato. In the exuberant aria "Ich will an den Himmel denken und der Welt mein Herz nicht schenken" ("I will think of Heaven and not give my heart to the world") there is a "step" rhythm in the bass, — prompted by the words "Wenn ich gehe oder stehe" ("If I go or stay"). The accompaniment to the aria "Man nehme sich in acht, wenn das Glücke lacht" ("Man, beware when fortune smiles") is accompanied by captivating, silvery laughter*.

One feature that these sister cantatas have in common is the making of an aria out of a chorale by giving the

* The theme of this aria is quoted on p. 78.

cantus firmus to solo voices, with a free orchestral accompaniment. In the first cantata it is the melody "Ich bitte dich, Herr Jesu Christ", to which the strings add a melancholy motive; in the second cantata the chorale verse:

"Und was der ewig' güt'ge Gott
In seinem Wort gesprochen hat,
Geschwor'n bei seinem Namen
Das hält und gibt er g'wiß fürwahr . . . ."

is sung, the orchestra adding a remarkably full and tense accompaniment in three parts, that excellently expresses the steadfastness of God's word*.

The same impression is given by the opening arioso "Wahrlich, ich sage euch! So ihr den Vater etwas bitten werdet in meinem Namen, so wird ers euch geben", which is worked out as a five-part fugue. As surely as the vocal melody takes its place as the fifth voice in the orchestral fugue, so surely will the prayer in the name of Jesus be fulfilled.

This cantata, with its two cheerful and delightful arias "Ich will doch wohl Rosen brechen" and "Gott hilft gewiss", is one of the most popular cantatas of Bach.

It is evident, again, that the two monumental music-dramas *Herr, gehe nicht ins Gericht* (No. 105) and *Schauet doch und sehet* (No. 46), written for the ninth and tenth Sundays after Trinity, originated at the same time. Their opening choruses are especially alike in this respect, that the tone-painting is relegated to the instrumental accompaniment, while the vocal part is noticeably simple. Here we have a quite new cantata type.

In the opening chorus of *Herr, gehe nicht ins Gericht*

* The melody of the chorale should not be sung by a soprano soloist, but by half a dozen fine boys' voices. In the accompaniment to "Und was der ewig' güt'ge Gott" the strings must reinforce the two oboes so as to give the figures the needful firmness. The bass should be strengthened by a bassoon, so as to make the *timbre* of the trio homogeneous.

the means employed are as simple as they are effective. In the bass we have a figure depicting anxious trembling —

The theme with which the two oboes accompany this is composed of two motives —

The second of these motives is a modification of the familiar motive of sighing. To explain the first motive we must look at other themes in the same syncopated style, when we shall see that they always embody the idea of something being drawn or dragged along*. If these syncopations and sighs are rightly accented, we can see the groaning and reluctant man being dragged before the judgment seat.

In the aria "Wie zittern und wanken der Sünden Gedanken" ("How thoughts of sin tremble and falter") the oboe reels about above the quavering figures in the strings—

During the recitative-arioso "Wohl aber dem, der seinen Bürgen weiss . . . wenn seine Sterbestunde schlägt" ("But well for him who knows his surety . . . when his last hour strikes") we hear the funeral bells, — not sounding sadly, however, but joyously. In the aria "Kann ich nur Jesum mir zum Freunde machen, so gilt der Mammon nicht bei mir" ("If Jesus be my friend, Mammon is nothing to me")

---

* Compare, for example, the theme of the aria "My Jesus, take me to Thee", cited on p. 150, from the cantata *Jesus nahm zu sich die Zwölfe* (No. 22).

the note of gladsomeness becomes one of unrestrained gaiety. It is as if a man were running wildly from captivity; the antagonism between the upper voice and the instrumental bass gives a sensation of precipitancy that is almost unbearable —

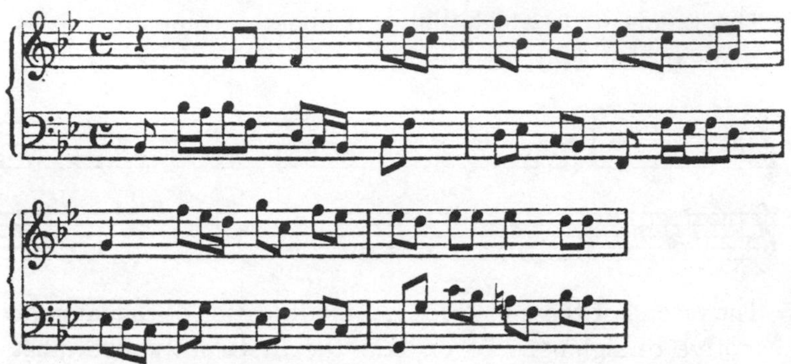

In the final chorale, "Nun ich weiss, du wirst mich stillen" ("Now I know that Thou wilt calm me") we can observe the transition in the orchestra from terrified trembling to peace —

The first part of the finely declaimed opening chorus of *Schauet doch und sehet, ob irgend ein Schmerz sei* (No. 46) seems like a sketch for the *Qui tollis* of the B minor Mass —

Schauet doch und se-het, ob ir - gend ein Schmerz sei wie mein Schmerz!

In the orchestra we have the violins sighing continually —

The flutes have the same motive, but in doubled motion —

The total effect is of a vast lamentation ascending to heaven.

In the recitative "So klage, du zerstörte Gottesstadt" ("Then lament, thou ruined city of God") the strings have long-drawn cries of woe, above which the flutes depict the "des Eifers Wasserwogen" ("waves of anger") that shall sweep over Jerusalem. An idea of the dreadful nature of the aria "Dein Wetter zog sich auf von weitem" ("Thy tempest gathered from afar") may be obtained from the figures in the bass —

The theme of the flute in the last aria —

illustrates the words "Doch Jesus will auch bei der Strafe der Frommen Schild und Beistand sein; er sammelt sie als seine Schafe, als seine Küchlein liebreich ein" ("But Jesus, even when suffering, will be the shield and succour of the godly. He will gather them lovingly as His sheep".)* This pastoral accompaniment, in which the oboe forms the bass, is extraordinarily beautiful; Bach has rarely written more heartfelt music. It forms the happiest contrast with the gloomy character of the preceding numbers. The fine

* The quavers in the aria should be played with a light staccato in order to get the proper effect.

painting at the words "Wenn Wetter der Rache" ("If tempests of vengeance") should be particularly noted.

Another of the dramatic cantatas is that for the first Sunday after Easter, *Halt im Gedächtnis Jesum Christ* (No. 67). The powerful opening chorus, — in which we may object to the threefold repetition of the "Halt" — is followed by the aria "Mein Jesus ist erstanden", — a movement of unusual charm, in which the boldly ascending figures speak eloquently of the resurrection. The finest part of the cantata, however, is the bass aria "Friede sei mit euch" ("Peace be unto you"). It begins with the "tumult" motive —

Then suddenly the uproar ceases, and the motive of transfiguration enters in tranquil majesty —

The world and all its woes sink out of sight. The risen Lord is with His disciples, consoling them with His "Peace be unto you". In vain does the world rage round them again; they sing through it all "Wohl uns, Jesus hilft uns kämpfen . . . Jesus holet uns zum Frieden . . . O Herr hilf und lass gelingen" ("It is well with us; Jesus fights for us . . . Jesus takes us to His peace . . . Help us, Lord, to victory"). And each time that He addresses them with His "Peace be unto you" the tumult is silenced.

It is less an aria than a symphonic tone-picture. The German Bach is trying to break through the mould of the decadent Italian art. His dramatic spirit leads him to seek the way back to the larger and simpler kind of art from which he started, and to create free forms for himself.

He is on the same path in the cantata for the third Sunday after Epiphany, *Herr, wie du willt* (No. 73), as may be seen in the freely-written aria "Herr, so du willt". The text of this is composed of three lines:

"Herr, so du willt, so preßt ihr Todesschmerzen die Seufzer aus dem Herzen . . . ."
"Herr, so du willt, so lege meine Glieder in Staub und Asche nieder . . . ."
"Herr, so du willt, so schlagt ihr Leichenglocken . . . ."
("Lord, if Thou wilt, the pangs of death will wring sighs from my heart".
"Lord, if Thou wilt, my limbs will fall in dust and ashes".
"Lord, if Thou wilt, the funeral bells will toll".)

In the first line we hear the sigh —

Then the voices descend as it were into the grave —

Finally the funeral bells are heard —

The opening chorus also is very impressive. The orchestra and organ have the following troubled motive —

that is formed from the commencement of the chorale melody; it bears a striking resemblance to the "Fate" motive in Beethoven's fifth symphony. The instruments try to force it upon the chorus, which is singing the chorale (interrupted by recitatives). The choir resists. Finally, as the motive returns with greater and greater urgency, the choir yields and repeats it three times, whereupon the movement ends. These dramatic beauties almost blind us to the charm of the tenor aria "Ach senke doch den Geist der Freuden dem Herzen ein", with its gentle semiquavers floating down.

But the fight of the giant for freedom was in vain. In the Michaelmas cantata *Es erhub sich ein Streit* (No. 19) he is beaten. The first chorus paints the struggle of Satan and his host against the archangel Michael*. The serpent-forms fling themselves upward in mighty contortions —

At the words

> "Aber Michael bezwingt,
> Und die Schar, die ihn umringt,
> Stürzt des Satans Grausamkeit."

("But Michael conquers, and the cruel host of Satan encircling him is cast down"), the motive is inverted, and the agitated and distorted mass falls precipitantly into the depths —

Then with one broad stroke of the pen Bach completely spoils the striking picture. At the finish, when Satan's host has

* Jude, verse 9.

fallen, the composer writes *Dal segno*, repeats the first part, "Es erhub sich ein Streit" ("Now there was war") and so concludes*. This *da capo* that he has inserted out of mere habit is of course a sin against both the text and the music: it shows how helpless this unique genius is against the formulæ and ordinances of his epoch. In this one *Dal segno* we have the whole tragic fate of Bach's art. There must be something in the nature of the pictorial conception of music to account for the fact that its two greatest representatives, Bach and Berlioz, are insensible to many things of which a quite mediocre talent would be conscious.

The music of the aria "Bleibt, ihr Engel, bleibt bei mir" ("Stay, ye angels, stay with me") is of course derived from the graceful "angel" theme —

The trumpet adds the chorale "Ach Gott, lass dein lieb' Engelein". This causes the movement to be unusually long, even for Bach. The marking of *adagio* therefore ought not to be taken too literally. The final chorale, "Lass dein Engel mit mir fahren", with its free orchestral accompaniment, is extraordinarily solemn in its effect.

Among the other dramatic cantatas of this period there are none that outwardly form so complete a whole as *Herr, gehe nicht ins Gericht* (No. 105) and *Schauet doch und sehet* (No. 46). They are composed of separate numbers; but these are often so powerful in effect that we are not conscious of the lack of an inner cohesion.

The first chorus of the two-part chorale cantata for the first Sunday after Trinity, *O Ewigkeit, du Donnerwort* (No. 20; first composition) is laid out in the French overture

---

* The succeeding recitative, "Gottlob! der Drache liegt" ("God be praised! the dragon is defeated") ought to have been sufficient to deter him from repeating the undecided battle!

form. The *vivace* commences with "O Ewigkeit, Zeit ohne Zeit"; it is rather short relatively to the *grave**. The effect of the chorus comes from the animation of the orchestral accompaniment and the extreme simplicity of the chorale-figuration.

The aria "O Ewigkeit, du machst mir bange" ("O eternity, thou fillest me with fear") is dominated by the "sigh" motive. In the aria "Wacht auf! Wacht auf! . . . eh die Posaune schallt" ("Awake, awake, ere the trumpet sounds") Bach of course employs that instrument. The fine trumpet part that he gives to it will exculpate him even in the eyes of the strictest musical æsthetician. In the alto aria "O Mensch, errette deine Seele, entfliehe Satans Sklaverei" ("O man, save thy soul, fly from Satan's bonds") the musical illustration of the text is quite excessive —

Nowhere else in music has the painful writhing of a body been so realistically depicted**.

The opening aria of the cantata for the ninth Sunday after Trinity, *Tue Rechnung! Donnerwort, das die Felsen selbst zerspaltet* (No. 168; text by Franck) is rather enigmatic. It is not clear what is signified by the agitated figure in the strings —

* The final words of the verse do not suit the return to the *grave.* In any case the employment of the overture form to the chorale chorus here is not very happy.

** The texts of the arias are partly taken from the remaining strophes of Rist's chorale.

It suggests most strongly the aria of the scourging in the *St. Matthew Passion*, "Erbarm es Gott". As a matter of fact the figure here also symbolises a succession of blows. Bach remembers the text that has been in the mind of his librettist, "Ist mein Wort nicht ein Hammer, der Felsen zerschmeisst" ("Is not my word like a hammer that breaketh the rock in pieces?")*, and accordingly depicts the hammer-blows in his music. When played with sufficient animation the movement is very impressive. If the music to the aria "Kapital und Interessen meiner Schulden gross und klein, müssen einst verrechnet sein" ("Capital and interest of my sins, great and small, must some day be reckoned up") does not affect us very deeply, that is not to be wondered at. On the other hand a fascinating effect is made by the titanic efforts expressed in the bass accompaniment to the aria "Herr, zerreiss des Mammons Ketten" ("Lord, break the chains of Mammon") —

In the opening duet of the cantata for the sixth Sunday after Easter, *Sie werden euch in den Bann tun* (No. 44) — ("They will put you under the ban") — the word "Bann" is expressed with dreadful force. The impression of horror is intensified by progressions of fifths in the instrumental basses —

which are made still more prominent by the figures in the second oboe. The choir enters with the words "Es kommt aber die Zeit, dass, wer euch töten wird".

The theme of the aria "Es ist und bleibt der Christen Trost" is a little confusing at first —

* Jeremiah XXIII, 29.

The jubilant triplets are explained, however, by the sequel, where mention is made of the "Lachen der Freudensonne" ("Laughter of the sun of joy"). Bach fastens upon these words because he sees the opportunity they give him for characteristic music.

In the opening chorus of the cantata for the third Sunday after Epiphany, *Alles nur nach Gottes Willen* (No. 72; text by Franck), the main musical theme is prompted by a word of quite subordinate importance. It is the word "Zeit" ("Time"), — "Alles nur nach Gottes Willen ... so bei gut als böser Zeit" ("God's will be done ... both in good and evil time"). Bach expresses it by the stroke of the pendulum, as in the cantata *Wer weiss wie nahe mir mein Ende, hin geht die Zeit, her kommt der Tod* ("Who knows how near my ending is; time flies, death is coming"). The monotonous rhythm in the bass, in which the rest of the orchestra also joins —

is accordingly maintained from beginning to end of the chorus. It is to this impressive tick-tack that the choir sings the moving text.

In the almost dance-like prelude to the aria "Mein Jesus will es tun" ("This will my Jesus do"), the upper voices several times pause suddenly on a chord, while the bass of the theme —

continues. The only other aria in which this occurs is "Wirf mein Herze, wirf dich noch in des Höchsten Liebesarme" ("Cast thyself, oh my heart, into the loving arms of God"), in the cantata *Mein Gott, wie lang, ach lange* (No. 155), in which passionate movement it depicts the heart at rest in God's arms. Bearing this musical identity in mind, let us look again at the text of the aria "Mein Jesus will es tun". The passage is at once seen to mean "Although thy heart is overwhelmed with heaviness, it shall rest gently in His arms". This is one of the cases where the meaning of Bach's music becomes clear by the comparison of two quite unconnected passages.

The theme of the opening aria of the cantata for Sexagesima, *Leichtgesinnte Flattergeister* (No. 181) runs thus —

It is never developed, but simply repeated. One is tempted to believe that Bach is painting the "Flattergeister" ("light-minded people") — the fowls of the air, that pick up the seeds — who are referred to in the Gospel for the day (Luke VIII, 4—15). We instinctively see a swarm of crows descending upon a field with beating wings and wide-stretched feet.

In the following aria, the "schädlichen Dornen" ("injurious thorns") are symbolised by the *staccati* in the bass. A final chorus of much beauty, "Lass Höchster uns zu allen Zeiten" compensates the hearer for the almost too drastic character of the other music.

The opening chorus of the cantata for the thirteenth Sunday after Trinity, *Du sollst Gott deinen Herrn lieben* (No. 77) — "Thou shalt love the Lord thy God" — is treated symbolically. Bach's knowledge of the Bible reminds him that Christ's answer to the question as to the greatest commandment in the law was that the whole of the law and the prophets was summed up in the commandment to love*. He expresses this in his music by surrounding the chorus that announces the new commandment with the *cantus firmus* of the chorale "Dies sind die heil'gen zehn Gebot" ("These are the sacred ten commandments") in the orchestra. The lesser commandments are represented by the theme in crotchets in the trumpet; the bass trombone of the organ gives it out in minims, signifying the greater commandments. The rest of the orchestra, with the opening motive of the melody, symbolises the least of the commandments, the jots and tittles of the law. Just as Jesus derived his new commandment of love from the old law, so Bach forms the theme of his chorus out of the first intervals of the old chorale. Unfortunately the further course of the text gave him no opportunity to write particularly striking music.

The poems of the two cantatas *Erforsche mich Gott* (No. 136; for the eighth Sunday after Trinity) and *Nimm was dein ist* (No. 144; for Septuagesima), seem to have stimulated him so little that he made them up almost entirely of old music, as we can see from the faulty declamation**. The only original portion that has any interest is the motet-like chorus "Nimm was dein ist und gehe

* Matthew XXII, 34—40. In the version in Luke X, 23-37,—which is the Gospel for the day, and on which the text of the cantata is founded — this concluding passage is lacking. Here we clearly see how far afield Bach sometimes goes in order to find characteristic ideas for his music, and how he does not hesitate to go past his real text if he sees what he wants outside it.

** The chorus "Erforsche mich Gott" is certainly not original. In the *In Gloria Dei Patris* of the A major Mass the effect is better, though even here he seems to have made use of some borrowed material. The strong proud theme of the duet "Uns treffen zwar der Sünden Flecken", again, is wholly alien to this text. Of the two arias of the cantata *Nimm was dein ist* we can say with confidence that Bach could not deliberately have declaimed them in this way, but that they are fully explained by another text having been fitted to the music at a later date.

hin" ("Take what is thine own and depart"), in which the instrumental basses dwell upon the representation of the "depart" —

The cantata for the second Sunday after Easter, *Du Hirte Israel, höre* (No. 104) takes us into a new world. Is the composer who here revels in the most delicate lyricism the same who elsewhere makes his music almost excessively characteristic? A charming triplet movement runs through the first chorus and the final aria, "Beglückte Herde". In the aria "Verbirgt mein Hirte sich zu lange . . . mein schwacher Schritt eilt dennoch fort" ("My Shepherd hides Himself too long, . . . yet I hasten with feeble steps") the oboes give a delightful picture of haste. The ravishing euphony and the perfect grace of this work ensure its immediate effect upon any audience; it is one of the most suitable for overcoming the common fear of Bach.

The cantata for Midsummer day, *Ihr Menschen rühmet Gottes Liebe* (No. 167) and that for the seventeenth Sunday after Trinity, *Bringet dem Herrn Ehre seines Namen* (No.148) are also full of simple charm. The final chorale of the former, "Sei Lob und Preis", with its joyous orchestral accompaniment, is particularly effective.

The fine text of the cantata for the Sunday after Christmas, *Gottlob, nun geht das Jahr zu Ende* (No. 28) is by Neumeister. The music shows that Bach worked at the text with pleasure. He accompanies the words that speak of the departure of the old year and the "glorious approach" of the new with a merry ballett in the minor —

Then comes a simple motet-chorus on "Nun lob' meine Seel' den Herren", in which the instruments merely reinforce the voices. At the end of this movement Bach has written "174 bars"!

The two choruses of the New Year cantata *Herr Gott, dich loben wir* (No. 16) are in a more popularly effective style. In the first, the orchestral basses keep up the rhythm of the "joy" motive —

In the second the *tutti* is broken by interludes for the solo bass.

The small amount of mysticism in the works of this epoch is due to the texts. Two cantatas glorify the longing for death. The first, *Ich lasse dich nicht, du segnest mich denn* (No. 157) — a solo cantata for tenor and bass — was written for the Feast of the Purification of Mary. The symphonic accompaniment to the opening duet reminds us of the first aria of *Jesus nahm zu sich die Zwölfe* (No. 22). Afterwards a joyous light streams with increasing brightness over the expectation of death. The aria "Ich halte meinen Jesum feste" is like a heavenly roundelay. The final aria, "Ja, ja, ich halte Jesum feste", is of almost extravagant cheerfulness.

From Picander's poems we learn that this fine cantata was produced on the 2nd February 1727, on the Feast of the Purification of Mary, and that Bach made use of it four days later at the funeral ceremony for the old chamberlain Johann Christian von Pönickau*.

Death and youth are the subjects of the cantata for the sixteenth Sunday after Trinity, *Liebster Gott, wann werd ich sterben* (No. 8), founded on the Gospel story of the widow's son of Nain (Luke VII, 11—17). The sun shines brightly on the fields as they bear the boy to the gate; the flowers of the meadow join in with the bell that peals

* See Spitta II, 411 ff.

from the tower; chirping and humming is heard from near and far. Spitta says of this orchestral tone-picture that it is woven out of the sounds of bells and the scent of flowers, and is filled with the spirit of a grave-yard in the spring.

In the aria "Was willst du dich, mein Geist, entsetzen, wenn meine letzte Stunde schlägt" ("Why wilt thou be afraid, my soul, when my last hour strikes"), the bells of death are heard in the minor, as if dark clouds were casting their shadows over the smiling meadow. These are driven away again in the aria "Doch weichet ihr tollen, vergeblichen Sorgen . . . mich rufet mein Jesus, wer sollte nicht gehn?" ("Away, ye mad, vain cares . . . My Jesus calls me; who would not go?"), in which the jubilant flute carries the strings and the voice along with it in a rapid gigue.

This splendid work should not be attempted except with a really good orchestra, that is familiar with Bach. It is one of the rather few cantatas in which the composer has most carefully marked the phrasing and the dynamic signs, — which indicates that he wanted special care in the performance of it.

CHAPTER XXVIII.

THE *TRAUERODE* AND THE *ST. MATTHEW PASSION.*

B. G. XIII[3]: The *Trauerode.*
B. G. IV: The *St. Matthew Passion.*

When Queen Christiane Eberhardine died, on the 7th September 1727, all Saxony mourned for her, not merely in the four months' public mourning ordered by the Court, but with sincere personal grief. After her husband had become a Roman Catholic in 1697, in order to gain the crown of Poland, she had lived far from him in quiet seclusion. The people had venerated the sufferer almost like a saint *.

The memorial ceremony, which took place on the 17th October in St. Paul's Church, was not arranged by the town council or even the consistory, but had its origin in a private impulse. A certain Hans Carl von Kirchbach, assessor to the upper court of mines at Freiberg, had asked permission of the Court to hold an "ovation" for the deceased. As St. Paul's Church, in which the ceremony was to take place, was the University church, the invitations came from the rector. The organiser of the ceremony had commissioned the text for the *Trauerode* from Gottsched. For the music he should really have gone to Görner, the director of the service at the University church. When the senate heard that he had ordered it of the St. Thomas cantor, it tried to force him to cancel the order. The end of the matter was that Bach received permission to write the composition, but it was expressly laid down that the permission was granted for that occasion only, and that he was not to deduce from it the right to compose the music for academic festivals, — and Herr von Kirchbach was to give Görner twelve thalers in compensation**.

The title of Bach's score runs thus:

"Trauer-Musik, so bey der Lob- und Trauer-Rede, welche auff das Absterben Ihro Königl. Maj. und Churf. Durchl. zu Sachsen, Frauen Christianen, Eberhardinen, Königin in Pohlen ... und Churfürstin zu Sachsen ... geb. Markgräfin zu Brandenburg Bayreuth, von dem Hochwohlgeb. Herrn von Kirchbach in der Pauliner Kirche zu Leipzig gehalten wurde, aufgeführet worden von Joh. Seb. Bach ao 1727 d. 18 Oct." ("Funeral music, given on the occasion of Herr von Kirchbach's address of praise and mourning for her royal majesty Christiane Eberhardine, Queen of Poland ... and Electoral Princess of Saxony ... née Margravine of Brandenburg Bayreuth, in St. Paul's Church at Leipzig, — performed by Joh. Seb. Bach, 18th Oct. 1727").

---

* On Queen Christiane Eberhardine see Spitta II, 613—615.
** See I. 121.

This date is wrong; it should be the 17th October*. At the end of the score there is the date 15th October; so that Bach finished his work only two days before the performance. It could therefore not have had much rehearsal.

Gottsched's ode is correct, but without poetry or depth. It is noteworthy that it does not voice the grief of the husband of the dead queen. The poet could not enlarge upon this, for everyone knew how unhappy the marriage had been, and how grievously the queen had been wronged by her husband.

Although the text was in strophic form, Bach resolved to handle it in a "modern" fashion, and compose the strophes in the form of Italian recitatives and arias. He very dexterously surmounted the technical difficulties thus placed in his way.

Forkel was enchanted with the music of the *Trauerode.* "The choruses of this work", he says, "are so attractive that no one who has begun to play through them can stop till he has gone to the end."**

The rhythm of solemnity runs through the first chorus, "Lass, Fürstin, lass noch einen Strahl", from beginning to end. The hearer is so affected by the majestic and sombre harmonies that he is unconscious of the length of the movement.

The two following movements are dominated by the motive of noble grief. In the aria "Verstummt, ihr holden Saiten" the violins maintain a continual sobbing and sighing —

* There is an account of the ceremony in Sicul's *Das thränende Leipzig* (1727). See Spitta II, 616.

** Forkel, p. 36. (The earlier part of the above citation is supplied from the context).

The recitative that speaks of the tolling of the funeral bells —

> "Der Glocken bebendes Getön
> Soll uns'rer trüben Seelen Schrecken
> Durch ihr geschwungnes Erze wecken,
> Und uns durch Mark und Adern gehn.
> O, könnte nur dies bange Klingen,
> Davon das Ohr uns täglich gellt,
> Der ganzen Europäerwelt
> Ein Zeugnis uns'res Jammers bringen"

is exceedingly affecting. While the alto sings these words, the bells are heard in the orchestra, — first of all the very small ones, then the larger ones, descending through the registers to the bass. Then the peals cease, the flutes and oboes being silenced in turn, then the violins and violas, until just the two gambas give out the tones, and finally the bass alone —

This representation of the beginning and the ending of a peal of bells is as realistic as that of the rapid waves of a river in the cantata *Christ unser Herr zum Jordan kam* (No. 7). On the other hand the tolling of the funeral bells in the cantata *Liebster Gott, wann werd' ich sterben* (No. 8) is a more idealised picture, which allows Bach to expand it into a large movement. In the *Trauerode* the brevity is an essential part of the effect of the picture, which comprises only eleven bars.

At the moment when "the bells' quivering tones" die away, death and its pangs are conquered; and henceforth the music is, as it were, transfigured. The theme of the gambas in the aria "Wie starb die Heldin so vergnügt" ("How happy was she in her death"), is like a smile of celestial serenity —

The succeeding recitative ends with the words "Ach selig, wessen großer Geist sich über die Natur erhebet, vor Gruft und Särgen nicht erbebet, wenn ihn sein Schöpfer scheiden heißt" ("Happy he whose great spirit is raised above nature, and is not terrified by the tomb, when his Maker bids him depart"). The peace that falls upon these victorious ones when they reach the shore of eternity is described by Bach in a wonderful tranquil figure in the bass, that persists from the beginning to the end of the movement —

The figures in the two oboi d'amore above these tranquil waves look like a transfiguration of the "joy" motive —

In the aria "Der Ewigkeit saphirnes Haus zieht, Fürstin, deine heitern Blicke von unsrer Niedrigkeit zurücke" ("From the sapphire house of eternity turn, oh princess, thy serene glance on our lowliness") Bach's mysticism finds exuberant expression. Over a simple accompaniment the flute has an arabesque that is like a saintly dance —

Besides these soli the work contains two splendid choruses, the one — "An dir, du Vorbild großer Frauen" — is in fugal form; the other, — the final chorus "O Königin, du stirbest nicht" — is in simple song-form, flowing along in gentle triplets.

In the orchestration of the *Trauerode* Bach endeavours, by the use of the oboe d'amore, gambas and lutes, to obtain a peculiar colour, which however is rarely realised in present-day performances, since gamba and lute players are scarce, and the parts have to be given to the ordinary strings. It is very interesting to note that having the lutes there, Bach employs them, when they are not playing obbligato parts, in strengthening the orchestral basses. This shows how much importance he attached to the prominence of these fundamental figures. Had he always had the lutes at his disposal, he would often have used them in the cantatas to reinforce the *continuo.*

The figured organ part has unfortunately been lost with the original parts of the score. The autograph score is almost illegible, and has evidently been written in great haste, as was to be expected in the case of so large a work composed in two or three weeks.

Rust did this splendid work the great service of adding to it, in the Bachgesellschaft edition, a new poetical version of his own for All Souls' Day, which is now generally used, — for every performance of the *Trauerode* cannot be given in memory of Christiane Eberhardine!

When Bach began the composition of the *St. Matthew Passion,* in the autumn of 1728, he received, in the middle of November, the news of the death of his friend Prince Leopold of Cöthen, and a commission for some music for the funeral ceremonies. These apparently took place some three months after the death of the Prince; the exact date is not known. Bach of course could not compose a new work so quickly at a time when he had the *St. Matthew Passion* on hand; so he asked Picander to write the text for the mourning ode in such a way that it could be adapted to the movements already written of the Passion. The work performed in honour of the Prince was thus made up of eight arias and the final chorus of the *St. Matthew Passion.* For the text of the opening chorus, "Klaget, Kinder, klagt es aller Welt", Bach used the first chorus of the *Trauerode,* which indicates that the opening chorus of the Passion was not finished at that time.

This was the mourning music for double chorus the score of which Forkel possessed. It is noteworthy that he does not seem to have observed the identity of this music with that of the *St. Matthew Passion*, for otherwise he would surely have remarked upon it. Spitta conjectures that Forkel had only a very superficial knowledge of the Passion. When an inventory was made of his musical manuscripts after his death in 1818, the autograph of the Cöthen mourning music was missing; nor has it since been found. The loss of one of Bach's finest works was long deplored, until Rust, in the preface to B. G. XX[2] (1870), proved from the nature of the text that we have the music in the *St. Matthew Passion*.

If we compare the two texts, we are astounded to find with what superficial agreement Bach was satisfied. Imagine, for example, the words "Geh', Leopold, zu deiner Ruhe" ("Go, Leopold, to thy rest") sung to the melody of the tenor aria "Ich will bei meinem Jesu wachen" ("I will watch by my Jesus") from the Passion! With the declamation treated in this way, we can easily understand that the new poem took not the least account of the poetic and pictorial intentions of the music. It is almost incredible that the Bach who had written the *St. Matthew Passion* is the same Bach who took this music, with all it expresses, and parodied it so grievously.

The text of the *St. Matthew Passion* has been put together with the greatest care. Bach may have had too poor an opinion of the Passion poem that Picander wrote for him in 1725* to give him a free hand on this occasion. We get the impression that he sketched the plan of the work in all its details, and that Picander worked literally under his observation.

From Brockes' Passion he took the "Daughter of Zion"**. For the texts of the arias Picander was allowed to employ

---

* See p. 172.

** Upon Brockes' Passion and its significance in connection with Bach see I. 93 ff.

certain poetic ideas from the poems of Bach's Weimar librettist, Franck. Some ideas from the Passion of 1725 were also taken up again and improved.

The dramatic plan is at once simple and ingenious. The story of the Passion is cast into the form of a series of pictures. At the characteristic points the narrative breaks off, and the scene that has just passed is made the subject of a pious meditation. This is effected in arias that are usually led up to by an arioso-like recitative. At minor resting-points the feelings of the Christian spectators are expressed in chorale verses. The choice of these fell to Bach, since no poet of that epoch who had any respect for himself would be troubled with a secondary task of that kind. It is just in the insertion of these chorale strophes that the full depth of Bach's poetic sense is revealed. It would be impossible to find, in the whole of the hymns of the German church, a verse better fitted to its particular purpose than the one Bach has selected.

Altogether the *St. Matthew Passion* falls into about twenty-four scenes, — twelve smaller ones, indicated by chorales, and twelve larger ones, marked by arias. The problem of representing the action of the Passion and at the same time of giving due weight to the devotional element is solved in the most perfect way imaginable. The more we realise the dramatic plan of the *St. Matthew Passion* the more we are convinced that it is a masterpiece.

Bach's coöperation was an excellent stimulus to Picander. In the *St. Matthew Passion* he has produced his best poem; the diction is animated and extremely rich in pictures; and there are few of those insipidities of his that annoy us in his other works. The situations are concisely described, and the reflections are simple but often really profound. The texts of the arioso-recitatives are indeed the best he ever wrote; they have a musical effect even when we merely read them.

Experience of the *St. Matthew Passion* makes us regret that Bach and Picander did not write a year's set of can-

Bach's Handwriting (Fair Copy)

Reduced facsimile of a page of the "St. Matthew Passion"

tatas in collaboration, the one contributing the depth of his devotion, the other the dexterity and the wealth of his diction.

Even when the text was completed Bach made alterations in it. Picander had cast the opening in the form of an aria with chorus, like the first movement in the Second Part. He thought the words "Kommt, ihr Töchter, helft mir klagen" ("Come, ye daughters, help me to mourn") and "Sehet . . . den Bräutigam! seht ihn . . . als wie ein Lamm" ("See, the bridegroom . . . like a lamb") should be sung by the daughter of Zion, while the chorus should only interject the "Whom? . . . How? . . . What?" Bach's musical sense made him think otherwise. He saw Jesus being led through the town to the cross; his eye caught sight of the crowd surging through the streets; he heard them calling to and answering each other. It was this vision that prompted him to cast the introduction to the Passion in the form of a great double chorus. The singular pronoun remains, —"Kommt, ihr Töchter, helft *mir* klagen" — as if to testify to the violence done to the text.

It is thus a mistake to conceive this double chorus as an expression of ideal grief, and to render it delicately and slowly. It is realistic in intention, and depicts a crowd moving excitedly about, crying aloud, roaring. The vocal parts are not coloratura, but a reproduction of the conflicting voices of a large crowd. This is evident from the nature of the first phrase for the sopranos —

12
8
Kommt - - - ihr Töch-ter helft mir kla - - gen!

If this conception be the right one, the orchestral prelude also should be played with heavy accents and a certain inward unrest, so that an impression of uneasiness may come from the pauses of the bass on the same notes and the dreadful inexorability of the harmonies. In any case the tempo here is usually too dragging; and the more we study the chorus the more we are convinced that the effect should come mainly from the drastic quality of the declamation rather than from factitious dynamic shading.

We have the same experience with the chorale-chorus "O Mensch bewein' dein Sünde gross" ("O Man, thy grievous sin lament") at the end of the First Part. The orchestral accompaniment is based on the motive of noble grief —

If we look at the instrumental part alone we are tempted to take the movement in a somewhat solemn tempo; but if we have regard to the chorus, we shall accelerate the tempo considerably. On closer examination we discover that the figuration of the separate lines of the chorale is most moving, and the effect of it is quite lost if it is not taken with some animation. So we are led to choose a tempo that perhaps appears too fast for the orchestral part, but at once justifies itself on the entry of the chorus. As the problem throughout is to reconcile two different tempi, the utmost possible flexibility is needed. It is therefore advisable to dispense with the usual *rallentandi* and *diminuendi* in order to avoid breaking up the text unnecessarily and preventing the hearer from perceiving the logical unity of the movement. The tempo should be slackened only where the words and the musical phrase demand it — e. g. at the words "unserer Sünde schwere Bürd" ("the heavy burden of our sins"). How the end of the movement should be rendered is doubtful. The *adagiosissimo* that Bach has noted in the last bar of the chorale prelude *O Mensch bewein' dein Sünde gross* (Peters V, No. 45) leads us to think that chorus and orchestra should here also die away softly in a slow *rallentando.*

The final chorus of the Second Part, like that of the *St. John Passion*, is conceived as a piece of burial music.

Here also the peculiar falling motives determine the character of the movement; the eye seems to follow the body into the grave. To bring out the full magic of the movement, the bass figures of this type —

should be brought out softly but clearly.

In the choruses of the people we see the great difference between the narratives of the Passion in John and Matthew, a difference which Bach has reproduced in his music. In the *St. John Passion* their predominant feeling is one of dramatic excitement; in the *St. Matthew Passion* the choruses have a certain epic tranquillity. They are shorter, and in some respects more musical, their objects not being, as in parts of the other Passions, to create the effect of long-drawn and conflicting cries. In the *St. John Passion* the people's choruses are the bearer of the action; in the *St. Matthew Passion* they are only a part of the narrative. Compare the "Crucify Him" in the two works, and note that Bach has not written any chorus upon the "Barabbas" passage.

In the choruses round the cross — "Der du den Tempel Gottes zerbrichst" ("Thou who destroyest the temple of God") and "Andern hat er geholfen" ("He helped others")— there is more of the dæmonic quality of the choruses of the *St. John Passion*. The words "So steig herab vom Kreuz" ("Then descend from the cross") are very effectively illustrated in the music. The bass figure runs thus —

Unfortunately much of the fine instrumental detail of these choruses of the people is generally lost in performance, our orchestras being much too weak in comparison with our choruses. Who can hear the arrogant laughter in the flutes at the words "Wahrlich, du bist auch einer von denen" ("Truly thou also art one of them")? Who can hear them in the "Crucify Him", in the "Prophesy unto us", in "What is that unto us", in "His blood be upon us"? Whereas the other instruments more or less agree with the voice parts, Bach, in these choruses, assigns a quite independent part to the united flutes. A good effect would often be made here, as in many of the choruses of the *St. John Passion*, by adding a piccolo.

It is strange how little thought is taken for the dramatic situation in our present-day arrangement of the choir. We actually hear four hundred singers giving out such passages as "Where wilt thou that we prepare the Passover", "Lord, is it I" (spoken by the twelve disciples), the "Truly thou also art one of them" (spoken by the two soldiers and the maid), and "Truly this man was the Son of God" (spoken by the centurion and the guard at the cross). Bach had three, or at most four, voices to each part. For the whole of the *St. Matthew Passion*, with its double choruses, he had to copy out only eight voice parts. None was doubled, though the violin parts were, in both choruses. Thus for Bach the question never arose of whether he should employ the whole or only a part of the choir; but it is decidedly a question for us, in view of the enormous choirs of today. Perhaps it will become the general practice to allot the above-mentioned choruses to a small choir of five or six voices to a part, for the sake not only of the dramatic situation but of the musical effect. We must get rid of the erroneous notion that only a large choir is effective in a church.

No analysis could do justice to the beauty and the consummate expressiveness of the recitatives of Christ and the Evangelist in the narrative of the Passion. It will be noticed that the words of Christ are set in a more arioso-like recitative than those of the Evangelist. They are also accompanied by the strings alone. At the entry of the soft and luminous harmonies of the violins we seem to see the halo round the head of the Saviour.

The declamation of the Evangelist is, as a rule, quite plain in character and objective in its painting. This gives all the greater effect to certain words that are underlined in the accompaniment or delivered in a melisma, such as the "and began to be sorrowful and very heavy", the "and fell on His face and prayed", in the Gethsemane scene, and the "wept bitterly" after the denial of Peter. The words of Jesus are set more elaborately; yet here again we wonder at the simplicity of the means employed. As a rule Bach needs only a simple cadence in order to throw a particular word into strong relief. Only rarely does the orchestral picture attract attention on its own account. The words of the crowd as it is dispersing are reproduced in a few diverging harmonies. In the verse "And when they had sung a hymn, they went out into the mount of olives", some heavy steps in the bass —

symbolise the Saviour setting out upon His path of sorrow. His gait is quite different later, when He has put off earthly form and appears transfigured. The orchestra suggests this buoyant tread in the moment when the Arisen One promises His disciples that He will go before them into Galilee —

If these pictorial details are not clearly and expressively brought out in the orchestra, the hearer cannot be conscious of them, e. g. in the accompaniment to the words of Jesus to the sleeping disciples at Gethsemane. In the motive —

we should be made to see the Lord, His heart full of anguish, shaking His disciples to rouse them from their sleep. As a rule, however, the violins take the passage and the trill so softly that none of the proper excitement is communicated to the audience. Again in the passage in which Jesus prophesies to the judge, "Ye shall see the Son of man sitting on the right hand of power, and coming in the clouds of heaven", the semiquaver figure that depicts the clouds that are to be His throne accumulating on the horizon hardly ever makes its proper effect.

The accompaniment to Christ's words at the supper does not express grief, but the triumphant confidence of the Lord, who, at this mournful last supper, promises His disciples that He will again drink of the fruit of the vine with them in heaven*.

For the performance of 1829 Mendelssohn orchestrated the accompaniment to "And behold, the veil of the temple was rent". This is contrary to Bach's intentions. All he is concerned with are the scale figures that represent the tearing. The organist should co-operate in these, as they never come out clearly enough in the violoncellos and basses alone; the chords should be played on another manual, with stops of an intense but not too strong quality. The widespread opinion that the organist here must indulge in a *fortissimo* fantasia has neither historical nor artistic foundation. In this place, as in the whole of the Evangelist's part, the chief thing is and must be the declamation of the narrative of the Passion; the accompaniment must only co-operate by means of suggestion. In the arias, on the other hand, the music is self-subsistent. It expresses ideas and represents events. Here we may almost say that the instrumental part is not an accompaniment to the voice part, but *vice versâ*.

On closer consideration of these movements, two things strike us; in the first place, the pictorial intention of the

---

* On this passage see also pp. 27 and 35.

themes is unmistakeable; in the second place, there is a thematic connection between the arias and the arioso-like recitatives. In many cases the theme of the aria is derived from the same musical idea as the accompaniment to the preceding arioso-recitative.

It goes without saying that these peculiarities of the "reflective" music in the *St. Matthew Passion* are not always equally evident. Where the text and the situation offer nothing that is specially pictorial, the music of pure feeling enters into its rights. This is particularly the case in the first and last solo pieces. In the arioso "Am Abend, da es kühle war" ("When evening brought the cooling shade") Bach expresses the tranquil peace of the falling twilight; the aria "Mache dich, mein Herze, rein" ("Oh, my heart, now make thee pure") expresses a joy that is exuberant and calm by turns. These two movements are unique of their kind. Again and again we ask ourselves what it is in these tones that makes them so perfectly suggest all that is mysterious and inexpressible in the holy mood that descends upon us when we think of the descent from the cross.

There is a thematic affinity between the earlier solo movements of the *St. Matthew Passion*, — the arioso "Du lieber Heiland", the aria "Buss und Reu", and the aria "Blute nur, du liebes Herz". In all three the text speaks of tears, sighs, laments; the music is therefore dominated by the "sighing" motive that is so characteristic of Bach —

Arioso-Recitative. "Du lieber Heiland, du".

Aria. "Buss und Reu".

Aria. "Blute nur, du liebes Herz".

The music here should really sob! To achieve this, however, the instrumentalists should bring out the tied notes and make them sound like veritable sighs, and generally realise all that Bach meant by his phrasing here. The singers, indeed, must bear their share of the guilt for the wrongful rendering of these movements; as a rule they take the tempo so slowly and make the rhythm so uncertain with their *rallentandi* that it is impossible to give the orchestral part its proper meaning.

In the aria "Blute nur" the tempo should be moderately fast. Particular care must be taken that the orchestra does not accent the theme on the strong beats, but brings out in the first bar the second quaver and the last crotchet, in the second bar the second and last crotchets, in the sixth bar the second and sixth quavers, and this in such a way that the other notes are almost lost by the side of them.

This music, in virtue of its fundamental motive and its affecting quality, stands on the borderline between the art of pure feeling and the art of representation. How quick Bach's imagination is, even here, to seize upon the slightest pretext for tone-painting may be seen from the fact that in the aria "Buss und Reu" he employs a motive characteristic of the dropping of tears at the words "Dass die Tropfen meiner Zähren" ("that my tear-drops") —

In the accompaniment to the arioso "Wiewohl mein Herz in Tränen schwimmt" ("Although my heart with tears o'erflow") the orchestra depicts the floods of tears —

The accents should fall not on the strong beats, but on the second, fourth, sixth and last quavers each time.

In the bright aria in G major, "Ich will dir mein Herze schenken" ("Lord, to Thee my heart I offer"), the laments for Jesus, that fill the earlier contemplative scenes of the *St. Matthew Passion*, terminate in a joyous confession.

In Gethsemane there are three scenes mainly characterised by devotional meditation, — Jesus' arrival with His disciples; His prayer; His capture.

The contemplative element enters in the verse "Meine Seele ist betrübt bis in den Tod; bleibet hier und wachet mit mir" ("My soul is exceeding sorrowful, even unto death; tarry ye here and watch with me"). The first half of the text, dealing with the agony of Jesus' soul, is expressed in the recitative "O Schmerz, hier zittert das gequälte Herz!" ("O grief! His tortured heart at last doth quail"); the second half, the prayer that they will stay and watch with Him, is devoted to the aria "Ich will bei meinem Jesu wachen" ("I stand beside my Saviour watching").

The first aria is accompanied by the anguished sighs of the flutes and oboes —

This is accompanied by a persistent semiquaver throbbing of the basses on the one tone. That these semiquavers express terror and trembling is shewn by their employment in the cantata *O Ewigkeit, du Donnerwort* (No. 60); moreover, they merely continue the throbbing of the quavers that, a moment before, accompanied the words of Jesus, "My soul is exceeding sorrowful unto death". The sense of the passage will only be properly conveyed in performance when the wood-wind have learned that the quavers are not to be played evenly, but with accents on two quavers only in each bar — the third and the seventh — all the rest, even those coming on a strong beat of the bar, being taken merely as preliminary or supplementary to these. Then not only shall we hear the sighs, but the accompaniment will become so transparent that the voice part can make itself heard without straining, instead of being buried under the flutes and oboes, as it generally is. If the bass is to be effective, it must be phrased thus —

It is the antagonism between the accentuation of the bass and that of the flutes that gives the music the pained unrest that Bach intended to suggest.

In the fine interjectory chorale, again, "Was ist die Ursach aller solcher Plagen" ("Why does He suffer all these bitter pains?") we must be conscious of the anguish and grief in the words of the faithful. It should be sung *pianissimo*, with a certain urgency of movement, the words being given out, as it were, in excited whispers.

The chorus "So schlafen unsre Sünden ein" ("Then laid to rest our sins will be") in the following aria must be breathed softly, as if in a dream; but care must be taken that the tempo is not too slow; it is determined not by the chorus but by the watchman's signal —

The significance of this motive will of course only be clear to the hearer when the wind emphasise not the semiquavers but the four constituent notes of the signal —

the last note taking the chief accent — the semiquavers being merely the filling-in of the pause.

The prayer in Gethsemane is treated in a recitative-arioso and aria. In the arioso "Der Heiland fällt vor seinem Vater nieder" ("The Saviour low before His Father falleth") the orchestra has an accompaniment of falling semiquavers —

Only after the words "dadurch erhebt er mich und alle von unserm Falle hinauf zu Gottes Gnade wieder" ("And thus by His own tribulation, for our salvation, our souls to God's great mercy calleth") is there a momentary reversion to ascending figures.

The theme of the aria "Gerne will ich mich bequemen Kreuz und Becher anzunehmen" ("Gladly will I leave him never, Cross and Cup be mine for ever") runs thus —

It symbolises humble obeisance; first there is a descent, then an attempt to rise, ending in a final descent. Similar motives with the same symbolical purpose frequently appear in the cantatas. The whole nature of the structure of the theme indicates that it is to be rendered — especially in the final descending passage — with a certain heaviness; then the hearer will really see before him a human body descending lower and lower.

In the duet "So ist mein Jesus nun gefangen" ("Betrayed is Jesus now, my Saviour") we must start out from the conception that Bach's music is before everything else the painting of a situation. His musical picture is decided by the words "Sie führen ihn, er ist gefangen" ("In bondage held, away they bear Him"). He sees the crowd moving about among the gloomy trees of Gethsemane, driving before it Jesus in bonds; and he imagines a number of the faithful following Him with their laments and cries of "Lasst ihn, haltet, bindet nicht" ("Leave Him, leave Him, bind Him not"). The music thus depicts a scene full of motion. Its two chief motives are so constructed that their co-operation gives a tense four-four rhythm —

Wind instruments. Strings.

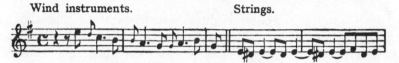

The almost march-like character of the whole piece is accentuated by the regular quaver-movement that relieves the syncopated motive and dominates the long-drawn *unisono* of the strings. Most decisive, however, are the crotchets, also in unison in the strings, that suggest the sound of footsteps. If we hear, at the words "Sie führen ihn, er ist gefangen", this progression —

clearly brought out, the meaning of the music is at once evident. As it is usually performed, however, we do not hear these steps, and are not made aware of the peculiar march-like movement of the piece. The excessive *rallentandi* that the singers spread over it deprive it of all rhythm; it has a merely vacillating effect, and the separate instruments tumble over each other, till everyone longs for the grateful moment when the chorus "Sind Blitze, sind Donner" ("Are lightnings and thunder") puts an end to the intolerable sound. The intended effect comes at once, however, if a firm and somewhat urgent rhythm be adopted, that carries the voices along with it. On closer examination one is even tempted to believe that the *coloratura* is meant to imitate the cries and laments upon the way.

To achieve a proper performance, again, we must restore to its rights the directions in the autograph score, "Violoncelli concordant violis". Rietz most inexcusably suppressed this indication in the edition of the *St. Matthew Passion* he brought out for the Bachgesellschaft, only mentioning it in a note in the preface, where he could be sure that it would not be seen. He omitted it from the score because he could not find a violoncello part for this chorus among the original orchestral parts. He never considered that Bach's cellists could play the part an octave lower, from the viola copies. The violoncellos must therefore be added to the *unisono* of the other strings in this duet if it is to have its proper foundation.

The aria "Ach windet euch nicht so, geplagte Seelen" ("Ah, writhe not so, tormented souls"), that was at one time in the *St. John Passion**, gives us a remarkable commentary upon this duet in the *St. Matthew Passion*. It has an exact parallel to the syncopated motive of the latter, in this form —

Here there can be no doubt that the motive is meant to symbolise the "Winden" ("writhing"). We may therefore assume that when Bach used it in the *St. Matthew Passion* he saw before him the captive Saviour writhing in His fetters.

The disappointment we so frequently experience in the chorus "Sind Blitze, sind Donner" ("Are lightnings and thunders") is generally the fault of the organist, who overwhelms everything with his continual *fortissimo* chords, and makes the strongest choir seem impotent. Of course the rolling semiquavers that suggest distant thunder —

* It will be found in B. G. XII[1], pp. 148—151

that are the foundation of the movement, are completely lost. The chief duty of the organist, — Bach's own score prescribes it to him — is to bring out these semiquaver runs; long-held chords should be played strongly on the third manual, and short chords, that are effective in holding the whole together, on the first. If the bass figure comes out clearly the effect of the chorus is assured.

The Second Part of the *St. Matthew Passion* opens again in Gethsemane. The tumult has died away. Night has fallen. The Daughter of Zion wanders through the lonely garden, seeking her Lord. "Ach! nun ist mein Jesu hin" she wails ("Ah, now is my Saviour gone"). The chorus of the faithful follow her and strive to console her. Bach reproduces this situation in his theme. It consists of two motives. The first —

depicts the steps of the Daughter of Zion as she rushes hither and thither, pauses, turns in another direction, again rushes forward, and again stands still and looks around. The meaning of the motive is assured by its affinity with many "step" motives in the cantatas. A conclusive proof may be had by comparing it with the bass theme of the aria "Ach, wo hol' ich Armer Rat" ("Ah, where shall I, wretched one, take counsel") in the cantata *Es ist nichts Gesundes an meinem Leibe* (No. 25), in which Bach is again depicting some one rushing about distractedly —

Notice also the "steps" in the accompaniment, e. g., —

The second motive, which is attached to the first, reproduces the laments and cries of the Daughter of Zion. In its first part we have the chromatic "grief" motive,

intensified and made more dreadful by the insertion here and there of intervals of the seventh, and sighs that culminate in wild shrieks. The passage runs thus —

The explanation of the theme gives the clue — otherwise missing — to the way in which it should be performed. At the commencement the first two quavers, as Bach himself indicates in his phrasing — must be detached from each other, the second receiving the main accent. Only in this way, and played heavily, will it suggest the steps. Later on, the trills are to be played vehemently; the penultimate note of the ascending run cannot be emphasised too strongly, so that the audience may really hear the awful sequences —

The end should not be played languishingly, but harshly, with a *crescendo* and a forward impulse. The tempo should be restless and urgent. Wherever the voice is silent, Bach has indicated *forte.* In the introductory bars the hearer should be horror-struck; he should see the distracted woman rushing about and wringing her hands in the gloomy wood. Nor should the characteristic rhythms and intervals be obscured even in the *piano* accompaniment to the voice. Conceived in this way, not only is the instrumental accompaniment made more effective, but the solo and the chorus make a finer effect if they are sung with some animation and a sense of anguish, instead of sentimental *rallentandi* and *accelerandi*.

The theme of the aria "Geduld, Geduld! wenn mich falsche Zungen stechen" ("Endure, endure! though lying tongues upbraid me") is also composed of two motives. The tranquil quavers symbolise the word "Geduld"; in the following bars we see the sharp tongues shooting forth—

The theme of the aria "Erbarme dich" ("Thy mercy show, oh God") is derived from the melisma of the preceding recitative "and wept bitterly" —

The contemplative words are thus sung to music in which we can recognise the weeping of Peter.

The aria "Gebt mir meinen Jesum wieder" ("Give me back my Lord beloved") affords us almost the best proof of how bent Bach is on reproducing in his music whatever the eye sees and the ear hears. The joyous music (G major) has apparently nothing to do with the reflections upon Judas' betrayal. Bach, however, has really derived it from his text. He fastens on the words "Seht das Geld, den Mörderlohn, wirft euch der verlorne Sohn zu den Füßen nieder!" ("Lo, the price for murder paid, now in guilty tribute laid"). In accordance with this he first of all writes a rapid ascending figure that suggests the entry of Judas and the motion of the hand with which he throws away the money, and then the rolling and clinking of the silver on the stone floor of the temple. Thus this theme also is a bipartite one. In estimating the first motive we must not forget that in the aria "Kein' Frucht das Weizenkörnlein bringt, es fall denn in die Erde" ("The wheat brings forth no fruit, let it fall then to the earth") in the cantata *Ach lieben Christen seid getrost* (No. 114), Bach represents the motion of the sower's arm. In performance Bach's own phrasing should be noted and the music accented in accordance with it.

Aria: "Gebt mir meinen Jesum wieder"; first motive.

Ditto: second motive.

When once the meaning of the music has been grasped, performers will not attempt to give the orchestral accompaniment an elegiac tinge by playing it tenderly and sentimentally; they will play it with the freshness and naturalness that belong to it, bringing out the *staccati* and the intermediary scale passages.

The recitative-arioso "Er hat uns allen wohlgetan" ("The Lord for all men good hath done") and the aria "Aus Liebe will mein Heiland sterben" ("Through loving my dear Saviour dieth") form a point of repose in this succession of very animated and pictorial movements. How Bach wished the aria to be performed is doubtful. Should it be sung tranquilly and radiantly, or more like a rhapsody, with a certain pathos in the declamation? The three following contemplative movements relate to the scourging of Jesus, His falling under the weight of the cross, and the hour of death on Golgotha. All are pictorial in conception. The motives of the recitative-ariosos and those of the arias depict the same situation.

First Scene. "Then released he Barabbas unto them; and when he had scourged Jesus, he delivered Him to be crucified."

During the arioso "Erbarm' es Gott! hier steht der Heiland angebunden. O Geisselung! O Schlag', o Wunden!" ("Have mercy, God! Lo, hand and foot their chains have bound Him! with cruel lash and scourge they wound Him") we hear, in the orchestra, the falling of the scourge —

As the aria "Können Tränen meiner Wangen nichts erlangen, o so nehmt mein Herz hinein" ("Though in vain be all my wailing, naught availing, oh receive this heart of mine") is also sung during the scourging, its theme contains a motive that likewise depicts the blows. Mingled with it now, however, are the imploring cries of the faithful soul; to the motive of scourging is appended a sequence of semiquavers that embody a shriek. This explains the peculiar form of the theme —

The significance resides in the final intervals. The two last notes cannot be thrown into too high relief, so that the cries

may literally pierce the hearer's soul. The meaning of the second motive is indicated in the fact that the vocal part is founded on it. The tempo should be as animated as possible; even when the accompaniment is toned down at the entry of the voice, the proper force must be given to the characteristic rhythms and intervals; the singer must let the orchestra carry her with it; then the movement will be most impressive in its effect.

Second Scene. "And as they came out, they found a man of Cyrene, Simon by name; him they compelled to bear His cross."

The accompaniment to the recitative-arioso "Ja freilich will in uns das Fleisch und Blut zum Kreuz gezwungen sein" ("Aye, surely now can flesh and blood atone, if the Cross hold them bound"), depicts the last tottering steps of Jesus under the cross. We see Him stumbling forward and at last falling —

For the motive to express what it is intended to, the quavers that follow the two semiquavers must of course be strongly accented.

In the aria "Komm, süsses Kreuz, so will ich zagen, mein Jesu gib es immer her" ("Oh blessed Cross, be mine to share it, my Saviour, grant this evermore"), the motive of falling notes is transformed into one of strength. Simon of Cyrene has taken the burden on himself, and strides out energetically under it, —

The *continuo* accompaniment gives the music a march-like character. That tempo is right that suggests a heavy, measured walk. The gamba solo should be played with a certain vigour, and the demisemiquavers properly accented.

Third Scene. "And sitting down they watched Him there . . . The thieves also which were crucified with Him cast the same in His teeth".

The mocking crowd has disappeared; the jeering thieves are silent. All is still around the cross. A great darkness rises towards heaven. The hour of death draws nigh. And just as on other occasions Bach represents the end by means of funeral bells, so here, in the recitative-arioso "Ach Golgatha, unsel'ges Golgatha!" ("Ah, Golgotha! unholy Golgotha!") the death of the Saviour is announced by the gloomy tolling of bells —

Then a ray of sunlight breaks through the clouds. A radiance of love and pity streams from the dying Redeemer. "Sehet, Jesus hat die Hand, uns zu fassen ausgespannt!" ("Behold, Jesus doth put forth His hand, giving strength whereby we stand"), sings the believing soul. The funeral bells are silenced, and the clear glad sound of the bells of salvation spreads over the earth. At the same time we see — in the figures mounting from the depths to the heights — the motion with which the Saviour draws mankind to Him on His Cross —

From the fact that the text of the *St. Matthew Passion* appears in the second part of Picander's *Ernst-scherzhaften und satyrischen Gedichten*, which was published at Easter 1729, we may conclude that Bach's work was produced on Good Friday — 15th April — in that year. The autograph score gives us no chronological clue; it was made for a later performance, about the beginning of the seventeen-forties.

We also possess the original parts, in which Bach has marked the dynamics and the phrasing. The parts include two complete sets for the organ; so that each choir had its own organist. The accompaniments could not have been given in this way, however, until after the positive of the St. Thomas's organ had been adapted for separate playing. At the first performance of the Passion the same organ accompanied both choirs.

If Bach placed the choirs with their respective orchestras on the two sides of the organ, we should have to assume that he placed the second choir in the little gallery opposite the great organ, the accompaniment being undertaken by the small organ that was situated there. This, however, is not very likely; the great distance between the two choirs would have put insurmountable difficulties in the way of their *ensemble.*

As the *St. Matthew Passion* cannot well be given entire at one performance, an afternoon should be devoted to it, with an interval of an hour or two between the two Parts. A method that is strongly recommended is to give the First Part on the Saturday evening and the Second Part on the Sunday afternoon, a Sunday during the Passion being selected if possible. The most appropriate way of all is to give the First Part on the evening of Holy Thursday, and the Second Part on Good Friday afternoon. If the work *must* be performed in one piece, none of the contemplative recitative-ariosos and none of the chorales should be cut out.

We do not know what impression the *St. Matthew Passion* made at its first performance; in all probability the work attracted no notice. On the same Good Friday, at the same hour, there was performed at the New Church a Passion by a certain Gottlieb Fröber, a candidate for the vacant post of cantor there. For the Leipzig public this was probably the event of the day, not the Passion of the cantor of St. Thomas's.

CHAPTER XXIX.

THE CANTATAS OF THE YEARS 1728—1734.

We have not many cantatas belonging to the years 1728 and 1729. This may partly be because a particularly large number belonging to those years have been lost; on the other hand it is possible that Bach had not much time for new cantatas while he was at work on the *St. Matthew Passion.* In any case he composed music to only a part of the cycle that Picander wrote for the church year 1728—1729. Of the nine cantatas belonging to this series that we possess, five, according to Spitta, fall into the period 1729—1730, and four in 1731.

The cantata for Christmas, *Ehre sei Gott*, has not come down to us in that form, Bach having incorporated the greater part of it in the Wedding Cantata, *Gott ist unsre Zuversicht* (B. G. XIII, No. 3). One wishes that at any rate the bass aria "O du angenehmes Paar" might be restored to Christmas music, for there is no cradle song anywhere else like this. It is scored for bassoon, oboe and two muted violins*.

For the New Year Feast of 1730 Bach wrote the cantata *Gott, wie dein Name* (No. 171). Its vigorous opening chorus pleased him so greatly that he afterwards turned it into the *Patrem omnipotentem* of the B minor Mass. The figures in the two violins in the aria "Herr, so weit die Wolken gehen, gehet deines Namens Ruhm" ("Lord, the glory of Thy name goes as far as the clouds") interlock so charmingly that we seem to see the white strips of cloud trailing across the heavens. The final chorale, "Dein ist allein die Ehre", with the interludes for the wind instruments, ought to figure in every New Year service**.

The cantata for the third Sunday after Epiphany, *Ich*

---

* The aria might be inserted in some other Christmas cantata. Its original text runs thus:

"O! du angenehmer Schatz,
Hebe dich aus deinen Krippen,
Nimm davor auf meine Lippen
Und in meinem Herzen Platz."

The aria "Vergnügen und Lust" likewise comes from this Christmas cantata. The first part of the Wedding Cantata also seems to have been derived from some other source.

** The soprano aria "Fort und fort" is an adaptation of a number, "Angenehmer Zephyrus", from the secular cantata *Der zufriedengestellte Aeolus* (B. G. XI², p. 189 ff.).

steh' mit einem Fuss im Grabe (No. 156)*, gives a characteristic example of Bach's method of representing motion. In the introductory sinfonia the strings suggest the steps of a man going to the grave; the bass has continual variants of the motive —

In the aria the descent into the tomb is depicted by a syncopated form of this motive —

The upper strings repeat it constantly with all possible rhythmical nuances —

so as to express quite clearly the picture suggested in the words "I stand with one foot in the grave; soon will my sick body descend into it". We could imagine that Bach had before his eyes Pigalle's celebrated memorial to the Maréchale de Saxe at St. Thomas's, Strassburg, where the motion of the hero stepping into the sarcophagus is so wonderfully portrayed. In order to mitigate the rhythmical unrest, Bach accompanies the song with the chorale "Machs mit mir, Gott, nach deiner Güt'".

The introductory duet-arioso of the cantata for Quinquagesima, *Sehet, wir gehen hinauf nach Jerusalem* (No. 159)** is also founded on a "step" motive —

* Solo cantata for alto, tenor, and bass.
** Solo cantata for alto, tenor and bass.

The interruption after the interval of the seventh is very impressive: Jesus pauses in His walk, turns to the disciples, and tells them of His approaching death. In the interludes for the alto the reflective soul accompanies the Saviour on the way to the cross. A splendid bass aria ends the work, which has a finely conceived text.

The first chorus of the Easter cantata *So du mit deinem Munde bekennest Jesum, dass er der Herr sei* (No. 145) is one of the most interesting specimens of Bach's declamation. See, for example, how he brings out the word "Herr". We may assume that the *tutti* of the chorus enters at the final passage "so wirst du selig", where the orchestra breaks out into the "joy" motive*.

The cantata for Septuagesima, *Ich bin vergnügt* (No. 84) certainly belongs to the year 1731**. It consists of two magnificent arias, one of them founded on the same rhythm of felicity that expresses, in the cantata *Halt im Gedächtnis Jesum Christ* (No. 67), the words "Peace be unto you". In the second aria, "Ich esse mit Freuden mein wenig Brot" ("I eat my scanty bread with joy") the sentiment of cheerful carelessness is expressed in a merry dialogue between the oboe and the violin. The text of this fine cantata is an adaptation of Picander's "Ich bin vergnügt mit meinem Stande". Spitta thinks that it was originally composed as a piece of domestic religious music for Anna Magdalena.

The cantata for the second day in Whit, *Ich liebe den Höchsten von ganzem Gemüte* (No. 174) is also written for solo voices only. To compensate the hearers for the absence of the chorus, Bach uses the first movement of the third Brandenburg concerto (B. G. XIX, p. 59 ff.) as an introduction to the work. As the movement was originally written for strings only, he adds two obbligati horns and

* Spitta cites this cantata by its opening chorale, "Auf, mein Herz! des Herren Tag". The powerful "resurrection" theme of the duet "Ich lebe, mein Herze", is quoted on p. 81.

** Solo cantata for soprano.

three oboes, in the most effective way. The theme of the aria "Greift das Heil, ihr Glaubenshände" ("Seize upon salvation, ye hands of faith") is of deliberate rigidity, as it is meant to symbolise the steadfastness of faith —

The basses move along in steady quavers. The movement is animated by the interposition of the "joy" motive, the music thus really expressing the joyous confidence of faith of which the poem speaks.

We have a thematic sketch for the first chorus of the Michaelmas cantata *Man singet mit Freuden vom Sieg* (No. 149) on a leaf of the score of *Phoebus und Pan* (1731). As there was hardly time, however, to work out an original composition, Bach had recourse to the music of the last chorus of the Weimar secular cantata *Was mir behagt, ist nur die muntre Jagd* (B. G. XXIX, p. 29 ff.), to which he added the new text*. The duet "Seid wachsam, ihr heiligen Wächter, die Nacht ist schier dahin" is accompanied only by an obbligato bassoon. We seem to see strips of light flickering about in a deep twilight. The aria "Gottes Engel weichen nie" is a masterpiece of musical charm.

According to a note on the score, the introduction to the cantata for the twenty-first Sunday after Trinity, *Ich habe meine Zuversicht* (No. 188)** is to be an organ arrangement of the concerto for clavier and orchestra in D minor —

The organ has an obbligato part also in the final chorus.

---

* For a performance of the secular cantata the figured bass can be played as in the later arrangement.

** Solo cantata for soprano, alto, tenor and bass.

What prompted Bach to use the organ in this way? It was formerly supposed that it was just at this time that the *Rückpositiv* of the organ at St. Thomas's was fitted with a separate manual that allowed it to be played independently of the great organ. It was thought that Bach seized the opportunity to accompany on this manual the more difficult numbers in his cantatas and to add extra parts to them. This was Spitta's conjecture; he founded it on an account that showed that in 1730 fifty thalers were expended in repairing the organ, and he imagined that this money was devoted to providing the new manual. In the *Bachjahrbuch* for 1908, however, B. F. Richter shews that this view is wrong. The archives of the Town Council shew that the fifty thalers were expended merely on the cleaning and better voicing of the instrument. Moreover, if Richter's chronology is correct, the cantatas with the obbligato organ part were not performed at St. Thomas's, but at St. Nicholas's. Bach therefore wrote them to give the organist of that church, Johann Schneider, whom he esteemed highly, an opportunity to display his art.

Besides the cantata *Ich habe meine Zuversicht* (No. 188) he wrote, about the same time, seven other cantatas for obbligato organ.*

If we come to these works with special expectations we are to some extent disappointed. In the first place they contain many movements that have been taken from

* *Erschallet, ihr Lieder* (No. 172; Whitsuntide): this is an arrangement of an earlier work (see p. 162); *Geist und Seele wird verwirret* (No. 35; twelfth Sunday after Trinity; solo cantata for alto); *Gott soll allein mein Herze haben* (No. 169; eighteenth Sunday after Trinity; solo cantata for alto); *Ich geh' und suche mit Verlangen* (No. 49; twentieth Sunday after Trinity; solo cantata for soprano and bass); *Wir danken dir, Gott* (No. 29; *Ratswahl* cantata for the 27th August 1731); *Wer weiss wie nahe mir mein Ende* (No. 27; sixteenth Sunday after Trinity); *Vergnügte Ruh, beliebte Seelenlust* (No. 170; sixth Sunday after Trinity; solo cantata for alto). See B. F. Richter's article *Über Seb. Bachs Cantaten mit obligater Orgel*, in the *Bachjahrbuch* for 1908, pp. 49—63. For further light on the problem see the section on the figured bass parts in the last chapter of the present book.

the instrumental works. Most of the pieces for organ and orchestra are derived from clavier concertos*. Even some of the arias are derived from instrumental movements. The aria "Stirb in mir", for example, from the cantata *Gott soll allein mein Herze haben* (No. 169) is merely the Siciliano of the clavier concerto in E major, to which Bach has added a vocal part. The arrangement is most masterly; but the music does not sound well, however fine it looks on paper. The cantata *Geist und Seele wird verwirret* (No. 35) is wholly made up out of previous instrumental movements, of the *provenance* of which, however, we cannot now be sure. This seems to be the case also with the numbers of the cantata *Ich geh' und suche mit Verlangen* (No. 49) in which the "concertising" organ is employed. Even the duet "Dich hab ich je und je geliebet" is a rearrangement, as may be seen from the imperfect declamation:

Dich hab'— ich je— und je— ge - lie - bet.

The alto aria "Willkommen will ich sagen", from the cantata *Wer weiss wie nahe mir mein Ende* (No. 27) is also anything but a model in this respect.

The solo cantata for alto, *Vergnügte Ruh, beliebte Seelenlust* (No. 170), seems to be composed mostly of original matter. The trio accompaniment to the aria "Wie jammern mich doch" is very interesting; the organ plays in two parts, and the united violins and violas take the third.

* The cantata *Ich habe meine Zuversicht* (No. 188) has for overture the D minor concerto, which itself is merely an arrangement of a violin concerto; the sinfonia of the cantata *Gott soll allein mein Herze haben* (No. 167) derives from the clavier concerto in E major; the finale of the same concerto becomes the sinfonia of the cantata *Ich geh' und suche mit Verlangen* (No. 49); the prelude to the *Ratswahl* cantata *Wir danken dir, Gott* (No. 29) is an arrangement of the first movement of the suite in E major for solo violin.

There is no bass foundation. It is unfortunate that the text of this work is utterly unsatisfactory.

The disappointing effect of these cantatas comes, however, from the way in which Bach has introduced the organ. It plays in two parts only. As the lower part is identical with the orchestral bass, it has really only one obbligato part, which runs from beginning to end with hardly an interruption. This quite uninteresting employment of the organ is not what we expect from Bach. There is no dramatic alternation between organ and orchestra, or any use of the effect to be derived from the opposition of the two so characteristic *timbres*. We ask ourselves how the master who, in his preludes and fugues, has revealed the special polyphony of the organ in all its richness, could here allot it so subordinate a task; and we are astounded that he did not think of making use, if only occasionally, of the effects derivable from the combination of organ and orchestra.

This does not imply that the works cannot be made effective. The preludes to *Gott soll allein mein Herze haben* (No. 169) and *Wir danken dir, Gott* (No. 29), for example, sound extremely well on the organ with a clear registration, with some silvery mixtures. In the accompaniment to the arias, however, the organ is less satisfactory, since it really only replaces a flute, and that not very profitably. Even the uncritical hearer feels, after a few bars, the inexpressiveness of this accompaniment.

Besides the "concertising" organ there was of course the great organ, which accompanied and played the figured bass. Thus the cantatas for obbligato organ really require two organs. Where only one is available, the "concertising" one must also play the figured basses. In this case it will be best to give the bass part to the pedal, and play the chords with the left hand and the obbligato part with the right. When Bach gave these cantatas at St. Nicholas's, where the *Rückpositiv* was not available, both organ parts would have to be played on one instrument. We know positively that this was the case with the *Ratswahl* cantata *Wir danken dir, Gott* (No. 29). We have a text-book for a later performance of the work at St. Nicholas's, in 1749. The first chorus is one of those in which he writes in a simple style resembling that of Handel. Whether the aria "Gedenk an uns" is or is not derived from the Siciliano of some instrumental concerto cannot now be settled.

The chorus of the cantata *Wer weiss wie nahe mir mein Ende* (No. 27) is very impressive. The strings and the bass illustrate the words "Hin geht die Zeit" ("Time passes away") by means of the rhythm of a slow inexorable pendulum —

Mingled with the choral voices as they sing of this flight of time are the wailing sighs of the oboes*.

The accompaniment to the final aria, "Gute Nacht, du Weltgetümmel" ("Good night, thou tumult of the world") is symphonic in character. The words "Gute Nacht" and "Weltgetümmel" are illustrated alternately, the former by means of a tranquil theme, the latter by means of the familiar "tumult" motive. The movement thus runs on exactly the same lines as the aria "Friede sei mit euch", from the cantata *Halt im Gedächtnis Jesum Christ* (No. 67).

In the end the obbligato use of the organ does not seem in the long run to have satisfied Bach himself; he wrote no more cantatas of this kind.

About the beginning of the thirties, too, he seems to have become conscious of the inadequacy of his cantata texts. He goes back to the chorale cantata. Picander first of

* Time is symbolised by pendulum-beats, again, in the cantata *Alles nur nach Gottes Willen* (No. 72). See p. 198.

all tries to effect a compromise between the free "modern" cantata and the chorale cantata, and to persuade Bach to compose texts in which the chorale verses are joined together by free poems. He interrupts, for example, the first verse of *Wer weiss wie nahe mir mein Ende* (No. 27) with contemplative recitatives. In the cantata for the fifth Sunday after Trinity, *Wer nur den lieben Gott lässt walten* (No. 93) he adopted this procedure in two verses of the hymn. One of them is couched in this form:

Recitative with chorale.

"What help to us are all our heavy cares?
. . . . *They only oppress the heart with a thousand pains and sorrows.*
What help to us are all our sighs of woe?
. . . . *They bring us only dire calamity.*"

Bach here treats the melody as Picander has treated the text. The themes of the soli are all formed out of the first notes of the *cantus firmus*. Even the volatile motive that expresses gay *insouciance* in the aria "Man halte nur ein wenig stille" is derived from the commencement of the melody —

The device may be very ingenious, but it gives no artistic satisfaction. It amounts to a disfigurement of the melody, and negates Bach's most individual principle; nowhere else does he handle the chorale verses in this way.

He gets a particularly fine effect in the chorus by first of all giving out each line in free style in a couple of voices, and then bringing in the whole choir with the same line. In the recitative "Was helfen uns die schweren Sorgen" the bass figure seems to be crushed under a heavy mass —*

* The "joy" motive of the basses in the aria "Er kennt die rechten Freudenstunden" is given on p. 112.

Yet Bach does not seem to have found much pleasure in this hybrid cantata. He now turns again to the simple chorale cantata. We have fifteen of these that appear to date from that epoch*. Some can be attributed with certainty to this period by reason of the quality of their organ parts, the arias and recitatives not being figured,

* 1. *Christus der ist mein Leben* (No. 95, for the sixteenth Sunday after Trinity).
2. *Der Herr ist mein getreuer Hirt* (No. 112, for the second Sunday after Easter).
3. *Ein' feste Burg ist unser Gott* (No. 80, for the Reformation festival).
4. *Es ist das Heil uns kommen her* (No. 9, for the sixth Sunday after Trinity).
5. *Gelobet sei der Herr* (No. 129, for Trinity Sunday).
6. *Ich ruf zu dir, Herr Jesu Christ* (No. 177, for the fourth Sunday after Trinity).
7. *In allen meinen Taten* (No. 97, for no fixed Sunday; perhaps used also as a wedding cantata).
8. *Lobe den Herren* (No. 137, for the twelfth Sunday after Trinity).
9. *Nun komm' der Heiden Heiland* (2nd composition, No. 62, for the first Sunday in Advent).
10. *Sei Lob und Ehr* (No. 117, for no fixed Sunday).
11. *Wachet auf, ruft uns die Stimme* (No. 140, for the twenty-seventh Sunday after Trinity).
12. *Was willst du dich betrüben* (No. 107, for the seventh Sunday after Trinity).
13. *Was Gott tut, das ist wohlgetan* (1st composition, No. 98, for the twenty-first Sunday after Trinity).
14. *Was Gott tut, das ist wohlgetan* (2nd composition, No. 99, for the fifteenth Sunday after Trinity).
15. *Was Gott tut, das ist wohlgetan* (3rd composition, No. 100).

The opening chorus of the third arrangement of *Was Gott tut, das ist wohlgetan* is identical with that of the second. The third arrangement was probably used as a wedding cantata. The first two seem to have been composed at periods not far removed from each other. Another chorale cantata, *Nun danket alle Gott* (No. 191, B. G. XLI) exists only in an incomplete form. The overture-form employed in the opening chorus of the cantata *In allen meinen Taten* (No. 97) makes it probable that it is based on a Weimar or Cöthen cantata.

but marked *Tacet**. This does not mean that the organ did not co-operate here, but simply that the player on the great organ ceased, and Bach played the accompaniment from the score on the separate positive. When the cantatas were repeated at St. Nicholas's, however, he had to supply the figuring in the chief organ parts, and he figured the *continuo* in full from the beginning. But at St. Thomas's he would, as before, accompany the solos on his positive.

All these cantatas have splendid choruses, especially *Was Gott tut, das ist wohlgetan* (No. 99), *Sei Lob und Ehr* (No. 117), *Lobe den Herrn* (No. 137), and *Gelobet sei der Herr* (No. 129). The last-named cantata has also a final chorale with an imposing accompaniment. These choruses all follow the same type. The soprano takes the *cantus firmus*, and the other voices the figuration. There is an independent orchestral accompaniment, though the motives of it are reminiscent of the chorale melody.

Here Bach's inexhaustible faculty of invention is plainly evident. He can write a number of choruses on the same principle, and yet give each of them such individuality that the similarity seems only destined to bring out more sharply the characteristic features of each of them. The arias in these cantatas are not so pleasing. Bach is contending with impossible texts. In a number of cases he tries to compose recitatives and arias to chorale verses. In this, however, he is unsuccessful; the regular form of the strophe is opposed to the plan of the aria; and its uniform metre admits of no proper theme. It goes without saying, also, that the strophic aria is wearisomely long**.

At other times Bach employs texts that are written round a chorale strophe; there are also free verses, though these do not appear to be by Picander, as they are remarkably heavy and unsuitable for music.

---

* See Nos. 97, 99, 129, and 177.

** The chorale strophes in cantatas Nos. 97, 100, 107, 112, 117, 129, 137, and 177 are composed in the form of arias and recitatives.

Thus few of the solo numbers of these cantatas make an immediate effect on the hearer. One of the very finest is the alto aria "Ich will dich all mein Leben lang, o Gott, von nun an ehren", in the cantata *Sei Lob und Ehr* (No. 117). In the bass aria in *Was Gott tut, das ist wohlgetan* (No. 100) the music in itself is splendid, but the declamation is somewhat banal; its faults are all the more noticeable as the declamation of the following alto aria is of a perfection rarely attained even by Bach.

The solos of these chorale cantatas are, however, extraordinarily rich in "characteristic" pictorial music. In the bass aria of the cantata *Was willst du dich betrüben* (No. 107) the solo violin has a series of wild scale passages, the tempo of which Bach has placed beyond doubt by his marking of *vivace*. The text runs thus: "Auf ihn magst du es wagen . . . du wirst mit ihm erjagen, was dir ist nütz und gut" ("Thou mayst venture on it with Him . . . thou wilt win with Him what is good for thee"). This example shows how, when Bach is fascinated by an image, he cannot resist the temptation to illustrate it, and for the sake of this he will pass over the general mood of the poem that he ought to be expressing in his music. The following tenor aria "Wenn auch gleich aus der Höllen der Satan wollte sich dir selbst entgegenstellen" ("Even though Satan himself should rise from hell and oppose thee") gives him an opportunity to depict the contortions of the body of the huge dragon —

The text of the aria "Leg ich mich späte nieder, erwache frühe wieder" ("I lay me down late, and awaken early"), in the cantata *In allen meinen Taten* (No. 97) is expressed by a motive suggestive of sinking down and rising again —*

If the majority of these chorale cantatas do not make an effective whole, the fault lies in the texts, which consist of a string of strophes without any inner dramatic coherence, and without sufficient musical distinction between them. Moreover there are too many strophes in most of the chorales. Cantatas worked out on these chorale lines require short hymns, in which every verse suggests a different musical characterisation. These ideal chorales are very few in number. When, however, Bach finds a text of this order, we get a dramatic art-work of the most perfect kind imaginable, as in the cantatas *Ein' feste Burg* (No. 80) and *Wachet auf, ruft uns die Stimme* (No. 140).

Ein' feste Burg was probably written for the Reformation festival of 1730; as this happened to be the bicentenary of the delivery of the Augsburg Confession, the festival was a particularly brilliant one. In the first chorus Bach builds up the "stronghold sure" on mighty lines, symbolising it by a gigantic choral fugue in the style of Pachelbel. Each of the separate fugues ends with a canon with the theme in augmentation, reaching from the pedal trombones of the organ to the trumpets of the orchestra. The movement runs to two hundred and twenty-eight bars.

In the second verse the fight on our behalf of the man whom God has chosen is depicted by the familiar "tumult" motive"—

---

* The extravagant "joy" motive of the first aria in the cantata *Gelobet sei der Herr* is quoted on p. 113. For the "tumult" motive of the aria "Streite, siege, starker Held", in the cantata *Nun komm der Heiden Heiland* (No. 62), see p. 91; and for the illustration of the text of "Wir waren schon zu tief gesunken", in the cantata *Es ist das Heil uns kommen her* (No. 9) see p. 83.

The sopranos join in with the chorale verse "Mit unsrer Macht ist nichts getan" ("With our own strength we can do nothing"), as if calling the hero to their aid; he answers with the song of triumph "Alles, was von Gott geboren, ist zum Siegen auserkoren" ("Everything that is born of God is chosen for victory").

The third strophe depicts the assault of the devil on the citadel of God. There peals out a signal formed from the opening notes of the melody, whereupon a host of horrid contorted bodies throws itself on the walls —

They mount, sink back again, recover themselves once more, again make the assault, again fall back into the depths — a wildly agitated mass, of the kind that Bach has painted also in the cantata *Es erhub sich ein Streit* (No. 19). Every now and then we hear shattering trumpet fanfares. From the battlements rings out the exultant song of the faithful:

> "Und wenn die Welt voll Teufel wär,
> Und wollt uns gar verschlingen,
> So fürchten wir uns nicht so sehr . . . ."

After a final effort the furious assault falls to pieces. This chorale verse is framed between the mystical movements "Komm in mein Herzenshaus" and "Wie selig sind doch die", from the Weimar cantata *Alles was von Gott geboren**.

* This cantata was intended for the third Sunday in Lent. Bach was unable to use it in Leipzig, as no cantatas were given there during the Passion time.

Lutheranism and mysticism — this was the confession of faith that the cantor of St. Thomas's brought to the Reformation festival.

The cantata *Wachet auf, ruft uns die Stimme* (No. 140) deals with the parable of the ten virgins, — the Gospel for the twenty-seventh Sunday after Trinity. This Sunday comes into the church year only when Easter falls very early; as a rule there are only twenty-six Sundays after Trinity.

The first chorus depicts the awakening. All is animation; the bridegroom comes; the virgins start up in dismay from their slumber, one raising the other —

In this chorus we can see very clearly the changes that have come over our conception of Bach's music. Julius Stockhausen, of Frankfort, used to bring in the orchestra *pianissimo* and work it up through a slow *crescendo*, as if distant noises were gradually coming nearer. Siegfried Ochs begins *forte* and with a very quick tempo, so as to suggest the sudden confusion caused by the "Wachet auf!" ("Awake!"). This is certainly the right way. To get the proper effect, the syncopated notes in the mounting semiquaver passages should be thrown into high relief. There need be hardly any fear of overdoing it; the more vehement the accents, the more clearly will the hearer apprehend the meaning of the motive*.

The second verse, "Zion hört die Wächter singen" ("Zion hears the watchmen singing"), is dominated by a simple dance melody —

* Spitta (II, 460) thinks that the semiquaver motive expresses "a feeling of mysterious bliss", that "overflows again and again in happy and expressive passages".

With this the chorale melody is combined dissonantly, as if it had nothing to do with it; the cry of the watchmen strikes into the music of the procession that is drawing nigh with the bridegroom. In order that this may have its proper rural quality, it is written for the strings *unisono*, with an accompaniment in the contrabasses*.

The procession arrives. In the festive hall the "Gloria sei dir gesungen" ("Glory now to thee be given") is sung. The foolish virgins are left outside in the night, in despair.

Not until Berlioz shall we meet with any dramatic-pictorial music comparable to this.

The middle verse of the chorale is framed between two mystical dialogues between Jesus and the soul. The consummate quality of these seems to point, like the contemplative parts of the cantata *Ein' feste Burg*, to an origin in the Weimar period.

These two cantatas taught Bach the advantage of short chorales for the composition of chorale cantatas. The idea now occurred to him to compile a chorale text out of characteristic stanzas from various hymns, and, in the cantata *Christus der ist mein Leben* (No. 95)** to employ chorales that express different aspects of death. The first of these —

"Christus der ist mein Leben,
Sterben ist mein Gewinn,"

---

* Of course the organ harmonies must be filled in. The chorale should be sung by several tenors, not a soloist; the text is "Zion hears the *watchmen* singing". According to Spitta "the mystical tone of the cantata here finds its fullest expression". He thinks "it is like the dance of the souls in bliss".

** For the sixteenth Sunday after Trinity.

speaks of the lassitude of death. The orchestra accompanies it with a melancholy funeral lullaby*, in which is interwoven a figure expressive of deep longing —

A recitative, "Mit Freuden will ich von hinnen scheiden" ("With joy I will depart"), during which the lullaby dies away, leads into the chorale "Mit Fried' und Freud' fahr ich dahin" ("With joy and peace I go thither"), in which the melody confidently wends its way above the quietly moving quavers in the bass. Then the sopranos** sing the joyous hymn of parting from the world, "Valet will ich dir geben" ("Farewell do I bid thee") the oboes accompanying it with a "joy" motive of almost excessive exuberance —

The figures in the basses symbolise the "Hinauf steht mein Begier" ("My longing is for heaven").

The same joyous mood in the face of death is expressed in the splendid tenor aria "Ach schlage doch bald, schlage doch bald, sel'ge Stunde!" ("Ah, strike soon, thou blessed hour"), the pizzicato of the strings giving a wonderful effect of distant bells. Bach's careful marking of the nuances here should be especially noted.

This beautiful cantata, with its simple choruses, is very seldom performed, for which Spitta's unjust estimate of it is probably answerable, — though perhaps the ex-

* The motive of this lullaby is quoted on p. 94.

** It is quite wrong to give the *cantus firmus* to a soloist, who cannot make herself heard above all the oboes and violins.

traordinary technical demands that the tenor aria makes on the singer may have something to do with it.

For the festival of the delivery of the Augsburg confession, which was lavishly celebrated in the Leipzig churches on the 25th, 26th, and 27th June, Bach did not write any new cantatas. He had recourse to the New Year cantata of 1724, *Singet dem Herrn ein neues Lied* (No. 190)*, and the two *Ratswahl* cantatas, *Gott, man lobt dich in der Stille* (No. 120)** and *Wünschet Jerusalem Glück*. The latter is lost. This was the time of Bach's conflict with the Council. Perhaps the disgusted frame of mind he was in accounts for him not having written a new work for the festival. He thus did not contribute any musical celebration to the two centenary feasts of the Reformed Church that came during his life-time. On the occasion of the bi-centenary of the beginning of the Reformation (31st October 1717), he had been in disgrace with the Duke of Weimar, and so the composition of the festival cantata had not been entrusted to him.

Closely related to the chorale cantatas are the chorale dialogues *O Ewigkeit, du Donnerwort* (No. 60)***, and *Ach Gott, wie manches Herzeleid* (No. 58)†.

The first of these is concerned with Fear and Hope. Fear (alto) sings the chorale "O Ewigkeit, du Donnerwort" ("Oh Eternity, thou awful word"), the orchestra painting its trembling. Then we hear the consoling voice of Hope (bass), reiterating incessantly "Herr, ich warte auf dein Heil" ("Lord, I wait for Thy salvation"). Both

---

* See p. 155.

** This cantata is partly identical with the mourning cantatas *Herr Gott, Beherrscher aller Dinge* (B. G. XIII[1]). The chorus "Jauchzet ihr erfreuten Stimmen", with its clear-cut motive of joy, is particularly beautiful.

*** Second composition, in D major. Solo cantata for alto, tenor and bass, for the twenty-fourth Sunday after Trinity (1732?).

† In C major. Solo cantata for soprano and bass, for the Sunday after New Year (1733?). In the B. G. edition it is called the second composition, although that in A major is perhaps later.

proceed along the road to death: "O schwerer Gang zum letzten Kampf und Streite" ("Oh saddest way to the last combat") ... "Mein letztes Lager will mich schrecken" ("I dread my last resting-place") laments the despairing soul, the passionately agitated orchestra adding a motive that reminds us of Peter's aria of despair in the *St. John Passion.* Hope sings consolingly "Mich wird des Heilands Hand bedecken" ("The hand of the Redeemer will protect me"). At the finish we hear the voice of the Holy Ghost in a wonderful arioso, "Selig sind die Toten, die in dem Herrn sterben, von nun an!" ("Blessed are the dead that die in the Lord, from now henceforth"). The cantata ends with Rudolf Ahle's beautiful hymn "Es ist genug, Herr, wenn es dir gefällt" ("Thy will, oh Lord, be done").

The other dialogue, *Ach Gott, wie manches Herzeleid* (No. 58) is constructed on similar lines. The opening duet, "Ach Gott, wie manches Herzeleid begegnet mir zu dieser Zeit ... Geduld, mein Herze! Geduld!") ("Ah Lord, how much sorrow of heart is now mine ... Be patient, my heart, be patient!") reproduces the musical mood of "Mein letztes Lager will mich schrecken". The marking of *adagio* must not tempt us to take the movement too slowly and too softly. The instrumental accompaniment must flame and glow with suppressed despair*. The final duet, on the other hand, cannot sound too joyful, notwithstanding the chorale "Ich hab' vor mir ein' schwere Reis' zu dir ins Himmelsparadies" ("I have a grievous journey before me to Thee in paradise"); the orchestra, in union with the voices, "Nur getrost, getrost, ihr Herzen! Hier ist Angst, dort Herrlichkeit" ("Be of good cheer, oh hearts! Here is anguish, there is glory") must dominate the lament. Note the animated steps of the basses, violas,

* All movements of this kind must be played heavily. The duet in cantata No. 60, "Mein letztes Lager will mich schrecken", again, is usually taken in such a way that the music does not express terror at all. On the problem of these duets see p. 98.

and second violins hastening joyously to the "Himmels-paradies", with the semiquavers of the first violins streaming before them.

If the idea of these two dialogues came from Picander, he did Bach's muse a great service. There is no mistaking the enthusiasm with which they have been written.

The unusually large number of Bach's solo cantatas at this time is easily explained by the poor state of the St. Thomas choir at the beginning of the thirties. With the two chorale dialogues we have eleven of these solo cantatas. Two of them are soprano cantatas, — *Falsche Welt, dir trau ich nicht* (No. 52), for the twenty-third Sunday after Trinity, and *Jauchzet Gott in allen Landen* (No. 51), for the fifteenth Sunday after Trinity.

The introduction to *Falsche Welt, dir trau ich nicht* is taken from the first Brandenburg concerto (B. G. XIX). The accompaniment to the first aria, "Immerhin, wenn ich gleich verstossen bin" ("Ever when I am cast off") is very characteristic. It illustrates the word "verstossen" in the most drastic style imaginable —

In the joyous theme of the final aria, "Ich halt' es mit dem lieben Gott, die Welt mag nur alleine bleiben" ("My part is with my dear Lord, I need not the world"), the music reminds us that it is the rejected one who has now found happiness in God.

The cantata *Jauchzet Gott in allen Landen* (No. 51) is a brilliant and spirited piece of *coloratura* for soprano and trumpet, the instrumental theme of the first aria being in this style —

For the last aria Bach uses the chorale "Sei Lob und Preis mit Ehren", the alleluia of which becomes a concerto for soprano and trumpet with orchestral accompaniment. All sopranos interested in Bach are recommended to practise this cantata daily. Its full effect, however, is obtainable only when it is sung by a clear boy's voice*.

The best known of the solo cantatas for alto is *Schlage doch, gewünschte Stunde* (No. 53). Strictly speaking it is not a cantata, but a "mourning aria", as it is called on the title-page of the old manuscript in which it has come down to us. As Bach employs two bells in this work, Forkel thinks that "it does not belong to the period of his purified taste."**

The other alto cantata, *Widerstehe doch der Sünde* (No. 54)*** begins with an alarming chord of the seventh —

The trembling of the basses and violas, and the sighs of the violins, between them give the movement a somewhat disturbing effect. It is meant to depict the horror of the curse upon sin that is threatened in the text. Of a similar character is the aria "Wer Sünde tut, der ist

* There exists another version of the text of this cantata, running thus, "Jauchzet Gott in allen Landen! Mit den Engeln lasst uns heut' unserm Gott ein Loblied singen", — which indicates that Bach at some time or other used this music for Michaelmas.

** Forkel, p. 62.

*** The copy does not state for which Sunday this cantata was intended.

vom Teufel" ("The sinner is of the devil"). It is a strict trio between the voice, the violas and the violins. The theme runs thus —

Harmonically the movement is of unparalleled harshness.

The opening aria of the solo cantata for tenor, *Ich armer Mensch, ich Sündenknecht* (No. 55) is, as a rule, phrased so inanimately that the whole sense of the despairing wail is lost. The characteristic accent should fall on the second beat. The orchestra must phrase thus —

This passage —

should be played with a strong *crescendo*, the last quaver being always heavily accented in contradiction to the beat, thus obstructing the rhythm, as it were. This motive belongs to the words "Ich geh' vor Gottes Angesicht mit Furcht und Zittern zum Gerichte" ("I go in fear and trembling into the presence of God"). It suggests painful striving, as in the theme of the introduction to the cantata *Herr, gehe nicht ins Gericht* (No. 105), of which it strongly reminds us*.

Finally the motive —

* See p. 189.

should also be phrased in opposition to the natural beat, the accent falling on the up-take quaver after the rest. The movement is only properly played when every suggestion of the charming $^6/_8$ rhythm is gone; the impression must be one of urgent unrest.

In the opening aria of the solo cantata for bass, *Ich will den Kreuzstab gerne tragen* (No. 56)*, it is doubtful whether we should accent thus —

The natural verbal accent indicates the latter. The first, however, is more characteristic, as it brings out the whole extent and all the severity of the ascending line by emphasising the final syncopated note**. For the rest, the accompaniment is wholly formed of the motive of transfigured grief. Perhaps the number is generally taken in rather too slow a tempo, so destroying the contrast with the final "Da leg' ich den Kummer auf einmal ins Grab" ("Then suddenly I lay my sorrow in the grave").

The fine "wave" motive*** that accompanies the recitative-arioso "Mein Wandel auf der Welt ist einer Schiffahrt gleich" ("My course on earth is like a voyage") does not make its full effect when given to a solo violoncello. It comes out calmly and clearly if a bassoon and a viola are added. In the *tutti* passages of the final aria, "Endlich, endlich wird mein Joch" ("At last, at last, is my yoke"), it is as well to add the violins to the oboe, so that the theme may give voice to all its ungovernable joy.

This is one of the most splendid of Bach's works. It makes unparalleled demands, however, on the dramatic

---

* For the nineteenth Sunday after Trinity.

** The distinction is of course only slight, as both the C sharp and the D are accented. The effect of the difference in accentuation between the orchestra and the singer is not displeasing.

*** Quoted on p. 75.

imagination of the singer who would depict convincingly this transition from the resigned expectation of death to the jubilant longing for death.

The bass cantata for the Purification of Mary, *Ich habe genug* (No. 82) also has death for its theme. It depicts the heavenly home-sickness of the old man who is already detached from all the things of this world. Inexpressible joy wells forth from the semiquaver passage with which the orchestra, in the first aria, accompanies the voice and the arabesques of the oboe. Then follows the glorious death-lullaby, "Schlummert ein, ihr matten Augen; fallet sanft und selig zu" ("Slumber now, weary eyes; close softly and happily") —

Here again, however, the last expression is that of ecstatic joy, that suddenly finds voice in the aria "Ich freue mich auf meinen Tod" ("I rejoice in my death").

Bach also transcribed this cantata for soprano, perhaps with a view to his wife singing it in their domestic concerts. He wrote the aria "Schlummert ein" in her *Klavierbüchlein* of 1725, only noting, however, the voice part in full. He would himself add a free accompaniment in performance.

We have a typical specimen of Bach's system of musical illustration in the cantata *Siehe, ich will Fischer aussenden* (No. 88)*. The orchestra accompanies the first half of the verse with flowing "wave" motives, as if to conjure up before the hearer the placidly heaving lake on which the fishers are embarking; at the words "Und danach will

---

* Jeremiah XVI, 16. Solo cantata for soprano, alto, tenor and bass, for the fifth Sunday after Trinity. It is also interesting to see that Bach accompanies the arioso "Fürchte dich nicht, denn von nun an wirst du Menschen fangen" ("Fear not, for from henceforth shalt thou be fishers of men", with the "joy" motive. See p. 112.

ich viel Jäger aussenden, die sollen sie fangen auf allen Bergen" ("And after will I send for many hunters, and they shall hunt them from every mountain and from every hill") this accompaniment suddenly ceases, and the horns strike in with gay fanfares.

One of the most perfect specimens of Bach's mood-painting is to be seen in the accompaniment to the first aria of the cantata *Was soll ich aus dir machen, Ephraim* (No. 89)*. The text is founded on Hosea XI, 8, and runs thus —

> "Was soll ich aus dir machen, Ephraim?
> Soll ich dich schützen, Israel?
> Soll ich nicht billig ein Adama aus dir machen,
> Und dich wie Zeboim zurichten?
> Aber mein Herz ist andern Sinnes;
> Meine Barmherzigkeit ist zu brünstig!"

("How shall I give thee up, Ephraim? How shall I deliver thee, Israel? How shall I make thee as Admah? How shall I set thee as Zeboim? Mine heart is turned within me; My repentings are kindled together.")**

This text is reproduced by means of three themes. The first, in the bass, symbolises the wrath of God —

The oboes give out wails and sighs —

* Solo cantata for alto, tenor and bass, for the twenty-second Sunday after Trinity.

** Admah and Zeboim were cities destroyed with Sodom.

The sorrowful question is put by the violins —

As these motives interwine and interpenetrate each other without coming to any conclusion, so God's heart is distracted by contradictory thoughts upon Israel.

That the theme in the violins is meant to suggest the sorrowful question is proved by the first chorus of the cantata *Ich elender Mensch, wer wird mich erlösen von dem Leibe dieses Todes?* (No. 48), where the orchestral accompaniment is constructed upon a theme that is almost identical with that of "Was soll ich aus dir machen, Ephraim?"

The first chorus of the cantata *Ich glaube, lieber Herr, hilf meinem Unglauben* (No. 109)*, is a marvel of polyphonic declamation. The distressful anxiety of the words is most movingly expressed. The aria "Wie zweifelhaftig ist mein Hoffen, wie wanket mein geängstigt Herz" ("How uncertain is my hope, how my anxious heart doth falter") is wholly taken up with the representation of some one walking uncertainly**. For this purpose Bach employs the heavy rhythm —

by means of which, in the aria "Komm süsses Kreuz", in the *St. Matthew Passion,* he depicts the man staggering under the weight of the cross. The cantata ends with the simply figured chorale "Wer hofft in Gott" ("He whose hope is in God") the peculiar tense orchestral accompaniment to which is probably intended to symbolise the certainty of the hope.

---

* For the twenty-first Sunday after Trinity.
** See p 93.

In the first chorus of the cantata *Herr, deine Augen sehen nach dem Glauben* (No. 102)* Bach gives a particular characterisation to each of the three sections of the text, so that the movement, apart from the final summary, is really composed of three choruses. Some idea of the splendid acerbity of this music may be had from the theme of the middle section, "Du schlägest sie, aber sie fühlen nicht" ("Thou smitest them, but they feel it not") —

The bass aria "Verachtest du den Reichtum seiner Gnade" ("If thou dost scorn the riches of His grace") begins with the leap of a seventh —

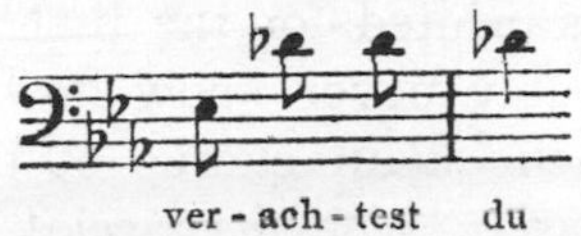

The orchestral accompaniment of the first chorus of the cantata *Es ist nichts Gesundes an meinem Leibe . . . und ist kein Friede in meinen Gebeinen* ("There is no soundness in my body . . . and no rest in my bones") (No. 25)** is constructed out of a series of sighs —

while the trombones, cornets and flutes play the chorale "Ach Herr, mich armen Sünder" ("Lord, I, a wretched sinner") in five parts.

The bass theme that accompanies the aria "Ach, wo hol' ich Armer Rat" ("Ah, where shall I, miserable one, find counsel") is interesting in that it reproduces exactly the

* For the tenth Sunday after Trinity.
** For the fourteenth Sunday after Trinity.

same hurried and faltering steps as we have in the theme of the aria "Ach, nun ist mein Jesus hin", in the *St. Matthew Passion.*

The final aria, "Öffne meinen schlechten Liedern", is dominated by a beautiful colloquy between the strings and oboes on the one side and the three flutes on the other.

At a performance of this work the recitative in which Picander compares the world to a hospital should be cut out. It goes beyond all endurable limits of tastelessness*.

The two cantatas last mentioned, — Nos. 102 and 25 — were performed by Emmanuel at Hamburg .. after he had corrected his father's errors. His revisions have been preserved; they do not throw a very favourable light on the understanding of Bach by his sons. In this partly disfigured form the cantata *Herr, deine Augen sehen nach dem Glauben* was printed for the first time in 1830.

We shall probably never know how Bach could bring himself to turn the main chorus of this cantata into a *Kyrie*, the alto aria "Weh der Seele!" into a *Qui tollis*, and the tenor aria "Erschrecke doch" into a *Quoniam tu solus***. More barbarous perversions cannot be imagined.

The blue sky seems to hang over the Ascension cantata *Wer da glaubet und getauft wird* (No. 37). It can easily be imagined how, in the final aria, Bach translates into musical motives the words "Der Glaube schafft der Seele Flügel, dass sie sich in den Himmel schwingt" ("Faith gives the soul wings that it may soar to heaven").

---

* Die ganze Welt ist nur ein Hospital, wo Menschen von unzählbar grosser Zahl
Und auch die Kinder in der Wiegen an Krankheit hart danieder liegen.
Den einen quälet in der Brust ein hitz'ges Fieber böser Lust;
Der andre lieget krank an eig'ner Ehre hässlichem Gestank;
Den dritten zehrt die Geldsucht ab und stürzt ihn vor der Zeit ins Grab ...

** See the small Masses in G minor and F major (B. G. VIII).

CHAPTER XXX.

THE SECULAR CANTATAS.

B. G. XI, Part II. (1861).
B. G. XX, Part II. (1870).
B. G. XXIX. (1879.)
B. G. XXXIV. (1884.)

The master of the secular cantatas was consigned to even longer oblivion than the master of the church cantata. Forkel knew only the Peasant Cantata*. The publication of the Bachgesellschaft edition brought to light several works of whose existence no one had had any notion. How many more must be irrevocably lost! Still we possess enough secular cantatas — about twenty — to be able to rejoice in the other side of Bach's genius.

His first secular cantata originated in the Weimar period. It is entitled *Was mir behagt, ist nur die muntre Jagd***; it was performed on 23rd February 1716, on which day Duke Christian von Sachsen-Weissenfels celebrated his fifty-third birthday by a great hunting party. Bach's master, Duke Ernst Wilhelm, was invited, and surprised his friend with a "fine table-music". The cantata was "musicized" during the banquet in the gamekeeper's lodge; Duke Christian would have probably found it hard to believe that the cantata would do more to preserve his name for future ages than all his own sovereign acts.

Bach evidently worked at it *con amore*. The text is by Salomo Franck, the secretary of the upper consistory at Weimar, for whose sacred cantata poems Bach had a high regard***. In accordance with the taste of the time, the poet goes back to mythology, making sundry great and

---

* Forkel, p. 62.

** B. G. XXIX, p. 3 ff.

*** It is printed in Franck's *Geistliche und Weltliche Poesien*, Part II, Jena 1716.

small gods pay their homage to the object of the day's celebration. The theme of the text is as follows. Endymion feels himself to be slighted by Diana, his beloved, and reproaches her. She makes the excuse that today she must follow the chase, and give her favourite hero Christian a congratulatory kiss, — to which arrangement Endymion has no objection. They are reconciled, and together sing the praises of the great sovereign. To give the work the necessary musical variety, the Pan of the country and Pales, the goddess of the flocks, are added, — which makes a cantata of half-a-dozen recitatives, eight arias, and two choruses.

The music is uncommonly expressive and of captivating freshness. The work begins and ends with brilliant fanfares. In the aria "Willst du dich nicht mehr ergötzen" Endymion sings his languishing love-lament over an animated *basso ostinato*. Pan's song, "Ein Fürst ist seines Landes Pan" is constructed on an imposing form of the rhythm of solemnity —

The aria of Pales, "Schafe können sicher weiden" ("Sheep can pasture in safety") is in the nature of a pastoral, and is accompanied by two flutes. At the finish Pan sings a dance-song in gigue-form, "Ihr Felder und Auen, sonst grünend euch schauen".

This cantata was turned to account more than once afterwards. It was given on the birthday of the music-loving Prince Ernst August of Sachsen-Weimar, the only alteration necessary being the substitution of the name of Ernst August for that of Christian. In the score the new name is simply written under the old one. Bach did not worry in the least over the fact that the names are accented differently, and that the declamation consequently became nonsensical. He calmly let his people sing* —

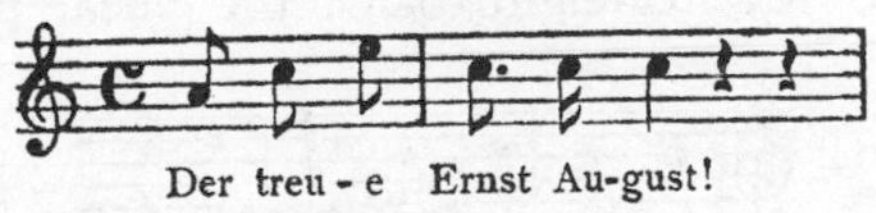

When the cantata was given at a later date by the Telemann Society, on the name-day of the Electoral Prince Friedrich August, Bach, — as we can see from a printed copy of the words that is attached to the autograph score— made only such changes in the text as were absolutely necessary. This time the work was entitled "Verlockender Götterstreit". It was again performed before Prince Christian von Weissenfels, at a feast he was celebrating with his wife Louise Christine (née Countess Stollberg). On this occasion the final chorus was sung to the following text:

"Die Anmut umfange, das Glück bediene
Den Herzog und seine Louyse Christine,
Sie weyden in Freuden auf Blumen und Klee,
Es prange die Zierde der fürstlichen Eh'
Die andre Dione,
Fürst Christians Crone!"

Our information as to all these different uses to which the cantata was put is derived from remarks in the score.

Some of the numbers were incorporated in church cantatas. The final chorus, "Ihr lieblichste Blicke" was transformed into the opening chorus of the Michaelmas cantata *Man singt mit Freuden vom Sieg* (No. 149). The hunting music and two arias are used in the cantata for Whit Monday 1731, *Also hat Gott die Welt geliebt* (No. 68); the bass aria of this, "Du bist geboren mir zum Guten" is derived from Pan's aria "Ein Fürst ist seines Landes Pan", and the well-known soprano aria "Mein gläubiges

* Again in the first recitative of Diana and Endymion (p. 9), in Pan's recitative (p. 11), and in the duet between Diana and Endymion.

Herze" is an enlarged arrangement of Pales' song, "Weil die wollenreichen Herden". The latter is expanded from thirty-six to seventy-eight bars; the vocal phrase —

is new; but the bass figure —

is derived from the secular cantata. The arrangement is not wholly satisfactory. The simple aria of the hunting cantata is in its own way more beautiful and better balanced than that of the Whit Monday cantata, in which we cannot help seeing ultimately that a new patch has been placed on an old garment*.

In Cöthen Bach had no choir at his disposal as he had in Weimar. For the birthday music *Durchlauchtster Leopold*, which he probably wrote for his master in his first year of service, he had to be content with a duet between soprano and bass**. In the two two-part arias, however, he tries to give the illusion that a choir is at work; he detaches the second violins and the violas from the rest of the orchestra, and makes them play second and third parts between the soprano and the bass.

There seems to have been no poet available there for the text. The mechanically rhymed prose reminds us somewhat of the kind that Bach himself used to write when he put his hand to poetry. It is therefore not unlikely

* Bach has written upon the same theme a small trio for violin, oboe, and clavier. See B. G. XXIX, pp. 250, 251.

** B. G. XXXIV, p. 3 ff. It is true that he has marked the two-part finale "Choro", but it was sung by his two soloists. The declamation is so curious, — e. g. on the words "Nimm auch", "Glücklich", and "sei dem Volke", — as to lead us to believe that the music was originally written to another text.

that the text of the serenata is his own. The charming music breathes of gaiety and happiness.

In order that it might not be wasted he used it for the church cantata for Whit Monday, *Erhöhtes Fleisch und Blut* (No. 173). The style of the textual transformation may be gathered from the first recitative —

Secular Cantata.	Whit Monday Cantata.
Durchlaucht'ster Leopold,	Erhöhtes Fleisch und Blut,
Es singet Anhalts Welt	Das Gott selbst an sich nimmt,
Von neuem mit Vergnügen,	Dem er schon hier auf Erden
Dein Cöthen sich dir stellt,	Ein himmlisch Heil bestimmt
Um sich vor dir zu biegen,	Des Höchsten Kind zu werden,
Durchlaucht'ster Leopold.	Erhöhtes Fleisch und Blut.

In 1725 the Duke of Cöthen took for second wife the Princess Charlotte Friederike Wilhelmine of Nassau. At that time Bach was settled in Leipzig; but he had retained his title of Cöthen Kapellmeister and his connection with the Court, and, of course, the duty of writing music for great occasions. On the 30th November 1726, the birthday of the Princess, he brought his best singers from Leipzig and performed the congratulatory cantata *Steigt freudig in die Luft, zu den erhabenen Höhen.* A little later on he used the same music for the birthday celebration of one of the Leipzig teachers, — probably the Rector Gesner. In this new form the cantata is entitled *Schwingt freudig euch empor**.

The music gives very characteristic expression to this idea of joyous soaring into the air —

The festive nature of the cantata impelled Bach to adapt it for the first Sunday in Advent; but he retained the opening words, as these were necessary for the music.

* We have the music in connection with this text. See B. G. XXXIV, p. 41 ff.

This was the origin of the sacred cantata *Schwingt freudig euch empor* (No. 36).

About the year 1733 the Cöthen secular cantata was again recast. It was adapted to the text *Die Freude reget sich*, and sung by the students on the birthday of the Professor of Law, Johann Florens Rivinus, who was very friendly with Bach*.

Another Cöthen cantata, *Mit Gnaden bekröne der Himmel die Zeiten* — perhaps written in 1721 — seems to have been performed at a New Year's festival or at some domestic celebration of the royal house**. It consists of solos and duets. At the end there is a chorus, but only of the simplest kind. This work also was converted into a church cantata with a new text, *Ein Herz, das seinen Jesum lebend weiss* (No. 134). It was intended for the third day of Easter.

A specially delightful piece of work is the secular Wedding Cantata for solo soprano, *Weichet nur, betrübte Schatten*, which Bach wrote as "table-music" for the wedding of some couple whose names we do not know***. It has survived only by accident; it would have been lost to us had it not been copied out by Rinck, a pupil of Peter Kellner.

The poem is much superior to the ordinary "occasional" text that came Bach's way. The theme is the passing of winter and the coming of spring. Phoebus and his horses gallop through the new world; Cupid runs through the fields whenever he sees a pair of lovers kissing; may the love-spring of the newly-wedded pair overcome and outlast the transitoriness of outward things.

To this expressive poem Bach has written some particularly beautiful music. The vaporous semiquavers ascending in the strings in the opening aria depict the mists vanishing before the breeze of spring —

---

* The four different texts will be found in B. G. XXXIV, Preface, p. 16 ff.

** B. G. XXIX, p. 209 ff. The commencement is mutilated. On the chronology of this cantata see Spitta III, 68, 284.

*** B. G. XI², p. 75 ff.

while the oboe sings a dreamy, yearning melody of the type of which Bach alone seems to have the secret*.

The aria that deals with the fleet steeds with which Phoebus flies through the newly-awakened world, begins in this way —

As the sketch for this theme is found in the final allegro of the sixth sonata for violin and clavier**, which was written in Cöthen, it is probable that the Wedding Cantata belongs to the same period.

When Bach settled in Leipzig he might have expected numerous commissions for "occasional" compositions. Such works were often called for in a town of that kind. Each great family festival, each birthday of any notable personality had to be accompanied by music specially written for the occasion. In addition there were many events in the university life, — "ovations" of students in

* It is quoted on p. 114.

** See I, 396. The sonata will be found in B. G. IX, p. 154 ff.

honour of favourite professors, the official festivals of the university, and the academic arrangements on patriotic occasions. Bach certainly counted on a substantial addition to his income from these sources. The ordinary remuneration for a piece of occasional music was about fifty thalers. This cannot be called brilliant for the circumstances of the time; but the presence or absence of two or three such commissions would count for something in the cantor's domestic exchequer.

It looks as if Bach were somewhat disappointed in this regard. He received practically no orders at all for official festivals at the university, owing to his having offended the academic authorities by his energetic action with regard to the services at the University Church*. He was out of touch with the students in the first few years, on account of his not conducting any of their *Collegia musica.* The public did not look upon him as a composer who could write graceful and sentimental melodies. Perhaps, too, the Cöthen-and-Weissenfels-Hofkapellmeister did not strike the Leipzig patricians as being sufficiently accommodating for a musician to whom they could give commissions for their festivals. We may therefore assume that Bach was entrusted with only a small portion of the occasional music performed during his residence in Leipzig. Görner and other third and fourth-rate great men, and, later on, his own pupil Doles, were much more in vogue than the master himself. Had he not undertaken, in 1729, the conductorship of the Telemann *Collegium Musicum,* he would have hardly made an appearance at all as a festival composer.

His poet for the secular cantatas was Picander, who served him better in wordly than in spiritual things. His heart was really in the former; for the church cantatas he could only string together phrases from the Bible and the hymn-books, without adding anything of his real self to them. In the secular cantatas he shewed real inventive

---

* See I, 120 ff.

power, and could always give a certain amount of interest to the mythological trappings of the situation. The richness of his diction in pictorial images was of great service to him in these works, and his sincere feeling for nature makes him, at certain happy moments, a real poet. If Bach's secular cantatas are not merely occasional compositions, but primarily art-works of genuine nature-poetry and only secondarily and by the accident of their origin "occasional" works, we must thank Picander for it.

His dexterity is evident in his first text, *Der zufriedengestellte Aeolus*, written for Bach in 1725 on the occasion of a students' celebration* in honour of the name-day (3rd August) of the Doctor of Philosophy August Friedrich Müller (1684—1761). In the cantata Aeolus proposes, on this particular day, to restore to the imprisoned winds their liberty, in view of the approaching end of the summer. They rejoice madly over the destruction they will work everywhere; Aeolus himself tells them what is permitted of them, and laughs in anticipation of what they will do. The gentle Zephyrus sings his song of farewell. Pomona enters and begs for a delay for the sake of her fruit-laden trees, but in vain. Pallas is more fortunate. She conjures the ruler of the winds not to disturb the feast that the muses are holding on Helicon, — the feast in honour of Herr August Müller. This entreaty Aeolus cannot resist. He recalls to their caves the already half-liberated winds. Pallas, Pomona and Zephyrus sing a happy trio, which is followed by a duet by the two goddesses. The finale is a brilliant chorus, "Vivat August"**.

The music is particularly vivacious. The first chorus and the recitative of Aeolus depicts the unbridled impetuosity of the scurrying winds***. The aria "Wie will

---

* The text of the Cöthen *Gratulation* Cantata *Schwingt freudig euch empor* (1726) is also by Picander. See p. 265.

** Bach's poet, of course, had in his mind's eye the well-known scene in Vergil's *Aeneid*.

*** See p. 58.

ich lustig lachen" ("How merrily will I laugh") is full of lusty laughter. A remarkable contrast to this strong music is afforded by the autumnal melancholy of the aria of Zephyrus, "Frische Schatten, meine Freude" —

In the aria of Pomona we see the leaves falling wearily from branch after branch.

What caressing grace, again, in the aria of Pallas! What restrained power in the air of Aeolus, with its accompaniment for wind instruments alone, "Zurücke, zurücke, geflügelte Winde!" What glorious sunshine in the G major theme of the duet of the goddesses —

And all this for Herr August Müller, who could have had no idea that Bach's music was a feast of the muses that would carry his name down to the remotest generations!

At a later date Bach himself sinned against this splendid work. When Friedrich August II. was crowned King of Poland at Cracow, on the 17th January 1734, Bach performed with the Telemann Society, in the same month, a festival cantata entitled *Blast Lärmen, ihr Feinde*, that is merely a perversion of the music composed in honour of August Müller. The text seems to have been rewritten by himself, for no author's name appears on the text-book printed by Breitkopf, — an omission that no poetaster of that day would have consented to*. The new version, in which "Valour", "Justice", and "Grace" appear, does not harmonise with the ideas and moods of the music, so that the combination is quite nonsensical. Spitta concludes from this that Bach certainly did not regard characterisation as the central point of his music**. This is an error. It merely proves in what a hurry Bach was to make sure that this Society should be the first to celebrate the coronation. The festival ode performed by the university in honour of the coronation, on the 19th February, was written by Görner.

The cantata *Vereinigte Zwietracht der wechselnden Saiten* was written in 1726 for the academic ceremony of the appointment of Dr. Gottlieb Kortte (1698—1731) as Professor of Roman Law***. The march with which the work opens was played by the wind instruments during the entry into the hall. For this reason it is not included among the orchestral parts of the cantata proper; we possess it in the score alone.

For this composition Bach made use of the second *Allegro* and the final Trio of the first Brandenburg concerto†. The *Allegro* became the opening chorus; the Trio, arranged for full orchestra, became an instrumental intermezzo (*ritornello*). The alto aria, "Ätzet dieses Angedenken", with its individual accompaniment, also seems to be borrowed from somewhere. The music takes no further account of the insipid allegory, in which all the possible virtues appear and admonish the youth of the university to follow the example of the new professor. What does it matter to Bach that it is tedious "Industry" that preaches to the sons of the muses in an aria, "Zieht

* This text is now in the Royal Library at Dresden. It is reprinted in Spitta II, 881 (German edition).

** Spitta II, 626.

*** B. G. XX², p. 73 ff.

† B. G. XIX, p. 16 ff., and 30.

euren Fuss nicht zurücke, ihr, die ihr meinen Weg erwählt" ("Draw not back, ye who have chosen my way")? All he sees is the musical image of the elastic step; so he sets the dull moral to a piquant piece of ballet music, which can be turned into a dance by simply substituting an instrument for the tenor voice —

To ensure the elegant performance of the movement, Bach took the trouble to indicate the phrasing and expression in the instrumental parts. The orchestra for the cantata consists of trumpets 1, 2, and 3, oboi d'amore 1 and 2, taille, violins 1 and 2, violas and *continuo*. Judging from the parts, each of the instruments, with the exception of the third trumpet and the drum, was multiplied — even the wind. For contrabass, cello and bassoon alone four unfigured *continuo* parts were written out.

Some time after 1733 — we cannot be sure of the exact date — this music was again adapted to the text *Auf, schmetternde Töne der muntern Trompeten*, for the name-day of August III*.

Several occasional compositions of that period must be regarded as lost. We merely know their titles, — and now and then their texts. Only by its title do we know of the cantata *Siehe, der Hüter Israels*, which is mentioned in Breitkopf's list for Michaelmas 1761 as a "graduation" cantata. On 5th June 1732 the reconstructed St. Thomas school was reconsecrated with great solemnity. For this occasion Bach wrote the cantata *Froher Tag, verlangte Stunden*, the text of which still exists in the

* The new text, with some newly-composed recitatives, is given in B. G. XX², p. 141 ff.

library of the institution*. The cantata *Entfernet euch, ihr heitern Sterne* was, as we learn from Sicul's *Das frohlockende Leipzig*, performed on the 12th May 1727, the birthday of King August II, about eight in the evening, in the market place, by the students of the university**. The monarch himself was in Leipzig, and listened to the work from a window in Apel's house. The music for the festival service in the University Church was written by Görner.

For the banquet at the wedding of the Leipzig merchant Heinrich Wolff and the daughter of Hempel, the Commissary of Excise in Zittau, on 5th February 1728, Bach wrote the cantata *Vergnügte Pleissenstadt*. The text is by Picander, who, in order to afford Bach an opportunity for musical painting, gives speaking parts to the rivers. At a later date Bach recast the text, substituted Apollo and Mercury for the Pleisse and the Neisse, and made them sing the praise of Leipzig and its Council***. When and for what occasion this revised version was performed we do not know. If it was during the period when Bach was at war with the Council, the composing of this libretto must have been even harder for him than the hammering out of the rhymes. The text is just what we might expect.

Der Streit zwischen Phoebus und Pan and the Coffee Cantata belong to the category of burlesque satire. Both were written about 1732.

The matter for *Phoebus und Pan* was derived by Picander from Ovid; but to ensure musical vivacity he made liberal additions of his own†. In the sextet, Momus, Mercury, Tmolus, Midas, Phoebus and Pan order the winds to withdraw to their caves, so as not to disturb the

* It is given in the Preface to B. G. XX², p. 51 ff. The text is by Bach's colleague, Magister Winkler.

** Given in B. G. XX², Preface p. 43. See also Spitta II, 628. There is a copy of the text in the Leipzig Town Library.

*** Both texts will be found in the Preface to B. G. XX², p. 46 ff. See also Spitta II, 634, 635.

† B. G. XI, p. 3 ff.

proposed contest of song. Bach, of course, did not let such an opportunity for pictorial music pass by him; we seem actually to see the clouds of whirling dust —

The tribunal is arranged. Phoebus chooses Tmolus for his advocate; Pan selects Midas. Thereupon Phoebus sings a melody in which we find embodied a number of themes which Bach uses to express unspeakable longing, —

Pan sings a peasant dance-tune, — "Zum Tanze, zum Sprunge, wie wackelt das Herz" — in which words and melody are both plebeian, as if sung at a Kermess —

The middle section is a *largo*, in which he parodies the elegiac theme of Phoebus in an angular $^4/_4$ rhythm —

The words run thus —

"Wenn der Ton zu mühsam klingt
Und der Mund gebunden singt,
So erweckt es keinen Scherz."

Tmolus awards the victory to Phoebus, and sings a song about music that is "born of charm". Midas, in an aria written in the style of a village cantor, gives the prize to Pan, justifying his verdict with the remark that Pan's music "fell thus on his ears". As a reward for his "mad ambition" he is given asses' ears. Mercury, however, announces that "arrogant presumption" always wins the "cap and bells of Folly" in the end, and we hear the bell jingling in the accompaniment to the aria —

Finally all unite in the praise of "charming music", that delights not only men but the gods, and for the sake of which we can calmly put up with "censure" and "jeers".

As early as 1856 Dehn, the well-known Bach student, conjectured that the satire is not a general one, but that Bach had some particular circumstance in view*. He thought that the cantata was directed against the Rector Biedermann, of Freiberg (Saxony). To the general discussion that took place, about the middle of the eighteenth century, as to whether, in the re-organisation of classical education, music was to keep its old place in the school course, this pedagogue had contributed, in 1749, a pamphlet entitled *De vita musica*, in which he maintained that not only was music prejudicial to education, but that it was usually the worst boys in the school who took up art. His object was to depreciate and annoy his cantor, Doles, who a year previously had won great success with a *Singspiel* on the centenary of the Peace of Westphalia. Bach had to endure from his own Rector just what his pupil Doles had to put up with from Biedermann. He consequently took a lively interest in the controversy that arose round

* *Johann Sebastian Bach als Polemiker,* in Westermann's *Monatshefte* for 1856.

the pamphlet, and in which every musician of note, especially Mattheson, fell furiously on the luckless author. Bach regretted that his health did not permit him to take up the pen himself; but he had an answer composed by a certain Schröter, of Nordhausen, a member of the musical Society. This pleased him so much that on the 10th December 1749 he wrote to Einicke, in Frankenhausen, that "he did not doubt that such *refutationes* would clean the author's dirty ear, and make it more fit to listen to music."*

It would be quite possible that Bach had attacked the malicious Rector in a satirical cantata. On closer examination, however, it becomes clear that *Der Streit zwischen Phoebus und Pan* does not relate to this matter; it is not directed against one who despises art, but against a superficial critic. A decisive point is that the text existed as early as 1732, when it was published in the third part of Picander's poems. It can therefore only refer to Bach's critic Scheibe**. It is true that the latter's views upon Bach's music only appeared in the *Kritischer Musikus* of 1737***. His animosity, however, dates from 1729, when Bach had not supported his candidature for the post of organist at St. Thomas's as Scheibe would have liked. He would not fail to speak offensively of Bach's music afterwards, so that the composer had good cause to ridicule him musically in the Telemann Society. This explains the character and the date of origin of the work. The points of the text are clear. Midas is Scheibe. The latter had charged Bach's music with being turgid and confused, and maintained that it must have been artificial and

---

* Spitta (III, 255 ff.) gives a full account of the controversy. The documents are to be found in Adlung and Marpurg.

** Otto Lindner controverted Dehn's hypothesis in an article on *Biedermann und Bach*, in the *Vossische Zeitung* for 1st and 8th July 1860. The correct theory is stated by Rust in the preface to B. G. XI[2], and by Spitta (II, 647, 648).

*** On Scheibe and Bach see I, 178 ff.

far-fetched, since it did not aim at an immediate appeal to the senses. This is why Midas sings —

"Ach Pan! wie hast du mich gestärkt!
Dein Lied hat mir so wohl geklungen,
Dass ich es mir auf einmal gleich gemerkt.
. . . . Der Phöbus macht es gar zu bunt,
Allein dein allerliebster Mund
Sang leicht und ungezwungen."

["Oh Pan! thy song was life to me!
My heart was stirred with strange emotion!
And as I listened, lo! it seemed to me
I heard the plaintive music of the woodland,
The sighing of the restless ocean!
Not Phoebus should receive the prize,
But thou, whose song in simple wise
Thy hearers all hath charmed."]*

The cantata is thus a product of the same spirit as Wagner's *Die Meistersinger*; Bach wrote it in order to rise superior, in his music, to the misunderstanding around him, and to place to his own lips the cheering and refreshing cup of high-souled irony — finding in this, like all great minds, strength to go on undisturbed with his work. Bach's heart was lightened when, in the aria of Phoebus and that of Tmolus, he had represented his art as that of godlike charm; the pessimism that had weighed on him since the production of the *St. Matthew Passion*, and that finds such bitter expression in the letter to Erdmann, was now overcome.

The cantata must have been performed again at the time of the Biedermann controversy. At that time Bach did not conduct any of the students' singing societies; but the circle of friends who felt themselves wounded with him by the attack sought out the work again and found refreshment in it. This accounts for our possessing a manuscript copy of the text-book with the date 1749. The last two lines of the final recitative were altered to fit

* Mr. Percy Pinkerton's translation, in Breitkopf and Härtel's English edition of the score. [Tr.]

the case of the malicious pedagogue. In 1732 they had been sung thus —

"Ergreife, Phoebus, nun die Leyer wieder
Es ist nicht Lieblicher's als deine Lieder."

("Take up thy lyre again, Phoebus; there is nothing more delightful than thy song").

They were now transformed thus —

"Verdopple, Phoebus, nun Musik und Lieder,
Tob auch Hortensius und ein Orbil dawider".

("Redouble, Phoebus, thy music and singing, even though a Hortensius and an Orbilius rage against them"). Orbilius is the Horatian schoolmaster, "ready to strike"; Hortensius, the Latin rhetor, is probably intended for Ernesti, the odious Rector of St. Thomas's, who was particularly devoted to Latin oratory.

The Coffee Cantata, *Schweigt stille, plaudert nicht**, is much more unassuming; it aims only at refreshment. In 1727 Picander had published, in the first volume of his poems, a story in which he had made merry over the increasing passion for coffee. The King of France, he says, has forbidden the beverage in Paris, which occasions general lamentation; the women die as if the plague were raging; this went on until the interdict was removed. It should be mentioned that the praise of coffee had been warmly sung in a collection of cantatas published in Paris about 1703. The text of the first German coffee cantata was by Gottfried Krause (1716); we do not know who wrote the music to it**.

---

* B. G. XXIX, p. 141 ff. The text is taken from Picander's *Ernst-Schertzhaffte und satyrische Gedichte*, Part III, Leipzig, 1732. The *Streit zwischen Phoebus und Pan* appeared in the same Part.

** See Spitta II, 641 ff. It is well known that in the eighteenth century many princes expressly forbade the public or secret drinking of coffee in their dominions. The Landgrave Friedrich of Hesse issued an ordinance of this kind in 1766; it was in force more than twenty years; the "coffee smellers" (Kaffeeriecher) who lodged information received one fourth of the fine. (See the *Frankf. Zeitung* for 26th July 1907.)

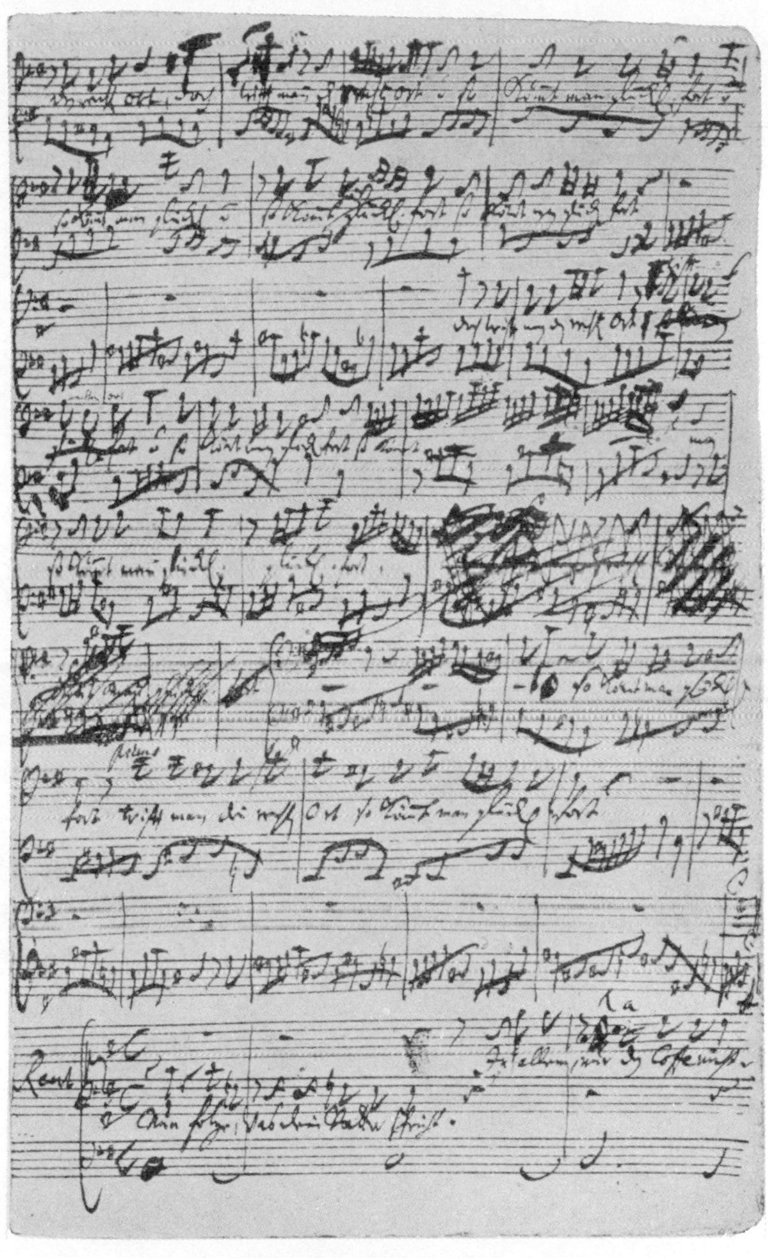

Bach's Handwriting (Rough Copy)

Reduced facsimile of a page of the "Coffee Cantata"

The theme of Picander's poem is as follows. Father Schlendrian (Routine) wishes to break his daughter Lieschen of the coffee habit*. "Oh father, be not so strict", she pleads. "If I do not drink my little cup of coffee three times a day I shall be like a dried-up piece of roast goat's-flesh." Her prayer is reinforced by a roguish aria in praise of the black beverage. All threats are in vain. She will give up her promenades, her wide and fashionable whale-bone skirt, even the silver-work ribbon for her cap. Not until she is engaged to a man will she consent to give up coffee. "So do it today, dear father," she says coaxingly in an aria. He has hardly gone out when Lieschen makes it known that "no wooer need come to the house unless he will promise, and have it put in the marriage settlement, that I may have liberty to make coffee when I will".

To this libretto Bach has written music that seems to come from Offenbach rather than from the old cantor of St. Thomas's. The work as it stands could be given as a one-act operetta.

On Tuesday, the 7th April 1739, a "foreign musician" (fremder Musikus) announced a concert in the Frankfort market house, "in which, among other things, Herr Schlendrian and his daughter Lieschen will appear."** This can only refer to Picander's poem. We do not know whether it was given with Bach's music, or whether the *fremde Musikus* had set it himself. If the former, then this is the only case which we can positively cite of a performance of one of his works in another town.

The soprano cantata *Von der Vergnügsamkeit* also probably dates from the early thirties***. It seems to have been written for Anna Magdalena, and was probably performed in the domestic concerts that Bach used to have as long as his elder sons were with him. It is not of great

* Bach always spells the word "Coffee", instead of in the usual German form of "Kaffee".

** *Frankfurter Nachrichten*, 1739. See Spitta II, 643.

*** B. G. XI², p. 105 ff.

musical value. It is significant that he should have been attracted by such a text. At first sight it merely seems to be concerned with the praise of a certain homely contentment and the art of putting away from us unnecessary cares and desires. But the religious note imperceptibly creeps in; the true contentment is peace and quietness in God. Thus the work that began in such banality ends with the praise of "divine sufficiency", that makes the poor rich and on the level of princes. This was the spiritual state of the great German mystic Bach, whose outward semblance was that of a comfortable citizen of the eighteenth century.

Yet even he strove after vain things. In 1733 he went to Dresden to receive the title of court composer. It is not surprising to hear that while waiting for this he performed some patriotic cantatas in order to bring himself before the friendly notice of the royal house. On 27th July he presented his petition; on 5th September he conducted in the Telemann Society a *dramma per musica*, — *Herkules auf dem Scheidewege*, — to celebrate the eleventh birthday of the Electoral Prince*. We learn this from Picander's poems, among which the libretto is printed; the autograph score merely has the title of "Glückwünschungskantate auf einen sächsischen Prinzen" ("Congratulatory Cantata for a Saxon Prince").

The subject is a familiar one. Pleasure and Virtue each try to capture Hercules, — who here represents the young prince. Warned by the faithful echo, he resists the former, and falls into the arms of Virtue, whereupon the work ends with the chorus "Lust der Völker, Lust der Deinen, blühe, holder Friederich!".

As the summer meetings of the *Collegium musicum* were held in Zimmermann's garden, before the city gate, we may assume that this cantata was given in the open air, — as was the case, indeed, with most of the large secular works he wrote in Leipzig.

---

* B. G. XXXIV, p. 121 ff.

The music Bach has written to Picander's poem is, with all its charm and urbanity, full of characterisation. As Spitta says, Handel's *Wahl des Herakles* is much inferior to that of Bach. It is not clear, however, what Spitta means by the reproach that the work is spoilt by an "excess of sentiment" that does not suit either the subject or the *genre**. He is always inclined, indeed, to under-appreciate Bach's secular cantatas.

Although the *Wahl des Herkules* is rarely performed in our concert halls, it is well known for all that, for the principal numbers — six in all — have been incorporated in the *Christmas Oratorio*, at which Bach was working at that time.

The opening chorus, "Lasst uns sorgen", is identical with the chorus "Fallt mit Danken" of the *Christmas Oratorio*.

The slumber song that Pleasure sings over Hercules became the lullaby for the infant Jesus. This is the well-known aria, —

The text of the original and that of the adaptation may be cited here for the purpose of comparison —

The Choice of Hercules;

Pleasure: "Schlafe, mein Lieber, und pflege der Ruh',
Folge der Lockung entbrannter Gedanken,
Schmecke die Lust
Der lüsternen Brust
Und erkenne keine Schranken."

The Christmas Oratorio;

"Schlafe, mein Liebster, genieße der Ruh',
Wache nach diesem für aller Gedeihen!
Labe die Brust,
Empfinde die Lust,
Wo wir unser Herz erfreuen."

---

* Spitta II, 629, 630.

The aria "Flösst mein Heiland" in the oratorio is also taken from *Die Wahl des Herkules*, where, in the aria "Treues Echo", the hero asks the echo to reply to him. Here the musical effect is justified by the text. In the corresponding number of the *Christmas Oratorio*, however, the echo effect is meaningless, the text having nothing to do with question and answer.

The aria "Auf meinen Flügeln sollst du schweben" corresponds to the aria "Ich will nur dir zu Ehren leben" in the *Christmas Oratorio*. Here again the music betrays how much of it is original and how much borrowed. In the aria in the cantata the motion of the floating wings is suggested; we seem to see an eagle soaring aloft with a few beats of his wings and then circling tranquilly in the air —

The text of the aria in the oratorio has no relation whatever to this wonderfully plastic theme. Why did not Bach take the trouble to ensure, by a corresponding pictorial figure, community between the words and the music in the new text?

So again with the aria "Bereite dich Zion" and its secular model "Ich will dich nicht hören". The theme of the middle section has meaning only in relation to the original. At one point the solo violin is silenced, and a curious figure enters in the basses —

What does this signify? It is the familiar motive by means of which Bach represents the winding motion of a serpent or a dragon. The text, in fact, speaks of the serpents that approached the youthful Hercules — "the serpents that tried to cajole me". In the *Christmas Oratorio* the bass figure has no justification.

The dialogue between Hercules and Virtue, "Ich bin deine", also loses its musical meaning when it becomes the duet "Herr, dein Mitleid" in the oratorio. No one acquainted with Bach's thematic invention can doubt that both the motives of the aria express joy of the liveliest kind —

In the original these themes are prompted by the text. Hercules' choice of Virtue is expressed in a sort of nuptial rapture —

> "Ich bin deine; du bist meine!
> Ich küsse dich; küsse mich!"

The text of the adaptation, however, is quite colourless, and would never have given rise of itself to music of this kind.

These examples of adaptations in a single work are typical for Bach. It is almost incredible that the same artist who insisted so strongly on characteristic expression in music could at another time constrain his music so barbarously to fit an alien text. "We can congratulate ourselves", says Spitta, "that with the exception of the final chorus and the recitatives, the whole of *Die Wahl des Herkules* has been incorporated in the *Christmas Oratorio*, written a year later."* To this we may rejoin that our good luck is somewhat doubtful, since the adapted move-

* Spitta II, 630.

ments make a notably uncomfortable impression upon us. Even the hearer who does not exactly know how the adaptations have been made will feel that the words and music do not agree. This makes full artistic enjoyment impossible. Spitta is secretly rejoiced at these superficial transcriptions, as they confirm for him his pet conclusion that the pictorial and the characteristic are only accidental, not essential, elements of Bach's art. The musician who is indifferent to all these theories will rather regret that the incorporation of *Die Wahl des Herkules* in the *Christmas Oratorio* prevents us hearing it in its original form.

On 8th December 1733, barely three months after *Die Wahl des Herkules*, Bach performed a new cantata in honour of the royal house, entitled *Tönet, ihr Pauken, erschallet Trompeten*, dramma per musica der Königin zu Ehren"*. Bach did not finish the work until the evening before the performance, as is shown by the note at the end of the autograph score — "Fine. DSGl. 1733. d. 7 Dec". It is interesting to observe that the majority of the cantatas in honour of the royal house, including *Die Wahl des Herkules*, bear the inscriptions J. J. (Jesu Juva — Jesus help) and SDGl. (Soli Deo Gloria — To God alone the glory'.

The text must be by Bach himself, since no author's name is given in the programme book printed by Breitkopf**. The quality and the quantity of the dialect in the text, however, would be enough to betray the real author. The first chorus may be quoted as an example of Bach's poetry:

"Tönet ihr Pauken! Erschallet Trompeten!
Klingende Saiten erfüllet die Luft!
Singet itzt Lieder ihr muntren Poeten,
Königin lebe! wie fröhlichst geruft.
Königin lebe! diss wünschet der Sachse,
Königin lebe! und blühe und wachse!"

---

* B. G. XXXIV, p. 177 ff. The 8th December was the Queen's birthday.

** The original imprint of the text is in the Royal Library at Dresden, showing that the programme books were sent to the Court.

The finest numbers of this work also have passed into the *Christmas Oratorio**. Here, however, the adaptations led to no violence being done to the music, both texts being of a general order and expressing the same joyous feelings.

In January 1734, for the coronation of August II at Cracow, the *Zufriedengestellte Aeolus* was rearranged for a new text, *Blast Lärmen ihr Feinde***.

In the autumn of the same year the King and Queen visited Leipzig. Bach hurriedly wrote the cantata *Preise dein Glücke, gesegnetes Sachsen*, which was performed in the market-place, before the windows of the royal pair, on the evening of 5th October***. "About 9 o'clock in the evening," says Salomon Riemer's Chronicle, "the whole of the students here performed before their Majesties a most submissive serenade, with trumpets and kettle-drums, composed by Hr. Capell-Meister Joh. Sebastian Bach, Cant. zu St. Thom. During it 600 students carried great torches, and four Counts, as Marshals, produced the music"†.

In the recitatives, allusions are made to contemporary events. One of these speaks of the exploits of the French in the War of the Polish Succession:

"In einer Zeit, da alles um uns blitzt und kracht,
Ja der Franzosen Macht (die doch so vielmal schon gedämpfet worden)
Von Süden und von Norden auch unserm Vaterland mit Schwert und Feuer dräut,
Kann diese Stadt so glücklich sein, dich, mächtgen Schutzgott unsrer Linden,
In ihrem Schoss zu finden."

* *Tönet, ihr Pauken.*	*Christmas Oratorio.*
1. Chorus. Tönet ihr Pauken.	1. Chorus. Jauchzet, frohlocket.
2. Aria. Fromme Musen.	2. Aria. Frohe Hirten eilt.
3. Aria. Kron' und Preis' gekrönter Damen.	3. Aria. Grosser Herr und starker König.
4. Chorus. Blicket ihr Linden.	4. Chorus. Herrscher des Himmels.

** See p. 270.

*** B. G. XXXIV, p. 245 ff.

† B. G. XXXIV, Preface, p. 30.

The texts of the sacred cantatas of that time also give expression to the anxiety caused by the war.

The music of this coronation cantata is somewhat unequal in quality. A number of the movements seem to be borrowed from other works. Only one number was taken from it for the *Christmas Oratorio**. The first chorus afterwards became the *Hosanna* of the B minor Mass.

Two days later, on the 7th October, the King's birthday was celebrated. For this festival Bach had long prepared a performance of the cantata *Schleicht spielende Wellen* at the *Collegium Musicum***. The text is by Picander, who again did Bach the service of supplying him with a poem exceedingly rich in musical motives. He manages this by making the Vistula, the Elbe, the Danube and the Pleisse laud the good fortune of the Saxon Poland through which they flow. This is all Bach needs; he lets the words of the text go where they will, and in almost every number depicts the changeful play of the waves.

In the first chorus their multiform motion is represented by the co-operation of three motives —

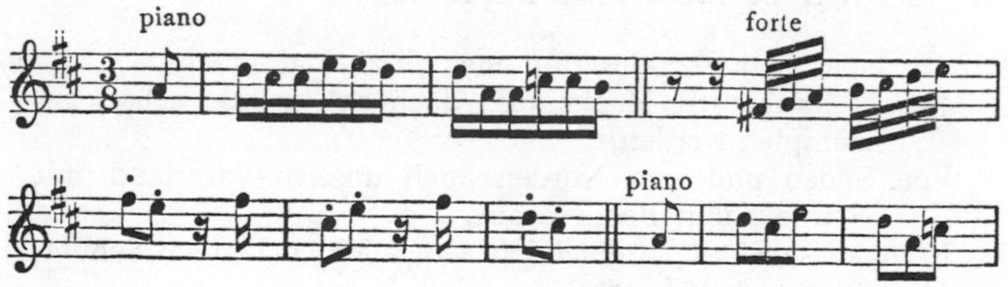

The truth of the picture to nature is astounding. All the irregularity and unexpectedness within a monotonous rhythm that give such fascination to the song of the waves is here achieved in tone.

---

* The adaptation is again barbarous. The aria "Durch die von Eifer entflammten Waffen" ("By the weapons inflamed with anger") is provided with the sacred text "Erleucht auch meine finstern Sinne" ("Lighten my darkened sense"). The text of the secular cantata is not by Picander; nor does it appear to be by Bach.

** B. G. XX[2], p. 1 ff.

The text runs thus:

> "Schleicht spielende Wellen und murmelt gelinde!
> Nein, rauschet geschwinde!"

("Glide along, ye waves in play, and murmur gently! No, rush along swiftly!")

As a great deal depends on the playing here, Bach has liberally sprinkled the original parts with dots, ties, and dynamic marks. They show us, down to the smallest detail, how he wished his music to be performed.

In the aria of the Elbe, "Jede Woge meiner Wellen ruft das goldne Wort August" ("Every one of my billows calls out the golden word Augustus"), the appropriate motion is rendered by a solo violin —

In the aria of the Danube the motion of the waves is represented in a very complex style. The motive of the aria of the Pleisse runs thus —

In the final chorus the motion is throughout tranquil and majestic —

Thus in thirteen months, — from September 1733 to October 1734 — Bach had produced five cantatas in honour of the royal house He could hardly have shewn more loyalty; nevertheless he had still to wait two years for the title he so eagerly desired.

After this the secular compositions became less and less frequent. The cantata *Thomana sass annoch betrübt*, performed on 21st November 1734 on the occasion of the induction of the younger Ernesti, is now lost. The dreary text is preserved in Riemer's Chronicle*.

Four years later (1738) another cantata of homage to the royal house was performed. Riemer's Chronicle speaks of it thus:

"On the morning of the 28th April, about 9 o'clock, Baron Woldemar von Schmettau gave a solemn discourse in St. Paul's church on the approaching marriage of the Princess Amelia and His Majesty the King of the two Sicilies. At nine o'clock in the evening the university students, with many torches, performed a fine *Nacht Musique*, with trumpets and kettle-drums, before Apel's house in the market, — a submissive drama composed by Herr Capell Meister Joh. Sebastian Bach; whereupon Count von Zierotin, Baron von Schmettau, Herr von Leipnitz and Herr von Marschall were so gracious as to submit the cantata most humbly to the Kings and the Princesses, and were allowed to kiss hands"**.

We are not told whether this honour fell to the composer also. Magister Birnbaum mentions this cantata in his defence of Bach against Scheibe (1739), adding it as a proof that "the Herr Court Composer writes movingly, expressively, naturally, symmetrically, and in accordance not with a depraved but with the best taste"***. The music is lost. The text glorifies August II and his father under the names of Solomon and David. The title of the cantata is *Willkommen, ihr herrschenden Götter der Erden.*

Altogether we have only three secular cantatas dating from Bach's last creative period. The first, *Angenehmes Wiederau*, belongs to the year 1737†. On 28th September

---

* See B. G. XXXIV, Preface, p. 58 ff. The aria "Hochgelobter Gottessohn" in the cantata *Bleib bei uns, denn es will Abend werden* (No. 6) seems to have been taken from this secular cantata.

** See B. G. XXXIV, p. 48 ff., where the text also is printed

*** See I, 182, and Spitta III, 252 ff.

† B. G. XXXIV, Preface, p. 36 ff. and p. 325 ff.

of that year Johann Christian Hennicke, a quondam lackey, who had prospered by the favour of Count Brühl, rendered homage at Wiederau on entering into possession of his land. Picander, who wished to curry favour with the parvenu, had written the text and asked Bach to compose the music. The opening chorus of the cantata — it is repeated at the end — is one of the most spirited movements ever written by Bach. We can easily understand him using it again for a festival work; it recurs in the cantata for Midsummer Day, *Freue dich, erlöste Schar* (No. 30). Four of the arias are also incorporated in the sacred work. The adaptation of the second is very imperfect, as will be seen from a cursory comparison of the two texts:

Angenehmes Wiederau.

Aria. "Was die Seele kann ergötzen,
Was vergnügt und hoch zu schätzen,
Soll dir lehn und erblich sein.
Meine Fülle soll nichts sparen,
Und dir reichlich offenbaren,
Daß mein ganzer Vorrat dein."

Freue dich, erlöste Schar.

Aria. "Kommt, ihr angefochtnen Sünder,
Eilt und lauft, ihr Adamskinder,
Euer Heiland ruft und schreit.
Kommet, ihr verirrten Schafe,
Stehet auf vom Sündenschlafe,
Denn jetzt ist die Gnadenzeit."

The cantata *Mer hahn en neue Oberkeet* was also written for an act of homage on entering into possession of land. It was performed on 30th August 1742, when the Chamberlain Karl Heinrich von Dieskau became Herr von Kleinzschocher*. The idea seems again to have come from Picander. As von Dieskau was his superior in the custom-house, he had good reasons for paying him

* B. G. XXIX, p. 175 ff.

attention. Perhaps, too, the gentleman was one of Bach's Dresden patrons. At any rate we find Frau von Dieskau, in 1752, mentioned as godmother to the first-born son of Wilhelm Friedemann*.

The idea of writing a piece of rustic music did not come inopportunely to Bach, for he had a strong *penchant* to burlesque. Almost all the movements are set in the form of dance-tunes; the overture is a potpourri of dances, terminating with a waltz. The action is simply this, — the village people come to congratulate the lord of the manor and offer him good wishes, after which they retire to drink free beer in the tavern. The text is skilfully put together by Picander. He gives Bach the opportunity to contrast the music of the town and that of the village. The composer also employs folk-melodies. One of these —

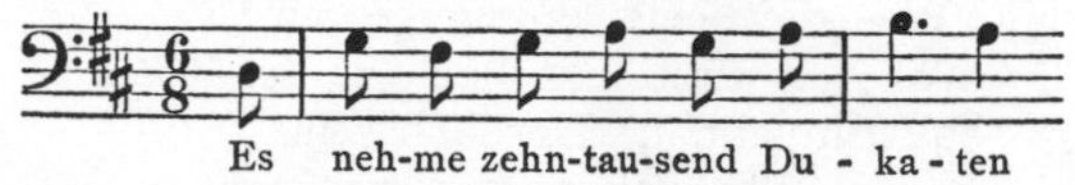
Es neh-me zehn-tau-send Du - ka - ten

had lately become popular with the words "Frisch auf zum fröhlichen Jagen"**. The other —

Gieb Schö - ne, viel Söh - ne von art - ger Ge - stalt

seems to have been well known as a cradle song. A third is used in the form of interludes in a recitative —

It is the same tune as appears in the Goldberg Variations. There may be other folk-melodies in the cantata, though we cannot be sure of them.

---

* Bitter, *C. P. Emmanuel und W. F. Bach,* II, 215.

** On its origin see Spitta III, 179 ff., where the other folk-tunes are also cited.

The orchestra usually consists of a contrabass, a viola, and a violin. In the song "Es nehme zehntausend Dukaten" a horn is added. The aria "Kleinzschocher müsse so zart und süsse" is instrumented in the town style, i. e. with flute and strings. Only Bach's fatal passion for borrowing can account for the fact that the number "Dein Wachstum sei feste und lache vor Lust" is not set to original music but to the prize song of Pan, "Zum Tanze, zum Sprunge"*; or was he so pleased with this that he wanted to hear it again?

The cantata *O holder Tag* was written as "table music" for a wedding feast**. If the text can be trusted, the wedded pair were musical. The question is discussed whether music ought to have any place in such a feast; at the end the answer is given in the affirmative, especially as a "patron" of the art is here concerned. The spouses each received a copy of the parts, written with extra neatness and fastened with silk; these are now in the Royal Library at Berlin.

This cantata probably belongs to Bach's last creative period; it is a specimen of that art of "charm" on which he prides himself in *Phoebus und Pan****. Charmingly roguish is the aria "Schweigt, ihr Flöten" ("Be silent, ye flutes"), in which the frightened flute cannot achieve a complete theme, but merely gives out short fragments, after each of which it stops timidly —

* See p. 274. The number will be found in its original form in B. G. XI², p. 38.

** B. G. XXIX, p. 69 ff. Like the other wedding cantata, *Weichet nur, betrübte Schatten,* it is written for soprano solo.

*** The aria "Grosser Gönner, dein Vergnügen" is taken from the cantata *Angenehmes Wiederau,* where it is set to the words "So wie ich die Tropfen zolle". See B. G. XXXIV, p. 338.

Soon after this first performance Bach provided the cantata with a new text, *O angenehme Melodei!* which sings the praise of art in general*. In this adaptation it was given at the house of Bach's Dresden patron, Count Flemming, and probably at a meeting of the *Collegium musicum*, — apparently at the one in 1749 at which *Phoebus und Pan* was revived. The new version of the occasional cantata seems to refer to the Biedermann controversy**. One recitative runs thus:

"Wiewohl, beliebte Musika, so angenehm dein Spiel so vielen Ohren ist,
So bist du doch betrübt und stehest in Gedanken da,
Denn es sind ihr'r viel, denen du verächtlich bist.
Mich deucht, ich höre deine Klagen selbst also sagen:
Schweigt, ihr Flöten, schweigt, ihr Töne . . . . ."

The final section of the opening recitative —

"Die Wissenschaften andrer Künste sind ird'nen Witzes kluge Dünste.
Du aber (— die Musik! —) bist allein vom Himmel zu uns abgestiegen;
So musst du auch recht himmlisch sein —"

is in the pure Bachian spirit.

Two Italian cantatas have come down to us, — *Amore traditore* and *Non sa che sia dolore****. The first is set for bass and clavier accompaniment — a unique case with Bach. In the second, for soprano solo, the accompaniment is for strings and flute. A splendid sinfonia opens the cantata. Neither work, as we might expect from Bach, makes any attempt at imitating the Italian style. The texts are written in Germanised Italian; the second, judg-

---

* The cantata will be found in this form in B. G. XXIX, p. 245 ff.

** See p. 275.

*** B. G. XI², p. 93 ff., and XXIX, p. 45 ff. The first is given in the B. G. with a good German translation. Another Italian cantata, *Andro dall colle al prato,* is lost. See Spitta II, 637.

ing from an allusion here and there, is meant to console an Italian artist who is leaving Germany and returning to his native land.

The fact that the secular cantatas are mostly only occasional works, written to order, is apt to prevent our doing them full justice. We are inclined to believe that with such an origin they must necessarily have been written hastily and mechanically, and so belong to a lower class of art. Bach and his generation, however, thought differently. When he had time, he wrote the works with particular pleasure and took great pains with the performance, as is evident from the careful way in which the parts have been revised, and the large number of phrasing marks and dynamic signs that they contain.

It is consequently time to clear away a misconception, and to make the Bach of "charm" known to the musical world. The majority of these works were published nearly a generation ago, yet only one or two of them have been given on rare occasions here and there. Works like *Phoebus und Pan*, *Die Wahl des Herkules*, *Der zufriedengestellte Aeolus*, *Weichet nur, betrübte Schatten*, *Schleicht, spielende Wellen*, and *O angenehme Melodei* should appear regularly on our concert programmes; even the *Coffee Cantata* and the *Mer hahn en neue Oberkeet* should be brought forward for other reasons than as mere curiosities.

It is curious that the experience of those who have produced the cantatas does not lead to further emulation. It has always been observed that the audience feels no sense of strangeness whatever, but is warmly enthusiastic. The Bach Society of Paris has had the courage to give some of the secular cantatas — including *Weichet nur, betrübte Schatten*, the *Coffee Cantata*, and *Mer hahn en neue Oberkeet* — at its very first concerts, and owes its remarkable success in no small degree to this course.

The question of the texts presents no particular difficulty. Certain fundamental alterations are necessary, — as August II and his family, and Herr Kortte, Herr Müller, and all the other lights of science, are of minor interest to us now, their names must be taken out of the poems. The proper method of adaptation is indicated for us in the music. The main thing is to see that the words embody the nature-poetry that have inspired the music. In *Der zufriedengestellte Aeolus* only a few recitatives and the final chorus need altering; in other works the changes will have to be more drastic. When shall we find the poet who will supply the music of *Schleicht, spielende Wellen* with that poetic song of the waves that Bach dimly perceived when he wrote the work? To the objection "Have we the right to undertake such adaptations of the text?" we may reply that Bach himself gives it us; he converted the Wedding Cantata, *O holder Tag*, into the hymn to music, *O angenehme Melodei*. The fate of the recitatives need not concern us. Bach himself, when making his adaptations, abandons them without scruple when he has no need for them.

Our singers, for their part, should pitilessly worry the conductors, great and small, until they are given the opportunity to sing the splendid music that Bach has provided for them in these works. The sopranos especially should plead for the solo cantatas *O angenehme Melodei* and *Weichet nur, betrübte Schatten*.

CHAPTER XXXI.

THE MOTETS AND THE SONGS.

B. G. XXXIX.

Of the motets that have come down to us with Bach's name, only six are by him, — *Singet dem Herrn ein neues Lied: Der Geist hilft unsrer Schwachheit auf: Jesu meine Freude: Fürchte dich nicht: Komm, Jesu, komm: Lobet* *den Herrn, alle Heiden**. The first, second, fourth and fifth are for double chorus.

We have autographs only of *Singet dem Herrn* and *Der Geist hilft unsrer Schwachheit auf*; the others exist only in copies. The credit of first publishing Bach's motets belongs to Schicht, one of his successors in the cantorate. He issued them in 1803 through Breitkopf and Härtel**.

Two motets were sung each Sunday both at St. Thomas's and St. Nicholas's, — at the commencement of the morning service and of vespers respectively. This would lead us to suppose that Bach must have written a large number of works of this kind. Had he done so some of them at any rate would certainly have survived. It appears, however, that he took no trouble over the ordinary Sunday motet, and always had the traditional ones sung. Those of his that we possess were in fact not written for the ordinary service but for special occasions. We learn by accident the origin of three of them; *Jesu meine Freude* is the music for the funeral of a certain Frau Reese (1723); *Fürchte dich nicht* was written for the funeral of Frau Winkler, the wife of the deputy mayor; *Der Geist hilft unsrer Schwachheit auf* is entitled, in the vocal parts, "Motet for the burial of Professor and Rector Ernesti", who died in October 1729.

The Sunday motets were usually sung at Leipzig in Latin. We possess, however, no Latin motets by Bach. Ernst Ludwig Gerber says that he heard a fine Latin motet of Bach's, for double chorus, sung at the Christmas

---

* The motet *Ich lasse dich nicht* is a work by Johann Christian Bach, of which Johann Sebastian made a copy. It is too fine a composition to remain unperformed merely because it is not "genuine". Of the other motets formerly attributed to Bach we may mention *Sei Lob und Preis mit Ehren; Lob', Ehre und Weisheit; Merk' auf, mein Herz, und singe; Unser Wandel ist im Himmel; Jauchzet dem Herrn alle Welt.* On the question of authenticity see Wüllner's excellent Preface to B. G. XXXIX.

** His edition contained six motets. *Ich lasse dich nicht* is given as a work of Johann Sebastian's. The other five motets are genuine; only *Lobet den Herrn, alle Heiden* is lacking.

service at St. Thomas's in 1767. In the old days, however, the term "motet" had such a general significance — even Zelter and Mendelssohn speak of motets when they mean cantatas — that we cannot deduce from Gerber's remark any positive conclusion as to the existence of Latin motets in the strict sense of the word.

All we can say, then, is that on the ordinary Sundays Bach gave other men's motets, not his own. The musicians of that time took no interest in the statutory portions of the service; they occupied themselves only with the "principal music", — the cantata. Certain hints in the documents relating to the Krause affair* almost lead us to suppose that Bach did not conduct the motet himself, but turned it over to the prefect. In his memorial of 19th August 1736 he speaks of having to conduct himself as something quite out of the ordinary course**.

The motets presented no text-problem, as Bach followed tradition in not setting original poems, but Biblical passages and chorale verses. His way of combining these shows the same mastery that we see in his choice of chorale verses for the Passions. A wonderful effect is made at the end of *Fürchte dich nicht* by the entry of the chorale "Herr mein Hirt, Brunn aller Freuden! Du bist mein, ich bin dein" ("Lord my shepherd, source of all joy! Thou art mine, I am thine") during the chorus "Fürchte dich nicht, ich habe dich erlöset; ich habe dich bei deinem Namen gerufen; du bist mein" ("Fear thou not, I have redeemed thee; I have called thee by thy name; thou art mine"). There is a similarly profound and moving stroke in the motet *Jesu meine Freude*, where Bach elucidates the verses of the mystical hymn by the intercalation of passages from the eighth chapter of the Epistle to the Romans. We may regard this text as Bach's sermon upon life and death.

---

* See I, 140.

** The memorial is given in Spitta III, 311.

The musical beauty of the motets was acclaimed by Mozart, who had the greatness of Bach borne in upon him in a flash during a performance of *Singet dem Herrn* *. Zelter writes to Goethe that if the latter could only be so fortunate as to hear a performance of a Bach motet he would feel that he was "in the very centre of the world"**. And truly when this music rings out we lose sight of the world with all its unrest, its care and sorrow. We are alone with Bach, who soothes our souls with the wonderful peace of his own heart, and lifts us above all that is, was and shall be. When the tones have died away we feel that we must sit still with folded hands, and thank the master for his legacy to mankind.

The question is still debated whether the motets are to be performed *a cappella*, or whether the voices should be supported by the organ or orchestra. We must remember that in Bach's time the pure vocal style had been quite lost by German composers. Their vocal works are written instrumentally. If, however, the voices are to be handled in this free style they must be supported in some way. By *a cappella* music was understood, at that time, and on this side of the Alps, not music for voices alone, but compositions in which the orchestra did not play an independent rôle. It was always taken for granted that the organ was to supply the harmonic foundation, and that instruments were to double the voices. The organ accompaniment in particular was regarded as indispensable. Mattheson, in his *Das beschützte Orchestre* (1717), shows that in his day there were no longer any vocalists who could sing without the support of the organ or the clavier; during Kuhnau's cantorate the St. Thomas boys who sang in the streets used to employ a small portable regal; Kirn-

* See I, 232 for Rochlitz's account of Mozart's sudden enthusiasm for Bach.

** See I, 241. It is possible, however, that by "motet" Zelter really means "cantata". We learn from Mendelssohn that Zelter used to give the cantatas before a small audience.

berger and Zelter are of opinion that all *a cappella* singing should be supported by the organ. Had Bach, therefore, performed his motets with the voices alone he would have been running counter to the practice of his epoch.

Moreover, in the case of one of his motets — *Der Geist hilft unsrer Schwachheit auf* — we possess a figured organ part and duplicate instrumental parts, all in Bach's handwriting. The first chorus is supported by the strings, the second by oboes, taille and bassoon. In the autograph score there is no hint of these additions, — which implies that Bach regarded the making of the instrumental parts as a matter of course, and that his practice would be the same in the other motets, only that there the instrumental parts have been lost. The motet *Lobet den Herrn, alle Heiden* was accompanied by at any rate the organ, as is shewn by the existence of a *continuo* part that is quite different from the bass of the choir.

Internal evidence, too, points to the fact that in the other motets the voices were supported by the organ; otherwise we can hardly believe that in *Singet dem Herrn* Bach would give the basses of the first chorus so long-held a note as this —

We must remember also that the motets for double chorus are so arranged that a *continuo* part can easily be made out of a combination of the two bass parts; Bach's *continuo* part in *Der Geist hilft unsrer Schwachheit auf* is constructed on this basis. How much he relies on the filling up of the harmonies here may be seen from the fact that where both basses are silent he makes the organist play with the tenor and work out the figured bass.

Further, the motets are merely the same kind of vocal music as Bach writes everywhere else. In the cantatas are a great number of movements that are really nothing else but motets*. They have no independent orchestral accompaniment; the instruments double the vocal parts. And these choruses prove how remote Bach was from the ideal of true *a cappella* singing. He will rather have too many orchestral parts than too few. Strings and oboes do not satisfy him; as a rule he employs four trombones — one to each voice-part.

Historical considerations thus make it practically certain that Bach had his motets accompanied by organ and orchestra**. In art, however, historical considerations alone are never decisive. It might well have been that Bach, with his feeble choir, regarded the co-operation of the instruments as indispensable, and that we, with our large and expert choirs, not only can but ought to dispense with them.

Here it must be unconditionally admitted that the double-choir motets in particular, when sung by a powerful and thoroughly efficient choir, are extraordinarily effective. But this does not settle the question. When we examine the works closely, and note the bold leading of the voices and the way harsh harmonies are piled up at the cost of a slight loss of beauty of tone, we are finally convinced that this freedom in the vocal writing is based on the

* For example, the chorus "Wenn aber jener, der Geist der Wahrheit kommen wird", in *Es ist euch gut, dass ich hingehe* (No. 108); the chorus "Wer an ihn glaubet, wird nicht gerichtet", in *Also hat Gott die Welt geliebt* (No. 68); and the opening choruses of *Christum wir sollen loben schon* (No. 121), *Wär' Gott nicht mit uns diese Zeit* (No. 14), *Aus tiefer Not schrei ich zu dir* (No. 38), and *Ach Gott vom Himmel sieh darein* (No. 2).

** We must not omit to mention that Gerber, who says he heard a Latin motet of Bach's at a service in Leipzig in 1767, remarks that the St. Thomas's choir sang it "without any accompaniment". The question arises whether this "without any accompaniment" bars out the organ also, or merely means that no other instruments took part in it. Kirnberger would not have been able to maintain positively that every chorus in the service was to be sung with the organ, if his teacher Bach had given the motets without the organ. It must be remembered, too, that in Lent, when the organ was silenced, the motets also were discontinued.

assumption of a harmonic substructure, and that the motets are best performed with a choir of moderate size — about sixty voices — with organ accompaniment.

If this view gains acceptance, the motets will be sung more frequently than they are now, since the opinion is at present widespread that only choirs of the utmost virtuosity dare venture to give them, and many a good Bach choir has not fulfilled expectations in the *a cappella* performance of a motet. If we are going to accompany the voices with instruments, we should employ not only strings but oboes and bassoons, as Bach always does in the motet choruses of his cantatas. If the instruments are numerous enough we get a peculiarly delightful *timbre*, and every detail of the part-writing comes out clearly. When the effect of an experiment with instrumental accompaniment is disappointing it is because strings alone have been used, and these on far too small a scale. The *cantus firmus* of the chorale may be accompanied by the trumpet.

Bach's work in the domain of the sacred song is principally known to us from Schemelli's hymn-book*. Of its sixty-nine melodies, twenty-four, according to the latest research, cannot be dated earlier than Bach. As the preface states that the melodies are "partly composed and partly improved in their figured basses by Herr Johann Sebastian Bach of Leipzig", these twenty-four are presumably his own**. As was pointed out in the chapter on the history

* On the subject of Schemelli's hymn-book, and Bach's share in it, see I, 22.

** The whole of the melodies in Schemelli's hymn-book will be found in B. G. XXXIX. Those supposed to be by Bach are: "Vergiss mich nicht"; "Dir, dir Jehova will ich singen"; "Mein Jesus, was für Seelenweh"; "Gott, wie gross ist deine Güte"; "Kommt, Seelen, dieser Tag"; "Kommt wieder aus der finstern Gruft"; "Komm, süsser Tod"; "Ach, dass nicht die letzte Stunde"; "O liebe Seele, zieh die Sinnen"; "Ich halte treulich still"; "Ich liebe Jesum alle Stund"; "Selig wer an Jesum denkt"; "Jesu, deine Liebeswunden"; "Beschränkt, ihr Weisen dieser Welt"; "Eins ist not! ach Herr dies eine"; "O finstre Nacht, wann wirst du doch"; "Dich bet' ich an, mein höchster Gott"; "Jesu, Jesu,

of the chorale melodies, they are sacred arias rather than chorale melodies. The best-known are "Mein Jesu, was für Seelenweh", "Kommt, Seelen, dieser Tag", "Komm, süsser Tod", "Liebster Herr Jesu, wo bleibst du so lange", and "Ich steh an deiner Krippe hier".

In the *Klavierbüchlein* of Anna Magdalena we find another and simpler melody to "Gib dich zufrieden" than that which Bach wrote for Schemelli, and the aria "Gedenke doch, mein Herz, zurücke ans Grab und an den Glockenschlag".

The dedication to his faithful life-companion, "Bist du bei mir", is especially moving*.

The melody of the beautiful long-song "Willst du dein Herz mir schenken" is presumably not by Bach. He copied it for his wife into the *Klavierbüchlein*, and inscribed it "Aria di Giovannini"**. The aria on the tobacco pipe however, seems to be his***. Like the two other songs from the first *Klavierbüchlein*, — "Bist du bei mir" and "Gedenke doch" — it contains a meditation on death.

---

du bist mein"; "Liebster Herr Jesu, wo bleibst du so lange"; "Ich steh' an deiner Krippe hier"; "So wünsch ich mir zu guter letzt"; "Auf, auf, die rechte Zeit ist hier"; "Ich lass dich nicht"; "Meines Lebens letzte Zeit".

* "Bist du bei mir, geh' ich mit Freuden zum Sterben und zu meiner Ruh.
Ach vergnügt wär' so mein Ende, es drückten deine schönen Hände
Mir die getreuen Augen zu."

** "Willst du dein Herz mir schenken, so fang es heimlich an,
Dass unser beider Denken niemand erraten kann.
Die Liebe muss bei beiden allzeit verschwiegen sein,
Drum schliess' die grössten Freuden in deinem Herzen ein."

*** "So oft ich meine Tabakspfeife, mit gutem Knaster angefüllt,
Zur Lust und Zeitvertreib ergreife, so gibt sie mir ein Trauerbild
Und füget diese Lehre bei, dass ich derselben ähnlich sei."

CHAPTER XXXII.

THE ORATORIOS.

B. G. V². The Christmas Oratorio.
B. G. XXI³. The Easter Oratorio.
B. G. II. The Ascension Oratorio (Cantata *Lobet Gott in seinen Reichen*: No. 11).

We possess the original score of the *Christmas Oratorio* and the parts, the latter carefully revised by Bach himself. How closely he went through these may be seen from the fact that he noted that the copyist had required a wind player to transpose in the middle of a solo, — whereupon he removed the error. The score and the parts, — now in the Royal Library at Berlin — once belonged to Emmanuel, who has written on the cover "composed in 1734, in the fiftieth year of the composer". We also have a text-book of the first performance of the work.

Bach's title of "oratorio" is misleading. An oratorio implies a Biblical action. This is lacking in Bach's work. It consists of lyrical meditations, held together by recitatives that tell the Christmas story as it is given in Matthew and Luke.

Moreover the work was never given under Bach as a whole and at one time, but in six parts, — on the three days of Christmas, New Year's day, the Sunday after New Year's day, and Epiphany. The *Christmas Oratorio* is therefore merely a collection of six cantatas which Bach wrote for the Christmas of 1734, and that only differ from other Christmas and post-Christmas cantatas in this respect, that the one mood runs through them all, and together they tell the full story of the birth of Christ.

He must have conceived the plan of such a collection of cantatas as early as 1733. It was the time when he was trying to support his petition for the title of Court Composer by a number of occasional compositions in honour of the royal house. It was out of the question that this music, after being performed, should be allowed to moulder in a drawer. The ceremonial and gladsome character of the choruses in these works made them specially suitable for the Christmas festival. We may thus almost say that Bach wrote the *Christmas Oratorio* in order that the finest movements of *Die Wahl des Herkules* and the *Dramma per musica* in honour of the Queen — *Tönet, ihr Pauken, erschallet Trompeten* — should not be lost. *Die Wahl des Herkules* had been given on 5th September 1733, the *Dramma per musica* on 8th December of the same year — both by the Telemann Society.

In the original score we can distinguish the borrowed movements from the new ones by the fact that the former are carefully and neatly written, while the remainder have been written hastily and are sometimes hardly legible. Besides the numbers taken from *Die Wahl des Herkules* and the *Dramma per musica*, there are some others that are evidently fair copies. It is practically certain that these also are not original, but are taken from occasional compositions which we cannot trace. The conclusion is that the great introductory choruses of the six cantatas and almost all the great solo numbers of the *Christmas Oratorio* are borrowed*.

* From the *Dramma per musica zu Ehren der Königin* are derived:

1. The chorus "Jauchzet, frohlocket" (1st cantata).
2. The aria "Grosser Herr und starker König (1st cantata).
3. The aria "Frohe Hirten eilt" (2nd cantata).
4. The chorus "Herrscher des Himmels" (3rd cantata).

From *Die Wahl des Herkules* are derived:

5. The aria "Bereite dich Zion" (1st cantata).
6. The aria "Schlafe, mein Liebster" (2nd cantata).
7. The duet "Herr, dein Mitleid" (3rd cantata).
8. The chorus "Fallt mit Danken" (4th cantata).
9. The aria "Flösst mein Heiland, flösst dein Name" (4th cantata).
10. The aria "Ich will nur dir zu Ehren leben" (4th cantata).

From the "Cantata gratulatoria in adventum regis", *Preise dein Glücke, gesegnetes Sachsen* — performed on 5th October 1734 — is derived:

We must neither overestimate nor underestimate the bearing of this fact on the artistic value of the *Christmas Oratorio*. Spitta underrates it, saying that the fact that the music was originally written for another text does not deprive it of any of its beauty. Others hold that the discovery of the *provenance* of the choruses and arias dissipates a good deal of the charm of the work. Against this it may be urged that a distinction must here be made between the choruses and the arias. The former are as good as original compositions could be; the declamation is excellent; the moods and ideas of the text correspond as exactly to the music as if the latter had been composed expressly to these particular words. The impression one gets is rather that their charm and beauty do not mate with the text of the secular cantatas.

The arias do not show the same happy agreement between the music and the words. The music to "Ich will nur dir zu Ehren leben", "Bereite dich Zion", and "Herr, dein Mitleid" in particular shows too clearly that it was prompted by other ideas and images than those of the present text*. The most artless hearer feels this discrepancy between the poem and the music; the majority of these arias do not affect him greatly. The declamation — thanks to the care with which the new text has been put together — does not often suggest adaptation, but it is

---

11. The aria "Erleucht auch meine finstern Sinne" (5th cantata).

The following come from unknown cantatas:

12. The aria "Schliesse mein Herze dies selige Wunder" (3rd cantata).
13. The chorus "Ehre sei dir, Gott, gesungen" (5th cantata).
14. The trio "Ach wann wird die Zeit erscheinen" (5th cantata).
15. The chorus "Herr, wenn die stolzen Feinde toben" (6th cantata).
16. The aria "Nur ein Wink von seinen Händen" (6th cantata).
17. The aria "Nun mögt ihr stolzen Feinde schrecken" (6th cantata).

* For further details see p. 282.

certainly not as natural as in other arias. All this, however, simply proves that the chief significance of the *Christmas Oratorio* is not to be sought in the arias, and that it is no crime to "cut" them.

The three choruses that belong to the action of the Christmas story — "Ehre sei Gott", "Lasset uns hingehen", and "Wo ist der neugeborene König" — are supremely beautiful. The commencement of the first reminds us strongly of the youthful freshness of the organ fantasia in G major (Peters IV, No. 11); in the others we are struck by their remarkable simplicity and concision. In performance, the beauty of "Lasset uns hingehen" is usually spoiled by too quick a tempo; people forget that the agitation and hurrying at the departure of the shepherds is already expressed in the semiquaver figure of the flutes and first violins, and that a quick tempo obliterates these runs and prevents the hearer perceiving their meaning. It may be suggested that the fine quaver-motive in the basses in "Ehre sei Gott" and "Lasset uns hingehen" would be brought out better by the addition of a few bassoons.

It was a very happy idea of Picander's to accompany the action with short meditative recitatives. They are well written, and have inspired Bach to some beautiful and fervent music. Especially fine are "So geht denn hin, ihr Hirten, gehet", "Immanuel, o süsses Wort", "Wohlan, dein Name soll allein in meinem Herzen sein", and the chorale with recitative "Er ist auf Erden kommen arm", — pastoral pipes playing round the last.

Perhaps the most moving effects come from the chorales with independent orchestral accompaniment. "Ach mein herzliebes Jesulein, mach dir ein rein sanft Bettelein, zu ruhn in meines Herzens Schrein . . ." ("Ah! dearest Jesus, Holy Child, make thee a bed, soft, undefiled, within my heart, and there recline"*) sings the chorus on the announcement that Mary has cradled the Child in a manger;

* [Mr. Troutbeck's translation, in Novello's edition of the oratorio. Tr.]

and we hear stately interludes in the three trumpets — a royal cradle-music for the Child in the stable at Bethlehem. The chorale "Wir singen dir in deinem Heer" ("With all thy hosts, oh Lord, we sing") is accompanied by the motive of the angels from the sinfonia at the commencement of the Second Part, since the preceding recitative indicates that it represents the combined song of angels and men. In the chorale "Jesu, richte mein Beginnen" the horn parts are of exquisite tenderness. The final chorale, "Nun seid ihr wohl gerochen", with its wonderful trumpet figures, is a song of triumph of inimitable grandeur.

Chorales with independent orchestral accompaniment are found in the cantatas of the first Leipzig period, but not in those belonging to the period of the *Christmas Oratorio*. There are so many other things in this work that remind us of the earlier ones, that if the date were not so thoroughly vouched for we should be tempted to believe it had been written ten years previously. This is a unique characteristic of Bach — the years have no effect on the artist in him. At fifty he can write as youthful music as at twenty-five.

Most hearers fail to perceive the beauty of the sinfonia that opens the Second Part; it gives them a slight feeling of disappointment. Instead of a tender pastorale, of the kind we have in Handel's *Messiah*, they get a movement into the mood of which they cannot quite enter. Even when played most tenderly it has a certain restlessness in it; it does not give the hallowed impression of the star-strewn heavens that we should expect from a prelude to the narrative of the shepherds who are watching their flocks by night. Probably there is no conductor who has not felt the difficulty of making so extremely animated a movement give the idea of the serene tranquillity of nature. Anyone who has had the truly painful experience of going through several performances of the sinfonia cannot help asking, in the end, whether Bach really intended to express the mood that his interpreters put into it*, and that never succeeds in performance.

But if the movement is properly understood it has quite a different meaning. No one who knows that the motive in strings and flutes is generally employed by Bach to symbolise angels**, and who notices that the movement is performed by two contrasted groups, — the four oboes having a theme of their own and being quite independent of the strings, whether they alternate or join with them — can have any doubt as to the meaning of the sinfonia. It represents the angels and the shepherds making music together. Bach is once more writing music that depicts a situation. The shepherds in the fields awake and blow their pipes; over them there hovers already the band of angels that is about to appear to them. Their music blends with that of the shepherds. Bach thus intends the movement to be an introduction to the recitative "And there were shepherds in the same country, abiding in the field . . . And lo, an angel of the Lord stood by them". If this be so, we need no longer take all the animation out of the sinfonia by playing it very softly and slowly; we can play it just as it is. The part for the flutes and violins must come out energetically if it is to suggest the joyous music of the angels. The oboes should play *piano* throughout, and in a tempo just a shade slower. Where the strings alone are playing, or interrupt the oboes for a moment, a *forte* is required; the short parentheses in particular must give the effect of a shout of joy. Where the strings play with the oboes, the former should, as a rule, play *piano*, as if the angels were listening to the pipes of the shepherds. In this way we not only give an admirable and natural variety to the movement, but we make it immediately intelligible to every hearer.

---

* According to Spitta, "the fundamental feeling" of the sinfonia is a combination of "the grace of the Eastern idyl with the severity of the starlit boreal winter's night". (Spitta II, 581.)

** See p. 80, where the two themes of the sinfonia are quoted.

It is desirable also that the violin motive be played with a somewhat heavy grace, the third and ninth quavers receiving a kind of secondary accent that detaches them, as it were, from the note that follows: —

For a full performance of the *Christmas Oratorio* two evenings are required. If possible the performance should be so arranged that the first comes in Advent or Christmas, and the second in Epiphany. If only one evening is available, it is better to "cut" the work freely rather than to hurry over it, for at the end the hearer is too tired to appreciate the beauty of the second part. It is a bad custom to make more cuts in the second part than in the first. The general principle to go upon is not to omit the great introductory choruses, the chorales, the recitatives, or anything relating to the action of the Christmas story; the cuts should all be in the arias*.

For a popular performance in church we can safely cut out almost all the arias without any risk of leaving a mere torso; as a matter of fact by so doing we shall make the action all the clearer and more beautiful**. The

* For example, the arias "Grosser König", "Frohe Hirten", "Schliesse mein Herze" and "Erleucht auch" might be omitted altogether, and big cuts made in the echo aria "Flösst mein Heiland" and the trio "Ach wann wird die Zeit". The short recitatives "Was Gott dem Abraham" and "Ja, ja mein Herz" might also be omitted.

** This refers only to the long and independent arias, — "Bereite dich Zion", "Grosser König", "Frohe Hirten", "Herr, dein Mitleid", "Schliesse mein Herze", "Flösst mein Heiland", "Ich will dir zu Ehren", "Erleucht auch meine schwachen Sinnen", "Ach wann wird die Zeit", "Nur ein Wink", and "Nun mögt ihr stolzen Feinde". The contemplative solo pieces, that bear on the action, must be retained. The proposal to sacrifice the independent arias in a church performance must not be taken as a depreciation of the arias in general. It simply means that small societies, that feel that they cannot give the *Christmas Oratorio* because of the expense of the soloists, will find the work very effective without the great solo numbers.

cradle song, "Schlafe, mein Liebster", should be retained, but it should be removed to the point in the action to which it really belongs, — at the end of the recitative "And they came with haste, and found both Mary and Joseph . . . But Mary kept all these things, and pondered them in her heart." Then it becomes the lullaby that the mother sings to the Holy Child when she is once more alone with Him*.

The Easter oratorio, *Kommt, eilet und laufet* (B. G. XXI[3]), is in its present form simply a large cantata. In its first form, as we see from the original parts, the work was a real oratorio. Mary the mother of James (soprano), Mary Magdalene (contralto), Peter (tenor), and John (bass) take part in it as active dramatic personages; the opening duet between tenor and bass represented the dialogue of Peter and John when running to the grave. At a later date the action struck Bach as insufficient for a religious drama; he took out the names of the characters, recast the opening duet in the form of a chorus, and left the middle movement only in duet-form. Unfortunately the orchestral parts of this third and definitive redaction that we possess are incomplete, so that Rust, when he was editing the work, felt compelled to mediate between the second version and the third. He gives the first main movement and the middle movement in the form of a choral duet, and does not bring in the four-part chorus until the end**.

The first movement contains a remarkable representation of running. It is interesting to note that the original

* In this case the recitatives "So geht denn hin" and "Ja, ja mein Herz" must also be cut out. It is incomprehensible how Bach could allow the cradle song to be sung after the bare annunciation of the angels. Even in performances in which the other arias are not sacrificed, the lullaby should be transferred to the point mentioned above.

** See his Preface to B. G. XXI[3]. It is fairly certain that the work was written about 1736. The date of the two revisions cannot be determined.

text originally was "Kommt, gehet und laufet" ("Come, go and run"); the later version of the words, which is much more animated and more singable, is by Bach himself.

There is a wonderful peace expressed in the tenor aria, "Sanfte soll mein Todeskummer" ("Easy my death shall be"). The voice is accompanied by the first and second violins *con sordini*, with the *flûtes à bec* doubling them; it is one of the most beautiful sacred lullabies that Bach ever wrote. We seem to be gazing in a dream over a gently-moving sea, towards the fields of eternity* —

The Ascension Oratorio, *Lobet Gott in seinen Reichen* (No. 11), — called by Bach an oratorio, though the text has scarcely a trace of Biblical action — probably belongs to the same period as the Easter Oratorio. Perhaps the music of the powerful and animated opening chorus was originally written for some secular festival cantata; this seems probable from some rather faulty pieces of declamation, such as this —

Sucht sein Lob— recht zu— ver - glei - chen.

and this —

Lo - bet Gott

They do not, however, diminish the effect of this spirited movement.

---

* The text should be altered somewhat; we hear a little too much of the "Schweisstuch Jesu" ("handkerchief of Jesus").

The final chorus takes the form of a chorale fantasia upon the last strophe of the hymn "Gott fähret auf gen Himmel":

"Wann soll es doch geschehen, wann kömmt die liebe Zeit,
Dass ich ihn werde sehen in seiner Herrlichkeit?
Du Tag, wann wirst du sein,
Dass wir den Heiland grüssen?
Dass wir den Heiland küssen?
Komm, stelle dich doch ein!"

The music to which Bach has set these words glows with ardent, mystic love. The accompaniment perpetually repeats this passionate motive —

CHAPTER XXXIII.

THE MASSES.

B. G. VI. B minor Mass.
B. G. VIII. Four small Masses.
B. G. XI[1]. Four *Sanctus*.

When Bach petitioned, on 27th July 1733, for the title of Court Composer*, he sent his sovereign the parts of the *Kyrie* and the *Gloria* of a Mass in B minor. He did not send the score; this he kept for himself. It was a frequent practice at that time to perform large works without a score.

These parts are now in the King of Saxony's private library at Dresden. As they show no signs of having

* See I, 139.

been used, it is doubtful whether the work that Bach wrote in order to secure the Kapellmeistership was ever performed. He had written out most of the parts himself, and added phrasing signs and marks of expression.

The *Gloria* consists not only of the "Gloria in excelsis et in terra pax hominibus bonae voluntatis", but comprises all the sections pertaining to this in the Mass — *Laudamus, Gratias, Domine, Qui tollis, Qui sedes, Quoniam, Cum sancto spiritu.*

It is curious that Bach should have described the *Kyrie* and *Gloria,* on the title-page of the original parts, as *Missa,* and designated the succeeding sections, — the *Credo, Sanctus* and *Osanna* — as independent parts, whereas, of course, it is the *ensemble* of them that constitutes the Mass. Emmanuel also enumerates the four parts separately in the catalogue of his musical library. Bach also entitles four smaller *Kyrie* and *Gloria* "Masses". His reason for this strange nomenclature is unknown. The designation of the *Kyrie* and the *Gloria* as "Masses" has nothing to do with the "Missa brevis".

Spitta thinks that the *Credo, Sanctus* and *Osanna* may have been written between 1734 and 1738. Bach does not appear to have sent these sections to the Court.

The parts of the *Credo* came into the possession of Emmanuel, who performed this section of the Mass in Hamburg, with an orchestral introduction of his own. We also possess the parts of the *Sanctus*; they are now in the Royal Library at Berlin. At the end of the original score of this section there is a note to the effect that the parts are with Count Sporck, in Bohemia.

Franz Anton, Count of Sporck*, was the Governor of Bohemia; he had close relations with the Leipzig artists and scholars. He seems to have been deeply interested in music; when he heard of the invention of the French horn in Paris he sent two of his servants there to learn

* See Spitta III, 42 ff.

how to play the instrument. He died in 1738 — during Bach's lifetime, that is to say — at his estate of Lissa. Bach would not fail to claim his property from the heirs, so that the parts in the Berlin Library are no doubt those from which the Governor of Bohemia used to have the *Sanctus* performed for him.

As a matter of prudence, and perhaps in the hope of finding the parts of the *Osanna*, the Bachgesellschaft, in 1854, requested the director of the Prague Conservatoire to make inquiries as to what had become of the Count's music. An official of the estate replied that "many years ago a lot of old music had been partly given away, partly lost; some of it had been given to the gardeners to wrap round the trees" *.

Thus we possess the complete original score of the B minor Mass, which belonged to Emmanuel, and the original parts of the *Kyrie*, *Gloria*, *Credo* and *Sanctus*.

The whole work was probably never given by Bach in a Leipzig service; but it is certain that he performed the separate sections. He would presumably give the *Credo* on Trinity Sunday; the *Kyrie* he could use in the principal services during times of mourning, as at these periods the cantata was omitted and the *Kyrie* was sung; of the *Gloria* we possess a score specially made in 1740, with the title "Festo nativitatis Christi" **.

It must be added that some of the sections of the B minor Mass are borrowed from other works. The *Gratias* comes from the cantata *Wir danken dir* (No. 29); the *Qui tollis* from *Schauet doch und sehet* (No. 46); the *Patrem omnipotentem* from *Gott, wie ist dein Name* (No. 171); the *Crucifixus* from *Weinen, Klagen* (No. 12); the *Osanna* from the

* See the Preface to B. G. VI. Whether the parts of the *Sanctus* are those that Bach sent to Count Sporck cannot now be accurately determined, the note at the end being undecipherable.

** For information regarding this *Gloria* see Spitta III, 40. This score was not available when the B. G. edition of the B minor Mass was prepared in 1855.

secular cantata *Preise dein Glücke*; the *Agnus Dei* from the cantata *Lobet Gott in seinen Reichen* (No. 11). These are not mere transfers, however, but rearrangements, often so thorough-going that it is more correct to speak of their being suggested by the original than borrowed from it. We can estimate the musical value of these numbers without the necessity of taking into account that they exist in other forms and other texts of the same nature.

The salient quality of the B minor Mass is its wonderful sublimity. The first chord of the *Kyrie* takes us into the world of great and profound emotions; we do not leave it until the final cadence of the *Dona nobis pacem*. It is as if Bach had here tried to write a really *Catholic* Mass; he endeavours to present faith under its larger and more objective aspects. Some of the splendid and brilliant chief choruses have quite a "Catholic" tinge. Yet in the other movements we get the same subjective, intimate spirit as in the cantatas, which we may regard as the Protestant element in Bach's religion. The sublime and the intimate do not interpenetrate; they co-exist side by side; they are separable from each other like the objective and the subjective in Bach's piety; and so the B minor Mass is at once Catholic and Protestant, and in addition as enigmatic and unfathomable as the religious consciousness of its creator.

The dual nature of the work is evident even in the earliest movements. The introductory *Kyrie eleison* is a large conception; it sends up a solemn supplication to God; the universal Christian church cries to its Father in heaven and bends before Him; we seem to see nation after nation pouring into the assembly and joining in the prayer*. The *Christe eleison*, on the other hand, is sunny and serene; it is the soul's glad and confident prayer to

* It is incomprehensible how some conductors can end this section *pianissimo* instead of *fortissimo*. The final entry of the theme in the bass cannot be too powerful.

its Redeemer. In the last *Kyrie* the gloom of the first is overcome; we no longer hear cries and entreaties, but a quiet, composed lament. The tranquil motion and the transfiguration of the bitter harmonies are like a symbol of the faith and hope that are mingled with this lament. The interludes with the animated —

in which we hear a reminiscence of the ardent supplication of the first chorus, are only there to throw into higher and higher relief the tranquility of the main theme —

There is some doubt as to how the *Gloria* should follow the *Kyrie.* There is a temptation to get a strong contrast by commencing the one immediately after the other. It is better, however, to interpose a fairly long pause between them, during which orchestra, choir and audience can traverse in silence the ground between the *Kyrie* and the *Gloria*, and ascend from the depths of the minor to the heights of the major harmonies from which, with the first D major chords, the world of praise and thanksgiving will be opened out before them.

It is not to the advantage of the movement to read too much into Bach's marking of *vivace.* The first section of the chorus must end without any perceptible *rallentando* and *diminuendo* before the *Et in terra pax.* That this second part is not to be taken *piano* is proved by the noticeably heavy orchestration. The length of the movement makes it undesirable to adopt so slow a tempo as the usual one. The build of the phrases in *Hominibus bonae voluntatis* shows that Bach wishes the *Et in terra pax* to be sung with a certain animation.

The fine violin accompaniment to the *Laudamus te* is a typical specimen of Bach's "joy" motive*. In the *Gratias agimus*, as in the last *Kyrie*, there is a conflict between the tempi of the two related themes. The wonderfully cheerful and tranquil theme expresses the opening words —

Gra - - ti - as a - - gi - mus ti - bi

The "propter magnam gloriam tuam" is set to a much more lively motive —

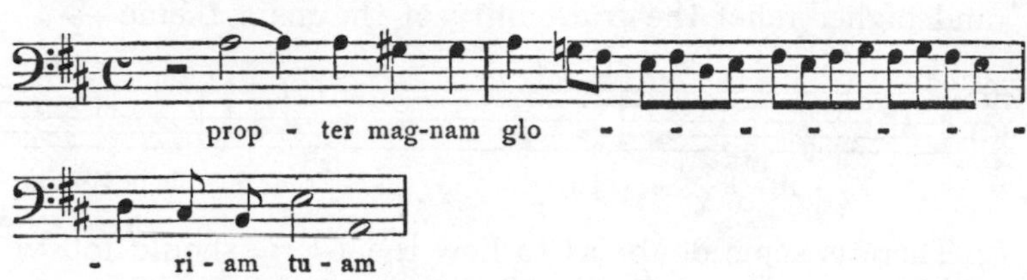
prop - ter mag-nam glo - - - - - - -
- ri - am tu - am

Their diversity is so great in Bach's eyes that as a rule he does not employ them together, but makes the chorus up of a succession of segments, constructed now on this motive, now on that. The charm and the difficulty in the performance of this movement consist in giving each of the segments its own appropriate tempo without impairing the unity of the tempo as a whole.

The *Gloria*, *Laudamus*, and *Gratias* constitute a single idea, and should not be separated by the slightest pause. After the *Gratias* we may pause for a moment, and then begin, with the *Domine*, the praise of Christ that continues to the *Credo*. The close connection of the texts here — the *Domine*, *Qui tollis*, *Qui sedes*, *Quoniam*, *Cum sancto spiritu* — must be reproduced in the succession of the movements.

The solos in these movements are generally taken much too slowly, so that, — especially when the singers indulge

* See p. 110.

liberally in *rallentandi* — the natural animation of the music suffers*. In the *tutti* parts of the *Quoniam* it is advisable to strengthen the two obbligato bassoons by two or more violoncellos. In the accompanied parts one would almost venture to recommend an alternation between two solo bassoons and two solo violoncelli.

Between the *Cum sancto spiritu* and the *Credo* comes the first large incision in the B minor Mass. From this point to the *Sanctus* all the sections are closely connected. They fall into three groups. The first, which relates to the Father, contains the *Credo* and the *Patrem omnipotentem*; the second, which relates to Christ, consists of the *Et in unum deum*, the *Et incarnatus est*, the *Crucifixus* and the *Et resurrexit*; the third, dealing with the Holy Ghost, embraces the *Et in spiritum sanctum* and the *Confiteor*. The three groups should be separated from each other by very short pauses; within each group the movements must follow each other without a break*.

The *Symbolum Nicaenum* is a hard nut for a composer to crack. If ever there was a text put together without any idea of its being set to music it is this, in which the Greek theologians have laid down their correct and dry formulas for the conception of the godhead of Christ. In no Mass has the difficulty of writing music for the *Credo* been so completely overcome as in this of Bach's. He

* I was particularly convinced of the preferability of a quick and tense tempo for these movements by a performance of the B minor Mass at Heidelberg under Professor Wolfrum. His tempi in general were the ideal ones for the work; it is to be wished that he would make them available for general use by giving the metronome numbers.

The remarks in the text as to the tempo in the solos being too slow applies to the whole of the B minor Mass. The *Laudamus te* is, as a rule, almost dragged.

** So much stress is here laid upon the right grouping of the numbers of the B minor Mass because it is of great importance to the effect, and many modern conductors do not know enough of the liturgy to avoid making false and capricious breaks in the continuity of the work.

has taken the utmost possible advantage of any dramatic ideas in the text; when emotion can be read into it he does so.

The external configuration of the text is itself masterly. The sections that lend themselves to brilliant tone-painting are worked out twice; others are compressed and treated continuously. The effect of the *Confiteor* mostly depends on the precise management and the close connection of the final periods of the *Credo*. One of the most striking features of the B minor Mass in general and the *Credo* in particular is Bach's excellent Latin declamation. His most daring *coloratura* are only the artistic intensification of the natural syllabic values and accents of the words.

The theologian Bach also had a hand in the composition of the *Credo*. He knew what the Greek fathers had in their minds when they took such pains to prove the identity of Christ with God and yet assert a diversity and independence of persons. To the dogmatist Bach the parallel passages of the *Et in unum Dominum* — "deum de deo" ("God of God"), "lumen de lumine" ("light of lights"), "genitum non factum" ("begotten, not made"), "con substantialem" ("of like substance") — were not merely empty sounds to be turned into music; he knew what the formulæ meant, and translated them into terms of music. He makes both singers sing the same notes, but in such a way that it does not amount to the same thing; the voices follow each other in strict canonic imitation; the one proceeds out of the other just as Christ proceeds of God —

Even the instruments take part in the canon. They signify in a special way the community of substance and difference of persons; the notes —

are always phrased two distinct ways in the different instruments; either —

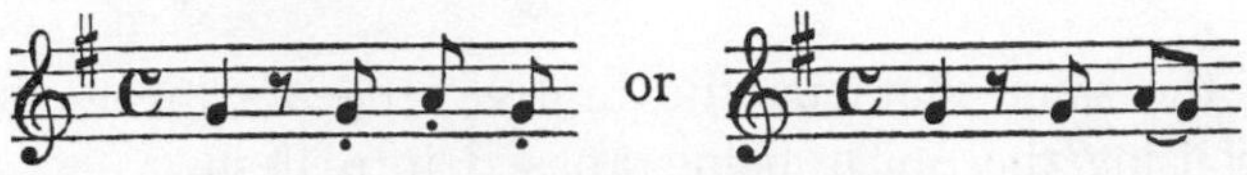

Bach thus proves that the dogma can be expressed much more clearly and satisfactorily in music than in verbal formulæ. His exegesis of these passages in the Nicene Creed has resolved the disputes that excited the Eastern world for many generations and finally delivered it over to Islam; his presentation of the dogma even makes it acceptable and comprehensible to minds for which dogma has no attraction.

In the dewy-fresh and flowing music of the *Et in unum spiritum sanctum* Bach's imagination had been fired by the word "vivificantem"; he depicts the Spirit as "that which makes alive" —

At the end of this movement, at the *Descendit de coelis* ("He descended from heaven") we get the motive of falling —

In the *Et incarnatus est* the Holy Spirit hovers over the earth as if in quest of a being into which it can enter —

At the words "Et homo factus est" it sinks to a restless conclusion —

At the same moment the motive appears in the bass, symbolising the Spirit being abased into flesh.

The *Crucifixus* is constructed upon a *basso ostinato* formed from the chromatic motive of grief; the choral writing is soft and vaporous, like that preceding it, so that the inexpressible sadness of the harmonies has a touch of the superterrestrial and the transfigured in it, as if the composer had had in his mind the "It is finished" of the dying Lord.

The *Et resurrexit* represents the victorious jubilation of redeemed mankind. Note should be taken not only of the fine line of the bold theme but of its perfectly natural declamation —

Et re - sur - re - xit re - sur - re - xit.

The chorus upon the *Credo* has for its theme the well-known splendid old intonation of the creed —

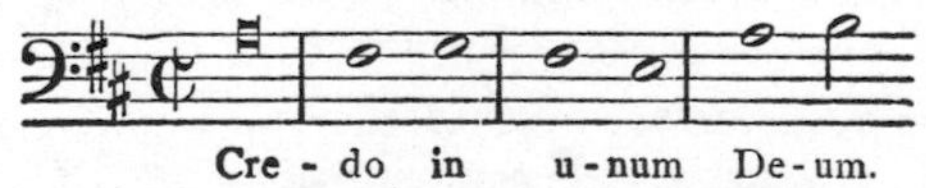
Cre - do in u - num De - um.

The steadfast and confident quaver-sequences in the bass symbolise the firmness of the faith. They are most effective when the individual notes are not tied but detached from each other, with an up-take grouping —

The tempo must not be too slow, or else the augmentation of the theme at the end, commencing in the vocal basses and extending to the whole movement, will not be perceptible to the hearer.

Bach could not base the *Confiteor* chorus on the old church tone, as this does not yield a theme capable of being developed polyphonically. He is thus compelled to invent a theme of his own; but he twice introduces the old intonation, — from the seventy-third bar onwards in a *stretto* between the bass and the alto, and again in triumphant breadth in the tenor. It runs thus* —

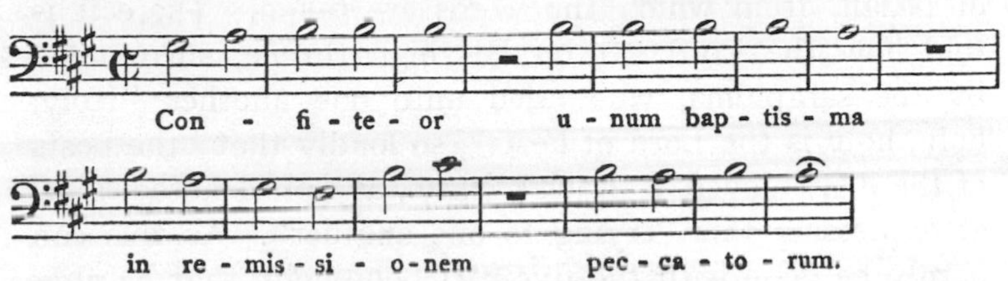

Very characteristic of Bach, again, is the setting of the *Et exspecto resurrectionem mortuorum.* We should expect music with something mysterious and a touch of longing in it; instead of this, the orchestra expresses, by means of the joyous "resurrection" motive, the exultation of the elect at the last day —

Bach lets himself be guided by the correct feeling that in the *Credo* everything presses onward to a big conclusion, which he must not retard by music of too intimate a kind. Note that in the *Patrem omnipotentem* he passes over the

* "I acknowledge one baptism for the remission of sins."

mystical suggestions of the word "invisibilium" — "Creator of all things, visible and invisible" — because he does not wish to interrupt the brilliant stream of music. Many conductors imagine that Bach, following his usual practice, meant to bring this word out saliently, and to express the mystery of the creation of the invisible underworld; and they try to rescue what there is to be rescued of the word, by having it sung *pianissimo* and with a *rallentando*, — or rather by wishing to have it so sung, for this method is so opposed to the structure of Bach's music that it always comes to grief, and only results in making the choir unsteady and the conclusion of the movement unintelligible.

For the *Sanctus*, Bach, who was a student of the Bible, has had in his minds' eye the beginning of the sixth chapter of Isaiah, from which the words are taken. There it is told how the Lord sat on His high throne, surrounded by the seraphims, who cried unto one another "Holy, holy, holy is the Lord of hosts", so loudly that "the posts of the door moved". Bach's music, as Spitta noted, aims at expressing this "crying to one another". As this can hardly be done with the five-part polyphony that he elsewhere employs in the Mass, he here writes the chorus in six parts. There is hardly anything else in all music that expresses so perfectly the idea of the sublime. The basses, that have to support these polyphonic triplets, move along in the most tranquil and powerful "step" motive to be found in all the scores of Bach —

A marvellous effect is made by the trumpets and kettledrums, which Bach employs with somewhat unusual discretion. In the *Pleni sunt coeli* and the *Osanna*, again, he observes a wise moderation in this respect that is of inestimable advantage to the whole movement.

In the *Benedictus* and the *Agnus Dei* we get perhaps the clearest light on the difference between Bach's conception of the Mass and Beethoven's. For Beethoven, the symphonist, these two sections are the culminating point of the drama of the Mass as he conceives it; for Bach, who thinks in terms of the church, they are the point at which it all dies slowly away. In Beethoven's *Agnus Dei* the cry of the pained and terrified soul for salvation is almost dreadful in its intensity; Bach's *Agnus Dei* is the song of the soul redeemed.

In the *Benedictus* he has probably made use of some previous composition of his, — so, at least, one assumes from the rather abrupt style and the repetitions of the words.

The *Dona nobis pacem* is also a confident and hopeful laudation of peace rather than a prayer for it. There is deep significance in the fact that Bach has these words sung to the music of the *Gratias agimus* ("We thank Thee"). A tender style of playing does not suit the character of the movement.

When the B minor Mass was published, the serious error was made of omitting the figuring of the *continuo* in the *Credo,* for the reason that it was in Emmanuel's writing, and could not be proved to have an authentic origin. Granting that the figuring is Emmanuel's own, it is at any rate better than none at all, since no one was in a better position to replace a lost original than he. Moreover it is almost certain that his *continuo* part is a copy of the original. The editor's suspicions were probably aroused by his noticing that the figured chords were not always congruous with those of the obbligato parts. But on these grounds he might have rejected many an original figuring by Bach, the genuineness of which is proved precisely by the fact of its independence. It is to be hoped that the error will be corrected by printing Emmanuel's figuring — which is in the Berlin Library — in the new edition of the

Bachgesellschaft*. Anyone who has had to accompany the B minor Mass on the organ knows how difficult it is even for the player familiar with Bach to divine the harmonies, especially in the solo pieces and the *Et incarnatus est*.

The Bachgesellschaft score is misleading again in the *Credo* and the *Confiteor*. According to this, the *Credo* is to be sung by the choir with organ accompaniment, while the first and second violins play the theme; in the *Confiteor* only the organ is to be employed. If the B. G. score is a correct reprint of the parts that once belonged to Emmanuel, then the error must be in these. Bach certainly did not desire these two choruses to be accompanied only by the organ; in the whole of his scores there is no other example of the violins alone playing an obbligato above the chorus in this fashion. The *Credo* and the *Confiteor* are to be given like the last *Kyrie*, i. e., the strings and wood-wind must double the voice parts. Further, if we consider how often Bach, in motet choruses of this kind, doubles the voice parts with the brass**, it is hardly credible that they would have been idle here, especially as the notes are long ones. It needs no proof that the two obbligato violin parts in the *Credo* should be supported by at any rate the wood-wind if they are to be heard; it is not less certain that the intonation of the *Credo*, that enters in augmentation in the basses towards the end, as well as the *Confiteor* intonation, — first in the basses and altos, then in the tenors, — cannot be heard even by the hearer who knows they are in the score, unless an instrument comes to the assistance of the voices***. Even then, with our heavy choirs, the in-

* On this question see also Seiffert's remarks in the *Bachjahrbuch* for 1904, p. 72 ff.

** See p. 299 ff.

*** At the performance conducted by Bach himself he told the instrumentalists by word of mouth to play from the vocal parts; he would not say so in the score because it was self-evident to him. This explains why the score and the parts give a wrong

tonations demand the support of the organ as well. In these passages the organist should play the *continuo* bass on the pedal, give the harmonies with one hand on a subsidiary manual, and with the other hand play the passages in question on the great organ with the eight and four-feet principals and mixtures; only in this way can these antique melodies come triumphantly through the mighty polyphony in the way that Bach contemplated.

The *Kyrie* and the *Gloria* were published in 1833 by Nägeli of Zürich, who had acquired the original score after the death of Schwenke, Emmanuel's successor; their poor reception was not of the kind to encourage Nägeli to bring out the whole work, and the remainder was first published in 1845 by Simrock, of Bonn. In a copy of the score of the *Credo* that was formerly in the possession of the Berlin Singakademie, Zelter has altered certain high passages in the trumpets with a view to making them more playable, and indicated some excisions. This suggests that he had performed this section of the Mass, or had intended to do so. The letters to Goethe throw no light on the matter. The first complete performance of the Mass was that of the Berlin Singakademie in 1834 and 1835*; perhaps the most perfect performance the work has ever had was that by the Berlin Philharmonic choir under Siegfried Ochs**.

---

idea of how Bach wished the work to be performed. Against these views it may be objected, with some show of reason, that in the *Patrem omnipotentem* and the *Et exspecto resurrectionem* Bach wishes to heighten the effect of the instruments by keeping them silent until then. The reply to this is that he would nevertheless have employed the strings and wood-wind to support the voice parts, and that the necessity of bringing out clearly the intonation of the *Credo* and the *Confiteor* certainly outweighed all other considerations. The scale is turned by the reflection that in the cantatas he always accompanies motet choruses of this kind with strings, wood-wind and trombones, and that in the last *Kyrie*, which is built on precisely the same lines as the *Credo* and the *Confiteor*, all the instruments previously employed are used to strengthen the chorus.

* Part I, 20th February 1834; Part II, 12th February 1835.

** On the 24th April 1896, in the Garrison Church.

When Bach received the title of Court Composer he sent four *Kyrie* and *Gloria* — which he called Masses — to the Court as tokens of his assiduity*. As he was in a great hurry, he did not waste time in writing new works, but to a large extent made these Masses up out of cantatas**. The adaptations are perfunctory and occasionally quite nonsensical. In the G minor Mass, for example, Bach adds the text of the *Gloria* to the gloomy music of the first chorus of the cantata *Alles nur nach Gottes Willen* (No. 72). The *Gloria* of the A major Mass is an arrangement of the bass solo with chorus "Friede sei mit euch", from the cantata *Halt im Gedächtnis Jesum Christ* (No. 67). Memory

* Two of the Masses — those in G major and A major, were certainly written about 1739. Spitta rightly supposes that the two others — in G minor and F major — belong to the same period. As Bach had no opportunities for the performance of Masses of this kind, we can only assume that he intended them for Dresden.

** The following movements can be traced to cantatas in our possession:

Mass in F major: The *Qui tollis* and the *Quoniam* are derived from *Herr, deine Augen sehen nach dem Glauben* (No. 102); and the *Cum sancto spiritu* from *Dazu ist erschienen* (No. 40).

Mass in A major: The *Gloria* is derived from *Halt im Gedächtnis Jesum Christ* (No. 67); the *Qui tollis* from *Siehe zu, dass deine Gottesfurcht* (No. 179); the *Quoniam* from *Gott der Herr ist Sonn und Schild* (No. 79); and the *Cum sancto spiritu* from *Erforsche mich Gott* (No. 136).

Mass in G minor: The *Kyrie* is derived from *Herr, deine Augen* (No. 102); the *Gloria* from *Alles nur nach Gottes Willen* (No. 72); the *Gratias, Domine,* and *Cum sancto spiritu* from *Es wartet alles auf dich* (No. 187).

Mass in G major: The *Kyrie* and the *Quoniam* are derived from *Siehe du, dass deine Gottesfurcht* (No. 179); the *Gloria* and the *Domine Deus* from *Gott der Herr ist Sonn' und Schild* (No. 79); the *Gratias* from *Warum betrübst du dich* (No, 138); and the *Cum sancto spiritu* from *Wer Dank opfert* (No. 17).

For further information see the Preface to B. G. VIII. The *Kyrie* of the Mass in A major, which Spitta thought might be original, also seems, judging from the occasionally strained declamation, to be taken from another work, — perhaps a lost cantata.

of the earlier work makes him reproduce, in the instrumental accompaniment to the new movement, the contrast between the unrest of the world in which the disciples live in alarm, and the peace that the risen Lord brings them. But in the new arrangement he does not trouble in the least about the significance of the music. He fits the instrumental accompaniment to a brisk chorus, and has the *Gloria in excelsis* sung to the "tumult" motive. In a number of these adaptations he does not even trouble to declaim the words in accordance with their sense.

Probably the only original section is the *Kyrie* of the Mass in F major. It consists of a short but admirable four-part chorus, which the horns and oboes accompany three times with the chorale melody "Christe, du Lamm Gottes", which Bach also employs in the cantata *Du wahrer Gott und Davidssohn* (No. 23). In the vocal basses we hear the final *Kyrie* of the Litany. The two melodies that run through the movement are as follows —

As the Litany was sung only in Lent and Advent, and on the first Sunday in Advent the *Kyrie* was sung to "concerted music", Spitta conjectures that the introductory movement of the F major Mass was composed for this Sunday. It represents a splendid blend of Catholic and Protestant church music.

The fact that Bach had to make up these Masses from his cantatas proves that he did not compose the sections of the Mass used in the Leipzig service. He copied out for this purpose Mass-movements and whole Masses of all kinds of composers, known and unknown, German and Italian*, but he felt no impulse to set these texts himself. He did not even compose the *Sanctus* that he had to use on feast days. Of the four settings of this text that have come down to us from him, — (B. G. XI[1]), C major, D major, D minor, G major — probably only one, — that in D major — is his own composition. We shall always regret that he did not write a short, concise Mass as a counterpart to the *Magnificat*.

CHAPTER XXXIV.

THE CANTATAS AFTER 1734.

We possess about seventy of the cantatas Bach wrote after 1734; about thirty of these belong to the years 1735 and 1736; the remainder, — chiefly chorale cantatas — were written between 1737 and 1745.

The cantata *Lobe den Herren, meine Seele* (No. 143; second composition) was probably performed on New Year's day 1735. The text of the aria "Tausendfaches Unglück, Schrecken" ("A thousandfold misery and fear") describes how grievously the neighbouring peoples had

* See the list of these copies given by Rust in the Preface to B. G. XI[1], and the corrections made by Spitta III, 29.

suffered from war and destitution during the previous months, while for the land in which this cantata was sung to the praise of God the preceding year had been one of blessing. This situation, as Spitta shows, agrees best with the year 1734, when almost the whole of Europe had been convulsed by the War of the Polish Succession (1733 to 1735), Saxony, however, being spared the horrors of war, and further having the gratification of seeing its sovereign enter Warsaw in December of that year as the bearer of peace. The text of the cantata is mainly made up out of three verses of Psalm 146 and two verses of the chorale "Du Friedefürst, Herr Jesu Christ". There is a particularly fine effect in the concluding chorus, in which the soprani sing the third strophe of the chorale and the other voices accompany them with alleluias. The orchestra comprises strings, bassoons, three horns and kettle-drums. In the aria "Jesu, Retter deiner Herde", which the strings accompany with the chorale, the bassoon and *continuo* bass have an interesting duet.

The cantata for the fourth Sunday after Epiphany, *Wär' Gott nicht mit uns diese Zeit* (No. 14), upon Luther's paraphrase of Psalm 124, also seems to belong to the year 1735. The first chorus is a fugal one in the style of Pachelbel. As in the chorale prelude *Wenn wir in höchsten Nöten sind* (Peters VII, No. 58), Bach here employs throughout the inversion of the melodic segments as counter-themes in the separate fugues that make up this skilfully wrought chorus. The *cantus firmus* is given to the instruments alone. This is one of the most difficult of Bach's vocal movements. If well done, the hearer will not be conscious of the ingenuity of the workmanship; all he will perceive will be the spirit of transfigured peace that breathes through the music.

The two arias contrast with the chorus by their strongly realistic character. In the first, "Unsre Stärke heisst zu schwach, unserm Feind zu widerstehn" ("Our strength is too weak to withstand our enemy") the orchestra depicts the tumult of the world-battle in which the faithful cry to God for help; in the second, "Gott, bei deinem starken Schützen sind wir von den Feinden frei" ("God, Thy mighty help hath set us free from our enemies"), the "mighty help" is represented in an angular but powerful trio between the two oboes and the *continuo* bass. The voice enters with a proud theme of its own, that appears to symbolise the word "free". The aria is a notable example of Bach's delineation of power. If its true character is to be preserved in performance, the marking of *vivace* must not be taken in an exaggerated modern sense*.

As the text of the Reformation cantata, *Gott der Herr ist Sonn' und Schild* (No. 79), also speaks of the miseries of war and salvation from them, it likewise seems to relate to the special events of 1735. In the first chorus the largely-planned symphonic accompaniment is built up out of two themes. The first, beginning as a fanfare in the horns, is apparently a solemn hymn of triumph —

Afterwards it is used as the accompaniment to the chorale "Nun danket alle Gott". The second theme is overpowering in its exultation —

The chorus goes its own way at the beginning and the end, tranquilly and majestically. In the middle section, however, the voices are caught up in the stream of exulta-

* Spitta justly remarks that at the commencement of the recitative we must read "Ja, hätte Gott es zugegeben" instead of "Ja, hätt' es Gott nicht zugegeben", as it is printed in the B. G. edition.

tion of the second theme*. The chorus is one of the most impressive ever written by Bach. A positively blinding radiance gleams from it; it is as if we were looking at a victorious battle in the rays of morning.

In the cry sent up in the midst of the battle, "Gott, ach Gott, verlass die Deinen nimmermehr" ("Oh God, forsake not Thy own"), the raging conflict is depicted by means of the "tumult" motive**. The musical picture strongly reminds us, as Spitta observed, of that in the aria with chorus "Mit unserer Macht ist nichts getan" in the cantata *Ein' feste Burg* (No. 80).

Among the cantatas written for the Sundays after Easter are nine of which the nature of the texts shows them to have been connected. They extend from the second Sunday after Easter to the third day in Whit. Spitta accidentally discovered the poems in the *Versuch in gebundener Schreibart* (Part I) of Marianne von Ziegler, published in 1728***.

In these texts the Biblical words play a much larger part than in Picander's; this gives Bach the opportunity to write fine ariosi and motet-like choruses. It would certainly be agreeable to him also to have the aria texts in free strophes rather than in the strict tripartite scheme of the *da capo* aria. As poetry the texts are greatly superior to those of Picander. As we read through the scores we fancy we can realise the delight with which Bach set to work on these new texts. He undoubtedly composed them

---

* Spitta (III, 74) thinks he sees "elaborate combinations of instruments" in this chorus, "down to the rhythm of the drums". This movement was afterwards turned by Bach into the *Gloria* of the G major Mass (B. G. VIII, p. 162 ff.).

** See p. 91.

*** In his biography Spitta conjectured that these libretti were by "a new poet", but he was unable to identify the poet until later, in his *Musikgeschichtliche Aufsätze* (Berlin 1892). Upon Marianne von Ziegler see I, 115. The texts of *Gott fähret auf mit Jauchzen* (No. 43) and *Ich bin ein guter Hirte* (No. 85) are not found among her poems, though their quality forbids us to attribute them to anyone but her.

all in one sequence. Spitta attributes them to the year 1735*.

The cantata for the second Sunday after Easter, *Ich bin ein guter Hirt* (No. 85) is written for a solo quartet It is in Bach's delightful lyrical style. Particularly fine is the simple, heartfelt tenor aria, "Seht, was die Liebe tut". The soprano aria "Der Herr ist mein getreuer Hirt" is in the form of a chorale prelude upon the melody "Allein Gott in der Höh' sei Ehr".

The powerful first chorus of the cantata for the third Sunday after Easter, *Ihr werdet weinen und heulen* (No. 103) — "Ye will weep and cry aloud, but the world will rejoice . .. Yet your mourning shall be turned into joy" — is based upon the continual antithesis of a theme in the rhythm of joy and a motive of wailing —

In the tenor aria "Erholet euch, betrübte Stimmen" ("Uplift yourselves again, ye grieving voices"), the "joy" motive carries away all the voices of the orchestra with

---

* See Spitta III, 70 ff. The cantatas are as follows: —

Ich bin ein guter Hirt (No. 85, for the second Sunday after Easter).

Ihr werdet weinen und heulen (No. 103, for the third Sunday after Easter).

Es ist euch gut, dass ich hingehe (No. 108, for the fourth Sunday after Easter).

Bisher habt ihr nichts gebeten (No. 87, for the fifth Sunday after Easter).

Gott fähret auf mit Jauchzen (No. 43, for Ascension).

Auf Christi Himmelfahrt allein (No. 128, for Ascension).

Sie werden euch in den Bann tun (No. 183, second composition, for the sixth Sunday after Easter).

Wer mich liebet, der wird mein Wort halten (No. 74, for the first day in Whit).

Also hat Gott die Welt geliebt (No. 68, for the second day in Whit).

Er rufet seine Schafe (No. 175, for the third day in Whit).

it in a wild dance. The music here expresses the words "O Freude, der nichts gleichen kann" ("Oh joy beyond compare"), which occur in the middle of the text.*

The text of the cantata *Es ist euch gut, dass ich hingehe* (No. 108), for the fourth Sunday after Easter, is founded on two beautiful passages from the farewell words of Jesus. Bach sets the first — "It is expedient for you that I go away; for if I go not away the Comforter will not come unto you" (John XVI, 7) — in the form of a bass arioso, in which the strings accompany the vaporous arabesques of the oboe d'amore with tender *staccato* quavers, representing the passing away of the transfigured Saviour. The orchestral picture reminds us of the musical illustration of the words "But after I am risen again, I will go before you into Galilee", in the *St. Matthew Passion.***

The second passage — "Howbeit when he, the Spirit of truth, is come, he will guide you into all truth" (John XVI, 13) — is set as a motet. In the tenor aria "Mich kann kein Zweifel stören" ("No doubt can disturb me") the semiquavers wandering aimlessly, as it were, in the solo violin, symbolise the doubt, while the firmly moving bass represents immovable faith. Then the joy of faith finds expression in the contralto aria "Was mein Herz von dir begehrt, ach, das wird mir wohl gewährt" ("Ah, what my heart desires of Thee, that wilt Thou give me"), in which the first violins give out the "joy" motive in every possible form. This cantata is a perfect expression of the mood of the farewell words of Jesus, as they are given in St. John.

These words are the basis also of the cantata for the fifth Sunday after Easter, *Bisher habt ihr nichts gebeten in meinem Namen* (No. 87)***. The bass arioso "In der Welt habt ihr Angst; aber seid getrost, ich habe die Welt überwunden" is as effective as it is simple. In the alto aria

* The bass motive of this aria is quoted on p. 113.
** See p. 215.
*** Solo cantata for alto, tenor and bass.

"Vergib, o Vater, unsere Schuld" ("Forgive, oh Father, our trespasses") the sighs and moans of the oboes are carried up to heaven by the ascending basses. The tenor aria "Ich will leiden, ich will schweigen", which closes the cantata, is one of Bach's most beautiful creations. The first violins circle about the voice as if in a saintly dance —

The form of this aria is interesting as being typical of a number of others written about the same time. It uses the tripartite *da capo* scheme, but departs from it to the extent that the vocal theme is different from that of the orchestra. The words are declaimed in a free arioso. Thus in these movements Bach partly emancipates himself from the Italian aria. The intermediate form which he creates is in many respects an ideal one.

In the large Ascension cantata, in three parts, *Gott fähret auf mit Jauchzen* (No. 43), the superiority of Marianne von Ziegler's texts, from a musical point of view, becomes quite clear. For the opening chorus she chooses the splendid verse from the Psalms, "God goeth up with a merry noise, and the Lord with the sound of a trumpet". Bach of course represents the "going up" by means of bold upward-striving lines; the chief figure in the violins covers two octaves in four bars. The soprano enters with this phrase —

to which the three trumpets add their fanfares. The concise form of the chorus makes the strength of the music all the more effective.

In the tenor aria "Ja tausendmal tausend begleiten den Wagen", the violins have a theme in unison, that rises and falls time after time in a manner suggestive of the peculiar melodic line of the aria "Gerne will ich mich bequemen", in the *St. Matthew Passion**. Here, as there, the fluctuations of the melody have their meaning. They are meant to symbolise the movement of earth and heaven, which, according to the text, "bend" beneath the chariot of the Lord.

The soprano aria "Mein Jesus hat nunmehr" resembles in its march-form the introductory arioso of the cantata *Es ist euch gut, dass ich hingehe* (No. 108)**. In the course of the text, mention is made of the "return" of the Son to the Father. Perhaps this explains the step-like rhythm that runs through the whole movement.

In the bass aria, "Er ist's, er ist's, der ganz allein", which is accompanied only by the trumpet, Christ's victory is described under the Old Testament image of the treader of the winepress. Bach of course does not let pass the opportunity to represent this proud stamping in his music, and he does not hesitate to write such progressions as these in the bass —

The alto aria "Ich sehe schon im Geist, wie er zur Rechten Gottes auf seine Feinde schmeisst" is at the first glance surprising. It looks as if the fervent music did not agree with the words ("Now I see in spirit how He sits on the right hand of God and smites His enemies"). The almost melancholy tone of the movement is explained by the final words of the text "Ich stehe hier am Weg und schau ihm sehnlich nach" ("I stand here by the way and

---

* See p. 221.

** See p. 333.

look towards Him with longing"). There is a kind of divine home-sickness in the dialogue of the two oboes. The movement is typical of the freer form of aria that Bach was employing at this time.

The smaller Ascension cantata, "Auf Christi Himmelfahrt allein" (No. 128)*, begins with a chorale chorus upon the melody "Allein Gott in der Höh' sei Ehr", to which the orchestra adds an independent accompaniment in upward-striving lines. The most striking of the instrumental motives is derived from the opening notes of the chorale —

The bass aria "Auf, auf mit hellem Schall" is a bravura piece for a solo trumpet. Its style — it is constructed on the "joy" motive — reminds us of the tenor aria "Erholet euch" in the cantata *Ihr werdet weinen und heulen* (No. 103). This second Ascension cantata also ends with an aria more thoughtful than brilliant.

In the cantata for the sixth Sunday after Easter, *Sie werden euch in den Bann tun* (No. 183, second composition; solo cantata for soprano, alto, tenor and bass), there is an antithesis between the other movements and the sombre introductory arioso "Sie werden euch in den Bann tun; es kommt aber die Zeit, dass, wer euch tötet, wird meinen, er tue Gott einen Dienst daran". They express the joyous anticipation of death. In the soprano aria "Höchster Tröster, heil'ger Geist, der du mir die Wege weist darauf ich wandeln soll", the confident setting-out upon the way that leads to death is accompanied by a cheerful dance theme —

* For the feast days Bach needed two cantatas, as the evening service also had to be musical.

The first chorus of the cantata for Whit, *Wer mich liebet, der wird mein Worl halten* (No. 74), is an arrangement of the opening duet of the Weimar cantata bearing the same title (No. 59). The music of the aria "Komm, mein Herze steht dir offen" is derived from the same source. The imperfect declamation of the first words is enough to show that Marianne von Ziegler's text has simply been written underneath it. In the arioso upon Christ's farewell words, "I go, but I shall return to you", the "step" progression —

must be made to stand out clearly through the quaver figures, or the accompaniment of the *continuo* bass will not tell its story. The last two arias are noticeable more for length than for depth.

In the cantata for the second day of Whit, *Also hat Gott die Welt geliebt* (No. 68), the two arias "Mein gläubiges Herze" and "Du bist geboren mir zugute" are taken from the Weimar secular cantata *Was mir behagt, ist nur die muntre Jagd**. The choruses are original. The first, upon the fine passage in John III, 16, is accompanied by the gently-swaying rhythm with which Bach loves to express the feeling of joyous serenity —

In the other, — a motet-like chorus, in which strings and wind are added to the voices — Bach writes peculiarly severe music to express the idea of the Last Judgment, already in process, of which St. John speaks in the passage "Whosoever believes in Him shall not be judged, but whosoever believes not is already judged".

* B. G. XXIX, pp. 25 ff. and 12 ff. See also *ante*, p. 263.

The cantata of the third day of Whit, *Er rufet seine Schafe mit Namen* (No. 175)*, begins with an arioso and aria for three flutes. In these two lovely pastorals Bach employed the *flûtes à bec*, not the traverse flutes. The bass aria "Öffnet euch" is accompanied only by two trumpets**.

Of the Easter cantatas written in the middle of the thirties we may mention two — *Erfreut euch, ihr Herzen* (No. 66), and *Bleib' bei uns* (No. 6), both intended for Easter Monday.

The great opening chorus of *Erfreut euch, ihr Herzen* (No. 66) is very agreeable in its sentiment. Even the orchestration is better than that of the other festival cantatas; only one trumpet is employed, and that most effectively. The accompaniment is dominated by the "joy" motive. It does not appear, however, in the middle section (marked *andante* by Bach), as the text speaks of "tears and fears and anguish".

The arias of this rather broadly-planned cantata are likewise written in a more pleasant style. The *forte*, *piano* and *pianissimo* that Bach has marked in the bass aria "Lasset dem Höchsten" are very instructive.

The solo movements of *Bleib' bei uns, denn es will Abend werden* (No. 6) are also somewhat lengthy. The most notable section is the opening chorus, a masterpiece of poetry in music. "Abide with us, abide with us", say the disciples at Emmaus, pleadingly and caressingly*** —

* Solo cantata for alto, tenor and bass.

** The aria "Es dünket mich ich seh dich kommen" comes from the secular cantata *Durchlauchtster Leopold* (B. G. XXXIV, p. 32); the chorale harmonisation of "Nun werter Geist" is taken from the cantata *Wer mich liebet, der wird mein Wort halten* (No. 59).

*** Note the curious accentuation of the "bei"; in the sequel the accents are varied thus — "*bleib'* bei uns"; "bleib' *bei* uns"; "bleib' bei *uns*".

At the words "denn es will Abend werden" ("for evening is nigh") the voices descend, as if the gloom of night were weighing upon them —

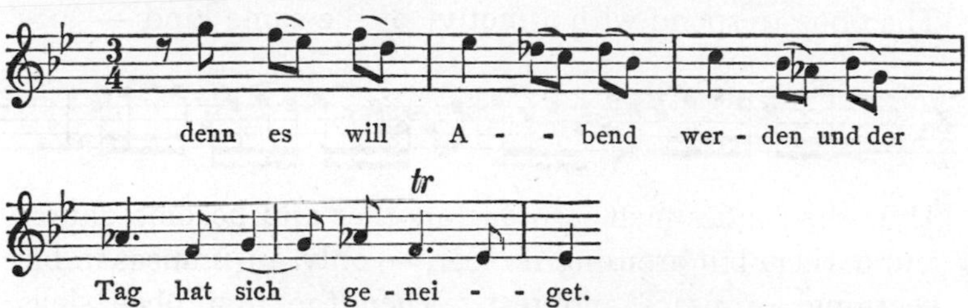

In the accompaniment we hear an anxious quivering —

In the andante of the middle section the triple rhythm gives way to $^4/_4$ time; the words "Bleib' bei uns" become still more expressive of entreaty and pain. Long-drawn cries resound from the gloomy fields; then all is still. Once more the prayer returns, in the caressing triple rhythm. The cadence suddenly slips into the major, and ends in bright colours, as if the Lord had intimated the granting of the prayer.

The same mood dominates the introductory sinfonia to the cantata for the first Sunday after Easter, *Am Abend aber desselbigen Sabbats* (No. 42), except that the anxiety expressed in the harmonies of the "Bleib' bei uns" is lacking here. In this remarkable movement Bach is painting the same evening calm that he has expressed in the accompaniment to the arioso in the *St. Matthew Passion** — "Am Abend, da es kühle ward". The string figures suggest the hovering shades of evening —

* What is meant by the words in this aria "Denn was aus Lieb' und Not geschieht, das bricht des Höchsten Ordnung nicht" will probably never be known. It is regrettable also that the poet has not taken further advantage of the dramatic situation, instead of indulging in not very profound reflections.

The oboes respond with a motive of the same kind —

Thus the shades melt into one another and become darker and darker, but arousing no fear, — only an immeasurable yearning for peace and rest. Then the first oboe sings a hymn of longing, that dies away in the night in long-sustained tones —

The second oboe answers —

The gloom deepens —

The movement ends in the minor. Then the Bible words are recited over a quivering bass accompaniment — "Then the same day at evening, being the first day of the week, when the doors were shut where the disciples were assembled, for fear of the Jews, came Jesus and stood in the midst". The Lord brings His distressed disciples the peace of evening; for this reason the accompaniment of the aria

"Wo zwei oder drei versammelt sind" ("Where two or three are gathered together") is composed of reminiscences of the sinfonia.

In the chorale duet "Verzage nicht, du Häuflein klein" the bassoon and violoncello have a theme that strides along in wide-spaced intervals, and in its fundamental idea reminds us of the theme of immovable faith in the chorale fantasia *Jesus Christus unser Heiland* (Peters VI, No. 30). It is also interesting by reason of the phrasing that Bach has indicated for it* —

The final aria, "Jesus ist ein Schild der Seinen", is an outburst of exultant joy.

Of the Michaelmas cantata, *Nun ist das Heil und die Kraft* (No. 50) only the first double chorus has been preserved; but this is so powerful in plan and execution that we can dispense with the remainder, and almost regard the lack of the solo pieces as a blessing. The theme is constructed out of the "strength" motive, — that occurs also in inversion — and the "joy" motive**. This choral double fugue is one of Bach's mightiest pieces of vocal music.

Bach wrote the cantata *Ich elender Mensch, wer wird mich erlösen von dem Leibe dieses Todes* (No. 48) upon the Gospel for the nineteenth Sunday after Trinity (Matthew IX, 1—9), in which Jesus heals the man sick of the palsy and forgives his sins. While the chorus sings the despairing words from the seventh chapter of Romans that give

* The whole cantata should be studied for the extremely careful way in which Bach has added the phrasing marks and dynamic signs. Hardly any other sacred cantata is so instructive in this respect as this.

** Quoted on p. 118.

the cantata its title — "Oh wretched man that I am! Who shall deliver me from the body of this death?" — the orchestral accompaniment incessantly repeats the sorrowful question —

while the trumpets and oboes play, in canon, the chorale "Herr Jesu Christ, ich schrei' zu dir".

The full sense of grief is given in the sinister harmonies of the chorale "Soll's ja so sein, dass Straf' und Pein auf Sünden folgen müssen"; but it exhausts itself at the words "Büssen" ("atonement"), with which the strophe ends. In the succeeding prayer to Jesus, "Ach lege das Sodom der sündlichen Glieder, sofern es dein Wille, zerstöret danieder", sorrow is quite overcome. The music breathes a serene longing for death. The theme anticipates the joyous and passionate animation of the following aria, "Vergib mir Jesus meine Sünden, so wird mir Leib und Seel' gesund". The theme of this last movement commences thus —

The last aria but one, therefore, should not be taken too slowly; the final aria can hardly be taken too quickly. It must be sung in a kind of wild ecstasy — no *rallentandi* in the cadences and no *diminuendi* in the transitions from *forte* to *piano*. That Bach's idea was that of haste almost breaking into a dance is shewn by the fact that in the cantata *O Ewigkeit, du Donnerwort* (No. 20) he employs similar music, but in the minor, to express the violent horror of the words "O Mensch, errette deine Seele, entfliehe Satans Sklaverei und mache deine Seele frei" ("Oh man, save thy soul; fly from Satan's bondage and make thy soul free").*

Perhaps it was at the direct inducement of Bach that Picander wrote a number of cantata poems which, like those of Marianne von Ziegler, took Biblical passages as their point of departure. He selected for this purpose, almost exclusively, verses from the Old Testament, preferring those of unusual length. Unfortunately the reflections he spins upon them are not so expressive as those of his model. We need have no scruple as to cutting out almost the whole of the recitatives in these cantatas.

The musical connection of these works** is evident at the first glance. They resemble each other not only in the large scale on which the choruses are laid out, but in the great — sometimes excessive — length of the orchestral introductions to the choruses and arias. There are hardly any concise solo pieces in these cantatas.

Three of these works are founded on two Biblical passages each, and are accordingly planned in two parts. They are *Brich dem Hungrigen dein Brot* (No. 39; for the first Sunday after Trinity); *Es wartet alles auf dich* (No.187; for the seventh Sunday after Trinity); *Es ist dir gesagt, Mensch, was gut ist* (No. 45; for the eighth Sunday after Trinity).

The finest of them, as a whole, is *Es wartet alles auf dich* (No. 187), which also has a satisfactory text. The first Biblical verse is set as a chorus; the second — the beautiful passage from the Sermon on the Mount, "Take no thought for your life, what ye shall eat or what ye

---

* This theme is quoted on p. 196.

** They are the following cantatas:

Brich dem Hungrigen dein Brot (No. 39).
Es ist dir gesagt, Mensch (No. 45).
Es wartet alles auf dich (No. 187).
Es ist ein trotzig und verzagt Ding (No. 176).
Wer Dank opfert (No. 17).
Unser Mund sei voll Lachens (No. 110).
Wir müssen durch viel Trübsal (No. 146).

shall drink" — is declaimed in a simple bass arioso. In the alto aria "Du Herr, du krönst allein das Jahr" the orchestra has a cheerful melody, in which Bach has marked the nuances almost from bar to bar. The first part of the soprano aria (*adagio*), "Gott versorget alles Leben" ("God nourishes every living thing") is founded on the rhythm of solemnity; at the words "Weichet, ihr Sorgen" ("Away, ye cares") — *un poco allegro* — the music breaks into flying figures*.

The peculiarly unsteady accompaniment in the first part of the chorus of *Brich dem Hungrigen dein Brot* (No. 39) — "Give the hungry man thy bread" represents the procession of the poor and the suffering, who are being supported and led to the house in accordance with the Biblical precept**; the second part abandons this motive, and is expressive of praise and thanksgiving. The arioso upon "Wohlzutun und mitzuteilen, vergesset nicht", which opens the *Seconda Parte* of the cantata, is not so satisfactory as the setting of the second Bible passage in *Es wartet alles auf dich* (No. 187).

Even Bach could not cast into a correct musical period the formless passage from Micah on which the first chorus of the cantata *Es ist dir gesagt, Mensch* (No. 45) is based. The many reiterations of the "It is said unto thee" at the commencement are quite disconcerting. It is incomprehensible why Bach should set himself the impossible task of making a chorus of this verse, instead of declaiming it in a simple arioso, as he does in the second part with Christ's words "Es werden viele zu mir sagen an jenem Tage".

We also possess the parts of this cantata, revised and corrected by Zelter***. They throw a doubtful light on

* The small G minor Mass (B. G. VIII) consists, from the *Domine Deus, Agnus Dei* onwards, entirely of movements from this cantata.

** On the problem of this chorus see p. 46.

*** Fragments from them are given in the Preface to B. G. X, p. 17 ff.

his way of relieving Bach's work of its thin tinsel and bringing out the "bright substance immediately underneath"*. His alterations are really ludicrous; we get the idea that his purpose was to substitute for Bach's intelligent declamation the most unintelligent that can be conceived.

The following cantatas deal with only one Biblical passage each — *Es ist ein trotzig und verzagt Ding* (No. 176; for Trinity); *Wer Dank opfert* (No. 17; for the fourteenth Sunday after Trinity); *Unser Mund sei voll Lachens* (No. 110; for Christmas); *Wir müssen durch viel Trübsal in das Reich Gottes eingehen* (No. 146; for the third Sunday after Easter).

The cantata *Wer Dank opfert* (No. 17) consists of a large and sharply-chiselled chorus and two interesting arias. The text, unfortunately, is a poor one.

In the first chorus of *Es ist ein trotzig und verzagt Ding* (No. 176) the orchestral parts of the accompaniment to the theme are marked first *forte*, then *piano*. This makes it probable that Bach had the chorus theme also sung *forte* at first, and *piano* from the middle onwards, thus —

On closer inspection the whole chorus is seen to be planned on the idea of this direct transition from *forte* to *piano*. This way of representing the antithesis between "trotzig" ("arrogant") and "verzagt" ("poor-spirited") may appear somewhat naïve; but the musical effect is natural and not without charm.

* See Zelter's remarks in a letter to Goethe, *ante*, I, 229.

The soprano aria "Dein sonst hell beliebter Schein" is set in march-rhythm, like a gavotte, the words being those that Nicodemus speaks to himself on his night journey to Jesus*.

The lengthy orchestral preludes to each of these cantatas explain how Bach came to employ many of his free orchestral compositions for church works. The chorus of the cantata *Unser Mund sei voll Lachens* (No. 110) is worked into the *allegro* section of the second D major overture (B. G. XXX[1], p. 66 ff.), and so framed between the first and final *grave***; the chorus of the cantata *Wir müssen durch viel Trübsal* (No. 146) is inserted in the *adagio* of the clavier concerto in D minor (B. G. XVII, p. 1 ff.), and is prefaced by an organ transcription of the *allegro*. In neither case has Bach made the arrangement without regard to the character of the text. The triplet rhythm of the D major overture seems really a musical representation of laughter, so that it has been conjectured, not without reason, that the overture may have originated at the same time as the cantata, and that the theme of the middle section was written with an eye to the words "Unser Mund sei voll Lachens" ("Our mouth is filled with laughter")***. The elegiac mood of the *adagio* in the D minor concerto harmonises excellently with the words "Wir müssen durch viel Trübsal in das Reich Gottes eingehen" ("We must through much tribulation enter into the Kingdom of God")†.

The solo movements of the last-named cantata are of extraordinary beauty; even their excessive length, which

* For an explanation of this curious movement see p. 47.

** On the insertion of this vocal movement in the overture see I, 410, where the theme of the *allegro* is quoted.

*** The duet "Ehre sei Gott" in this cantata is a transcription of the "Virgo Jesse floruit" that originally formed part of the Magnificat in D major. See B. G. XI[1], p. 110, and Preface, p. 11.

† The *allegro* of the clavier concerto in D minor goes splendidly on the organ, where a beautiful tone-colour, not too strong, can be obtained.

they share with the other arias of this period, cannot prejudice us against them. In the soprano aria "Ich säe meine Zähren mit bangem Herzen" ("I sow my tears with a heavy heart"), the two oboes let fall a tear in each bar —

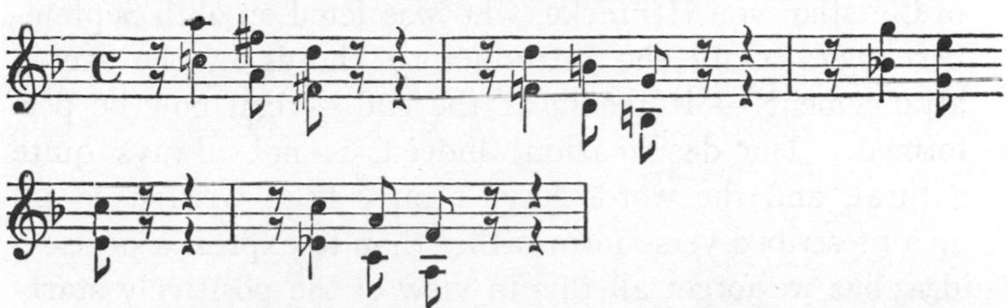

The duet between tenor and bass, "Wie will ich mich freuen" is one of the loveliest and sweetest of the movements constructed on a "joy" motive.

The cantata for Whit, *O ewiges Feuer* (No. 34) is shewn by the existence of a set of older parts to be founded on a mourning cantata of the same title*. The semiquaver figures of the first violins run through the whole of the first chorus like the lambent flames that are to set the heart on fire —

The exquisite lulling music of the alto aria "Wohl euch, ihr auserwählten Seelen" is not fully explained by its present text. This is one of the cases in which the mere knowledge of Bach's musical language is sufficient to make us decide that the music was originally written for another text**.

* The declamation of the revised text is not always faultless, as may be seen from the first chorus.

** The theme belongs to the category of the "cradle-song" motives.

The splendid chorus "Friede über Israel" seems to have been abbreviated from its original form.

The music of the cantata for Midsummer Day, *Freue dich, erlöste Schar* (No. 30) is derived from the secular cantata *Angenehmes Wiederau*, which Bach wrote in honour of Christian von Hennicke, who was fêted on 28th September 1737. Only the introductory chorus of the sacred arrangement — it recurs at the end — can now be performed. The declamation, indeed, is not always quite natural, and the words have clearly been written to fill up a prescribed verse-form rather than to express a poetical idea; but we forget all this in view of the positively startling force of the music. Perhaps no other of Bach's works equals this in fire and splendour of sonority. Anyone who could supply the music with a new and singable text, — suitable, say, for Christmas, — would be doing Bach a great service.

In the solo numbers the fitting-in of the text is so outrageous from the musical and declamatory point of view as to be unendurable. Some magnificent music is thus going to waste. It would be a worthy task for some poet to provide the secular cantata with an expressive poem, and so restore this grand music to the world*.

The few solo cantatas of this period — the end of the thirties — that we possess relate almost exclusively to Christmas and Epiphany**.

---

* The secular cantata can easily be restored from the cantata *Freue dich, erlöste Schar* (B. G. V[1], pp. 323—395) and the supplement (pp. 399—408). Of course there is no necessity to preserve all the recitatives.

** *Selig ist der Mann* (No. 57; for soprano and bass; for the second day of Christmas).

Süsser Trost, mein Jesus kommt (No. 151; for soprano, alto, tenor and bass; for the third day of Christmas).

Liebster Jesus, mein Verlangen (No. 32; for bass and soprano; for Epiphany).

Meine Seufzer, meine Tränen (No. 13; for soprano, alto, tenor and bass; for the second Sunday after Epiphany).

Es reifet euch ein schrecklich Ende (No. 90; for alto, tenor and bass; for the twenty-fifth Sunday after Trinity).

In the cantata *Selig ist der Mann* (No. 57) there is a dialogue between Jesus (bass) and the believing soul (soprano). The first bass arioso delivers in expressive music the words "Blessed is the man that endureth temptation; for when he is tried he shall receive the crown of life"; the orchestra adds a symphonic accompaniment. Bach would have worked out his solos wholly in this ideal form had not the *da capo* aria been the fashion of the day. The moving lament of the soul, "Ich wünschte mir den Tod, wenn du, mein Jesu, mich nicht liebtest", is set in the same free arioso style. An idea of the overwhelming sorrow expressed in the accompaniment can be had from the opening bars for the first violin —

In the succeeding *vivace*, which is somewhat in the style of an aria, Jesus comforts the soul with the song of triumph "Ja, ja, ich kann die Feinde schlagen". The words of the middle section, "Bedrängter Geist, hör auf zu weinen" ("Cease to weep, oh afflicted soul") are set to wonderfully expressive music, the violins having a motive suggestive of sighs. "Ich ende behende mein irdisches Leben", sings the joyous soul, happy to meet its death, in an aria with an animated $^3/_4$ rhythm, as if it were hastening from this world to its Redeemer, leaping and dancing on its way*.

The cantata for the third day of Christmas, *Süsser Trost, mein Jesus kommt, Jesus wird anitzt geboren* (No. 151, for soprano, alto, tenor and bass) consists, apart from the recitatives, simply of two arias and the final chorale. In the first aria the strings *(piano sempre)* sing a lullaby over the infant Jesus —

* It is not clear why Spitta should regard this cantata as "domestic religious music" rather than music for the church. There is nothing in Bach's works to justify a distinction of this kind.

to which the flute adds exuberant runs and figures —

The theme of the alto aria, *In Jesu Demut kann ich Trost, in seiner Armut Reichtum finden*, is constructed on the same lines as that of "Gerne will ich mich bequemen" in the *St. Matthew Passion*. It represents humility ("Demut"); it sinks, rises, sinks again, again recovers, and in the final cadence quite goes to pieces, as it were. The ties that Bach has marked for the instruments here are particularly instructive. The indications in the orchestral part as to the co-operation of the strings and the oboe are interesting in themselves, and no doubt applicable to many other scores. They play *unisono* until a *piano* comes, when the violins cease, leaving the oboe to continue alone.

The opening aria of the cantata *Liebster Jesu, mein Verlangen* (No. 32; dialogue for bass and soprano) reminds us strongly of the first movement — so full of longing — of the secular cantata *Weichet nur, betrübte Schatten* (B. G. XI[2]). In the final duet — *vivace* — between the believing soul and Jesus, all care is driven away before the joyous rushes of the instruments. The theme runs thus, the oboes always hurrying alone with the strings —

The second violins and the violas fly about in loud *staccato* quavers throughout the movement.

In the bass aria of the cantata for the second Sunday after Epiphany, *Meine Seufzer, meine Tränen* (No. 13, for soprano, alto, tenor and bass), we have one of Bach's most remarkable dual themes. It begins with the "sigh" motive, which is immediately followed by the motive of joy. The text that Bach wished to express by means of this juxtaposition runs thus: "Groans and piteous weeping bring no relief to care; but he who looks towards heaven will find a joyous light shining in his sorrowful bosom"*. The introductory aria and the chorale with orchestral accompaniment, "Der Gott, der mir hat zugesprochen", are very sombre in tone.

In the first aria of the cantata for the twenty-fifth Sunday after Trinity, *Es reifet euch ein schrecklich Ende* (No. 90), Bach declaims the word "schrecklich" ("dreadful") several times in this fashion —

In the passionate final aria, "So löschet im Eifer der rächende Richter den Leuchter des Wortes zur Strafe doch aus" confused demisemiquaver passages fly up and down in the various instruments like a flame struggling against the storm-wind. Even Spitta frankly admits Bach's pictorial intention here.** It is one of the most powerful symphonic accompaniments to be found in all Bach's works.

The most glorious feature of these solo cantatas is that the German Bach here finds free expression. It is true that for many movements he still retains the *da capo* form. We are hardly conscious of it, however, for it is so changed

---

* The theme is quoted on p. 106.

** Bach has represented the flickering of flames in other places.

that he seems to have risen superior to it. Where he still employs the repetitive scheme of the *da capo* aria he very often does away with the identity of the vocal and the instrumental theme. He thus makes a peculiarly delightful type of aria. The texts of these solo cantatas are as a rule expressive.

At this very time, — about 1736, — Bach became weary of the search for "free" poems for his "church pieces", and definitely resolved to revert to the chorale cantata and to write a cycle of works in this *genre*. We may probably assume that this kind of cantata struck him as being the most suitable to the church, and that consequently he wished to make a year's cycle of this kind the culminating point of his labour for the service.

By an evil fate he halted half-way on the path that led back to the chorale cantata. The admirable older cantata, with its text compounded out of chorale verses and Biblical passages, does not enter his mind now. What he wants is a chorale cantata that will permit him to retain the "speaking" recitative and the *da capo* aria. He will not again endeavour to set hymn strophes as recitatives and *da capo* arias, as he did at the beginning of the thirties. Picander offers to cast the chorale strophes into madrigal form for him*. Bach agrees, and so seals the fate of the cantata texts to which he devotes his final labours.

Nor is it comprehensible from the purely musical standpoint how Bach could remain satisfied with this kind of chorale cantata, as it compelled him to renounce all freedom in the choice of the form for his choruses. We rather get the impression that the sacrifice was not a serious one for him. He seems to have wearied of looking for pictures in which he could express his ideas, and felt a certain relief in being absolved from the search and having simply one task before him — to keep a chorale melody going as a *cantus firmus* in the soprano, and to build up the other

* These cantatas also contain "free" aria-texts.

voices line by line in motet form. Indeed, while all these choruses are plainly signed with his name, no two of them are alike, in spite of their having the same scheme in common; each of them has a personality of its own.

Bach accepts as a necessary evil the fact that in choruses of this kind he can introduce the text only in melodic segments separated by interludes, and so has to dismember sentences that are one and indivisible from both the declamatory and the intellectual point of view. Moreover he can give only limited expression in his choruses to the poetry of the text, since he cannot employ themes of his own invention. Thus it comes about that the main work of musical representation in these choruses devolves upon the orchestra, which as a rule has no concern at all for the melody, but weaves round the chorale and its figuration a free fantasia in which the basic idea or emotion of the text finds characteristic expression. The themes and motives of this orchestral accompaniment throw a great deal of light on the nature of Bach's musical language.

In the arias of these chorale cantatas he is more than usually dependent upon his poet. Very often the latter gives him a mere formless and senseless mass of ideas compiled out of one or more chorale verses, quite unsuitable for music, and moreover necessitating arias of excessive length. Now and then, however, Picander has succeeded in fastening upon the characteristic point of the verse and expressing it concisely, so that the cantatas contain some arias of surpassing beauty.

Many of these cantatas do not form a poetic whole, the text being lacking in natural dramatic structure. In the cantatas that are more lyrical in feeling this defect is not so noticeable, which explains our finding the pearls of the collection among them. In all these chorale cantatas, however, we have not only the last but the deepest expression of Bach's piety. His music shews how deeply he has been penetrated by these hymns. He has chosen them as the basis of his cantatas because he lives and moves and has his being in them, and finds in them all his thoughts and emotions in their fullest form. And as Bach, the man of piety, feels thus, it hardly occurs to Bach the artist that he is renouncing his freedom.

The scores of this year's cycle of chorale cantatas became Friedemann's at the division of his father's property, as we learn from a letter of Forkel, dated 3rd April 1803*:

> "I have had in my house the whole year's cycle that was in the possession of Wilhelm Friedemann Bach, — the one that is so excellently written upon chorale melodies. Friedemann Bach was at that time in great distress, and asked me twenty louis d'or for the complete property in the cycle, or two louis d'or for the loan of them. I was not rich enough then to put down the twenty louis d'or all at once, but I could afford the two. As it would have cost me more than twenty louis d'or to have had all the cantatas copied that half-year, I resolved to copy some of the best movements myself for my two louis d'or. I consequently possess now only two works written upon the chorales "Es ist das Heil uns kommen her" and "Wo Gott der Herr nicht bei uns hält". Both are extraordinarily beautiful. The whole collection, for which I was asked twenty louis d'or, Friedemann was compelled by want to sell for twelve thalers. I do not know who bought it."

B. F. Richter conjectures**, not improbably, that the purchaser was Doles, the cantor of St. Thomas's. It is more than doubtful, however, whether the cycle was then complete. Rochlitz mentions only twenty-six chorale cantatas of Bach as belonging to Doles.

The parts of these cantatas remained in the possession of Bach's widow. When, in 1752, she asked the Council for a grant, she was given forty thalers "on account of her poverty, and in return for certain pieces of music". According to Richter, these were the parts of the cycle of chorale cantatas, which, however, appear not to have been complete.

---

* Quoted in Preface to B. G. XXXV, p. 29. Dörffel, who communicates this fragment, does not tell us the name of the addressee of the letter from which it is taken.

** See, on this question, his interesting article *Über die Schicksale der der Thomasschule zu Leipzig angehörenden Kantaten J. S. Bachs,* in the *Bachjahrbuch* for 1906, pp. 43—73.

Some of these chorale cantatas were intended, according to Spitta's chronology, for the year 1735 *, — for example the New Year's cantata *Jesu, nun sei gepreiset* (No. 41). The "joy" motive dominates the orchestra in the first part of the chorus, the two trumpets working out the following splendid figuration —

At the words "dass wir in guter Stille", where the praise gives way to prayer, the "joy" motive ceases in the accompaniment and does not return until near the end, where the prayer "Behüt Leib, Seele und Leben hinfort durchs ganze Jahr" is repeated. The final chorale is interwoven with the trumpet fanfares of the first chorus. The two arias rank among the most beautiful of Bach's lyrics.

In the accompaniment to the first chorus of the cantata for the ninth Sunday after Trinity, *Was frag ich nach der Welt* (No. 94) — which also seems to date from 1735 — Bach gives flying figures to the flute and first violins, while the other strings have *staccato* quavers. This is how he elsewhere depicts some one running — the *staccato* quavers are especially characteristic. He is therefore not expressing here the rather contemplative mood of the text, but the hastening of the soul to withdraw itself from the world. Only when we know the meaning of the or-

* It is quite possible that some chorale cantatas of an earlier date, such as *Ein' feste Burg* and *Christus der ist mein Leben*, also belonged to this cycle. Bach did not arrange his works to suit the season, as he was always performing the older cantatas again. He made up the present yearly cycle of chorale cantatas by taking up a number of pre-existent works of this kind, and adding others for the Sundays that were lacking, until the cycle was complete. Of the five cycles that he left at his death, two must have consisted of chorale cantatas. Those of which the St. Thomas's School possessed the parts — the cantatas now to be discussed — belong without exception to his later years.

chestral accompaniment can we find the right tempo for this superb and closely woven movement, and the right way of performing it.

The first chorus of the cantata for the nineteenth Sunday after Trinity, *Wo soll ich fliehen hin* (No. 5), contains a similar piece of orchestral painting. In the aria "Ergiesse dich reichlich, du göttliche Quelle, ach walle mit blutigen Strömen auf mich" ("Pour forth abundantly over me, oh divine stream of blood"), a solo viola keeps up a delightful flowing and murmuring obbligato. The chief motive of this accompaniment recurs in the great orchestral symphony to the first chorus of the cantata *Christ unser Herr zum Jordan kam* (No. 7). The aria "Verstumme, Höllenheer" is also extremely effective. The solos in the cantata *Was frag ich nach der Welt* (No. 94), however, suffer from the poor quality of the texts.

The cantata for the third day of Christmas, *Ich freue mich in dir* (No. 133) seems also to have been written for the year 1735. The scantily figured chorale is sung to a simple orchestral accompaniment, based on the naïve "joy" motive, consisting of continuous semiquaver passages, of which we have a typical specimen in the chorale prelude *Lobt Gott, ihr Christen, allzugleich* (Peters V, No. 40). This mode of expressing joy is frequently used in the Christmas chorale cantatas.

This chorus shows us the risks that the declamation has to run even in the simplest chorale figuration; in two places Bach phrases thus —

In the chorus of the cantata *Was frag ich nach der Welt* (No. 94) there is a passage in which, if he does not divide the syllables of a word by a pause, as in the foregoing example, he separates the words in a way hardly less objectionable —

Wenn ich mich nur an !dir

The two arias of the Christmas cantata are very characteristic. The first begins with the cry —

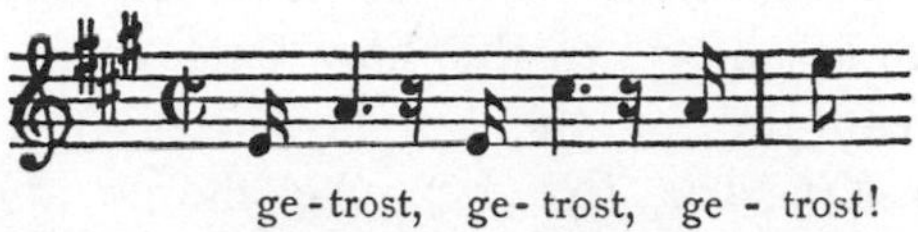
ge-trost, ge-trost, ge - trost!

In the second, — "Wie lieblich klingt es in den Ohren, dies Wort: Mein Jesus ist geboren" ("How exquisitely do these words ring in the ear: My Jesus is born") — Bach cannot forbear making the violins illustrate the "ringing" at the words "klingt es in den Ohren".

Tutti.

We possess three Christmas cantatas belonging to this cycle. The cantata *Gelobet seist du, Jesus Christ* (No. 91) is intended for the first day. The chorus is naturally based on the "joy" motive. The tenor aria, accompanied by three oboes, is a charming lullaby. In the duet "Die Armut, so Gott auf sich nimmt" ("God takes poverty on Himself") the violins have a *unisono* theme in the rhythm of solemnity*, symbolising the celestial majesty of Jesus, while the voices tell us of the "human form" that makes us equal to the angels.

In the cantata for the second day of Christmas, *Christum wir sollen loben schon* (No. 121) the chorus is treated in pure motet style. The orchestra duplicates the voices. One is inclined to regret that Bach did not employ this

* Quoted on p. 95. When performing this fine work it is best to leave out the recitative with chorale, "Der Glanz der höchsten Herrlichkeit".

form more frequently in his chorale choruses. The curious music in the aria "Johannis freudevolles Springen erkannte dich, mein Heiland, schon" can only be explained on the supposition that Bach is representing the leaping of the child in Elisabeth's womb at the greeting of Mary*. The barbarous declamation in the tenor aria is in itself sufficient to show that the music has been taken from another source; it is incomprehensible how Bach could listen to it.

In the cantata for the Sunday after Christmas, *Das neugeborne Kindelein* (No. 12), the chorus and orchestra have some lullaby music about the performance of which Bach was so particular that he has supplied it most carefully with phrasing marks. This movement is especially instructive with regard to the echo effects that he uses in his orchestral works. The theme, the beauty of which comes to a great extent from the splendid symmetry of its form, begins thus —

In the recitative "Die Engel, welche sich zuvor vor euch, als vor Verfluchten scheuten, erfüllen nun die Luft im höhern Chor", the chorale is played by the three flutes. The chorale trio "O wohl uns" (for soprano, alto, and tenor), in which the alto has the melody, is accompanied by the orchestral basses with the "angel" motive, Bach taking it to represent the song of the angels in the "höhern Chor" ("choir on high")**.

The cantata for Epiphany, *Liebster Immanuel* (No. 123) is one of the finest expressions of Bach's mysticism. Its first chorus reminds us a good deal of that of the cantata

---

* See p. 86.

** See the motive on p. 81. It is identical with those of the pastoral symphony of the *Christmas Oratorio* and the accompaniment to the chorale "Wir singen dir in deinem Heer" (in the same work), which ends the angels' song "Ehre sei Gott in der Höhe".

Du Hirte Israel (No. 104). "Liebster Immanuel! Liebster Immanuel!" cry the orchestra, all the instruments repeating continually the opening phrases of the melody

It suggests a crowd of people appealing to the Lord, Whose glory has just been revealed in baptism, to be allowed to kiss the hem of his garment.

The text is very beautiful: —

"Liebster Immanuel, Herzog der Frommen,
Du meiner Seelen Heil, komm nur bald!
Du hast mir, höchster Schatz, mein Herz genommen,
So ganz vor Liebe brennt und nach dir wallt.
Nichts kann auf Erden mir Lieb'res werden,
Als wenn ich meinen Jesum stets behalt."

After this chorus the tenor sings of the "cruel way to the cross", the two oboi d'amore adding an expressive lament. At the end comes the joyous march-song "Lass, o Welt, mich aus Verachtung", in which the soul bids the world farewell. Unless we know, from other scores of Bach, what is meant by the *staccato* quavers in the basses and the hurrying figures in the flute we are apt to render this music wrongly, failing to perceive the joyousness and urgency of it, and reading into it the rather elegiac mood of the text.

The first chorus of the cantata for the first Sunday after Epiphany, *Meinen Jesum lass ich nicht* (No. 124) must be sung with particular delicacy in order that it may not cover up the runs of the oboe d'amore *concertante*, in which Bach has expressed the whole of the fervour that he has seen in the text. In the moving aria "Und wenn der harte Todesschlag" ("And when the cruel blow of death"), the terrors of death are three times overcome by the words "Ich lasse meinen Jesum nicht" ("My Jesus will I never leave"). The strings incessantly accompany the poignant song of the oboes with the "blow of death" —

This ceases each time the words "Ich lasse meinen Jesum nicht" recur.

This movement only makes its full effect when the strings give a really terrifying expression to their semiquavers, with a heavy accent on each note. The final duet between soprano and alto, "Entziehe dich eilends, mein Herze, der Welt", is more effective when sung by several voices*.

This method of performance may be recommended again for the joyous final duet, "Wenn Sorgen auf mich dringen", of the cantata for the second Sunday after Epiphany, *Ach Gott, wie manches Herzeleid* (No. 3; second composition). In the first chorus of this work the *cantus firmus* is in the bass, — an unusual position. In the sorrowful orchestral accompaniment we hear with especial clearness the sighs of the first violins —

The march-like character given to the movement by the remaining strings and the orchestral basses has been suggested to Bach by the text, which speaks of the narrow and calamitous way that leads to heaven. In the recitative with chorale, "Wie schwerlich lässt sich Fleisch und Blut zwingen zu dem ewigen Gut", the stubborn *basso ostinato* symbolises the word "zwingen" ("to force").

In the cantata for the third Sunday after Epiphany, *Was mein Gott will, das g'scheh allezeit* (No. 111), the spirited accompaniment (founded on the "joy" motive) to the

* Simple duets and trios for the final numbers are characteristic features of many of these later chorale cantatas.

introductory chorus shows that Bach interpreted the words of the beautiful chorale ("God's will be done") not in the sense of quiet submission but in that of joyous and confident faith. The chorus, in which the violins have runs of this kind —

must be sung jubilantly and triumphantly.

The duet for alto and tenor, "So geh ich mit beherzten Schritten, und wenn mich Gott zum Grabe führt" ("I go with courageous steps, even though God be leading me to the grave") is like a gladsome, stately march. The voices are accompanied at their entry by the following figures in the first violins —

All the music for the Feasts of Mary in this cycle has survived. The cantata *Mit Fried' und Freud' fahr' ich dahin* (No. 125) was written for the Purification. In the first chorus we seem to hear the weary uncertain steps of the pilgrim of heaven —

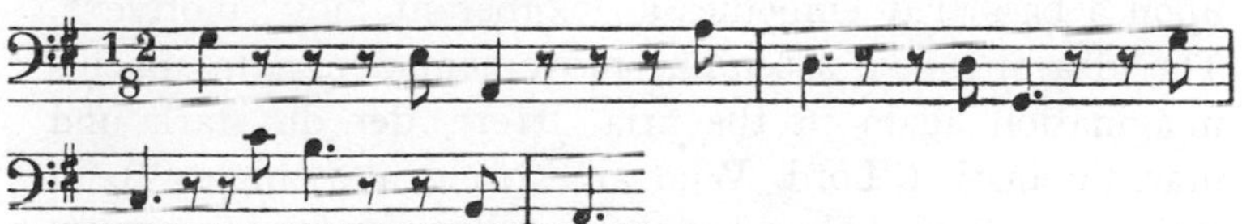

The other instruments have a similar motive, alternating with a triplet figure that is full of inexpressible felicity. In the beautiful aria "Ich will auch mit gebrochnen Augen" we almost get the impression that Bach is continuing to depict the steps, only that the music now, as in the duet "So geh ich mit beherzten Schritten", in the cantata last mentioned, represents a more assured and joyous procession.

The accompaniment to the recitative "O Wunder, dass ein Herz vor der dem Fleisch verhassten Gruft sich nicht entsetzt" ("Oh wonder, that a heart does not shrink from the detested grave") is very characteristic of Bach's pictorialism. The "not shrinking from the grave" becomes, in the orchestra, a matter of positive rejoicing; it is with the "joy" motive that the voice is accompanied —

In this cantata, again, it is best to allot the final duet to several voices.

In the first chorus of the cantata for the Annunciation, *Wie schön leuchtet der Morgenstern* (No. 1) Bach uses two obbligato violins. His music converts the text into an expression of mystical exuberance. In the orchestral accompaniment the themes of the separate lines of the chorale are largely employed as motives. The arias, too, are masterly; in the last of them he again makes use of two obbligato violins*.

The powerful first chorus of the cantata for the Visitation of Mary, *Meine Seel' erhebt den Herrn* (No. 10) — written upon the German Magnificat — is constructed upon a bass that embodies an exuberant "joy" motive**. The idea of a bold ascending movement dominates Bach's imagination again in the aria "Herr, der du stark und mächtig bist" ("Lord, Who art strong and mighty"), in which the first violins have the following free figures —

* In the first, "Erfüllet, ihr himmlischen, göttlichen Flammen, die nach euch verlangende, gläubige Brust", we can almost believe that Bach is trying to give the impression of a flickering flame.

** It is quoted on p. 111.

The proud semiquaver figures in the bass should be noted.

In the *basso ostinato* of the aria "Gewaltige stösst Gott vom Stuhl" ("God casts the mighty down from their seat") the motive of falling and that of haughty strength are combined in one theme*. In the duet between alto and tenor with the *cantus firmus* of the Magnificat — which Bach afterwards made into a chorale prelude (Peters VII, No. 42) — the voice parts should be increased.

The imposing music to the first chorus of the Michaelmas cantata, *Herr Gott, dich loben alle wir* (No. 130) reminds us strongly of the kind of chorus that Bach used to write in his first Leipzig period. In the bass aria "Der alte Drache brennt vor Neid" ("The old dragon is consumed with envy") he tries to show the hearer the powerful body of the serpent working its way upward in furious contortions —

This movement is accompanied by three trumpets and the kettledrum; to make it sound well in performance is one of the most difficult of the problems presented by Bach's scores**.

In the instrumental accompaniment to the cantata for Midsummer Day, *Christ unser Herr zum Jordan kam* (No. 7), Bach has employed on a large scale the method of painting he had already used in his chorale preludes upon this chorale (Peters VI, Nos. 17 and 18)***. The representa-

* Cited on p. 90. Upon the meaning of the semiquaver figures in the strings in the recitative "Was Gott den Vätern allen Zeiten", see p. 76.

** The simple tenor aria, "Lass o Fürst der Cherubinen" should be sung by several voices to each part, the first and second violins, in this case, being added *unisono* to the flute.

*** See pp. 58, 59. See also the fine representation of rapid waves in the first chorus of the secular cantata *Schleicht, spielende Wellen* (B. G. XX^2).

tion of the rhythm and the sound of the moving water is as realistic as it could be. We see great waves and little ones; some overtake the others and break over them; the rapid song of the flutes is bright and gloomy in turns; then the monotony of the even motion is again broken for a moment by a mighty surge of the greater waves. The following are the chief of the themes and motives by means of the succession and interlocking of which Bach depicts so wonderfully the animated play of the waves —

The recitative "Merkt und hört ihr Menschenkinder", which proclaims the promises of baptism and calls for faith in them, is accompanied by a theme that has been prompted by the idea of firm and assured steps. Here again, as in the chorale prelude *Jesus Christus, unser Heiland* (Peters VI, No. 30)*, Bach's purpose is to represent immovable faith in the marvel of the sacrament.

* See p. 61.

In the great chorus of the cantata *Ach wie flüchtig, ach wie nichtig* (No. 26; for the twenty-fourth Sunday after Trinity) Bach again paints a picture for which he had made the sketch in a chorale prelude upon the same melody (Peters V, No. 1)*.

As a rule the accompaniment to this chorus is played much too loudly for it to suggest the flying and undulating mists. The best effect is ensured by having only a few voices to each part and making the orchestra play *piano* throughout. This will permit of a much quicker tempo than is customary. The phrasing must be the one plainly indicated in the bass figure —

Particular care should be taken not to accent the first semiquaver in the fourth beat. If it receives the very slightest emphasis the upward motion of the melodic line is impeded.

The two arias are also conceived in very characteristic style, and their tone-colour is particularly effective. In the first, "So schnell ein rauschend Wasser schiesst, so eilen unsers Lebens Tage" ("The days of our life hasten away like rushing water"), Bach depicts the "hastening" in much the same style as at the commencement of the Easter oratorio, *Kommt, eilet und laufet* (B. G. XXI[3]); in the last he expresses the words "An irdische Schätze das Herze zu hängen ist eine Verführung" ("It is a deceit-

* The sketch and the complete picture are shown on pp. 57, 58.

ful thing to fix the heart on earthly treasures") by means of a theme founded on the "joy" motive, making it a cheerful song of freedom from the world. But as soon as the words "rauschen und reissen die wallenden Fluten" ("The floods rush overwhelmingly along") or "in Trümmer zerfällt" ("falls in ruins") occur, the orchestra at once re-produces these pictures in appropriate motives.

In the cantata for Septuagesima, *Ich hab' in Gottes Herz und Sinn* (No. 92), Picander was particularly anxious to please the composer, so he besprinkled the text liberally with pictures and images. He interrupts the second chorale verse with a recitative, in which "mit Prasseln und mit großem Knallen die Berge und die Hügel fallen" ("the mountains and hills fall with a great crash"), and the flowing waves are also invoked. He was not deceived in his expectation that Bach would seize upon these opportunities for tone-painting, — as he gladly does again in the aria "Seht, wie bricht, wie reisst, wie fällt, was Gottes starker Arm nicht hält" ("See, how breaks, how splits, how falls, whatever God's strong arm doth not uphold")*.

Very characteristic, again, is the bass accompaniment to the aria "Das Brausen von den rauhen Winden" ("The roaring of the boisterous winds"). In the final aria,

"Meinem Hirten bleib' ich treu,
Will er mir den Kreuzkelch füllen,
Ruh' ich ganz in seinem Willen,
Er steht mir im Leiden bei",

Bach expresses this superterrestial serenity of soul in a kind of spiritualised dance-melody —

The same spirit breathes through the first chorus. Unfortunately the tasteless recitatives that fill out the chorale strophes are a serious drawback to this cantata.

---

* See p. 82.

Hans Sachs's fine hymn, which Bach uses in the cantata *Warum betrübst du dich, mein Herz* (No. 138; for the fifteenth Sunday after Trinity) is also so disfigured by Picander's poetical additions that it can hardly be performed without alterations. Moreover the interrupting recitatives in the first two chorale choruses are very unfortunate from the purely musical standpoint, to say nothing of the quality of the passages that have been inserted. It is a pity that the beautiful und expressive music of the first chorus, in which the chorale motives are used also in the orchestral accompaniment, has been so disfigured. At the finish the chorale is sung without any interruptions, the orchestra adding a rich and animated accompaniment*. This chorale cantata stands alone in the peculiarity of its structure. We get the impression — Spitta expresses the same opinion — that Bach had set to work upon it without any very clear plan.

The accompaniment to the first chorus of the cantata for Quinquagesima Sunday, *Herr Jesu Christ, wahr'r Mensch und Gott* (No. 127), is wholly based on the rhythm of solemnity. It will be remembered that in an aria of the cantata *Gelobet seist du, Jesu Christ* (No. 91) Bach employs this rhythm to express the text "God takes poverty on Himself", which likewise deals with the divine and human nature of Jesus. Thus the music in each case represents the divine majesty. As Quinquagesima Sunday, however, introduces the period of the Passion, in the cantata for that day Bach makes the strings and wind give out alternately the chorale "Christ, du Lamm Gottes", in a solemn rhythm.

In the soprano aria "Die Seele ruht in Jesu Händen, wenn Erde diesen Leib bedeckt . . . ach, ruft mich bald, ihr Sterbeglocken" ("The soul reposes in Jesus' hands,

* The fine bass aria "Auf Gott steht meine Zuversicht", which is accompanied by the "joy" motive, was utilised by Bach for the *Gratias agimus* of the G major Mass (B. G. VIII, pp. 178 ff). Hans Sachs's chorale is found in the Wittenberg hymn-book of 1586.

even when the earth covers my body . . . Ah, call me soon away, ye bells of death") the tolling of the funeral bells is heard in the flutes, the oboe adding a strain of ecstatic yearning. The lengthy final arioso gives Bach an opportunity to depict the terrors of the Last Judgment and of the destruction of the world. He does so with the same enthusiasm as in the cantatas of the first Leipzig period.

There is a striking resemblance between the magnificent principal choruses of the cantatas *Ach lieben Christen, seid getrost* (No. 114; for the seventeenth Sunday after Trinity) and *Mache dich mein Geist bereit, wache, fleh' und bete* (No. 115; for the twenty-second Sunday after Trinity). In each of them Bach expresses the idea of some one raising and comforting himself by means of many repetitions of a short soaring motive that is seen also in the first chorus of *Wachet auf, ruft uns die Stimme* (No. 140) —

Cantata: "Ach lieben Christen seid getrost".

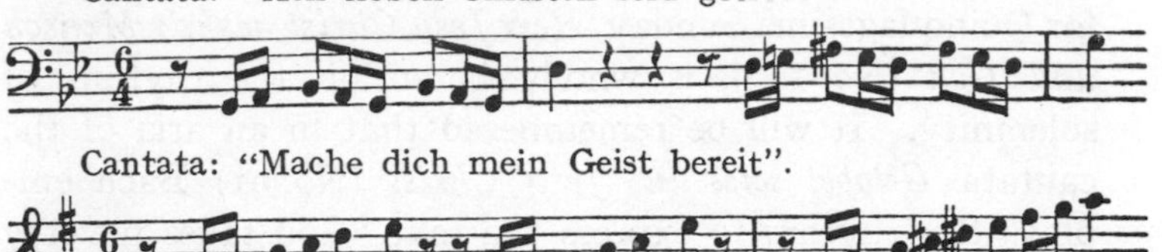

This motive gives a bright and joyous complexion to the musical expression of the text. Bach takes account only of the words "bereit" ("ready") and "getrost" ("confident"), not troubling in the least about the fundamental mood of the verses, which is almost a sombre one. This is especially noticeable in the first chorus of the cantata *Mache dich mein Geist bereit.* It should be mentioned that we possess also another commencement of the chorus, extending as far as the fifth bar, which Bach rejected in favour of the present version*. These choruses must of course be taken in a brisk and energetic tempo.

* See Preface to B. G. XXIV, p. 24.

The solos in both cantatas are beautiful and impressive. In the aria "Ach schläfrige Seele, wie? ruhest du noch? Ermuntre dich doch!" ("Ah, drowsy soul, dost thou still sleep? Come, rouse thyself!"), in the cantata *Mache dich mein Geist bereit*, the orchestra has a lulling slumber-song, through which we hear the warning and terrifying call of the alto voice. In the *allegro* passage at the words "Es möchte die Strafe dich plötzlich ereilen" ("Chastisement may suddenly overtake thee") there is a momentary start of terror in the accompaniment; at the end, however, where the text speaks of the eternal sleep of death, the slumber-song returns. There is a wonderfully intimate feeling in the soprano aria "Bete aber auch dabei", which Bach has marked *molto adagio*.

The solos in *Ach lieben Christen seid getrost* aim more at the characteristic. "Wo wird in diesem Jammertale für meinen Geist die Zuflucht sein" ("Where, in this vale of sorrow, can my spirit find refuge") asks the tenor. The sorrowful flute accompaniment seems to suggest the confused uncertain beating of wings —

But when the answer comes, "Allein zu den Vaterhänden will ich mich in der Schwachheit wenden" ("In my weakness will I turn to my Father's hand alone"), the soul also finds the path along which it is to take wing; it glides through the air with a uniform and easy motion —

In the chorale "Kein' Frucht das Weizenkörnlein bringt, es fall' denn in die Erden" ('If the grain bring forth no wheat, let it fall to the earth") the *basso ostinato* symbolises the motion of the arm as it flings the grain away, and the falling of the latter —

We possess also the sketch for this curious figure. The theme occurred to Bach when he was working at the opening chorus. Dreading lest he should forget it, he wrote it down on an empty line of the score, where it runs thus —

As will be seen, the pictorial idea is fully contained in this sketch; in the improved version, however, it is made much more characteristic. The $^4/_4$ rhythm and the pauses give the theme the abruptness and the angularity that are typical of the motion of the sower's arm as seen from a distance. Thus Bach's notion of "improving" it is to make it more realistic. This accidental light upon his way of transforming a theme is very instructive as to the nature of his art.

Further, in order, that the hearer's attention may not be distracted from the pictorial figure, Bach admits no obbligato instrument in the accompaniment. The violas can be used effectively here to assist the *continuo* bass at the interval of an octave. The organist, by means of one or two four-feet stops, should brighten the *timbre* of the manual on which he is playing with his left hand. Scrupulous care should also be taken to accent strongly the quavers that terminate the semiquaver run, since otherwise the meaning of the figure will be obscured. In the chorale half-a-dozen clear boys' voices should be employed.

The transfigured music of the alto aria, "Du machst, o Tod, mir nun nicht ferner bange", is all the more impressive in virtue of its contrast with the realism of the preceding movement.

When performing the cantata *Aus tiefer Not schrei ich zu dir* (No. 38; for the twenty-first Sunday after Trinity), it is as well to omit the solitary aria it contains. The unendurably wretched declamation proves the music to have been borrowed from another work. The first chorus is in the form of a concise chorale motet. The final trio has also a motet character; it should, of course, be performed by a small chorus, not by the soloists.

The splendid motet upon "O Jesu Christ, meins Lebens Licht", which is printed in the B. G. edition as cantata No. 118, was not originally written for the church, but was performed in the open air, at a funeral ceremony. For this reason it is accompanied by wind instruments alone. Nothing precise can be learned from either Mattheson or Walther as to the instrument called the "Lituus" that is here employed twice. It probably belonged to the cornet family. The work could be re-orchestrated for church use. We possess another score of it, used by Bach for a performance in a building. In this he replaces the cornetto and the three trombones by strings, to which, perhaps, the wood-wind were added.

In the first chorus of the cantata *Allein zu dir, Herr Jesu Christ* (No. 33; for the thirteenth Sunday after Trinity) a sunny confidence is expressed by means of a "joy" motive in uninterrupted semiquavers. The energetic "step" motives in the accompaniment probably symbolise steadfast faith; perhaps they are specially prompted by the passage "Allein zu dir, Herr Jesu Christ, mein' Hoffnung steht auf Erden" ("My hope on earth, Lord Jesus Christ, is fixed on Thee alone"). The most sharply characteristic of these motives runs thus —

In the aria "Wie furchtsam wankten meine Schritte" ("How fearful and uncertain were my steps") the violins give it out in an uncertain and feeble form, —

the other strings adding their *pizzicato* in a march-rhythm. In the themes we should of course accent the syncopated quavers, not the strong beats of the bars, if we are not to destroy the pictorial suggestion of the motion*.

In the bass aria "Bald zur Rechten, bald zur Linken lenkt sich mein verirrter Schritt" ("My wandering steps turn now to the right, now to the left"), in the cantata *Herr Christ, der ein'ge Gottessohn* (No. 96; for the eighteenth Sunday after Trinity), Bach depicts the reeling gait by means of intervals of a similar kind —

At the words "Gehe doch, mein Heiland, mit" ("But let my Saviour go with me") the stumbling accompaniment ceases in all the parts, and is replaced by a short and delicate march. The chorus of this cantata is exceptionally beautiful. It receives an individual physiognomy through the animated semiquaver figures in the *flauto piccolo* and

* The final duet should be sung by several voices.

violino piccolo, that run through the whole movement. The *cantus firmus* is here in the alto.

The first chorus of the cantata for Sexagesima, *Erhalt' uns, Herr, bei deinem Wort* (No. 126), is an expression of confident joy. Besides the rhythm of joy, a descending semiquaver figure runs through the accompaniment. It reminds us very much of the one in the Michaelmas cantata, *Es erhub sich ein Streit* (No. 19), that represents the falling of the vanished hosts of hell. In the Sexagesima cantata the motive has a similar poetic significance, as may be seen from the fact that the basses have this semiquaver figuration at the words "die Jesum Christum, deinen Sohn, stürzen wollen von seinem Thron" ("Who would cast down Jesus Christ, Thy Son, from His throne").

The bass aria "Stürze zu Boden, schwülstige Stolze" ("Fall to the ground, thou swollen pride") is accompanied by a theme composed of two motives. The first depicts the falling; the second, in an ascending motion, paints the huge effort to rise again, which is ended by a new fall*. In this realistic cantata Bach introduces, as he so often does, a movement wholly composed of spiritualised music. The duet of the two oboes in the tenor aria "Sende deine Macht von oben" seems like a heavenly choir singing the praise of God.

There is mystic feeling again in the gentle triplet motion that runs through the great introductory chorus of the cantata *Schmücke dich, o liebe Seele* (No. 180; for the twentieth Sunday after Trinity). We feel that Bach is at work upon one of his favourite melodies. In lively contrast to this thoughtful chorus is the tenor aria "Ermunt're dich, dein Heiland klopft, ach öffne bald" ("Arouse thee and open; thy Saviour knocks"), in which the flute represents the joyous hastening by means of an extremely animated version of the "joy" motive —

* The theme is quoted on p. 83.

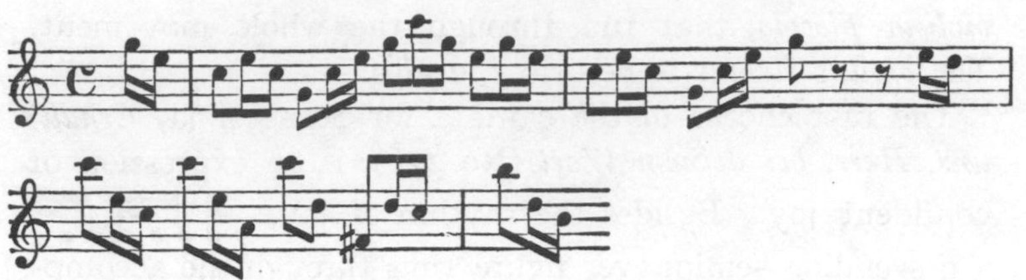

The soprano's hymn of praise, "Lebenssonne, Licht der Sinnen", is accompanied by the orchestra in majestic, flowing, wave-like lines.

The first chorus of the cantata *Wo Gott der Herr nicht bei uns hält* (No. 178; for the eighth Sunday after Trinity) is accompanied by the rhythm of solemnity in the orchestra. In the solos Bach's pictorial conception of the text is almost too evident. The accompaniment of the bass aria "Gleichwie die wilden Meereswellen" ("Like the wild waves of the sea") flows along in agitated wavy lines; the chorale "Auf sperren sie den Rachen weit" ("Their jaws open wide") is accompanied by a motive that is the exact inversion of the one in the arioso of the *St. Matthew Passion,* "Der Heiland fällt vor seinem Vater nieder" ("The Saviour falls before His father"); in the tenor aria "Schweig' nur, taumelnde Vernunft" ("Be silent, reeling reason"), Bach is chiefly concerned to represent the reeling in the most drastic way, by figures of this kind —

How strongly Bach's imagination is influenced by pictorial images in these last cantatas may be seen from the cantata *Wohl dem, der sich auf seinen Gott* (No. 139; for the twenty-third Sunday after Trinity). In the aria "Das Unglück schlägt um mich ein zentnerschweres Band; doch plötzlich erscheint die helfende Hand; mir scheint des

Trostes Licht von weitem" ("Misfortune overwhelms me on every side as with heavy bonds; but suddenly appears the helping hand, and the light of comfort shines on me from afar"), three principal motives are used in succession. The first symbolises the entwining of the heavy bonds —

The second represents the rescuing hand that raises the fallen soul to heaven —

The third symbolises the flickering light that has become visible in the distance —

The third motive has already appeared in the prelude to the aria; it also ends the movement.

It may be observed that the excessive pictorial tendency in the ageing Bach is noticeable not only in his thematic invention, but to an even greater extent in the fact that he no longer works the motives out musically, but is satisfied with the perpetual repetition of them.

The cantata *Nimm von uns, Herr, du treuer Gott* (No. 101; for the tenth Sunday after Trinity), is one of those that are sadly disfigured by the excessively tasteless recitative-passages that are dovetailed into the chorale text. Bach himself was unconscious of the wretched quality of this text. He worked at it with extraordinary devotion. Fortunately Picander had left the first strophe intact. Bach makes a double motet of it. One of these, worked out upon themes of his own, is given to the orchestra; the other, upon the splendid melody "Vater unser im Himmelreich") is given to the choir. We cannot help wishing that Bach had left us more chorale-choruses of this type. The theme that accompanies the final duet, "Gedenk an Jesu bittern Tod; nimm, Vater, deines Sohnes Schmerzen" ("Think of Jesus' bitter death; oh Father, take away Thy Son's sorrow") has a basic affinity with the sobbing, sighing theme of the aria "Erbarme dich" in the *St. Matthew Passion.* It is also interesting from the fact that Bach himself has marked the phrasing, which is very instructive —

The first chorus of the cantata *Ach Gott vom Himmel sieh darein* (No. 2; for the second Sunday after Trinity), is in the form of a simple motet. In the aria "Tilg, o Gott, die Lehren, so dein Wort verkehren" ("Extirpate, oh God, the wise ones who pervert Thy word"), the "perversity" is painted in the typical Bach style. The music of the final aria seems to be derived from some other work.

The beautiful music to the tenor aria "Tröste mir, Jesu, mein Gemüte", in the cantata *Ach Herr, mich armen Sünder* (No. 135; for the third Sunday after Epiphany) was also probably written originally for another text, judging from the imperfection of the declamation. In the bass aria "Weichet all' ihr Übeltäter, weicht" ("Away, ye evildoers"), the rushing away is depicted in a manner as perfect from the pictorial as from the musical point of view*. The first chorus — upon the melody "O Haupt voll Blut und Wunden" — is extremely effective in its wonderful simplicity. The *cantus firmus* is in the bass. The orchestra is occupied only with a motive formed out

* The chief theme of this interesting movement is quoted on p. 88.

of the first notes of the melody, as if it were repeating incessantly the words "Ach Herr! mich armen Sünder!"

The solos in the cantatas of the last period are remarkable not only for their length but for the character of the instrumental accompaniment. Bach seldom employs the orchestra for this purpose; as a rule he contents himself with one or two solo instruments and the *continuo*. The solos in the cantata for the eleventh Sunday after Trinity, *Herr Jesu Christ, du höchstes Gut* (No. 113) are typical in this respect. The chorus of the cantata is in extremely simple style; the voices sing the plain chorale to an orchestral accompaniment.

The chorale used by Bach in the cantata for the fourteenth Sunday after Trinity, *Jesu, der du meine Seele* (No. 78) begins thus —

"Jesu, der du meine Seele
Hast durch deinen bittern Tod
Aus des Teufels finstrer Höhle
Und der schweren Seelennot
Kräftiglich herausgerissen . . . . ."

("Jesus, who hast by Thy bitter death mightily torn my soul from deep distress and the gloomy pit of the devil"). The bitter death and the distress of soul are depicted by Bach in a theme based upon the familiar chromatic sequence —

The "mighty tearing" of the soul from the gloomy pit of the devil is symbolised in this figure —

The whole movement is constructed out of these two themes. The extraordinarily rich detail makes the chorus one of the most expressive ever written by Bach

The fine solos of this cantata run to considerable length. In the duet "Wir eilen mit schwachen, doch emsigen Schritten" ("We hasten with feeble yet diligent steps") the bass of course does not fail to reproduce the motion suggested in the words.

The latest cantata of Bach's that we can date is *Du Friedefürst, Herr Jesu Christ* (No. 116). Its two recitatives contain allusions to the bitter hardships of war.

> "So strecke deine Hand
> Auf ein erschreckt geplagtes Land,
> Die kann der Feinde Macht bezwingen,
> Und uns beständig Frieden bringen" —

so concludes the second recitative. This can refer only to the Prussian invasion in the autumn of 1744. The cantata was performed on the twenty-fifth Sunday after Trinity, which in that year fell on the 15th November.

The music is eloquent of the depth of feeling from which it came. There is a whole world of sorrow in the alto aria "Ach unaussprechlich ist die Not" and the trio "Ach wir bekennen unsre Schuld". Yet even in these melancholy days Bach's joyous faith does not desert him. In the first chorus the orchestra has a gladsome, animated, aspiring motive, that reminds us of that in the cantata *Ach lieben Christen, seid getrost* (No. 114) —

To this accompaniment the choir sang to the afflicted congregation the hymn of the Prince of Peace, who is a strong "helper in man's need". Did the Leipzigers understand, that Sunday, the sermon the cantor was preaching to them from the organ gallery?

CHAPTER XXXV.

THE PERFORMANCE OF THE CANTATAS AND PASSIONS.

A lively contest rages at present as to the way to perform Bach's vocal works; the main point in dispute is whether the cantatas and Passions are to be given according to the original scores, or whether we should make more or less drastic modern arrangements of them.

Perhaps this discussion attracts far too much attention to itself, so that another and elementary question receives less consideration than it deserves, — the question, that is, of the phrasing.

When time pressed, and Bach could only look hastily over the orchestral parts, he marked the phrasing, but not the dynamic nuances. He attached more importance, indeed, to the phrasing than to the correctness of the parts. Many a time he has inserted ties and left wrong notes unaltered, though he must have perceived them had he read the score with ordinary care*.

In present-day performances we are not nearly careful enough as to the phrasing; the majority of conductors do not as yet sufficiently appreciate its significance to insist on the instrumentalists phrasing properly. As they find no phrasing marks in most of the cantatas, they think that Bach had no particular wishes in this respect, and that it is enough if the notes are strung together in any seemly fashion. Even when a cantata is being given in which the parts are covered with Bach's own ties, both players and conductor very often think they are following his directions when they are not realising his wishes in the slightest.

* E. g., in the cantatas *Christus, der ist mein Leben* (No. 95), and *Ich bin ein guter Hirt* (No. 85).

The first thing necessary to give life and rhythm to Bach's themes and periods is his own phrasing. It has a character of its own. If this is disregarded, if instead of the authentic phrasing we adopt a general one that is applicable to any kind of music, the work becomes peculiarly heavy and inert. The colour of it fades; the outlines are effaced; the hearer can no longer follow the several voices; all he hears is an inextricable and wearisome medley; the work makes no vital impression.

If we look merely at this or that cantata with Bach's phrasing marks, it is impossible for us to realise the importance and the bearing of them. For this we need to examine a large number of works of which he has carefully revised the parts. The chief of these are the Brandenburg concertos, the *St. Matthew Passion*, the B minor Mass, the *Christmas Oratorio* and the *Easter Oratorio*; the following secular cantatas — *Phoebus und Pan*, *Schleicht, spielende Wellen*, and *O holder Tag*; and the following church cantatas, — *Wer sich selbst erhöhet* (No. 47), *Herr, gehe nicht ins Gericht* (No. 105), *Liebster Gott, wann werd' ich sterben* (No. 8), *Ach Gott, wie manches Herzeleid* (No. 58), *O Ewigkeit, du Donnerwort* (No. 60), *Ich habe genug* (No. 82), *Ich will den Kreuzstab* (No. 56), *Christus, der ist mein Leben* (No. 95), *Ihr werdet weinen und heulen* (No. 103), *Erfreut euch, ihr Herzen* (No. 66), *Bleib bei uns* (No. 6), *Am Abend aber desselbigen Sabbats* (No. 42), *Es wartet alles auf dich* (No. 187), *Süsser Trost, mein Jesus kommt* (No. 151), *Liebster Jesu, mein Verlangen* (No. 32), *Meine Seufzer, meine Tränen* (No. 13), *Christ unser Herr zum Jordan kam* (first chorus; No. 7), *Nimm von uns, Herr* (No. 101)*.

Anyone who has carefully studied these works, or a number of them, feels that a new light has been thrown for him upon the question of the grouping and the sequences of notes. He becomes aware of a wealth of tonal combina-

---

* Of course not all the numbers in these cantatas are phrased to the same extent.

tions that were previously undreamt of by him. The most wonderful thing, however, is that this multiplicity is not the product of accident or caprice, but seems to come from certain basic ideas as to the combination of a complex of notes in a long musical period.

Characteristic and individual as this phrasing seems, it is quite natural when we see the origin and nature of it. It comes from the idea of the natural use of the somewhat slackened bow. It is characteristic of Bach that he demands it of the wind instruments also, and to a certain extent of the clavier and organ as well.

The first principle* we can deduce from the parts that Bach himself has revised is this, that his phrasing has generally an up-take character. Instead of conceiving in one group the strong beat and the notes of the following weak beats, he groups the latter with the succeeding strong beat. Speaking in general terms, the axiom is that in Bach the accented note is as a rule not the commencement but the end of the group. The grouping that is usual elsewhere  is the exception with him; the grouping that is unusual elsewhere  is with him the rule.

The other possible groupings of the four notes are also more frequent with him than the simple linking of the last three to the first. He prefers figures of this kind: ; ; ; .

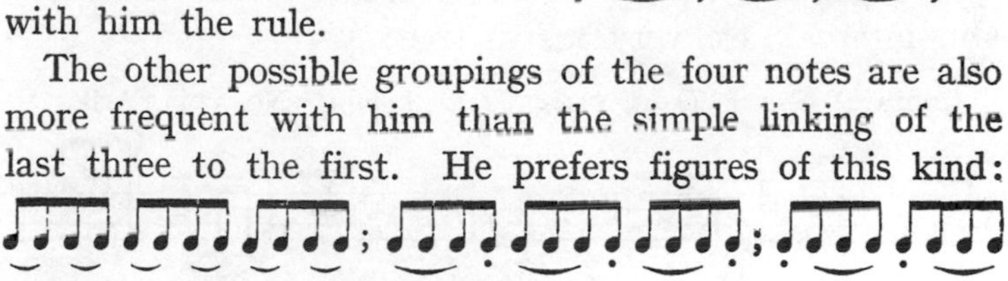

It is unnecessary to quote examples to illustrate this fundamental rule; anyone who will glance through a few of the cantatas named above will at once meet with a dozen of them, and will then understand why the ordinary

* The general principles of the Bach phrasing are given in I. 365 ff.

phrasing can have no other result than the disfiguring of Bach's music.

The second rule is that the intervals which interrupt the natural succession of the notes are to be detached from the tie and played *staccato*, whether they begin or close the period. The following are typical examples:

Ratswahl cantata: *Wir danken dir, Gott* (No. 29). Aria.

Cantata: *Ich habe genug* (No. 82). Aria.

Secular cantata: *Preise dein Glücke* (B.G. XXXIV). Aria.

The cases in which the phrasing alters in the same passage, owing to a change in the position of the characteristic interval, are very instructive:

Cantata: *Süsser Trost, mein Jesus kommt* (No. 151). Aria.

It is equally important to remember that when a larger interval enters in a sequence that is grouped on a definite principle, it does not submit to the preceding phrasing, but abolishes it —

Cantata: *Herr wie du willst* (No. 73). Aria.

Cantata: *Liebster Gott, wann werd' ich sterben* (No. 8). Aria.

Cantata: *Wer sich selbst erhöhet, der soll erniedrigt werden* (No. 47). Aria.

These examples derive their force from the fact that a modern instrumentalist who had them placed before him without any phrasing marks would not play them as above, but on an exactly opposite principle, — tieing the largest intervals; so that a conductor might say to the cellists who asked him as to the phrasing of a run, "Play it in just the opposite way to what you think is correct; then you will be right."

The study of the parts that Bach himself has revised shows us moreover the senselessness of the supposed Bach "tradition" that when the tempo is not very fast the notes of the instrumental bass should be detached from each other so as to come out the more clearly. Only certain basses, consisting of natural sequences in uniform quavers or crotchets, are to be played in this way, especially in passages where the music expresses walking or running. In cases of this kind Bach usually indicates the *staccato* points for the first bars, or marks the movement *staccato sempre.* As a rule, however, he demands the same vitality in the grouping of the bass notes as in the other parts. We can even say that the phrasing in the bass is almost more important than elsewhere. If the bass figure is not perceptible to most of the hearers, this is generally due to the fact that it is not phrased in accordance with Bach's intentions, but as a characterless succession of notes.

How Bach wishes his basses to be played can be seen from the aria "Blute nur", in the *St. Matthew Passion.*

At the commencement of the middle section he phrases the bass thus —

In motives constructed on formulas of this kind and the final quavers or crotchets are, as a rule, to be separated from each other.

In figures founded on the rhythm we must carefully discriminate as to the form to which the phrase belongs*. The "solemnity" rhythm and the "passionate" rhythm must be phrased in such a way that the short note is heavily accented, and drawn, as it were, towards the long note that succeeds it, thus

But if the motive is one expressive of charm or peace, the short note must be quite without accent, and drawn towards its predecessor, thus.

In triple rhythms the customary phrasing, in which the unaccented notes are linked in a uniform succession to the preceding acccented note, , is rather more frequently met with than in the quadruple rhythms; nevertheless there are some very significant combinations of other kinds, such as $\frac{3}{8}$;

* On the various forms of the rhythm and their meanings see pp. 94 ff.

One peculiarity of the figures in the triple rhythms is that Bach more frequently introduces *staccato* interrupting notes, and more of them, within the ties, than he does in the quadruple rhythms. The following are typical cases —

Cantata: *Wer sich selbst erhöhet, der soll erniedriget werden* (No. 47).

Cantata: *In allen meinen Taten* (No. 97) Aria.

Cantata: *Nimm von uns, Herr, du treuer Gott* (No. 101). Aria

It is noticeable, again, that in the triple rhythms Bach very often introduces variants into the phrasing, as if desirous of breaking a monotony that might spoil his tonal figures. In most cases the change is made in the bass. In the bass of the aria "Jede Woge meiner Wellen", in the cantata *Schleicht, spielende Wellen* (B. G. XX[2]), he opposes to the normal phrasing the following ; in the bass of the aria "Fromme Musen", in the secular cantata *Tönet, ihr Pauken* (B. G. XXXIV), the normal rhythm and the other are placed side by side —

The variants in the phrasing in the upper parts are not so sharply antithetical as this, but are all the richer and more interesting. In an aria with accompaniment for a solo violin in the secular cantata *Der zufriedengestellte Æolus* (B. G. XI[2]), Bach indicates the following groupings — , and ; in the aria "Seht, was die Liebe tut", in the cantata *Der Herr ist mein getreuer Hirt* (No. 85), he groups the last six quavers against the first three —

The intention is so delicate that the instrumentalists, as a rule, are not aware of it, and simply play three uniform and connected triplets.

In the runs in the alto aria in the cantata *Es wartet alles auf dich* (No. 181) the antagonism between the natural rhythm of the bar and that of the phrasing is very marked—

The following examples will give an idea of the delightful variety of phrasing by means of which Bach tries to overcome the monotony of triple rhythms:

Secular Cantata: *Schleicht, spielende Wellen* (B. G. XX[2]). Aria with solo violin.

Christmas Oratorio: Air with flute accompaniment.

Cantata: *Liebster Jesu, mein Verlangen* (No. 32). Aria.

A number of varieties in the phrasing are found in the prelude to an aria in the cantata *Lobe den Herrn* (No. 137), of which three bars may be quoted here* —

In $^{12}/_{8}$ time, again, which is a combination of the triple and the quadruple, Bach varies the phrasing in several ways —

* The cantata *Schleicht, spielende Wellen* (B. G. XX[2]) may be specially recommended for a study of Bach's phrasing in triple times.

Cantata: *Liebster Gott, wann werd' ich sterben* (No. 8). Bass aria.

In the rhythms in common time Bach does not introduce so many varieties of phrasing, though they are plentiful enough for all that, as may be seen in the alto aria "Schliesse mein Herze" in the *Christmas Oratorio*, where we find passages like this in the solo violin part —

Generally speaking, however, in $^4/_4$ time he simply differentiates the ties and indicates the natural alternations of *staccato* and *legato*. It should be noticed, however, that almost every one of his ties and dots has for its object to ensure the freedom of the phrases as against the ordinary metre of the bar, and to diminish the authority of the strong beats. A typical example of this tendency may be seen in the cross-tieing of the notes in an aria in the cantata *Ach Gott, wie manches Herzeleid* (No. 58) —

Certain other phrasings that alternate regularly between *staccato* and *legato* have the same end in view. There is a very significant case of this kind in an aria in the cantata *Schweigt stille, plaudert nicht* (B. G. XXIX) —

Other movements in which the transition from *legato* to *staccato* can be studied are the arias "Blute nur, du liebes Herz" and "Gebt mir meinen Jesum wieder", in the *St. Matthew Passion.* The full wealth of Bach's blending of the two in semiquaver passages is seen in the orchestral accompaniment to the first chorus of *Christ, unser Herr, zum Jordan kam* (No. 7).

On the whole we may say that single notes that interrupt the natural flow of the phrases are to be played *staccato*, especially when they are separated from the other notes by large intervals. If they form a large group of their own, then *staccato* and *legato* must alternate within this.

In rhythms of this formula $\frac{2}{4}$ ♪ ♩ ♬ | ♪ ♩ ♬ the question as to whether the second note is to be attached to or separated from the first must be settled in each case by the nature of the motive. In the aria "Schlummert ein", from *Ich habe genug* (No. 82), Bach phrases thus —

while he marks the violin solo in the *Laudamus te* of the B minor Mass thus —

If the first two notes form a large or striking interval, they must, as a rule, be played without *legato*.

It will be generally noticed that Bach's ties and *staccato* points aim at bringing out as saliently as possible the rhythmic individuality or peculiarity of the phrase, while the ordinary phrasing rather tries to tone down the characteristic quality of the melody, as if it were excessive.

No one who has tried to understand the essence of Bach's own phrasing can ever again place unphrased parts before the orchestral players; he will mark the proper ties and dots in the works that have come down to us without them. The task is a long and weary one, but the reward is great.

We meet with fewer insoluble problems than we should expect, since a little research into the original parts that have been phrased will always afford us a number of analogies that will elucidate the obscure case. These researches will convince us that Bach's phrasing is throughout deliberate and rational. His ties and dots are always explicable from the nature and the function of the rhythms and the intervals; the conviction grows upon us that this phrasing is "inevitable", — rules can even be found for the variations. His markings in the *Christe eleison* of the B minor Mass — ; ; ; ; ; — can astonish only those who regard this one movement alone; as soon as we collect analogous cases we see that Bach could not, without being untrue to himself, have phrased in any other way than he has done. It is easy, again, to discover, why, in the *Et in spiritum sanctum* of the Mass he writes at one time  , and at another  ; and a little practice will enable us to understand why, in the same movement, he phrases thus  and again thus  .

The difficulty in some cases would be to decide upon the correct distribution of *legato* and *staccato*; absolute certainty is not always to be expected here. Very instructive examples of the rather rare employment of an uninterrupted *staccato* may be seen in the cantatas *Liebster*

Jesu, mein Verlangen (No. 32) and *Wo soll ich fliehen hin* (No. 5).

Too much care cannot be taken to ensure the up-take phrasing of the basses. Our instrumentalists are so unaccustomed to it that they do not even observe it when the notes plainly indicate it, as e. g. in the *Credo* of the B minor Mass.

The conductor should not only mark the dots and ties in the parts but should often instruct his players as to the nature of Bach's phrasing. Until the players acquire the instinct of grouping Bach's phrases according to their sense rather than according to the bar divisions, it is hopeless to expect a faithful performance of any of his works.

If our instrumentalists are to bring out Bach's phrasing properly they must understand that it goes along with a great multiplicity of accents, that cannot be brought out too sharply. If our orchestras so often think they have fulfilled Bach's intentions when they have done nothing of the kind, it is because they have had regard only to the external aspects of the ties and dots, and have mostly missed the accentuation that can alone convert the separate notes into organic groups.

In no composer, as was remarked in connection with the phrasing and accentuation of the clavier works*, are the dynamic values of the notes so relative as in Bach; no one makes such play as he with light and shade. But ill luck will have it that the dogma of the dynamic equivalence of the notes in his music is hardly disposed of even yet.

The importance of the right accentuation of two tied notes cannot be sufficiently strongly insisted upon. One of them must always be played comparatively heavily, so that the other seems to disappear. If the sequence of notes is in the normal rhythm of the bar, the accent must be given to the first, thus —

* On the general principles of Bach accentuation see I. 375 ff.

The more we take from the second note in these cases, the closer we come to Bach's intentions. Passages like those in "O Mensch, bewein dein' Sünde gross" (in the *St. Matthew Passion*) and the *Domine, Qui tollis,* and *Qui sedes* of the B minor Mass are always played much too cumbrously.

If the succession of the two tied notes is contrary to the normal rhythm of the bar, then the second is to be accented even more strongly, if possible, than the first was in the preceding case —

In the first chorus of the B minor Mass this cross-accentuation must place the normal $^4/_4$ accent quite in the shade —

A very instructive light on the question of the treatment of three tied notes is afforded by the introductory numbers of the cantatas *Es ist nichts Gesundes an meinem Leibe* (No. 25) and *Jesus schläft, was soll ich hoffen* (No. 81). The orchestral accompaniment has quite a different effect when accented thus —

with a certain obtrusiveness of emphasis, instead of the notes being made practically uniform.

Bach's purpose here is the same as in the orchestral accompaniment to the first *Kyrie* in the B minor Mass. He wants to throw a strong counter-accent on to the second and fourth beats, and by means of the antagonism between this and the natural bar-accent to ensure the animated variety of rhythm that is necessary for the "elasticity" of his figures.

This method of treating $^4/_4$ time is very common with him. It is one of the distinguishing characteristics of his style. A comparison of Handelian and Mozartian pieces in common time with those of Bach will show that in the two former there is hardly a trace of these continual rhythmic contrasts; in Beethoven they are more frequent, but not so frequent as in Bach, who indeed always intends them where he indicates or presupposes phrasings of this kind —  or  or 

The general rule may be laid down that Bach's tie mostly means that a strong accent must fall on one of the inner notes comprised within the tie. This gives uncommon force to the correct accentuation of the up-take phrasing. A bass in a regular motion, of the outline of which the hearer is never conscious when it is accented in the ordinary way, becomes unexpectedly plastic when it is phrased and accented thus —

The most instructive example in this respect is the *Credo* of the B minor Mass, the majestic bass figure of which is generally lost upon the hearer, owing to its up-take character not being properly brought out by means of the accentuation. If, however, it is phrased in this way —

it will come out clearly, without there being any necessity to strengthen the instruments.

The basses in the chorus "Sind Blitze, sind Donner", in the *St. Matthew Passion*, should be played in this manner —

if they are to stand out prominently. The result will show that this is how Bach conceived them.

There are thus innumerable cases in which Bach's fine bass figures can be made to tell, by letting the hearer perceive them, as it were, through the breaks in the normal accentuation of the bar.

Retardations, syncopations and all other notes that have any rhythmical peculiarity should be brought out strongly, especially in the triple times. In this regard, however, our worthy instrumentalists are curiously coy; it costs endless trouble to get them to play such passages properly, even in the most striking rhythms. In the characteristic passage in the theme of the aria *Qui sedes*, in the B minor Mass —

it is difficult to persuade them that the natural accent of the first quaver is to be regarded only as a preliminary accent to that of the third.

Motives constructed on this formula, ♪ ♩ ♬ | ♪ ♩ ♬ are to be accented contrary to the normal rhythm of the bar. The strong accent which we necessarily associate with the first note must be regarded as a kind of spring-board to the main accent on the second note. At the commencement of the aria "Ach, nun ist mein Jesus hin", in the *St. Matthew Passion*, we should accordingly play thus —

Notes of small value, especially when they precede an accent, are generally made most effective when played with a certain heaviness, as if we were afraid they might pass by unobserved. This remark holds good in particular for certain motives that are founded on the rhythm of solemnity or passion ♪. ♬ ♪. ♬.

It should be recognised that the Bach *staccato* means, in the majority of cases, not a lightening but a certain weighting of the note.

These rules as to the accent in Bach, founded as they are on his own phrasing marks, are confirmed by what we know of the nature of his themes and motives. It has been already remarked, in connection with the clavier works, that their structure is not always clear from the natural rhythm of the bar, their real form very often only becoming apparent in the main accent that comes at the end. This is true of the themes of the cantatas to an even larger extent; they are much freer and bolder in their construction than the clavier themes, Bach having kept in view, in the latter, the limited possibilities of phrasing and accentuation on a keyed instrument.

All the earlier notes strive as it were towards the principal accent. Before its entry we have the impression of chaos; when it comes it relieves the tension and makes everything clear in a moment; the restlessness is at an end; the theme stands before us in plastic outlines; we perceive the musical period as an organic whole. If we do not experience this sense of tension followed by relief, the theme has not been properly played; it has been phrased in the ordinary rhythm of the bars, instead of in its fundamental rhythm.

It is important to observe that in the mighty periods in which Bach conceives his themes the principal accent is led up to and from by one or more preliminary or supplementary accents, the former process, however, being as a rule longer than the latter. We must therefore emphasise the characteristic intervals and the notes that form the culminating point or the conclusion of a melodic line, whether they fall on a strong or a weak part of the bar. In general this rule will coincide with the one previously formulated as to the accenting of retardations, syncopations and other salient notes in the rhythm.

The difference made to a Bach theme by not accenting the strong and semi-strong beats of the bar can be studied to advantage in the final chorus of the First Part of the *St. Matthew Passion.* If the instrumentalists are allowed to play the ascending semiquaver passage —

in the way that seems most natural to them, they will accent the *E* at the commencement of the third beat, in which case the hearer will not get the sense of the interval of the seventh that is the basis of the passage. If however the accent is thrown on the *A* of the beginning of the fourth beat, the line makes its proper effect on him. In the former case he will hear —

in the latter case —

Nor should we play thus in this chorus —

but thus —

If we accent in this way the final points of the lines and the characteristic intervals, we get a certain rhythmical tension between the upper parts — violin, violas, oboes and flutes — and the basses, which keep to the normal bar-accentuation. Only in this way can the hearer be made conscious of the wailing motives of the upper parts; previously they were lost in the bar-rhythm; he no longer gets the impression of monotony which he could not ward off when the movement was rendered in the ordinary way.

Special attention should be given to the melodic lines that Bach traces with the "joy" motive. Take, as a typical example, the splendid motive —

from the instrumental accompaniment to the first chorus of *Was mein Gott will, das g'scheh allzeit* (No. 111). The usual accentuation — on the first and third beats — does not bring out the meaning of the passage; if, however, we accent the second and fourth beats, in such a way that the main emphasis falls on the last beat of the second bar, the hearer gets a sense of the heaven-storming, joyous faith that Bach desires to express in the motive.

The effects that can be made by the appropriate accentuation of even small melodic lines may be seen in the first chorus of *Wachet auf* (No. 140), by accenting according to its real nature the semiquaver motive that depicts the hurried wakening, instead of according to the normal $^3/_4$ scheme —

In this chorus, again, we can study how to bring out clearly those themes of Bach that are based on scale figures. Much can also be learned in this respect from the first chorus of *Ach wie flüchtig* (No. 26)*.

The characteristic accentuation of complete themes may be illustrated by two examples from the *St. Matthew Passion.* The commencement of the aria "Gerne will ich mich bequemen" should be played thus —

This accentuation prepares the way for the principal accent in the remainder of the theme —

When we accent the theme in this way, bringing out heavily the descending notes after the preliminary accent and between the main accent and the succeeding accent, the theme strikes the hearer as a connected whole; and

* See p. 365.

at the same time he understands how it expresses the obeisance implied in the words "Gerne will ich mich bequemen". With the ordinary accentuation both the form and the sense of the theme are completely lost*.

For the first period of the theme of the aria "Gebt mir meinen Jesum wieder" we should disregard the $^4/_4$ metre, and accent thus —

The second period should be played on analogous lines. Bach's desire to have the second and fourth beats accented throughout is clearly shown by his ties, and by the way in which he makes the other instruments accompany the solo violin**.

We need have no fear that by bringing out strongly the greater and smaller outlines, and by accenting the characteristic notes in what often seems at first an almost unnatural way, we shall give the melody a restless and unrhythmical character. We shall always observe that when the theme is rightly accented the bar-rhythm is still felt to be implicit.

When we ask for this kind of phrasing and accentuation from an orchestra with merely a superficial knowledge of Bach, the instrumentalists feel like a man who is asked to "declaim" instead of speaking in the ordinary way. But just as the latter comes to see in time that what seemed affected to him at first is the correct thing, and what seemed natural is merely a negligent way of speaking, so it happens with the players; what they thought unnatural at first becomes more and more self-evident to them. At the same time they begin to realise how much Bach's music asks

---

* On this theme see p. 221.

** The phrasing and accentuation of a number of themes have been already discussed in connection with the works in which they occur.

of them; they see that each of them must feel himself to be a soloist, and that a correct performance is impossible unless each of them realises from moment to moment the true connection of the notes, internal as well as external. An orchestra that is merely a herd of driven beasts is of no use for playing Bach. We often hear very good orchestras play the accompaniments to the cantatas and Passions in mediocre style, simply because the players have no idea of the demands that this music — which is not difficult in itself, especially as regards the strings — makes upon the musical imagination of each individual. On the other hand we shall find that ordinary orchestras sometimes play Bach excellently when they really try to do so. A conductor with the gift of inspiring enthusiasm will not shrink even from performing the cantatas occasionally with military bands*.

With regard to the tempo markings a distinction exists between the earlier and the later works. In the former, Bach usually indicates the tempo; in the latter he only does this occasionally, even in the cantatas the parts of which he has carefully revised**. The appropriate tempo for a movement is as a rule not hard to find if we examine the text and the nature of the music. The old tempi were generally rather too slow, which did some injustice to the more passionate of Bach's movements. Even today many arias ought to be taken much more quickly than they usually are. A hurried tempo, however, must always be

* I have often assisted as organist at performances of the cantatas in small garrison towns in Alsace, such as Kolmar, Weissenburg, and Saarburg, and have always been astonished to find how well the strings and wind could play the less difficult Bach works after a little training.

** Among the cantatas partly or wholly provided with tempo indications we may mention *Gottes Zeit* (No. 106), *Du wahrer Gott und Davidssohn* (No. 23), *Nun komm' der Heiden Heiland* (No. 61), *Weinen, Klagen* (No. 12), *Selig ist der Mann* (No. 57), *Süsser Trost* (No. 151), and *Mache dich mein Geist bereit* (No. 115). The tempi are also marked in the B minor Mass and many of the secular cantatas.

avoided. It should be noted how simple the vocal part is in certain movements of a passionate character; this seems to indicate that Bach wishes them to be taken quickly*.

Sometimes the problem of the proper tempo for a movement can only be solved by long experiment. Some movements, again, are enigmas; we shall never be quite clear as to the tempo they require.

We may formulate the general principle that the tempo is correct when the details and the *ensemble* are equally perceptible and equally effective. Here again, as in the clavier and organ works, we must remember that the hearer who is listening to a work of Bach's for the first time often feels a moderate tempo to be a quick one, if the modulations are very rich and the contrapuntal writing very complicated.

The real difficulty in Bach's music lies not in choosing the tempo but in maintaining it. No one who knows the scores of the cantatas can doubt that Bach demands great elasticity in the tempo, — the unity of which, however, must not be impaired. If the hearer perceives the nuances too clearly, he at once gets an impression of unsteadiness and a lack of rhythm.

Our singers especially have not sufficiently realised this as yet, — otherwise their performances would be more frequently satisfactory on the rhythmical side than they are at present. They are particularly at fault in their treatment of the cadences. They draw them out to excessive length, and insist too much on even the most unimportant transitional cadences, — which results in the arias being torn into separate fragments. The hearer

---

* Examples of a very quick tempo will be found in the duet "Lass, Seele, keine Leiden", from *Ärgre dich o Seele nicht* (No. 186) and the arias "O Mensch, errette deine Seele", from *O Ewigkeit, du Donnerwort* (No. 20), and "Wirf mein Herze, wirf dich doch", from *Mein Gott, wie lang, ach lange* (No. 155). The tempi of the Passions, the B minor Mass, and the Magnificat have been discussed in connection with the analyses of these works.

with a sense of rhythm is nervously affected by this; as soon as he scents a cadence coming from afar he realises that the tempo will infallibly be slackened, that there will be a discrepancy between the voice and the accompanying instruments, that the orchestra will try to get back to the original tempo in the interludes, and that at the next cadence the game will begin all over again, and be repeated six or seven times before the aria comes to an end.

The art of transition, of which Wagner speaks in one place, should be the ideal that every Bach singer should keep before him with regard to the tempo. Much will be attained if we can first of all get rid of the mistaken notion that every cadence must be taken in a slower tempo. The next thing desirable is that where *rallentandi* seem called for in the cadences, they should be applied circumspectly and with moderation. The *ensemble* of singer and orchestra should never be in the slightest degree impaired. Many *rallentandi* that seem possible from the point of view of the vocal part are impossible to the orchestra. In this respect Bach's arias differ from those of the Italians. The orchestra with him does not merely accompany the singer; it is a separate entity; it cannot bow to the caprices of the singers. These must realise that they have to declaim their part expressively to a symphonic orchestral movement, and that the tempo must not vary very much, the effect being rather obtained by the finest nuances of tempo and rhythm.

The tempo can be perceptibly varied where the verbal sense requires it. An excellent example of this is the soprano aria "Ich folge dir gleichfalls", in the *St. John Passion*. Here the usual *rallentandi* are wrong, as they negate the joyous urgency of the music; the only justifiable *rallentandi* are those required by the words "Höre nicht auf, selbst an mir zu ziehen, zu schieben, zu bitten" ("Cease not to draw near to me and pray"), — the music here depicting the effort of "bringing back". But to overdo this *rallentando* in the least is to endanger the effect of the aria.

In Bach's arias it is advisable not to carry a *rallentando* through to the end, but to lead imperceptibly into the normal tempo again at the conclusion of the cadence, so that when the orchestra enters with the interlude it has not to fall abruptly into another tempo.

Practically these considerations all amount to this, that the customary stereotyped *rallentandi* in Bach's music are bad, and that only those are justifiable that proceed from proper reflection upon the musical and poetical nature of the work. This implies that the conductor and the singer should come to an understanding as to the tempo and its variations, and the general conception of the work *before*, not at, the rehearsal. They must not shrink from long rehearsals and much correspondence; both will bear rich fruit. Every thoughtful conductor and singer knows, to his sorrow, that one of the greatest obstacles to a good performance of a Bach cantata or Passion is the too limited time devoted to the rehearsal of the solos.

Our singers probably sin most against Bach's tempi in the recitatives; they take them much too slowly, and with "expression" in the bad sense of the term, slowing down at each word that they wish to throw into relief, and introducing *rallentandi* in the cadences at the end of the subordinate sections, so that the hearer gets the impression only of a series of fragments, not of a connected whole. But if the singer aims simply at reproducing the verbal period as Bach has written it, he instinctively avoids any dragging, indulges in no senseless *rallentandi*, and tries to make his effect chiefly by means of the declamatory prominence of the most characteristic words. This or that section must be sung in a special tempo only when the sense of the text demands it; and in these cases the art of transition must be called into play so as to preserve the general unity of the tempo. No improvement in the delivery of the recitatives is to be looked for until our singers see clearly that they must not so much be "sung" as "spoken" with a certain musical feeling. How far the average singer is from this ideal as yet may be seen from the way he renders the recitatives in the Passions. His drawling mode of delivery often prolongs the performance by almost half an hour; but that is the least evil he works. Far worse than this is the fact that he is always "depicting" instead of narrating, wearies the audience with his false pathos, and neutralises the effect of the glorious occasional passages in which Bach has given the evangelist a situation to paint. It would be a good thing if our "Evangelists" would now and then recite from memory the story of the Passion; this would save them from many of the stereotyped errors in the delivery of Bach's recitative. The ultimate reason for the unsatisfactory performance of the part of the Evangelist is very often the fact that the singer does not know the story of the Passion by heart.

If Bach employs two themes in a movement, the artistic problem is to ensure to each its proper tempo without destroying the unity of the general tempo. The charm and the difficulty of this problem may be realised from a study of the first chorus of *Ihr werdet weinen und heulen* (No. 103). There are many choruses in which Bach has expressly marked more tempi than one*. It goes without saying that the middle section of the choruses and arias should be taken a shade faster or slower than the main sections, conformably to the sense of them. It is certain also that we can allot a special tempo to this or that segment of a passage; in the final chorus of *Christen ätzet diesen Tag* (No. 63) Bach himself has marked the words "Aber niemals lass geschehen" *adagio*. Markings of this kind,

---

* E. g., the first choruses of *Der Himmel lacht, die Erde jubilieriet* (No. 31) — *allegro, adagio, allegro* —, and *Jesu, nun sei gepreiset* (No. 41), in which Bach has marked the two middle sections *adagio* and *presto*. In the choruses of his youthful works he almost always prescribes more than one tempo, as in these cantatas he is specially bent on composing the text line by line. In the analysis of the B minor Mass (p. 315) examples are given in which the tempo of a movement is the product of a contest between two different motives.

however, give no warrant for the capricious *rallentandi*, merely designed for effect, by which certain conductors think they lend an added interest to Bach's music, even in the chorales.

Where Bach has sharply contrasted two motives in obedience to the poetic idea, it would be wrong to tone down the antithesis by passing gradually from the one tempo to the other. In the final aria with chorus of the cantata *Halt im Gedächtnis Jesum Christ* (No. 67) a *rallentando* in the concluding bars of the passages that are constructed on the "tumult" motive must necessarily weaken the effect of the entry of the "peace" motive in the wind instruments; even a *diminuendo* is out of place here; the more abrupt the transition is the better*; the instrumental basses must still give out the last bar of their "tumult" motive *forte* even after the wind have entered *piano*. In the antiphonal cries, again, of the chorus, "Wohl uns" and "O Herr", there should be no gradual mediation between the two tempi.

The question of ornaments presents no special difficulty with regard to the cantatas and Passions, since Bach almost always adopted the principle of writing out in full the complicated or even the simple ornaments. The signs he employs are to be interpreted in the light of the general principles laid down by Emmanuel, Quantz and Türk on this subject**.

As a rule the trills are taken too quickly and irregularly. Our instrumentalists find a strange difficulty in entering into the spirit of Bach's style. It would be as well if the conductors would write out the signs in full in the orchestral parts. This would at any rate ensure a certain uniformity in the performance, which at present is sadly lacking, in spite of all explanation.

---

* On this aria see p. 192.

** See the detailed exposition of Bach's ornamentation in I. 345 ff. Rust discusses the ornaments of the cantatas in particular in the Preface to B. G. VII.

Too much importance cannot be attached to a simple and quiet rendering of the trills. The following mode of realisation may be suggested for the trills in the bass accompaniment to the aria "Mein teurer Heiland" in the *St. John Passion* —

Very often the context shows that the trill is best realised as a simple *Pralltriller*; an example may be seen in the oboe duet in the aria "Sehet, Jesus hat die Hand", in the *St. Matthew Passion.*

As many of the trills that Bach has marked are barely possible or quite impossible on the wood-wind of to-day,— and must have been even more so on the imperfect instruments of that period — Rust* conjectured that the sign *t* or *tr* in these cases signified a kind of *tenuto*. This hypothesis can hardly be maintained. On closer examination we get the impression that by the trill sign Bach very frequently intended the single or double *Pralltriller*. In any case the acceptance of this view might solve many difficulties.

As regards the realisation of the ornaments in the violin solo of the aria "Erbarme dich", in the *St. Matthew Passion*, it is first of all to be observed that the opening bars, according to the score and the parts, are not written

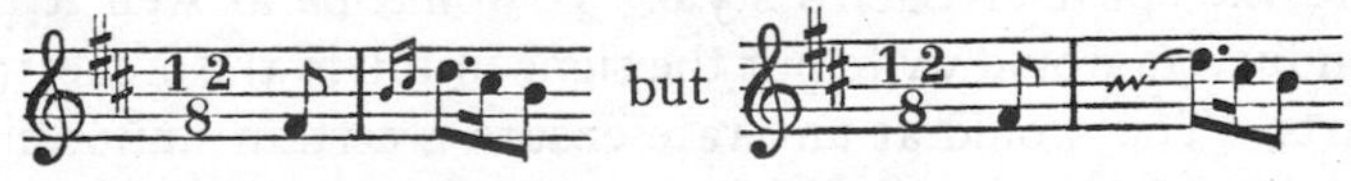

Since in the vocal part of the aria "Was willst du dich, mein Geist, entsetzen", from *Liebster Gott, wann werd' ich sterben* (No. 8), the score has the sign ~⌒ and the voice part has the small notes, this realisation of the sign may pro-

* Preface to B. G. VII, p. 18 ff.

bably be regarded as authentic*. The only question is whether Bach meant this slur to be part of the beat, or to be regarded as a *portamento*, outside the beat, between the *F* sharp and the *D*. The former is the more natural; but in the later part of the solo we meet with passages of this kind —

in which the slur is written out; it is therefore a probable assumption, — and one that has been put forward by connoisseurs, — that Bach's notation in the opening bar implies another kind of slur, *not* included in the beat**. There ought to be little difficulty in coming to an agreement as to the difference between the long and the short *Vorschlag* in this movement; the long *Vorschläge* are merely those that come before a dotted or undotted crotchet; all the rest are short. It goes without saying that in each case the accent falls on the small note of the *Vorschlag****.

The appoggiatura, in the narrower sense of the term, gives unnecessary trouble to inexperienced singers. It is well known that in the vocal cadence Bach and his contemporaries did not write the falling second or the falling fourth as such, but wrote the final note twice, or the equivalent of twice. The following recitative in the *St. Matthew Passion* —

* The B. G. editors have made the mistake of printing the realisation in the text and the authentic sign in the Preface (p. 27), instead of *vice versa*. In the aria "Ach schläfrige Seele", from *Mache dich, mein Geist, bereit* (No. 115), and in other places, the B. G. edition rightly prints ⁓.

** Stockhausen, for example, held that the Bach slur must not always be included in the beat. Whether this opinion can be historically justified is doubtful.

*** See I. 348 ff.

must therefore be sung thus —

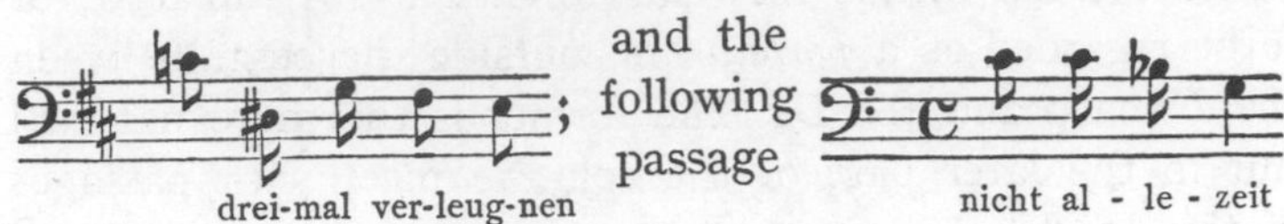

thus —

This method of notation, in which, as in the Hebrew "Q're-K'thib", we have to read something else than what is written, is explained by the reluctance of the old musicians to write out retardations in full; for the same reason they wrote the *Vorschlag* thus —

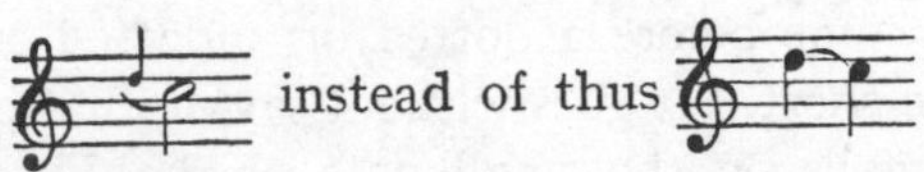

The laws of euphony were not extended to the eye. The appoggiatura in the narrower sense is therefore simply a matter of the three *Vorschläge* involved in a vocal cadence. It was not notated in the ordinary way, but omitted altogether, in order that the organist or cembalist, who had the voice part written out partially or in full above his figured bass, might not be put out by the retardation when he came to play his final chord. The terrors that this method of notation has for the laity vanish as soon as the reason for it is explained.

It should be observed that nowadays it is not the custom to take every interval of a third in a vocal cadence as an appoggiatura, — by the mediation of the second. Julius Stockhausen, for example, very often disregarded the appoggiatura in a transitional cadence*.

---

* I owe this information to Herr Theodor Gerold, teacher of singing in Frankfort, who was associated for many years with Stockhausen in his teaching work.

Many singers think it necessary to distinguish between two short *Vorschläge*, — an accented and an unaccented one, i. e. one not taken in the beat. The authentic traditions of the eighteenth century seem to give no warrant for this view; and practical experiment will show that the short accented *Vorschlag* is always more natural in its effect than the unaccented one.

It is still a matter for investigation whether the rule that the trill must begin with the subsidiary note holds good without exception in Bach's vocal music. The answer would probably be in the affirmative. In certain cases the trill commencing with the principal note may have a charm of its own; as a rule, however, we should render it in the traditional way more frequently than is the custom now. It is hardly credible that Bach conceived the vocal trill differently from the instrumental. Every singer is bound to be pleased with the result when he takes the trill in the correct way. A particularly good method is to pause slightly on the principal note before beginning the trill with the subordinate note, and then gradually increase the tempo; thus —

On short notes the sign *tr* mostly indicates only a *Pralltriller* or double *Pralltriller*.

For the dynamics of Bach's vocal music the following works may be recommended for study: the secular cantatas *Schleicht, spielende Wellen* (B. G. XX²) and *O holder Tag* (B. G. XXIX), and the church cantatas *Ach ich sehe, jetzt da ich zur Hochzeit gehe* (No. 162), *Herz und Mund und Tat und Leben* (No. 147), *Mein liebster Jesu ist verloren* (No. 154), *Schauet doch und sehet* (No. 46), *Herr, gehe nicht ins Gericht* (No. 105), *Liebster Gott, wann werd' ich sterben* (No. 8), *Ich bin vergnügt mit meinem Glücke* (No. 84), *Christus, der ist mein Leben* (No. 95), *Erfreut euch, ihr Herzen* (No. 66), *Am Abend aber desselbigen Sabbats* (No. 42), *Es wartet alles auf dich* (No. 187), *Süsser Trost, mein Jesus kommt* (No. 151), *Liebster Jesu, mein Verlangen* (No. 32), *Ich elender Mensch* (No. 48), *Ich freue mich in dir* (No. 133), *Gelobet seist du* (No. 91), *Das neugeborne Kindelein* (No. 122).

Among these movements are some in which Bach distributes *forte, piano* and *pianissimo* in the subtlest way,—e. g. the first chorus of *Das neugeborne Kindelein* (No. 122), and the arias in *Ich freue mich in dir* (No. 133) and *Es wartet alles auf dich* (No. 187). As a rule, however, he is content with simple alternations of *forte* and *piano*. In the majority of the arias the nuances mean very little, since the *piano* in the orchestral parts merely indicates the entry of the voice. Nevertheless it would be a mistake to think that Bach wished for no more nuances than he has usually marked. Proof to the contrary may be had in the movements which he has liberally sprinkled with *forte, piano* and *pianissimo*. Moreover we must always remember that he revised his parts only for his personal use, not for publication or for performances by other people*. He relied principally on verbal directions. Nor must we forget that the singers and players, being constantly engaged in performing his works under his own direction, were intimately acquainted with his intentions, and would do the right thing of their own accord.

These considerations determine our own course of action with regard to the parts in a performance. Whatever authentic marking exists must be attended to; but beyond this we can venture upon many things which must not be regarded as unauthorised though they are not written

---

* The scores contain no indications for phrasing and no dynamic marks; even the figuring of the *continuo* is omitted. How Bach marked the parts when it was a case of performance by some one else may be seen from the *Kyrie* and *Gloria* of the B minor Mass; the phrasing is indicated in the most precise way, while the dynamics are merely suggested.

in the parts, for they correspond to what Bach would tell his players by word of mouth. The parts must accordingly be elucidated and explained.

The nuances that Bach has marked must be carried out, as in the clavier works and the Brandenburg concertos, with a certain abruptness. He loves the immediate antithesis of *forte* and *piano*; generally speaking he does not provide for the transition of one into the other by means of a *diminuendo* or *crescendo*. This is especially true with regard to the arias. The orchestral preludes and interludes must be played in a solid *forte*; at the entry of the voice the instruments suddenly pass into *piano*. This abrupt transition cannot be successfully managed at the first attempt; some practice in it is required. No conductor, however, will regret making the attempt to get his orchestra to enter into the spirit of the old tradition; moreover this is the best way of weaning the instrumentalists from the false kind of *rallentandi*. It has the further advantage that a number of transitional bass figures, that were formerly lost in the *diminuendo*, now make their proper effect.

Among the peculiarities of Bach's dynamics, which can be studied in the parts that he has so carefully marked with nuances, are the echo effects. He often introduces, by way of contrast, two or three *pianissimo* bars where it would not occur to us to do so. At the first glance the device seems artificial and pedantic; but as many themes and passages are calculated on it, it is one of the most natural and most telling effects that we can introduce into the accompaniment of the arias. As has been already mentioned, the players in Bach's time probably rendered these passages by slackening the hairs of the bow*. The curious change of *timbre* obtained in this way unfortunately cannot be obtained with the modern bow.

---

* See I, 209.

Bach gives us no indications as to the nuances he employed in the arias after the entry of the voice. He would regard this as belonging to the province of correct declamation. He would certainly permit every *crescendo* and *diminuendo* that was needed to give expression to the words. All nuances, therefore, that have a natural musical or poetical justification may be regarded as not only permissible but necessary. From the character of Bach's music it is clear that nothing could be more odious to him than a lifeless delivery of an aria. The more dramatically it can be sung the better. Even the purely lyrical movements in the cantatas gain in performance by the infusion of a certain inward vivacity.

In proportion, however, as the singer attains to a more profound conception of the text will he adopt a simple style of performance. Many an effect that he thought fine at first will come to seem bad and factitious as he understands the music better.

If the singer articulates clearly and declaims with natural feeling, and the instrumentalists — even when they are playing *piano* — put life into their phrasing and accentuation, the dynamic problem solves itself. It will be observed that in Bach the question is generally not one of long periods of *crescendo* and *diminuendo*, but of throwing single words into high relief, — notwithstanding that examples can be adduced in which the guiding idea of the music has apparently been an increase or decrease of tone.

Perhaps it is not superfluous to remind singers that it is always bad to force the voice in performing Bach.

Good Bach singers are comparatively rare. The majority fail because they lack the necessary technical foundation. Their conception may be right, but their voices are not fully obedient to them. The often-repeated opinion that Bach's works do not need the *bel canto* is utterly false. They need this — but something more as well. It would be well for every Bach singer to devote some time to acquiring the lightness that is aimed at in the Italian and French schools, for which an acquaintance with good Italian vocal music is indispensable. It must not be forgotten that Bach formed himself on the Italian style of singing, and presupposes this in his music. Present-day singers, as a rule, perform it too heavily.

To this external art of singing has to be added the other art of natural poetic declamation, that is so necessary in German music. Bach's *coloratura* has really hardly anything in common with that of the Italians. It is not an end in itself, but the servant of the declamation, — which makes it harder, not easier. The singer must be superior to every technical difficulty if he is to render the runs simply and with a certain naturalness that is indispensable to their proper effect, — for they should not impress us as *coloratura* but as fine enunciation. In passages of this kind a certain urgency of tempo is preferable to dragging.

The directness of delivery that suits Bach's music so well really demands a perfect technique. Few of our singers, apparently, realise the mischief done by inappropriate *crescendi*, or they would not prolong so unnaturally and embellish as they do every sustained note, even the shortest. In Bach's arias and recitatives we should not be conscious of the art of singing as such, no matter how indispensable it may be; on the contrary the singing should be fresh, ingenuous, and "youthful" in the best sense of the word. It should not be forgotten that the parts were written, without exception, for boys and very young singers. Bach's style was naturally influenced by the fact that these were the only interpreters he had at his disposal.

The feminine delicacy with which very many of our singers render the arias is therefore foreign to Bach's ideas, and does harm to his music. It is to be hoped that a time will come when more attention will be paid than at present to the natural lightness of the boy's voice, and more use made of boy singers in performances of Bach. We shall then probably find that the current prejudice as to the inexpressiveness of a boy's singing is not justified. Has not every musician discovered from his own experience that his artistic sensibility developed in an extraordinary way from his twelfth to his fifteenth year, and that later on he had to acquire afresh what at that time came naturally to him? Why should boys at that age merely play the piano well? Why should they not achieve something in the much more natural art of song? Every one who has studied Bach's scores carefully knows that there are many movements in them that can never be fully effective except with the freshness and the *timbre* of the boy's voice. Perhaps the day will come when we shall once more hear the soprano cantata *Jauchzet Gott in allen Landen* (No. 51) again sung by the fresh voice of a boy.

That beautiful boys' voices are the ideal for the Bach choruses will not be disputed by anyone who has heard a good boys' choir in one of the cantatas. Schreck has shown, with the St. Thomas boys of today, what can be done with an *ensemble* of this kind. The advantages of the boys' choir are the natural ease of the voices in the higher register, the clarity of the *timbre* of the soprano and alto, and, above all, the homogeneity of the voices as a whole. The glorious outlines of Bach's alto parts cannot be followed properly except in a boys' choir.

The difficulties of getting boys to perform Bach must not be overrated. The easier cantatas can be given by any good college choir after careful rehearsal. Certain of the secular cantatas, such as *Der zufriedengestellte Æolus* seem to be written for a choir of this kind. Perhaps the practice of Bach's works will bring about a new era in the rather sorry state of singing in our high schools.

The conductor who has a few good boys' voices in his choir should use them to support the women's voices. It cannot be too strongly urged that the *cantus firmus* of the chorales, — even in the chorale arias — should always be sung by boys. Anyone who has heard boy sopranos in the introductory choruses of the chorale cantatas can hardly imagine them again without these. Not many voices are required; half a dozen of them, together with the women's voices, are sufficient to bring out the melody in broad, plastic lines.

Boys' voices are very effective, again, in the *canti fermi* of the final chorales. There need be no fear that they will impair the fineness of the expression here, as will be evident to anyone who makes the experiment rationally. On the contrary it is a matter for wonder that we have been so long satisfied to have the chorale melodies sung by women's voices, that lack the full, penetrating, "objective" tone that is here required.

There is still considerable difference of opinion as to the best way of rendering the final chorales. One view is that they should be given *a cappella*, without the accompaniment for strings and oboes that Bach has indicated or presupposed — to which the flutes and even the brass may sometimes be added. It is urged that Bach's purpose was merely to support his rather inefficient singers, and that our large modern well-trained choirs can dispense with this assistance. It would be a pity if this view should gain ground. There is a great danger in the *a cappella* performance of the chorales by a large choir; it is very easy to achieve falsity by exaggerating the dynamic shadings. It is indisputable that a great effect can be made on an audience by four hundred voices delivering one line of a chorale *fortissimo* and the next in a hardly audible *pianissimo*; but it is almost equally indisputable that this is not the right way. The simple and beautiful outlines of the chorale melody are lost in these mighty *crescendi* and *decrescendi*, the *rallentandi* that they almost of necessity bring with them, and the long holding of the *fermate* for the sake of effect. We lose the sense of the chorale as a whole, and only perceive the fragments. What should we say if any other simple melody were sung by a chorus in the same coarsely effective style? Yet it is permitted in chorales which are not only simple but full of piety!

For these exaggerated nuances we should substitute a simple but impressive declamation, studiously avoiding anything like sentimentality or excitement. The choir should almost speak rather than sing, the dynamic shadings being obtained, as it were, within a gamut of a sharply defined recitation; care should be had with regard to the endings of words and of sentences; the *fermate* should be no more than natural breath-pauses, short or long as the sense of the line requires; this method will bring us nearer artistic truth than the present style. If after this the chorale does not affect the audience, it will at all events give it a deeper artistic conception of the nature of the sacred melody.

In a performance of this kind the instruments are neither a hindrance nor a superfluity, but a necessity*. They afford a golden background for the declamation; they work out the melodic outlines and permit the voices to attend almost exclusively to the clear delivery of the text. It should be noted that the harmonies in Bach's chorale movements aim not so much at large dynamic effects as at bringing out separate words and syllables. The enunciation of our large choirs in *pianissimo* passages is often very defective, the audience hearing neither singing nor speaking, but only a confused murmur, — which cannot be agreeable even to an uncritical hearer.

These views must not be taken to mean that under no circumstances must the chorales be sung *a cappella* by large or small choirs; there are occasions when it would be wrong to throw away the opportunities thus afforded for a striking effect. Each case of the kind, however, should be able to show its own justification. For the rest, we should

---

* The instruments must co-operate in places where they are not prescribed in the B. G. edition. If they are not indicated in the chorale, this simply means that the parts of the cantata are lost. Bach comparatively rarely marks the instrumentation of the final chorale in the score, and does not even take the trouble to write the text in there, often inserting no more than the first line.

never approach the problem of the performance of Bach's music in a narrow-minded spirit.

It is often debated whether large choirs are an advantage in the cantatas and Passions. It is hardly possible to give an unequivocal answer. It is obvious that Bach's music, with its complicated polyphony, does not aim at the same massive effects as Handel's. It would even be easy to name a number of works that for purely external reasons call for a choir of only moderate dimensions, — the cantatas, that is to say, in which Bach employs a solo violin or solo oboe with the chorus. In other works, internal considerations forbid the use of a large choir; by their very essence they are a kind of sacred chamber music. The works in which Bach wrote simply for the choir usually at his service — with three or four voices to a part, — are really much more numerous than is generally supposed. Further it must be acknowledged that even Bach's largest and most powerful choruses are extremely effective with a small choir of really good voices — say six or eight to a part. Julius Stockhausen's experiences in this way with a choir of his pupils, in the *St. John Passion*, are extremely encouraging. The desire to hear Bach's works more frequently with the "original equipment" is therefore well justified. It is certain that his polyphony shows to the best advantage under these conditions.

On the other hand it would be a mistake to deny that there is some reason in, and some justification for, our large choirs, to which we have become so accustomed, and which are often called for by the size of the building in which we are giving Bach's work. Bach indeed never dreamed of a performance of the *Gloria*, the *Et resurrexit* and the *Osanna* of his B minor Mass by three or four hundred singers; nevertheless we may venture to perform them in this way, and it has been done successfully. We ought to recognise, however, that it is all a matter of chance. Even with a choir of hundred and fifty voices there is a danger of the lines of the vocal polyphony coming out too thickly and heavily in a way directly opposed to the nature of Bach's music. Audience and conductors often show, in this regard, a happy simplicity and modesty. They are satisfied with choral performances that are really more like a confused din than the polyphony of Bach, and that have not even the saving grace of mechanical precision. Siegfried Ochs has conclusively shown that this danger can be avoided, and that the same clarity, precision and delicacy can be obtained with large choirs as with small. In this respect the performances of the Berlin Philharmonic are an event in the history of Bach interpretation.

With our large choirs, the dynamic nuances necessarily seem more sharply defined than in performances on the scale of those of Bach himself. In reality, only the broad and simple dynamic plans can come out. The conductor discovers, in the case of almost every work, that when the orchestra and organ enter he has to resign himself to the loss of many interesting nuances that he had set his heart on at rehearsal. In the choruses, as in the chorales, the range of dynamic possibilities is finally limited by the vivacity of the declamation. Opportunities for the usual big *crescendi* and *decrescendi* are not too plentiful. There is no excuse, however, for introducing nuances for the mere sake of variety. On the other hand the more we work at Bach the more convinced we become of the importance of clear enunciation, down even to the finest detail.

A certain *martellato* — used with discretion and in moderation — is very effective in the *colorature*, as it brings them out more clearly than the customary strict legato, in which the successive notes flow smoothly one into the other. The least exaggeration, however, is bad.

If the choir can declaim well, and the orchestra phrase and accent well, the hearer will feel no desire for a number of pronounced dynamic shadings. The leading of the voices, if it be sufficiently spirited, compensates for everything; the piling-up of the parts produces a *crescendo*, and a natural *decrescendo* comes as they diminish in number. False nuances frequently have no other effect than to obscure for the hearer the natural dynamic impression that Bach's polyphony ought to give him. Special care must be taken not to pursue any dynamic chimæras in the opening choruses of the chorale cantatas.

Bach gives hardly any direct dynamic instructions in his choruses. Valuable hints for *forte* and *piano* can be had, however, from a consideration of the instrumental parts. If the full orchestra co-operates, the movement is usually meant to be taken *forte*; if this wholly or partially ceases, the movement is generally intended to be *piano*. As a rule the greater *crescendo* and *diminuendo*, which we are inclined to get dynamically, are produced by Bach by adding or subtracting instruments, — i. e., by increasing or diminishing the number of obbligato parts. This fact is of great importance for the proper interpretation of his scores.

In the cantatas Bach often uses, as in the Brandenburg concertos, a *tutti* and a solo ensemble, not only in the orchestra but in the chorus. As a rule he would say verbally when the *ripieno* players* were to enter or leave off. Fortunately, however, some indications of this kind are found in the parts. He desires the alternation of the solo and the *tutti*, for example, in the opening choruses of *Die Himmel erzählen* (No. 76), *Ich glaube, lieber Herr* (No. 109), and *Gott ist mein König* (No. 71); in the chorus "Was betrübst du dich" from *Ich hatte viel Bekümmernis* (No. 21); and in the chorus "Alles nun, was ihr wollt" from *Ein ungefärbt Gemüte* (No. 24). For the first chorus of *Unser Mund sei voll Lachens* (No. 110) he even writes out special *ripieno* vocal parts. If he thus worked with two tonal masses with the small choirs he had at his disposal, how much more would he have done so with the large choirs we have today!

---

* For the explanation of this term see I, 124.

The *piano* and *forte* obtained by stronger or softer singing can never replace those resulting from the increase or diminution of the number of voices. The latter means is the more natural one where the effect desired is not one of transition, but of the contrast of tonal degrees. It achieves this excellently; the leading of the voices comes out much more clearly in a *piano* of a small choir singing with moderate force than in the sustained *pianissimo* of a large choir, where indeed it is often far from distinct. Bach aims at effects of this kind. Why do we always fight shy of them? In any case there is one thing we should insist upon, — that in the middle movements of the choruses, where the instruments are silent, only a portion of the choir shall sing. The effects to be made in the fugues by means of successive increases of the number of voices at decisive entries, and in the lyrical choruses, such as those of *Du Hirte Israel* (No. 104) and *Liebster Immanuel* (No.123), by means of the alternation of various choral masses, and the effect of shadings of this kind in the large choruses of the festival cantatas — all this offers a rich field for interesting experiment.

The absurdities that follow from the continual employment of a large chorus in the Passions have already been mentioned.* In the chorales the best effect is often obtained by the use of some thirty or forty good voices.

On the other hand it may be argued that not all the movements which we regard as solo numbers were allotted to soloists by Bach himself. For him solo singing and choral singing passed over into each other in a way to which there is no parallel now. We must remember that his choristers were soloists, and his soloists choristers. The best of them were skilful in *coloratura*. Perhaps it is not too hazardous a view to take that, as boys' voices blend so well, he did not scruple to have solos sung by two, and if necessary three, of his choristers. We sometimes wonder how he

* See p. 213.

could orchestrate an aria or a duet in such a way that the best singers cannot hold their own against the orchestra*. Is the solution of the enigma to be found, perhaps, in the doubling of the solo voices? Anyone who has happened to hear boys' voices in a church, without seeing the singers, will have observed that it is almost impossible to say whether solo passages are being taken by one or two voices. Voigt rightly remarks, when discussing, from the practical standpoint, the possibility of allotting the solo numbers to more than one voice, that Bach's solos "do not express individual sentiments, as opposed to the general sentiments of the chorus", and that "they should not be allotted to definite individual singers"**.

It will not be denied that the opening duet of the *Easter Oratorio* (B. G. XXI^3) presupposes a choral performance; that a number of simple duets and trios in the latest cantatas give one the same impression, and are certainly more effective when sung by several voices, has already been argued in connection with the discussion of these works***.

The understanding of the scores is of the greatest importance for the orchestral parts. The *piano* in the instrumental parts of the arias not only means that at the entry of the voice the orchestra is to play softly, but that the *ripieno* also has to cease. Thus the instrumental *piano* also is obtained by a diminution of the number of the players.

* Who can boast that he has ever heard the opening duet of *O Ewigkeit, du Donnerwort* (No. 60) even fairly well done? A glance at the score shows that it can never be sung properly by any two voices, even those of the best singers.

** W. Voigt, *Erfahrungen und Ratschläge bezüglich der Aufführung Bachscher Kirchenkantaten*, in the *Bachjahrbuch* for 1906, pp. 1—42.

*** See, for example, the simple but splendid duets and trios in the cantatas *Allein zu dir, Herr Jesu Christ* (No. 33); *Aus tiefer Not* (No. 38); *Du Friedefürst, Herr Jesu Christ* (No. 116); *Gott der Herr ist Sonn' und Schild* (No. 79); *Meinen Jesum lass ich nicht* (No. 124); *Mit Fried' und Freud' fahr' ich dahin* (No. 125); *Meine Seel' erhebt den Herren* (No. 10); *Herr Jesu Christ, du höchstes Gut* (No. 113); *Jesu, der du meine Seele* (No. 78).

This natural use of the *tutti* — for the preludes and interludes — and the *Senza Ripieni* — for the accompaniment to the voice — is coming slowly into acceptance. It is beginning to be recognised how much more effective is the *piano* obtained by the use of a few instruments as compared with the *pianissimo* playing of a larger number. It carries better; it is capable of more modulation; the leading of the voices is quite clear. As there is no need to play *pianissimo*, — a normal tone-strength being all that is required — we can get better phrasing and accentuation; the nuances also can be made more pronounced. At first this kind of accompaniment strikes the hearer as curiously thin; he soon becomes accustomed to it, however, and is pleased to have lost his perpetual fear that the voice is about to be submerged by the orchestra.

In the halls in which we are accustomed to perform Bach, however, it is not advisable to employ too few instruments. For string accompaniments the following will be found best as a rule — two desks for the first and second violins and violas, and one desk each for the cellos and double basses*. In the accompaniment of a recitative in *Ich liebe den Höchsten* (No. 174) Bach prescribes three string instruments to each part.

The *piano*, however, does not merely signify that the *ripieno* instruments concerned are to cease; it refers also to the instruments in the *tutti* that have been playing the same parts. In the opening number and in the duet "Ich hab' vor mir ein' schwere Reis'", from *Ach Gott, wie manches Herzeleid* (No. 58), the three oboes, in the *tutti* passages, play with the strings; in the passages where the voice enters they are marked *tacet*, the strings alone

* At a very interesting performance of the *St. Matthew Passion* in the cathedral at Basel, in 1906, I observed that many of the instrumental parts did not come out, there being too few desks of them for the space; this was especially noticeable in the accompaniment to the music of Jesus. In other passages, however, the advantages of the principle were fully manifested.

accompanying; the third oboe goes to the support of the soprano, which sings a chorale. There is a similar case in the alto aria in *Süsser Trost, mein Jesus kommt* (No. 151). This is accompanied by the oboe d'amore; in the *tutti* passages, however, this part is played by the whole of the violins and violas. In the first chorus of *Was frag' ich nach der Welt* (No. 94), Bach, in order to get certain echo effects, sometimes makes the oboes play with the violins, and sometimes silences them.

It is a mere accident that these indications have come down to us; Bach has for once entered in the parts the instructions he was accustomed to give by word of mouth. In arias in which the oboes and violins play in unison, *piano* probably often means that either the wind or the strings are to cease. This rule may be tested in the cantatas *Ich will den Kreuzstab gerne tragen* (No. 56) and *Ich armer Mensch, ich Sündenknecht* (No. 57), in the opening numbers of which, according to the Bachgesellschaft editions, the oboes should play from beginning to end with the strings, whereas, as a matter of fact, the voices ought probably to be accompanied only by the strings or only by the wind, or by the one or the other in turns.

In the aria "Sanfte soll mein Todeskummer", from the *Easter Oratorio* (B.G. XXI[3]) the violins are doubled by the *flûtes à bec* in the octave. It is more than doubtful, however, whether Bach had the flutes played throughout, or whether they ceased in the accompaniment to the voices.

The fact that the parts of the instruments that merely double others in the *tutti* are written out in full is only an apparent contradiction of the views here advanced. The obbligato parts were copied out; the conductor would say to what extent the instrument in question was to play from them. It was only in rare cases that separate parts were made for the *ripieno* instruments.

The false conclusions to which we can be led by a literal following of the score and its markings may be seen in connection with the bassoon. At the beginning of one cantata is a note to the effect that the bassoon is to play with the cellos. To do this throughout the movement would be a gross error; it merely means that the bassoon must co-operate in the chorus, and now and then in the *tutti* of a strongly scored aria.

On the other hand the absence of any indication as to the co-operation of the bassoon does not imply that we are not to employ it to strengthen the basses, at any rate in the choruses. In the majority of choruses it is really essential; and if the choir is a large one it is as well to employ not merely one but two or three bassoons. It should even be used in the *tutti* passages of the aria where it will be effective, — at any rate wherever the violins and violas are reinforced by the wood-wind.

We may venture upon still other courses that are not indicated either in the score or in the parts, but which were probably pursued by Bach himself. We must consider the circumstances at the performances in St. Thomas's. It was a case of doing with the smallest possible number of written parts; even in the choruses there was usually only one copy for each vocal part. The instrumentalists mostly played standing; they half knew their parts by heart. Thus it was quite practicable for other instruments to play at times from the same part in the *tutti* of the arias.

When the Bachgesellschaft edition indicates an oboe accompaniment to an aria, this does not always imply that the part is to be played by merely one oboe from beginning to end. We may be sure that when Bach had one or two oboes at his disposal he did not let them remain idle, but made them join in the *tutti* when he came to a vigorous theme. Nor is it unlikely that he supported the oboe with two or more string instruments, which would play in the *tutti* from the same part.

Even these historical considerations are unnecessary; often the music itself shows that in the *tutti* of the arias that were accompanied by the wind, the "solo instruments" were either doubled, or supported by strings, or both. We cannot help feeling it to be ridiculous when a bold and proud theme is suggested, rather than actually given out, by a single oboe or flute. Every assistance is permissible, and indeed imperative, that makes the obbligato part more effective, — for it is of the part, not the instrument, that Bach thinks in the first place.

Two oboes are prescribed for the instrumental duet that accompanies the chorale aria "Und was der ewig güt'ge Gott", in *Wahrlich, ich sage euch* (No. 86); but even the best players cannot perform these haughty runs in such a way that the introduction has its desired effect. For the *tutti*, therefore, we must double the oboes and add the whole of the violins. It is to be observed that in many themes that are marked for oboes alone, the phrasing is so string-like in quality that the right grouping and accentuation of the notes are quite impossible without the cooperation of the violins. Thus in the *tutti* passages of the opening numbers of *Sie werden euch in den Bann tun* (No. 44) and the first aria of *Jesu, nun sei gepreiset* (No. 41), for example, we may add the strings in the oboe duet and the oboe trio*. It is frequently necessary to add the strings in the *tutti* passages even in an aria for solo oboe.

How much has to be added to the received scoring may be seen from the arias in which, according to Bach's score, the oboes are to play with the first and second violins. We may reasonably wonder why he leaves the violas without the support of the taille, which, with Bach, takes the place of the third oboe. He, however, would have wondered that anyone should think him capable of such an inconsistency; he presupposes, indeed, the co-operation of the taille in just the same way as that of the oboes;

---

* Another case that justifies the support of the oboe by the strings is the chorale aria "Valet will ich dir geben", in *Christus, der ist mein Leben* (No. 95). It should be mentioned, too, that in large halls the strings may also be sometimes used to advantage with the oboes in the vocal accompaniments, when there is no danger of the voice being drowned.

the only difference is that his marking calls for the writing of special oboe parts, whereas the taille was played from the viola part. Or else ... at that time, to his sorrow, he had no third oboist.

If the theme requires it, the solo flute should be supported in the *tutti* passages by the oboe or the violins, or by both together. Perhaps the best example of the necessity of this rule is the aria "Lass, o Fürst der Cherubinen", from *Herr Gott, dich loben alle wir* (No. 130).

It is very frequently desirable to strengthen the oboes by the flutes. The fact that both instruments played from the same part* in the cantata *Jesus schläft, was soll ich hoffen* (No. 81) makes it practically certain that where Bach writes flutes he intends the oboes also to play, and *vice versâ*. The first and last arias sound particularly well in this arrangement.

The employment of flutes in the oboe accompaniments to choruses — sometimes an octave higher — cannot be too strongly recommended; this is often the only means of ensuring that the oboe shall be really heard. It has already been said, in connection with the Passions, that the flutes themselves must sometimes be reinforced by the piccolo if their runs are to come out clearly.

We ought not to shrink from any combination of instruments that will bring out the obbligato parts properly; these combinations are all to be found in Bach's scores. In the opening chorus of *Herr, gehe nicht ins Gericht* (No.105) he even adds the horn to the first oboe in order to make the latter part stand out better.

Perhaps it is even justifiable to try the experiment of allotting the violin soli in certain movements to two or more desks in the *tutti*. Bach's reason for marking a movement "solo violin" was frequently simply this, — that the part was much too difficult for his ordinary players.

* See the acute remarks of Rust in the Preface to B. G. XX^1, p. 14.

As our orchestras contain many violinists with a technique sufficient for the solo, Bach himself, in these circumstances, would probably be the first to give the part to a number of the players in the *tutti* passages, when the themes are of a powerful nature. This experiment should be tried sometimes with the *Laudamus te* of the B minor Mass.

The question as to whether the foregoing proposals can be adopted must be decided anew for each individual case. There are *tutti* in which any reinforcement of the solo instrument would be a flagrant error, many parts being conceived so absolutely in terms of the flute or the oboe that the whole effect would be ruined by the addition of any other instrument. It will seldom do harm, however, to double the instruments.

The indispensable pre-requisite, however, is the recognition of the fundamental fact that a conductor must interpret a Bach score discreetly and moderately. No one who knows how Bach's works have come down to us will raise much objection to the principle. Bach wrote obbligato parts, not parts for particular instruments. The subjectivity of the instrument only slightly influences his writing. He does not orchestrate in the modern way, but just as he registers on the organ; what he has in view is the particular *timbre**. No violence is done to his intention, however, when this *timbre* is simply made more effective by means of the occasional co-operation of other instruments. We must remember that many scores have come down to us without any indication as to the orchestration. If in these cases the parts are lost, the realisation of the score is sometimes puzzling even to a Bach expert.

---

* This is speaking broadly; the necessary qualifications of the statement, through which alone it can be rightly understood, will be self-evident to every one who knows the scores. To others it would be of no use to mention them, for this would necessitate the enumeration of many examples, the bearing of which would not be understood.

Nor must we think that when Bach repeated a cantata he did not sometimes substitute one solo instrument for another. Frequently circumstances would compel him to do so. What else could he do when he had, say, no good flute player, and the cantata he was repeating had a difficult solo for that instrument? In his memorial of 1730 he says that at times he had neither a third trumpet, nor a third oboe, nor a flutist, nor a viola player, nor a cellist, nor a contrabassist, nor sufficient violinists, and that for the bassoon he had to call upon a member of the town band!*

The foregoing suggestions, therefore, do not open the door to caprice, but simply indicate that we should deal with the instrumental parts just in the way that Bach himself would have done had he had sufficient space and competent players. Many justifiable complaints as to the poor effect of Bach's music will cease when once we have got rid of the mistaken notion that the few orchestral parts that have been transmitted to us give a correct idea of the performance Bach had in his mind, and that we must keep strictly to these if we wish to be right. The nature and the extent of the freedom we can import into our interpretations are not to be settled by theories, but by repeated experiments. Whatever sounds well and is impressive, and does not aim merely at external effect, has always some kind of artistic justification.

When once the hearer has become used to the ordinary Bach orchestra of the cantatas it gives him undisturbed pleasure. The metallic clang that results from the continual co-operation of wood-wind and strings soon becomes so agreeable to him that he cannot dispense with it. A good example of splendid orchestration is the cantata *Liebster Immanuel* (No. 123), the introductory chorus of which is accompanied by two flutes, two oboi d'amore, and strings.

---

* See I, 134, and Spitta II, 264 ff.

If this simple orchestra does not suffice, Bach strengthens the wind. In the first chorus of *Wie schön leucht' uns der Morgenstern* (No. 1) he adds two horns to the two oboes, the two concertante violins and the remaining strings; in the opening chorus of the cantata *Es ist nichts Gesundes an meinem Leibe* (No. 25) a choir of four brass wind and three flutes gives out a chorale to the accompaniment of the strings and oboes; in the cantata *Lobe den Herrn* (No. 143) he adds three horns to his orchestra.

His festival orchestra was distinguished from the ordinary one by the addition to the strings and wood-wind of four trumpets. The instrumentation of *Preise Jerusalem* (No. 119) is typical, — four trumpets, two flutes, three oboes, and three strings.

Bach's fondness for the wind is particularly shown in his accompaniments to the solos. For the first two numbers of the cantata *Er rufet seinen Schafen* (No. 175) he employs three flutes; the instrumental part of the bass aria is played by two trumpets. A recitative in the cantata *Sie werden euch in den Bann tun* (No. 183; second composition) is accompanied by two oboi da caccia and two oboi d'amore. In the first aria of *Herr Gott, dich loben alle wir* (No. 130), and in the aria "Heiligste Dreieinigkeit" from *Erschallet, ihr Lieder* (No. 172), the voice has to struggle against three trumpets and the kettledrum; a recitative in *Preise Jerusalem* (No. 119) is accompanied by kettledrum, four trumpets, two flutes and two oboes; in the aria "Ach, es bleibt in meiner Liebe", from *Du sollst Gott deinen Herrn* (No. 77), Bach is satisfied with one trumpet. His fondness for clangorous sound is shewn again by the fact that in a number of motet-choruses he doubles the voices with the brass*.

Bach proceeds upon the basis of the old town band, so that many of the instruments he uses are no longer known to us today. This raises the question of the necessity of

---

* See p. 299.

rearranging his scores. Can we perform them as they are written, or is it better to touch them up in such a way as to get the effects and *timbres* he wanted by a certain amount of modern re-instrumentation?

The modern orchestra has developed from the old by a process of selection. From each orchestral group,— strings, wood, and brass,— there have fallen out a number of "intermediate" instruments. Only the ones that were most perfect and capable of the most varied uses have stood their ground. People gave up the idea of having the same instrument in all possible registers and qualities. This reform, which at the same time implies a certain impoverishment, came from the Italians. Bach, although he was contemporary with this reform, ignored it. He employed instruments that were already becoming obsolete in his own day. Handel wrote for what was then the modern and more simplified orchestra. The brass instruments were naturally most affected by the reform; but a number of string instruments also fell into disuse. Bach still uses the violino piccolo, a small *Quartgeige* (three-quarter violin); he makes it play in octaves with the ordinary violin. It plays a special rôle in the cantata *Herr Christ, der ein'ge Gottes Sohn* (No. 96), in which it has an obbligato part in conjunction with the piccolo flute.

The gamba, which Bach employs in the Passions, is a six-stringed instrument, occupying a place between the cello and the viola; the viola d'amore, which he uses in the *St. John Passion*, somewhat resembles the viola. It had seven strings; under the gut strings touched by the bow, — the three deepest being overlaid with metal — were seven metal strings which increased the resonance; these gave the instrument its peculiarly beautiful *timbre*.

The larger string instruments gave Bach a lot of trouble. Our contrabass as yet did not exist. The violone and the violone grosso, which he sometimes used in large choruses, were so imperfect that it was impossible to play his bass runs on them*. The player was content to perform the principal notes, leaving the remainder to the celli and the other string instruments that co-operated an octave higher—the viola pomposa**, invented by Bach, and the violoncello piccolo. In the cantatas of Bach's later period he often gives solo passages to the latter instrument***.

What is the bearing of these facts on modern performances? The viola pomposa and the violoncello piccolo can easily be dispensed with. Bach employed them to bring out the bass more clearly. This can be done in other ways; it is partly secured, indeed, by the perfection to which the contrabass has now been brought. The violoncello piccolo solos can be played by any good cellist on his own instrument; when necessary they can be divided between the cello and the viola. The loss of the viola d'amore is felt as a misfortune only in the *St. John Passion*.

---

* Bach's violone could not play such basses, for example, as those in the first chorus of *Sei Lob und Ehr' dem höchsten Gut* (No. 117). We must remember, too, that often his cello and violone players were merely students, as is clearly seen from his memorial of 1730 to the Council (Spitta II, 246 ff.). As a rule the violone players and the inexpert cellists gave as many of the notes of their part as they could. Sometimes, however, Bach wrote out a simplified part for them, and we consequently find two basses in the score, — a rudimentary one surrounded by a richly figured one. Examples may be seen in the sinfonia of the Wedding Cantata *Der Herr denket an uns* (B. G. XIII[1], p. 73 ff.) and the aria "Kraft und Stärke" from *Man singet mit Freuden vom Sieg* (No. 149). At other times the basses exhibit a certain independence of each other, as in the chorale duet "Verzage nicht" from *Am Abend aber desselbigen Sabbats* (No. 42). They are quite independent in the aria "Ach, wann kommet der Tag", from *Wachet, betet* (No. 70). See also the cantata *Bereitet die Wege* (No. 132) and the secular cantata *O holder Tag* (B. G. XXIX).

** See I, 204, 205. This instrument is never indicated in the scores. Perhaps the viola pomposa and the violoncello piccolo are identical; in this case the latter would simply be the name used in the score for the instrument invented by Bach.

*** It sounded an octave deeper than it was written, as is proved beyond doubt by the orchestral parts of *Jesu nun sei gepreiset* (No. 41; see Preface to B. G. X). There is a solo for violoncello piccolo in *Ich geh' und suche mit Verlangen* (No. 49).

It would be an advantage, however, if gamba playing were cultivated again, the cello and the viola, or the two together, being poor substitutes for the solos on this instrument. It will be noted that we are already beginning to realise the poverty of our string instruments and trying to remedy it. Viola players who can also play the gamba will probably be the rule in the future. The necessities of our modern orchestra will also compel us to look for string instruments with a higher range than the violin. Then we shall be able to perform the violin parts in many of Bach's scores in the way that makes them most effective, though he has not marked them so, — i. e. by doubling them with the octave above. In general the arrangement that is equivalent to drawing a corresponding four-feet register is quite in Bach's spirit; he himself doubles the cello in the octave with the violoncello piccolo, and the violin with the violino piccolo.

Bach uses both the transverse flute and the *flûte à bec*. In his employment of the latter he probably stood alone among the musicians of his time; he even uses it in his later works, — e. g., the cantata *Herr Jesu Christ, wahr'r Mensch und Gott* (No. 127), which dates from the end of the thirties*.

The disappearance of the *flûte à bec* is not a very great misfortune. It is one of the family of long flutes; it was constructed like the open flute pipe of the organ, and blown in precisely the same way. A number of finger-holes — six to eight — made it possible to produce various tones from this primitive instrument; some of them were always rather impure, being obtained by only half closing the hole. The overtones being completely lacking, the *timbre* was soft but inexpressive**.

---

* For further examples of the use of the *flûte à bec* see the *Actus tragicus* (No. 106) and the cantata *Jesus schläft* (No. 81).

** There were various kinds of *flûtes à bec*, including heavy bass instruments. See Ernst Euting's *Zur Geschichte der Bassinstrumente im XVI. und XVII. Jahrhundert*, Berlin, 1899.

The parts for *flûte à bec* hardly suffer at all from being played on the modern transverse flute. With regard to the general question of Bach's flute parts it may be asked whether the metal flute is not preferable in many cases to the wooden flute. The metal flute, which the French mostly use, has the advantage of speaking more easily. In many solos it is certainly more effective than the wooden flute, which is almost exclusively used in Germany. In the choruses, however, the full round tone of the wooden flute is greatly to be preferred. It is thus best to employ them together.

The question of the oboe in Bach performances is not nearly so complicated now as it was a little while ago. Formerly the oboe da caccia and the oboe d'amore had both to be replaced by the cor anglais, which does extremely well for the oboe da caccia, but is a poor makeshift for the oboe d'amore, the tone of the instrument Bach had in view being much softer and more tender*. In the meantime the oboe d'amore has come into use again in the modern orchestra. Five instruments of this type are now made, which any reasonably good oboe player can master without much difficulty**. The many beautiful passages for the oboe d'amore in Bach's works are only truly expressive when played as he intended them. Even the ordinary hearer at once perceives the difference.

The question of the brass instruments is a very complicated one. Bach employs the trombone, the cornetto, the trumpet and the horn.

In his epoch there was a complete family of trombones,—

* The oboe d'amore is practically an alto oboe, the oboe da caccia a tenor oboe; the taille, — the third oboe — can easily be replaced by the cor anglais, which instrument is merely an improved form of the old oboe da caccia. Max Seiffert, in his interesting article on *Praktische Bearbeitung Bachscher Kompositionen*, in the *Bachjahrbuch* for 1904, p. 5 ff., contends that a practical experiment would decide us against, rather than for, the retention of the old instruments. He cannot have had the oboe d'amore in his mind when he said this. It is constructed on a perfectly sound principle.

** A good oboe d'amore costs about £ 10.

soprano, alto, tenor and bass*. These instruments were capable of much purer tone than the trumpets, but could only be used in long-drawn passages; the town musicians employed them in choruses. Similarly Bach does not use them in the orchestra, but only to accompany motet-like choruses. Each vocal part has its corresponding trombone; see, for example, the opening chorus of *Ach Gott vom Himmel sieh darein* (No. 2).

Bach frequently substitutes the cornetto for the discant trombone, — in this again following the practice of the town bands. The cornetto was an instrument with a bell-shaped mouth-piece, and usually an S-shaped tube of wood, wrapped round with leather. The "serpent" was a member of this family, — it was simply the bass cornetto**. The discant cornetto had seven holes, so that, as with the *flûte à bec*, the player had to get the full scale by only partially closing some of the holes. Under these circumstances several of the tones were bound to be impure.

The cornetto had a clear and not very strong tone, — a mixture of the *timbres* of the trumpet and the wood-wind. Bach certainly used it to support the *cantus firmus* in the large chorale choruses in many places where it is not indicated either in the score or the parts, — for the wind players of course, knew the chorale melody by heart.

In the motet-choruses accompanied by the wind it is best to employ the bugle for the soprano and alto trombones; the parts for the tenor and bass trombones can be played on the original instruments, the slide trombones being preferable to the valve trombones***. It should be observed that the trombones of that day, being smaller,

---

* The trombone slide is first mentioned by Zarlino, in 1588. See Euting's *Blasinstrumente*, 1899.

** The Lituus, used in the cantata *O Jesu Christ, mein's Lebens Licht* (No. 118), probably also belonged to the cornetto family.

*** In England the slide trumpet that is still in use there can probably be employed; this corresponds directly to the discant trombone. The slide trumpet was known in Bach's time; he means this instrument when he writes *tromba da tirarsi*.

were not so strong as ours, but had a brighter tone; as our choirs are much heavier than those of Bach's day, however, the proportions are preserved.

If it is impossible to employ the brass, these motet-choruses may be supported simply by the wood-wind and strings, the former in as large numbers as possible; in any case the effect will be satisfactory*. If the upper part is a chorale, the trumpet way always take this.

There can hardly be any doubt that all the chorale melodies used in the choruses — with the exception of the final chorales — should be reinforced by the trumpet. even where the score has no indication to this effect.

There used to be the most confused opinions current upon the trumpet and upon the technique that Bach demanded of its players; this confusion was ended by the thorough researches of Eichborn**. One error in particular needs to be cleared away, — that things were possible on the old natural trumpet that are impossible on the present valve trumpet. The runs that Bach writes for his players were about as difficult on their instruments as they are on ours. The only difference is that his players were well practised in them, while ours are not.

The natural trumpet — the only one known in those days — consisted of a cylindrical tube with a thin conical opening at the top; it was generally bent and curved something like the cavalry trumpet of today. The C and D trumpets were the most frequently used. The open tube of a trumpet of this kind gave the ground tone, the octave, the fifth, the pure fourth, the major third, the minor third, the minor seventh, the major second, then a diatonic scale, not quite pure, in the fourth octave and

* In this case the experiment may be tried of adding the reeds of the organ.

** Hermann Eichborn, *Die Trompete in alter und neuer Zeit* (Leipzig, 1881); *Das alte Klarinenblasen auf Trompeten* (Leipzig, 1894). The above remarks are based on these studies. I owe a good deal of valuable technical information to Herr Wilhelm Riff, the teacher of the trumpet at the Strassburg Conservatoire.

a chromatic scale in the fifth octave from the ground tone. These notes have been retained in the trumpet and can be produced theoretically — by varying degrees of force in the breath pressure and the varying movements of the lips, which here correspond to the reed mouthpiece of the oboe. As the two lower octaves are poor, use was made only of some tones in the middle and the penultimate (diatonic) octave. The diatonic octave could be still further enriched, as on the C trumpet F could be blown F sharp, G, G sharp, and B flat, B natural. The practicable tones were therefore the four notes of the third octave, reckoned from the ground tone, the diatonic scale of the fourth octave, with F sharp, G sharp and B*; of the fifth (chromatic) octave the first four diatonic notes were the most important, since the other intervals, though theoretically complete, could not be obtained, owing to the difficulty of getting the necessary fineness of lip-pressure. Yet in the second Brandenburg concerto Bach demands from the solo trumpet the fifth diatonic note of this octave, — the g.

Eichborn gives the following as the scale:

The mysterious art of "clarino playing"** therefore consisted of nothing more than the mastery of these tones

* The diatonic octave could have been further enriched by "stopping", — a device derived from the technique of the horn. In Bach's time, however, this was not thought of.

** In the seventeenth and early eighteenth centuries a distinction was made between the players of the upper and of the lower trumpet parts, the former being called "clarino", the latter "principale". [Tr.]

by incessant practice from youth upwards. Bach's reason for writing his parts so high was that these were the only notes that were at all complete on the instruments of that epoch.

The player was helped by the easy "speaking" of his simple and delicately constructed instrument and its narrow dimensions*. Moreover he employed a special mouthpiece for playing in the high register. The smoother this is, and the sharper its angle, the easier and more certain are the attack and the articulation of the high notes. According to Eichborn, the following would be the ideal shape for the mouthpiece in clarino playing. 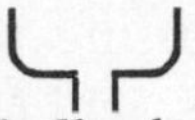 As a matter of fact it does not alter the tone wholly for the better; in the higher register it becomes dry and lacking in expression.

We cannot therefore suppose the contemporary rendering of Bach's trumpet parts to have been ideal. As the above table shews, a number of tones remained impure even in the best circumstances; others were uncertain; the *timbre* in the upper register was not beautiful, resembling that of a child's trumpet. The one advantage of the instrument — and it is a very great advantage with regard to Bach's orchestration — was that its tone was weaker than that of the trumpet of today; an oboe, or certainly two oboes, could hold their own against it quite well.

After the practice ceased of writing scores in purely obbligato parts — that is to say, after the middle of the eighteenth century — there was no motive for the study of clarino playing. About the same time the town bands also became extinct. At the end of the century valve-trumpets began to be made in England and Germany; from these there developed the modern instrument. Our trumpet really unites several instruments in one, the

* The narrower the trumpet, the easier are its high notes, and the more difficult its lower ones. The former are of fine quality, while the middle and lower register are "dry".

arrangements of crooks and valves allowing the player to lengthen or shorten the tube at will*. By combining the serviceable diatonic notes of these various trumpets we get the complete chromatic scale. The nature of the trumpet is not altered in any way. As before, the performer plays on the "natural" trumpet, only that by a pressure of the finger he places to his mouth each time the trumpet that produces the desired note most easily and most purely**; and on this adaptable instrument he can do whatever is possible on the "natural" trumpet. Of course the other conditions must be fulfilled. When some musicians were discussing the possibility of playing Bach's trumpet passages, and expressing every possible theory on the subject, Gevaert, the director of the Brussels Conservatoire, drily interjected that it was "une question d'embouchure et d'entraînement". That is the whole point; it is simply a question of mouthpiece and technique.

With the ordinary mouthpiece Bach's higher notes cannot be easily and surely played. Flatter ones make them possible. It is a matter of finding the right type, and of our players' lips becoming accustomed to it. It cannot be too flat if beauty of tone is desired***.

Of course the art of producing the high notes purely and easily is not to be learned in a day; still less can a Bach trumpet part be played at sight at rehearsal, nor,

---

* The three valves of the modern trumpet correspond, in their combinations, to seven positions.

** It should be observed, however, that the lower third cannot be produced on the valve-trumpet as a natural note.

*** After some years of research and experiment the trumpeter of the Brussels Conservatoire has constructed a special mouthpiece for performing the Bach and Handel trumpet parts. He uses the D trumpet, described by Gevaert in his *Traité d'Instrumentation* (p. 281 ff.); though at historical concerts he is able to play the parts on the natural trumpet. But he plays no other trumpet, so as not to spoil his embouchure for this particular mouthpiece. To make it possible for him to do this, an administrative post has been found for him at the Conservatoire. [See also Grove's Dictionary, new edition, V, 271, column 2.] [Tr.]

when this proves impossible, should it be declared unplayable. If there ever comes a generation of players who practise Bach from the commencement, and make a special study of the higher register and of the lip-technique demanded by the flat mouthpiece, people will be astonished at the long prevalence of the view that Bach wrote unplayable trumpet parts*.

It must be admitted that the valve-trumpet, as it is constructed today, rather increases the difficulty of blowing. The complicated path taken by the column of air as it passes through one of the crooks hinders its free vibration; the attack of the note is not so natural as in the normal trumpet, where the air-path is not so circuitous. This inconvenience, however, can be greatly diminished by making the tubes as thin and delicate as possible, and by avoiding all superfluous apparatus for the evacuation of moisture and all unnecessary solderings. By these means the vibratory capacity of the valve-trumpet may be made not much less than that of the natural trumpet.

The proper performance of Bach's trumpet parts demands therefore very lightly-built and narrow valve-trumpets, special mouthpieces, tested in every detail, and particularly practised players**.

We may affirm, however, that even the ordinary performances of the present day are in many respects better than those of Bach's players, the tones being purer and more certain. We can therefore put up with a certain sluggishness of tone in the higher notes.

---

* Gevaert wrote me a few years ago that he believed that as regards facility in the higher register the pupils of the present day were already often superior to their teachers, owing to their having practised it from the commencement.

** It must not be forgotten that the trumpeters of Bach's day had a much more practised ear than modern players have for the intervals that are produced solely with the lips. A trumpeter informs me that modern players find such difficulty in the higher register not only because they are deficient in lip-technique, but because their ear is not sufficiently fine.

Until the ideal Bach trumpet comes we should employ, in the cantatas, the trumpet in D, for which Bach usually writes. The trumpets in high D made by Alexander, of Mainz, may be recommended. They not only greatly lighten the task of the player who is accustomed to them, but produce a tone which, particularly in the higher register, is much softer than the ordinary. It has already been remarked, in discussing the Brandenburg concertos, that this firm's trumpet in high F is the best for the second concerto*. But a good player should not despair if he cannot play the part easily on the new instrument after several weeks' practice. Familiarity is a matter not of weeks and months, but of years.

It is more than doubtful whether Bach had trumpet parts of this kind performed by one player only. Eichborn draws attention to the number of trumpets employed in an orchestra in that epoch, and conjectures, perhaps rightly, that they shared difficult passages between them, each of them taking a short section. Whether this view be right or wrong historically, the plan recommends itself. It is barbarous to expect our trumpeters to play a Bach part from beginning to end. From artistic considerations alone we ought to employ two, since the moment a wind-player becomes ever so little fatigued he loses his certainty in high passages.

The demands made on the trumpeters in a Bach performance are so severe because the same player, if he belongs to an orchestra, has so recently had to produce the deeper tones required from the trumpet in modern compositions. We shall probably come to a time when wind-players will specialise for Bach and Handel, and will be as much sought after and as well paid as the solo singers.

When no good trumpeters are to be had, it is always best to give the higher trumpet part to two or three C or

* The cost of a D trumpet is £ 3—5, that of an F trumpet £ 5. Either of them can be hired for a month for £ 1.

D clarinets, or at all events to resort to the assistance of these in the high notes*.

It should be mentioned that in his earlier works Bach writes for the trumpet in a more fanfare-like and less obbligato style than in his later ones. These early parts are really the finest and most effective that he ever wrote for the instrument; an example may be seen in the cantata *Es erhub sich ein Streit* (No. 19).

Whether, even with good instruments and good players, we can ever be made to "enjoy" the arias accompanied by two or three trumpets, is another question. But till this time comes we must not revolt at the device of substituting the wood-wind for the brass, out of pity for the voice when there is only one singer.

The question of the horn is similar to that of the trumpet. It was only a little time before Bach's death that the muting of the horn was achieved by the Bohemian Anton Hampel. Bach is acquainted only with the simple corno da caccia — the hunting horn — that had come into use in Paris at the end of the seventeenth century and beginning of the eighteenth. Thus the hornist, like the trumpeter, had to use special mouthpieces for the high notes. In connection with Bach it is therefore more correct to speak of a trumpet in the form of a horn than of a real horn**. The *timbre* of the modern horn is somewhat duller than what Bach had in view. If the part is a high one, it is as well to divide it between horn and trumpet, since only the finest horn virtuosi can produce the upper tones well. The bugle, if the player is at all master of his instrument, gives better results than one is commonly inclined to suppose. It may be observed that even ex-

* See the instructive remarks of Voigt in his able article *Erfahrungen und Ratschläge bezüglich der Aufführung Bachscher Kirchenkantaten*, in the *Bachjahrbuch* for 1906, p. 8 ff. His suggestion to transpose certain high notes into the lower octave must not be blindly condemned as mere heresy. The unprejudiced hearer will in any case not be much disturbed by this procedure.

** See Eichborn, *Die Dämpfung beim Horn*, Leipzig, 1897.

perienced musicians among the audience wonder at the flexibility of the runs, without suspecting that it is not the ordinary horn that is playing*.

As the tone of the modern trumpet and horn is stronger than that of the instruments of Bach's day, we must see that we get the right relation between the brass on the one side and the strings and wood on the other. Every voice in a Bach score counts for as much as the others. But this is true not only of the orchestral parts among themselves, but of these in relation to the voice parts. The flute part must come out just as clearly as that of the soprani in the choir. The true essence of a Bach score does not consist in the accompaniment of the chorus by the orchestra, but in the co-operation of a vocal mass and an instrumental mass of equal significance with it. In the performances under Bach himself, indeed, the orchestral part was in the ascendant; in a festival cantata there were eighteen or twenty instruments to twelve singers**. But even on ordinary occasions he had at least as many first and second violins as soprani and alti, — if not more — as is shown by the fact that the parts for those instruments are frequently written out in duplicate, which is not often the case with the vocal parts; nor must we forget that the slighter tension of the bow in those days led to a much smaller tone being drawn from the violin than is customary today.

It is in this light that we must consider our present practice of performing Bach's cantatas with choirs of two hundred voices. It was mistakenly assumed to be self-evident that the orchestra should be quite weak in comparison with

---

* This, of course, is only a makeshift, until such time as our hornists shall again be expert in the higher registers. Even today there are a few viruosi who can play the first horn part of the F major Brandenburg concerto exactly as it is written. The part should only be divided between the horn and the trumpet when there is no good bugle player available, since horn and bugle blend much better than horn and trumpet.

** On the question of the chorus and orchestra that Bach had at his disposal see I, 123 ff.

the choir, and should be practically inaudible when the latter entered. Those who were conscious of this disproportion felt the need for re-orchestration of the works, which they often carried out. The most natural solution of the problem, however, is to strengthen the instrumental parts in proportion to the numbers of the choir. There was nothing in the modern view to negate an increase in the number of the strings; but the advocates of re-orchestration made merry over the proposal to employ with a large choir a dozen oboes, a dozen flutes and half a dozen bassoons, and ridiculed the idea of asking a modern audience to listen to a "bellowing" of this kind. This, however, did not disconcert the advocates of performances in accordance with the original score. Siegfried Ochs in particular fought gallantly both with word and deed for the right principle; his performances have shown that it is possible to get an instrumental equivalent to a large chorus without any re-orchestration, simply by using the proper number of instruments, and that an orchestra of this kind, if efficiently handled, is not in the slightest degree unwieldy.

The old notion that Bach's music cannot be performed just as it is written will probably die out by degrees. We still, however, occasionally meet with a choral conductor who, when a beautiful cantata is recommended to him, immediately asks "whether there is an arrangement of it published" — which shows how our self-reliance has been destroyed by these "arranged" editions.

As the tone of our instruments is much stronger than that of the older ones, and some of the numbers of our mixed choirs do not count at full strength, something like the following disposition of the orchestra may be recommended for a choir of fifty to eighty voices: six first violins, six seconds, six violas, four cellos, two contrabasses, two flutes and two oboes for each part. For a choir of a hundred to a hundred and fifty voices the following would be the ideal: ten first violins, ten seconds, ten violas, six cellos, four contrabasses, six flutes and six oboes for each part. Even at the end of the eighteenth century it was taken for granted that the orchestra was to be hardly numerically weaker than the choir. Hiller had an enormous orchestra at the famous performance of the *Messiah* at Berlin in 1788.

After the size the disposition of the orchestra is of prime importance. The customary arrangement, with the orchestra thrust like a wedge into the choir, is perhaps not the best for a Bach performance. The strings and wood-wind are better placed in front of the choir; only in this way can the proper effect be secured*.

It is a mistake for the conductor to make the orchestra play *piano* at the entry of the chorus — which he sometimes does in accordance with modern custom, or because the instruments sound too loud where he is standing. It is very seldom that a listener in the church or the concert room finds the orchestra too loud in a Bach chorus; it much more frequently happens that he simply does not hear it at all. It cannot be too often repeated that in a Bach performance it is not a question of an *accompanying* orchestra, but of the co-operation of a vocal choir and an instrumental choir, the latter playing, if anything, the leading rôle.

The correct proportions of the instrumental forces, however, are not enough; the correct realisation of the figured bass is also essential. Bach's obbligato parts, absolutely free as they are in their movements, presuppose a harmonic foundation; the harmonies resulting from the combination of these parts necessarily contain retardations, dissonances and consonances that arise from the casual meeting of the themes rather than from the harmonic ground-plan of the whole. If the hearer perceives only the obbligato parts, he will get — even when the writing

* To increase the effect of the wood-wind, they should be placed in the forefront, before the violins. See Voigt's article, already cited, in the *Bachjahrbuch* for 1906.

is in four or five parts — only a confused and incomplete sense of the harmony that Bach had in his mind; the essential is mixed up with the accidental.

It is in the figured bass that Bach has indicated the real, decisive harmonic sequences. This figured bass is not an abstract of the harmonies made by the obbligato parts, but occupies a quite independent position with regard to these, — sometimes so independent that at the first glance one might doubt the correctness of the figuring, which does not seem to agree with the orchestral parts. In a Bach work, therefore, we have to take account of a kind of "final" harmony, resulting from the combined activities of the fundamental harmony of the figured bass and the "moving harmonies" of the obbligato parts.

It is only on the presupposition that the firm ground-harmony defining the course of the piece will be brought out elsewhere that Bach can venture to let the voices go their own way unhindered, without anxiety as to the general harmonic "stability" of this or that bar. It is with his music as with the façade of the Strassburg Cathedral. The rich filigree ornamentation that covers this like a veil of fine lace carved in stone would not have the needful firmness and consistency unless it were supported by a whole network of delicate iron bars. Bach's obbligato parts are held together in the same way by the fundamental harmonics of the figured bass. The first thing he did after finishing a cantata was to prepare the figured *continuo* part.

When Bach's works began to be revived, no account was taken of the figured bass, even in cases where only the bass and a solo instrument were playing together, — which seems almost incomprehensible when we reflect that at that time Zelter and other musicians with a knowledge of the traditions of the old school were still living. In the first pianoforte edition of the *St. Matthew Passion* (1830) not a note of the figured bass is given even in the arias! The performances were of the same character. The public was treated to a dialogue between a contrabass and a flute, or even to a contrabass monologue, and it was all put down to the account of the good old times! If the conductor found it unendurable, he cut these passages out of the arias, or did away with the aria altogether. It was only after the issue of the great Bachgesellschaft edition that the musicians who were interested in Bach learned of the existence of the figured bass. It was an unexpected revelation for them: their feeling of salvation is described for us in Robert Franz's open letter to Hanslick*.

---

* *Offener Brief an Eduard Hanslick: Über Bearbeitungen älterer Tonwerke, namentlich Bachscher und Händelscher Vokalmusik,* Leipzig, 1871.

Even in the modern piano editions there is no figured bass part: see, for example, the Peters edition of the *St. Matthew Passion,* which takes no notice of the harmonies indicated by Bach. If the instruments do not happen to enter in the upper parts until the second beat, this edition gives the bare bass, but not the chord that Bach intended. This practice turns a movement like "Ich will bei meinem Jesu wachen" into mere caricature. Bach conceived it with rich harmonic sequences; in the piano edition it sounds thin and empty. There is the same procedure, followed by the same result, in the Breitkopf piano editions, e. g. in the first aria of "Jesu schläft, was soll ich hoffen" (No. 81).

Our piano editions are very unsatisfactory in other respects. They do not show the authentic bass figure of the contrabasses and cellos, or where it ceases; frequently we are given a purely fantastic bass, compiled by the editor from the cello and contrabass part and that of the violas; still more frequently it is disfigured by absolutely wrong notes; octaves are introduced — even when they make the whole figure unrecognisable — as if these were the one thing needful; the authentic phrasing is very often not regarded; the editor mixes up his own dynamic marks with those of Bach, so that it is impossible to distinguish one from the other; the instrumentation is very frequently not indicated.

All lovers of Bach must unite in energetically demanding that these piano editions shall some day wholly be withdrawn, and replaced by critically correct editions, based on the following principles: (1) Everything that is not authentic — phrasing signs, dynamic indications, octave doublings — must be omitted; (2) along with the obbligato parts there should be printed, in smaller type, the notes resulting from the figured bass, so far as they are not already contained in the obbligato parts; (3) the figuring should be given beneath the line; (4) if there is no authentic thorough-bass part, and the harmonies have to be conjecturally reconstructed, this must be indicated at the commencement, along with the orchestration.

The new impulse was so strong, however, that it overshot its mark. The figured bass began to be regarded merely as a license for all kinds of experiments, the object of which was to eliminate every trace of "Zopf" and to obtain an orchestral tone that should be as rich and varied as possible. Thus Robert Franz became the father of the "arrangement" theory. His piano editions and "practical editions", and those that followed his lead, became the standard among lovers of Bach, and to some extent still remain the standard. The hearer now got a modern substitute for the figured harmonies, instead of the harmonies in their original form and on the original instrument.

This discussion, which is not yet settled, has therefore two questions to decide. The first is: shall the figured harmonies be given to the instrument for which Bach intended them or to the orchestra? The second, which is bound up with the first, is whether we ought to realise the harmonic sequences in accordance with Bach's own indications, or whether we should be coming closer to his ideas by setting our imaginations to work upon the harmonies.

As both Rust and Spitta have remarked, the only original instrument to be considered in connection with the realisation of the thorough-bass is the organ, — on both historical and practical grounds*. There is no evidence that Bach used the cembalo for the vocal solos**. We must remember that while in every cantata of which we possess the parts there is a figured *continuo* part — generally in Bach's own handwriting — transposed a tone lower for the organ***,

* For the benefit of the lay reader it may be pointed out that "thorough-bass part" and "*continuo* part" are identical terms, signifying the copy of the instrumental bass part in which Bach has indicated the harmonies by means of figures.

** See Voigt's strictures (in the *Bachjahrbuch* for 1906, p. 11 ff.) on Seiffert's hypotheses (*Bachjahrbuch* for 1904, p. 64 ff.). There are some valuable reflections in Richard Buchmayer's article *Cembalo oder Pianoforte?* in the *Bachjahrbuch* for 1908, pp. 64—93.

*** At that epoch the pitch of the instruments differed from that of the organ. Moreover, the pitch in which vocal and instrumental works was performed was at that time about a semitone lower than ours.

it is only rarely that we have a thorough-bass part that is untransposed and therefore suitable for the cembalo*.

It is a question therefore of either organ or orchestra. And here it must certainly be admitted that there is a very strong temptation to entrust the working-out of the

---

* There was certainly a cembalo in the organ gallery; we still possess the description and the accounts of the installation and tuning of it. It may have been used at rehearsals; perhaps Bach played the basses on it, perhaps even gave the harmonies. But whatever may be thought of this hypothesis, it is certain that the fact of the cantata being accompanied throughout by the organ remains unshaken. The organ undertook the realisation of the figured bass. The only movements planned without organ accompaniment are those that are also without natural basses, — e. g. the aria "Jesu, lass dich finden", from *Mein liebster Jesu ist verloren* (No. 154); the aria "Doch Jesus will", from *Schauet doch und sehet* (No. 46); the aria "Wir zittern und wanken" from *Herr, gehe nicht ins Gericht* (No. 105); the aria "Aus Liebe will mein Heiland sterben", in the *St. Matthew Passion.*

When Bach did not wish for any harmonies, as is now and then the case, he writes *tasto solo.* They must have been supplied everywhere else, even at the commencement of the choral fugues, where only one voice-part enters. If we omit them here, some of the instrumental parts, such as that of the flutes in the opening bars of "Lass ihn kreuzigen", in the *St. Matthew Passion,* are simply left suspended in the air.

The sign *tacet* in separate numbers of a cantata — see e. g. cantatas Nos. 97, 99, 129, 139, and 177 — does not mean that the organ was silent, but that the part was played on the great organ from another part than that of the accompanist. This accounts for the concertante accompaniments in the cantatas for concertante organ not being figured. It seems to indicate that at these times Bach himself took the organ, and played from the score. Or was a special part written for the concertante accompaniments by the organist of St. Nicholas's, for whom, according to Richter's theory (see II, 237) these cantatas were written? The probability is that we have not yet mastered the problem of the cantatas with concertante organ. In spite of Richter, I am more and more inclined to think that Bach composed these concertante numbers for himself.

If the figuring is lacking throughout a cantata, it implies that the parts, — or at any rate the transposed *continuo* part — have been lost. If a transposed *continuo* part exists, but without any figuring — as, for instance, in the case of the cantata *Siehe, ich will viel Fischer aussenden* (No. 88) — this probably indicates that Bach played the whole accompaniment on the positive.

harmonic foundation to the orchestra. No one who knows Bach's music and is versed in modern orchestration can help imagining the effect to be obtained by enriching the harmonies with orchestral colour and interesting rhythms, and so bringing out, by means of this "accompanying orchestra", at once the great thematic and dynamic lines of the chorus and the body of tone made by the obbligato instruments. Only pedantry can be blind to the artistic charm of a problem of this kind; only a prejudiced critic can close his eyes to the fact that in certain modern arrangements of Bach the problem has to some extent been solved in brilliant fashion.

No amount, however, of reflection or admission can alter the final conclusion that it does not become us to play Bach's music otherwise than as it was conceived. It is no use always saying what Bach himself would have put into his scores had he had the resources of the modern orchestra. It is sufficient that he had not those resources; he did not think "coloristically"; he tries to get all his effects, even the "modern" ones, by the co-operation of obbligato parts; for the realisation of the harmonic substratum he calculated on soft flue-work; and therefore his works are most likely to achieve their native effect by our not tampering with the principle of them. We do the hearer more service by educating him to understand and enjoy this simple beauty than by presenting Bach's works to him in such a way that they are neither ancient nor modern.

With regard to the question as to whether the figuring should be realised simply or freely, a remark of Rochlitz's has caused a lot of mischief. He says that in Bach's time the accompanying cembalist or organist "did not merely strike the chords, but freely added melodic sequences of his own in the upper part and ingenious combinations in the middle parts," and that Bach himself particularly excelled in this art*. From this it seemed to go without

* Rochlitz, *Für Freunde der Tonkunst*, II, 375 ff.

saying that Bach's figuring really only served the player as a harmonic starting-point for an original accompaniment conceived in the general spirit of the work*. Rochlitz's remark is correct as far as it goes; only he forgets to add that it refers to what Bach used to do with the meagre and imperfect figurings of others, not to his practice with regard to his own thorough-bass, which, with its rich and uninterrupted figuring, of itself supplies the "fantasy" he desired in the accompaniment of his works.

No comparison is possible between Bach's figured basses and those of Handel. The latter merely give simple and often rather uninteresting chordal sequences; the former represent a strict four- or five-part movement, in which each voice is an obbligato part. Bach did not permit his pupils to interpret the basses as they liked. The precise rules for realising the figuring have been transmitted to us; we have figured basses of Bach's that have been worked out by Kirnberger, presumably in the spirit of his master**.

---

* This is the opinion expressed by Robert Franz in his open letter to Hanslick. It was on this principle that he and his successors made their pianoforte arrangements, and up to quite recently organists who had to accompany in Bach's works accepted this theory almost as a dogma. Anyone who expects to find in Franz's dissertation a clear exposition of the principles of "arrangement" will be greatly disappointed. The cardinal problems are not touched upon at all, and for the rest are always settled by reasoning from Handel to Bach, — an error still customary today.

** The following are the main documents on the question of the realisation of the figured basses: (1) the rules given in Anna Magdalena's *Klavierbüchlein* (see I, 108, and Spitta III, 118, 347 ff.); (2) Peter Kellner's copy of precepts dictated to him by Bach (see I, 218, and Spitta III, 315 ff.); (3) the Albinoni violin sonata, the figuring of which Gerber worked out under Bach's guidance (see I, 218, and Spitta III, 388 ff.); (4) Kirnberger's realisation of the thorough-bass in the trio from the *Musikalisches Opfer* (see I, 421, 422; given in B. G. XXXI², pp. 52—57). This realised accompaniment by a Bach pupil is, with the rules that have come down to us from Peter Kellner, probably the most instructive thing of the kind that we possess. There is also much valuable information on the subject of thorough-bass accompaniment in the writings of Mattheson and Quantz and the pianoforte schools of Emmanuel Bach and Türck.

Anyone who really tries to construct the figured bass part according to these principles will soon see that they generate a finer "fantasy" than any we can invent for ourselves.

This holds good also of the movements that are accompanied by the *continuo* alone. If Bach, in these places, gives only the bass figure to the instruments, and the upper voices to the organ, it is not because he is too indolent to write something for the other instruments, but because the bass figure is so important and so independent that the hearer's attention must not be distracted from it by any other instrumental parts. Observe, however, what simple and beautiful melodic upper parts can be obtained by the proper realisation of the figuring! The pity is that these movements are so disfigured in our piano editions*.

The realisation of the *continuo* part in the choruses is affected by the fact that our forces are different from those of Bach's day. Orchestra and choir are much larger than they were then; if we realise the thorough-bass on the same scale it sounds too loud; while if we tone it down too much it does not fulfil its purpose. Long experiment is necessary before we hit upon the proportions in which choir and orchestra will blend properly. Of course the problem of the modern organist — owing to the situation created by our huge forces — is different from that of

* What violence can be done to the intentions of the composer may be seen in the fanciful realisation of the figured bass of the aria "Gewaltige stösst Gott" from *Meine Seel' erhebt den Herrn* (No. 10) in Breitkopf and Härtel's piano edition; the demisemiquaver runs have all been added to Bach's text by the editor. In the arrangement of the aria "Geduld, wenn mich falsche Zungen stechen", in Peters' edition of the *St. Matthew Passion*, again, too many accessories have been added. That the simple realisation of the figured bass of itself gives a beautiful melodic upper part may be seen from the aria "Ich gehe hin", from *Wer mich liebet, der wird mein Wort halten* (No. 74); and every organist who has had to accompany the aria "Öffne dich", from *Nun komm' der Heiden Heiland* (No. 61), knows how difficult it is to add upper parts to the bass in the absence of any figuring.

the organist who accompanied under Bach himself. He has to help the parts to stand out and to make choral effects tell. A very great deal depends upon his co-operation. He has this advantage over Bach's organist, that he can study his part in advance from the score. The conductor and he should come to a complete understanding, before the first rehearsal, as to the rôle the *continuo* accompaniment is to play in the choruses of the work.

The organ must always play where there is a figured bass, — therefore also in the chorales and the recitatives that are accompanied by the orchestra. Even when the organ harmonies are so discreetly filled in that the hearer does not perceive them independently, and cannot be certain of the organist's co-operation, they still ought to be there, since they form the substratum that supports the instrumental harmonies, giving these not only composure and steadiness but also a peculiarly soft colouring.

Unfortunately the voicing of our organs is an obstacle to proper accompaniment; the excessive wind-pressure produces too dull a tone, and one that blends neither with the voices nor with the instruments*. The organ *timbre* should be the soft harmonic ground against which the lines of the obbligato parts can group themselves; instead of this it rather serves to confuse these lines and efface them. As soon as we happen to accompany a Passion or a cantata on a good Silbermann organ we realise for the first time how unsuitable the modern organ is for that purpose. On our instruments we have to experiment for a long time until we have found a number of registers which, when properly blended, give the desired quality of tone. Organ accompaniment as we so often hear it is simply calculated to disfigure Bach's music; and we cannot blame the advocates of the "arrangement" theory if they substitute the orchestra for the heavy, — and often heavily-

* The general unsuitability of our modern organ-tone for Bach's music has been discussed in Chapter XIV.

handled — instrument, and merely call upon the organ for assistance here and there.

In the accompaniment of the soli we have to take into account this drawback, that the swell-chest manual which we use for this purpose is placed high up and at the back, and so is a long way off the platform with the soloists and orchestra, which renders impossible not only an exact *ensemble* but any kind of blending of tone. In a big performance, therefore, there should be substituted for the large organ, in the recitatives and arias, a small portable positive, placed among the instruments. It must be remembered that the positive of the main organ, on which Bach had the soloists accompanied, came out into the church.

The proposal to substitute the harmonium for the old portable positive is incomprehensible. Bach wants the "wide" tone of the "Musikgedackt" and the salicional of his day; and for this we would substitute the narrow, nasal tone of the harmonium — replace an instrument with proper flue-pipes by one in which the vibrations are produced by metal tongues!*

The tone of the portative organ we meet with today is, indeed, not calculated to prove the possibility of using this instrument, though it alone has historical justification. One would think the sole purpose of the builders had been to show what a coarse tone can be produced even on a miniature organ. If they would only make again portative organs voiced in the Silbermann style, people would be astounded at the ideal support this delicate tone gives to the singer and the instruments, and how perfectly it "carries". In case of need a one-manual portative with bourdon 8′ and salicional 8′ will suffice. The ideal would be a two-manual instrument with bourdon 8′, salicional 8′, and flute 4′ on the second manual, and bourdon 16′ and

* Even connoisseurs of the old instruments, such as Gevaert and Seiffert, have unfortunately become the advocates of the harmonium.

principal 8′ on the first. It should be observed that a portative organ is not relatively any dearer than a harmonium*.

Almost more important than the question of the harmonies is that of bringing out the bass. With Bach the bass is not, as with other composers, merely a harmonic foundation-line; it is at the same time an obbligato part, of the detail of which the hearer must be just as conscious as of those of any other part. In the church or the concert-room the bass is usually not heard at all, or only in fragments; and for this the conductors and organists are answerable, who give far too little attention to this question. The large size of our orchestras and choirs increases the difficulty of bringing out the bass. How is it possible to produce in the lower part a real equivalent to such salient upper parts? Not by any increase in the number of the contrabasses; too many of them, or too forcible playing, is rather a disadvantage, as it gives a peculiar buzz to the tone. It is much better to add to the number of the cellos and to reinforce them with bassoons. Sometimes also a few violas will be very effective — playing the bass part an octave higher, instead of the violoncello piccolo. But all this does not suffice with a large chorus and orchestra; the tone lacks the necessary consistency.

The arrangers of Bach's vocal works have been acutely conscious of this problem, and have tried to solve it with the deep brass instruments. This, however, is practicable only in the rare cases where Bach has written tranquil basses; and even there the brass is much too heavy. The only solution is the employment of flue-work stops in the lower register; and for this only the organ is of use. Only

* Of course the present-day portative should be fitted with a Venetian shutter swell, so as to make *crescendi* and *diminuendi* possible. A pedal is also desirable. The Alsatian organ builders Dalstein and Härpfer (Bolchen) supply portative organs of the type described above, with the Silbermann voicing, at about £ 70 for the one-manual and £ 140 for the two-manual instrument. A two-manual, with bourdon 8′ and salicional 8′ on the second keyboard and principal 8′ on the first, costs about £ 120.

when strings and flue-work stops play the bass figures together can the latter, without becoming obtrusive, hold their own against the vocal and orchestral upper parts, having now a tone-colour adequate to the whole mass.

The proper rendering of the organ part therefore consists in letting the left hand play the bass part note for note — and with the right phrasing — on a stronger manual, while the right takes the figuring on a softer manual. This is the tradition; it is also the course suggested by practical experiment. The pedal is not in itself requisite in accompanying. Naturally, however, a good player will make use of it, and find many opportunities to turn his dexterity to account. For example, if he wishes to bring out with appropriate force the lower voices in a chorus, he will employ three basses, — one for the passages with orchestra alone; a somewhat stronger one for the ordinary combination of chorus and orchestra; and a strong one for the *forte* passages. He will draw a bass on the chief manual and one on the pedal, and let the three basses separate or combine, using either the manual or the pedal or both together, — it making no difference, in the latter case, whether he couples or plays the same part with the left hand and the feet. This shading in the bass was not desired by the accompanist in Bach's day; it is rendered necessary, however, by the size of our modern forces. And of course the player will employ the pedal also in cases where — as in the chorale cantatas — he has to reproduce a *cantus firmus*, or where he strikes the chords on the great organ in order to bring out special effects, or where he plays the harmonies on two different manuals so as to bring a part out more clearly.

He must never forget, however, that he is solely responsible for the proper effect of the bass figure; the trouble it gives and the combinations it demands are well known to every organist who has had to perform this task in the chorale chorus "O Mensch, bewein' dein' Sünde gross", in the *St. Matthew Passion.*

Care should be taken that the registration is not too dull. Bach's bass figures are conceived in eight-feet tone; and therefore too many contrabass and sixteen-feet stops are bad, as they make the part sound an octave too low, and leave a gap between it and the next highest part — that of the violas. Eight-feet stops should therefore be used throughout, even in the pedal; one or two sixteen-feet stops will be enough; frequently none at all are necessary in the manual on which the left hand is playing*. On the other hand it must not be forgotten that Bach, as is shown by his instrumentation, counts on the four-feet tone also for the bass figure: in *forte* bass parts two or three fine and clear four-feet stops are extremely effective. Nor should we shrink from the use of mixtures and reeds if they happen to be good. In general we should aim at a clear and intense rather than a thick tone-colour, if only for the sake of precision.

For the arias also we must have in readiness two bass *timbres* — one for the *tutti*, the other for the accompaniment passages. It depends upon circumstances whether we shall draw a soft bourdon 16′ or not. We must remember that if the bass contains many sustained notes, — as in the recitatives, for instance — the sixteen-feet tone easily becomes obtrusive, and an unpleasant hollow is left between the bass and the harmonic parts. A good eight-feet bourdon, in the deep octave, will often be better. In any case the organ bass should never cease, even in the solo movements; as soon as it does so — even if we have not

---

* In the first chorus of *Ein' feste Burg* (No. 80), for example, the bass should be played with eight-feet stops alone, and the sixteen-feet only employed when the *cantus firmus* enters in the lower part. In the opening chorus of the cantata *Du sollst Gott deinen Herrn* (No. 77) it is clear from the clefs Bach has used that with the exception of the *cantus firmus* the whole bass is to be played with eight-feet stops. It goes without saying that when the *cantus firmus* enters in the bass it must be reinforced by a trombone. Bach assuredly posted a trombone player by the organ, to join in these passages.

been conscious of hearing it before — the cellos and contrabasses also disappear, since their foundation is now lacking.

The movements in which only the bass and the organ accompany may generally sound so badly because the four-feet tone which gives the necessary clearness and distinctness is missing from the bass. It may be remarked that, according to some parts that have come down to us, and sundry indications in the scores, Bach had the contrabasses and cellos supported in these passages by the violas, or the violas and violins, — at any rate in the *tutti*. We shall probably not go wrong if we observe this rule in many solos that are accompanied by the *continuo* alone*.

In performances under Bach himself the violone seems very often to have ceased upon the entry of the solo voice, and to have only joined again in the *tutti***. This, however, is no reason why we, if we have one or two good contra basses at our disposal, should not let them join in *piano*.

For a long time it was thought pedantic to use contrabass and cello for accompanying the recitatives. Many who tried to dispense with these instruments, e. g. in the part of the Evangelist, ultimately had to revert to the old practice, since the organ bass alone is not sufficiently clear and precise, even for simple chord-progressions. It does not allow of accents in the basses. In the fine quaver-figures of the bass of arioso movements an excellent effect

---

* In the aria "Hasse nur", from *Die Himmel erzählen* (No. 76), the gambas play with the bass; in the aria "Streite, siege, starker Held", from *Nun komm' der Heiden Heiland* (second composition; No. 62), Bach writes *"violini e viola sempre col continuo"*. The importance of this marking consists in the fact that it is only inserted because of the *sempre*; it was self-evident that the violins and violas in these passages should play from the *continuo* part, but not that they were to continue *sempre*, i. e,. in the *piano* passages as well, where the voice entered; it therefore had to be marked so.

** Authentic information as to this may be had, e. g., in the alto aria in *Was Gott tut, das ist wohlgetan* (No. 100). Bach's principles on this point may be studied most fully in the secular cantata *O holder Tag* (B. G. XXIX), which is richly provided with *con violone* and *senza violone* marks

is obtained by strengthening the cellos; and a discreetly used bassoon often does good service.

The gaps that are created when the proper *continuo* accompaniment ceases may be realised in such a cantata — very fully orchestrated throughout — as *Ich will den Kreuzstab gerne tragen* (No. 56), which is often performed in the concert-room with a harmonium. In the *St. Matthew Passion* we see from the score that in the recitatives of Jesus the strings enter with the organ and continue with it; if we go contrary to Bach's intentions here, we must take into account the restless and peculiarly flickering quality of the chords that are sustained by the strings alone; the softest bourdon or salicional — so soft as not to be audible in the *ensemble* — gives them a quite new character — much quieter and more uniform — without the accompaniment being at all strengthened by the device*.

The accompanying organist usually lays for too little store by precision. We still hear the organ after chorus and orchestra have ceased; in the arias and recitatives it is always a shade too late. The player, however, thinks he is perfectly in time. He has forgotten that the lower register, in which he duplicates the bass, necessarily "speaks" somewhat more slowly, and that a certain delay is caused by the distance between the first orchestral desks and the organ, which is often considerable owing to the size of our choirs, — to say nothing of the fact that very many organists follow not the conductor but their own ear, which doubles and trebles the chances of error. Precision in accompaniment is possible only when the conductor's beat is scrupulously obeyed, and care is taken always to be the merest trifle ahead in pressing down and releasing the keys; the organist must always feel that he is entering or ceasing a shade too

---

* A very interesting example of the joint performance of chords by orchestra and organ may be had in the recitative "Verdoppelt euch demnach", from *Christen, ätzet diesen Tag* (No. 63). The organ binds them together in crotchets; the orchestra separates them by means of quavers with rests between.

soon; if it sounds quite right to him, he may be sure that in the hall or the church the organ sounds too late.

As the full effect of Bach's music depends upon the proper bringing out of the harmonic basis of the obbligato parts, and of these again among themselves, conductors and organists should try to discover, at rehearsal, how things sound from various parts of the hall; otherwise, as it is impossible for them to judge of the relative strength of the various parts from where they sit, they will frequently err as to the real effect of this or that passage. To discover whether his registration is right, the organist should temporarily give up his seat at rehearsal to a pupil; he will then have some valuable experiences, and will realise how the smallest detail is often of the utmost importance. It may happen that the proper *timbre* depends upon the drawing or closing of a soft four-feet register, the presence or absence of which seems of no consequence whatever.

For a good player perhaps the best organ part is a piano score, in which he has entered the thorough-bass figuring and the main lines upon which he will work it out. He must not forget, however, to revise the basses, or else he will unconsciously play a number of false notes in every cantata. With experience he will learn to get his effect not by motley successions of tone-combinations, but by fine transitions between various degrees of strength and tonal nuances. In the recitatives much harm is done by the chords being too massive and too loud in comparison with the voice. Organ accompaniment is a matter of temperament. An impetuous, unreflecting temperament, however, often does the wrong thing; the right thing comes only from a temperament that is thoughtful and refined.

The following are some of the cantatas most frequently performed — *Gottes Zeit* (No. 106); *Ich hatte viel Bekümmernis* (No. 21); *Ein' feste Burg* (No. 80); *Wachet auf* (No. 140); *Ich will den Kreuzstab gerne tragen* (No. 56); *Gott der Herr ist Sonn' und Schild* (No. 79); *Ach wie flüchtig, ach wie nichtig* (No. 26); *Halt' im Gedächtnis* (No. 67).

Other works, equally fine, are seldom or never given. Breitkopf and Härtel have not yet engraved the parts of many wonderful cantatas, having never yet been asked for them. The explanation of this unequal appreciation of Bach's works is that very few conductors possess the complete edition, and so are in a position to make a free choice; the others keep to the cantatas of which arrangements are published, or which they have heard, or seen in some programme or other*. It sometimes happens, too, that choir conductors make a bad choice through ignorance, selecting a too difficult cantata for a not very expert choir simply because they do not know the easy ones; or they give a public imperfectly acquainted with Bach a cantata that is not calculated to make it understand and love him more, but rather to frighten it. It goes without saying, too, that in choosing a cantata the quality of the text should be taken into consideration.

The following lists, without pretending to be complete, may be of assistance in making a proper selection. They include only works that are effective as a whole, and of which the texts are satisfactory.

Cantatas particularly suitable for performance:

Komm, du süsse Todesstunde (No. 161); *Himmelskönig, sei willkommen* (No. 182); *Wachet, betet* (No. 70); *Erwünschtes Freudenlicht* (No. 184); *Herr, gehe nicht ins Gericht* (No. 105); *Schauet doch und sehet* (No. 46); *Liebster Gott, wann werd' ich sterben* (No. 8); *Es erhub sich ein Streit* (No. 19); *Christus, der ist mein Leben* (No. 95); *Herr, deine Augen* (No. 102); *Es ist nichts Gesundes an meinem Leibe* (No. 25); *Gott fähret auf mit Jauchzen* (No. 43); *Am Abend aber desselbigen Sabbats* (No. 42; some of the recitatives should be "cut", and the middle section of the first aria should be provided with new words); *Nun ist das Heil und die Kraft* (No. 50); *Es wartet alles auf dich* (No. 187; the text is very fine); *Jesu, nun sei gepreiset* (No. 41; very

* See Voigt's remarks in the *Bachjahrbuch* for 1906, p. 2 ff.

large choir); *Gelobet seist du, Jesu Christ* (No. 91); *Meinen Jesum lass ich nicht* (No. 124): *Meine Seel' erhebt den Herren* (No. 10); *Mache dich, mein Geist, bereit* (No. 115); *Ach, lieben Christen, seid getrost* (No. 114); *Du Friedefürst, Herr Jesu Christ* (No. 116).

The following are easy to perform, and are of a more popular character:

Aus der Tiefe (No. 131); *Uns ist ein Kind geboren* (No. 142); *Nun komm' der Heiden Heiland* (No. 61; first composition); *Seht welch' eine Liebe* (No. 64); *Es ist das Heil uns kommen her* (No. 9); *Wer da glaubet und getauft wird* (No. 37); *Das neugeborne Kindelein* (No. 122); *Aus tiefer Not* (No. 38; omitting the aria "Ich höre", which is borrowed from another work); *Ach Herr, mich armen Sünder* (No. 135; without the tenor aria, which is probably borrowed).

The following cantatas are useful for winning over a public that is musically cultured but not yet intimate with Bach:

Die Himmel erzählen (No. 76); *Sie werden aus Saba alle kommen* (No. 65); *Du wahrer Gott und Davidssohn* (No. 23); *Herr, wie du willt* (No. 73); *Du Hirte Israel* (No. 104); *Ihr werdet weinen und heulen* (No. 103); *Ich elender Mensch* (No. 48); *Liebster Immanuel* (No. 123); *Was mein Gott will* (No. 111).

Of the solo cantatas the following may be mentioned:

Mein Gott, wie lang, ach lange (No. 155; alto, tenor, bass); *Meine Seele rühmt und preist* (No. 189; tenor); *Schau, lieber Gott, wie meine Feind'* (No. 153; alto, tenor, bass. Very popular); *Mein liebster Jesus ist verloren* (No. 154; alto, tenor, bass); *Erfreute Zeit im neuen Bunde* (No. 83; alto, tenor, bass. The text is very fine); *Wahrlich, ich sage euch* (No. 86; soprano, alto, tenor, bass. Easily understood; text very fine); *Wo gehest du hin?* (No. 166; alto, tenor, bass. Easily understood; text very fine); *Ich lasse dich nicht, du segnest mich denn* (No. 157; tenor, bass); *Sehet, wir gehen hinauf nach Jerusalem* (No. 159; alto, tenor, bass); *Ich habe genug* (No. 82; bass); *Jauchzet Gott in allen Landen* (No. 51; soprano); *Schlage doch, gewünschte Stunde* (No. 53; alto); *Ich armer Mensch, ich Sündenknecht* (No. 55; tenor); *Was soll ich aus dir machen, Ephraim* (No. 89; soprano, alto, bass); *Siehe, ich will viel Fischer* (No. 88; soprano, alto, tenor, bass); *Ich bin ein guter Hirt* (No. 85; soprano, alto, tenor, bass); *Bisher habt ihr nichts gebeten in meinem Namen* (No. 87; alto, tenor, bass); *Selig ist der Mann* (No. 57; soprano, bass); *Süsser Trost, mein Jesus kommt* (No. 151; soprano, alto, tenor, bass); *Liebster Jesu, mein Verlangen* (No. 32; soprano, bass); *Meine Seufzer, meine Tränen* (No. 13; soprano, alto, tenor, bass); *Es reifet euch ein schrecklich Ende* (No. 90; alto, tenor, bass); *Meine Seele rühmt und preist* (No. 189; tenor. Short and simple); *Der Friede sei mit euch* (No. 158; bass. Very simple; the accompaniment consists only of *continuo* and a solo violin); *O Ewigkeit, du Donnerwort* (No. 60; second composition; alto, tenor, bass); *Ach Gott, wie manches Herzeleid* (No. 58; second composition; soprano, bass).

It is hoped that these lists may be of assistance not only to choir conductors but to musical amateurs who can sing, and that they may help to introduce the cantatas into the home. In Mendelssohn's time these works were given in small circles — often with a modest choir, — with a pianoforte accompaniment; in this way many came to learn their Bach. This practice has unfortunately ceased, just at the time when Bach's cantatas can be had so easily and so cheaply; we seldom find amateurs in possession of any but those that have been performed in their neighbourhood; our amateur singers wait for collections of Bach's arias, instead of getting a number of cantatas containing the finest arias for their peculiar kind of voice*. Even

* In this respect the solo cantatas mentioned above should first be taken into account. Of the others may be mentioned Nos. 25, 31, 52, 68, 72, 94, 115, 127, 133, 146, 149, as containing particularly fine soprano numbers; Nos. 20, 108, 114, 115, 125, 148, 161, 187 for particularly fine alto numbers; Nos. 1, 19, 22, 48, 65,

many professional singers have only a limited knowledge of the works that concern them. If it should come about that the cantatas are performed publicly, but at the same time fall into disuse in domestic circles — in which the first enthusiasm for Bach sprang up about a century ago — we should have won only half the victory. Perhaps the finest feature of Bach's destiny is that, without his ever having dreamt of it, he has provided the world with a spiritual domestic music. The performances of the cantatas by a few singers with pianoforte accompaniment may be imperfect; but if the performers only have their heart in their work they are fully conscious of the beauty of the music, and their souls feel the consecration of it perhaps more than in listening to the most perfect performance.

The reason for so few cantatas being given, especially by the church choral societies, is sometimes economic. Bach's almost invariable practice of writing for four soloists makes the works costly to produce. This, however, need be no hindrance. Quite good performances of the cantatas can be given with only two soloists, or even one. The inner connection of the separate numbers of a cantata is often very loose; it is not a crime, therefore, to construct out of the choruses and solos of four or five cantatas of the same internal spirit a kind of ideal cantata that will fill out the evening, arranging it in such a way that only particular voices — say alto and bass, or soprano and tenor — are required for the solos and duets. A performance of this kind ranks much higher artistically than the ordinary one, in which three or four cantatas are strung together without regard to their textual connection.

75, 85, 91, 95, 96, 114, 123, 124, 161, 172, 180 for particularly fine tenor numbers; and Nos. 27, 46, 66, 69, 73, 75, 104, 145 for particularly fine bass numbers. Splendid duets for alto and tenor will be found in Nos. 63, 80, 111; for alto and bass in No. 106; for soprano and bass in Nos. 140, 152; for soprano and alto in Nos. 172, 184, 186.

Of course there are a number of cantatas that should be produced intact, since they constitute complete religious "dramas of ideas"; on the other hand there are dozens* that have so little inner cohesion, and of which the texts are so unequal in quality, that a full performance would merely serve to reveal their poetic imperfections.

In a cantata made up out of several others, the choruses and chorales will predominate over the solos, and the total picture will be richer and more varied than that of the single Bach cantata; but this ought not to be regarded as a disadvantage. In the last resort we have done nothing more than reach past the uninteresting Neumeister cantata-form — which Bach adopted because no one would give him any other texts — to the rich German cantata of an older day.

In any case intelligent musicians everywhere ought to acknowledge the claim that when cantatas are performed together they should have some kind of poetic connection among themselves, and that even in these unecclesiastical days the particular church period should not be so disregarded in our programmes as it everywhere is at present. Art like Bach's can only make its way as a religious and liturgical barbarity of this kind gradually falls into discredit; and the time will probably come when our concert performances of his music will be arranged in accordance with the season — All Saints Day, Advent, Christmas, New Year, Epiphany, the Passion, Easter or Whit. The Trinity cantatas can be grouped according to definite poetic or religious ideas, or connected with cantatas pertaining to the feast time.

There are more specimens in the cantatas than is commonly imagined of simple service music within the capacities of church choirs that would not be equal to Bach as a whole, so that he could be made use of in simple liturgical

---

* This refers only to the chorale cantatas of the last period. See p. 353.

ceremonies much more frequently than he is at present. This is especially true of the motet-like choruses in the cantatas Nos. 2, 8, 12, 28, 37, 38, 64, 116, 118, 121, 144, 150, and 179; they could be given, in case of need, with organ alone, or with the addition of a very modest orchestra.

Other choruses of a simple kind are the following:

"Weinen, Klagen" from No. 12; "Aller Augen warten, Herr" from No. 23; "Nimm von uns, Herr" from No. 101; "Das neugeborne Kindelein" from No. 121; "Meinen Jesum lass ich nicht" from No. 124; "Aus der Tiefe" from No. 131; "Ich will den Namen Gottes" from No. 142; "Wenn es meines Gottes Wille" from No. 161; "Rühre, Höchster, unsern Geist" from No. 173; "So lasst uns gehen in Salem der Freuden" (No. 182).

Besides these there are a number of simple or plainly figured chorales with orchestral accompaniment. Fine specimens will be found in the cantatas Nos. 1, 15, 22, 23, 24, 29, 33, 46, 75, 76, 79, 98, 99, 101, 105, 107, 109, 113, 124, 133, 138, 142, 147, 167, 171, 172, 173, 186, and 190. The wind instruments in the accompaniment to the chorales in the cantatas Nos. 31, 41 and 100 could be replaced by the organ, as the parts are very simple. For use in liturgical services, again, the unison chorale melodies with instrumental accompaniment are appropriate; they could be sung by several good boys' voices. Numbers of this kind will be found in cantatas Nos. 6, 36, 51, 85, 86, 92, 95, 130, 140, 143, 166, 178.

Further there are many simple and easy solos that could be put to good use in the church service, — for example:

"O Menschenkind", duet for alto and tenor, from No. 20; "Gott, der du die Liebe heisst", duet for tenor and bass, from No. 33; "Nun komm' der Heiden Heiland", duet for soprano and alto, from No. 36; "Entziehe dich eilends, mein Herze, der Welt", duet for soprano and alto, from No. 124; "Lass, o Fürst der Cherubine", tenor solo, from No. 130; "Händen, die sich nicht verschliessen", duet for soprano and bass, from No. 173; "Jesu, lass durch Wohl und Weh", tenor solo, from No. 182; "Barmherziges Herze der ewigen Liebe", duet for soprano and tenor, from No. 185; "Darum sollt ihr nicht sorgen", bass solo, from No. 187; "Jesus soll mein alles sein", duet for tenor and bass, from No. 190.

Many duets and trios are so simple that, as has already been pointed out, they could be sung by the choir with several voices to each part, — for example:

"Er denket der Barmherzigkeit" (alto and tenor) from No. 10; "Herr Gott, Vater" (for soprano and alto) from No. 37; "Wenn meine Trübsal" (soprano, alto and bass) from No. 38; "Wir eilen mit schwachen" (soprano and alto) from No. 78; "Gott, ach Gott, verlass" (soprano and bass) from No. 79; "Ach, wir bekennen" (soprano, tenor and bass) from No. 116; "Ist Gott versöhnt" (soprano, alto and tenor) from No. 122; "Zedern müssen von den Winden" (alto, tenor and bass) from No. 150.

When the great Bachgesellschaft edition was being prepared, subscriptions were chiefly expected from the church choirs; but these did not respond. Nor have they as yet done what may be expected of them in the way of performing the cantatas. This was mostly due to the mistaken notion of the conductors that Bach could not be performed in the original form; they waited for the time when the whole of Bach should be issued in an "edition for practical use", and meanwhile sat with their hands folded. It is hardly credible that they will continue to hold back in this way; from articles by Seiffert (*Bachjahrbuch* for 1904) and Voigt (*Bachjahrbuch* for 1906) they can learn that they can make the practical arrangement out of the score for themselves, to suit the capacity and numbers of their choirs. On the whole, articles of this kind, recounting experiences and giving suggestions for the study and performance of Bach's works, are what is most needed at present. It is desirable that many other Bach experts should contribute to the discussion of this question in the

Bachjahrbuch. What results, for example, might not be hoped for if an æsthetician and practical man like Kretzschmar would take a dozen cantatas, and discuss in detail everything that concerned the study and performance of them with the modest forces of the ordinary choir!

We must not, of course, expect complete agreement upon the many points involved in the performance of Bach's works. We are still in the experimental epoch. But if people will take the experiences of others and examine them, form their own opinion of them, and carry them still further, we shall attain to principles that are universally valid, the fruit of all-round examination. Without inquiry and discussion of this kind there can be no progress. The problem of the correct way of performing Bach can be solved only by artistic experiments conducted with a consciousness of the end in view.

But even when we attain to a general understanding as to the technical questions, a diversity of opinion upon the artistic conception will still have to be reckoned with. This will proceed not only from us but from Bach's work itself. "Bach", says a distinguished student of him*, "has at present a Janus head; one face looking back to the epoch of formal architectonic structure, the other turned towards the future, — towards the freest subjectivity of inward speech." We cannot help modernising him; on the other hand, experience has led us back to the point of striving more than ever to bring out the architectonic form. We get a different Bach according as we stress the modern or the formal element in him.

"It is with Bach's music", Gevaert once wrote**, "as with the Gospel: we know it only according to Matthew, or Mark, or Luke, or John; the Evangelists deviate widely from each other, and yet they give us the 'Gospel'; anyone who seeks for this in them can find it, and can com-

---

* Von Lüpke, — in a letter to the author on the subject of Bach - æsthetic.

** In a letter to the author.

municate it to others. So is it with Bach's works; the only thing is that we must seek Bach, not ourselves, in them, and have a reverent consciousness of offering mankind something precious not only for the artistic sense but for soul and spirit; then it is always the true Bach, no matter in how many different ways he sounds."

Bach's music depends for its effect not upon the perfection but upon the spirit of the performance. Mendelssohn, Schelble and Mosewius, who were the first to waken the Cantatas and Passions to new life, were able to do so because they were not only musicians but sincere and deep-feeling men. Only he who sinks himself in the emotional world of Bach, who lives and thinks with him, who is simple and modest as he, is in a position to perform him properly. If the director and the performer do not feel themselves in a consecrated mood, they cannot communicate such a mood to the hearer; something cold will settle upon the music and deprive it of its best strength. "One thing is needful", said Mosewius in 1845, when he was trying to interest the world in Bach's cantatas; and it is perhaps more needful now than ever it was. "An inner unity of soul", he says at the end of his essay, "is absolutely indispensable in performing Bach; and every individual chorister must not only have thoroughly mastered the work technically but must preserve his spiritual forces unbroken throughout."

May this perception penetrate everywhere; then will Bach help our age to attain the spiritual unity and fervour of which it so sorely stands in need.

INDEX.

BACH'S WORKS.

VOCAL WORKS.

Chorale Preludes, Fantasias, etc.

Clavier Works.

Orchestral Works.

THE CHURCH CANTATAS ARRANGED NUMERICALLY.

B. G. I.

No. 1. Wie schön leuchtet der Morgenstern.
- 2. Ach Gott, vom Himmel sieh darein.
- 3. Ach Gott, wie manches Herzeleid. Erste Bearbeitung.
- 4. Christ lag in Todesbanden.
- 5. Wo soll ich fliehen hin.
- 6. Bleib' bei uns, denn es will Abend werden.
- 7. Christ unser Herr zum Jordan kam.
- 8. Liebster Gott, wann werd' ich sterben?
- 9. Es ist das Heil uns kommen her.
- 10. Meine Seel' erhebt den Herrn!

B. G. II.

No. 11. Lobet Gott in seinen Reichen.
- 12. Weinen, Klagen, Sorgen, Zagen.
- 13. Meine Seufzer, meine Tränen.
- 14. Wär' Gott nicht mit uns diese Zeit.
- 15. Denn du wirst meine Seele nicht in der Hölle lassen.
- 16. Herr Gott, dich loben wir.
- 17. Wer Dank opfert, der preiset mich.

No. 18. Gleich wie der Regen und Schnee vom Himmel fällt.
- 19. Es erhub sich ein Streit.
- 20. O Ewigkeit, du Donnerwort. Erste Bearbeitung.

B. G. V.

No. 21. Ich hatte viel Bekümmernis.
- 22. Jesus nahm zu sich die Zwölfe.
- 23. Du wahrer Gott und Davids Sohn.
- 24. Ein ungefärbt Gemüte.
- 25. Es ist nichts Gesundes an meinem Leibe.
- 26. Ach wie flüchtig, ach wie nichtig.
- 27. Wer weiss, wie nahe mir mein Ende.
- 28. Gottlob! Nun geht das Jahr zu Ende.
- 29. Wir danken dir, Gott, wir danken dir.
- 30. Freue dich, erlöste Schar.

B. G. VII.

No. 31. Der Himmel lacht, die Erde jubilieret.
- 32. Liebster Jesu, mein Verlangen.
- 33. Allein zu dir, Herr Jesu Christ.
- 34. O ewiges Feuer, o Ursprung der Liebe.
- 35. Geist und Seele wird verwirret.

No. 36. Schwingt freudig euch empor.
- 37. Wer da glaubet und getauft wird.
- 38. Aus tiefer Not schrei' ich zu dir.
- 39. Brich dem Hungrigen dein Brot.
- 40. Dazu ist erschienen der Sohn Gottes.

B. G. X.

No. 41. Jesu, nun sei gepreiset.
- 42. Am Abend aber desselbigen Sabbats.
- 43. Gott fähret auf mit Jauchzen.
- 44. Sie werden euch in den Bann tun.
- 45. Es ist dir gesagt, Mensch, was gut ist.
- 46. Schauet doch und sehet, ob irgend ein Schmerz sei.
- 47. Wer sich selbst erhöhet, der soll erniedrigt werden.
- 48. Ich elender Mensch, wer wird mich erlösen?
- 49. Ich geh' und suche mit Verlangen.
- 50. Nun ist das Heil und die Kraft.

B. G. XII.

No. 51. Jauchzet Gott in allen Landen.
- 52. Falsche Welt, dir trau' ich nicht.
- 53. Schlage doch, gewünschte Stunde.
- 54. Widerstehe doch der Sünde.
- 55. Ich armer Mensch, ich Sündenknecht.
- 56. Ich will den Kreuzstab gerne tragen.
- 57. Selig ist der Mann.

No. 58. Ach Gott, wie manches Herzeleid. Second Composition.
- 59. Wer mich liebet, der wird mein Wort halten. First Composition.
- 60. O Ewigkeit, du Donnerwort. Second Composition.

B. G. XVI.

No. 61. Nun komm, der Heiden Heiland. First Composition.
- 62. Nun komm, der Heiden Heiland. Second Composition.
- 63. Christen, ätzet diesen Tag.
- 64. Sehet, welch' eine Liebe hat uns der Vater erzeiget.
- 65. Sie werden aus Saba alle kommen.
- 66. Erfreut euch, ihr Herzen.
- 67. Halt' im Gedächtnis Jesum Christ.
- 68. Also hat Gott die Welt geliebt.
- 69. Lobe den Herrn, meine Seele.
- 70. Wachet, betet, seid bereit allezeit.

B. G. XVIII.

No. 71. Gott ist mein König.
- 72. Alles nur nach Gottes Willen.
- 73. Herr, wie du willst, so schick's mit mir.
- 74. Wer mich liebet, der wird mein Wort halten. (2nd enlarged arrangement.)
- 75. Die Elenden sollen essen.
- 76. Die Himmel erzählen die Ehre Gottes.

No. 77. Du sollst Gott, deinen Herrn, lieben.
- 78. Jesu, der du meineSeele.
- 79. Gott der Herr ist Sonn' und Schild.
- 80. Ein' feste Burg ist unser Gott.

B. G. XX.

No. 81. Jesus schläft, was soll ich hoffen.
- 82. Ich habe genug.
- 83. Erfreute Zeit im neuen Bunde.
- 84. Ich bin vergnügt mit meinem Glücke.
- 85. Ich bin ein guter Hirt.
- 86. Wahrlich, ich sage euch.
- 87. Bisher habt ihr nichts gebeten in meinem Namen.
- 88. Siehe, ich will viel Fischer aussenden, spricht der Herr.
- 89. Was soll ich aus dir machen, Ephraim?
- 90. Es reifet euch ein schrecklich Ende.

B. G. XXII.

No. 91. Gelobet seist du, Jesu Christ.
- 92. Ich hab' in Gottes Herz und Sinn.
- 93. Wer nur den lieben Gott lässt walten.
- 94. Was frag' ich nach der Welt.
- 95. Christus, der ist mein Leben.
- 96. Herr Christ, der ein'ge Gottessohn.
- 97. In allen meinen Taten.
- 98. Was Gott tut, das ist wohlgetan. First Composition. B flat major.
- 99. Was Gott tut, das ist wohlgetan. Second Composition. G major.

No. 100. Was Gott tut, das ist wohlgetan. Third Composition.

B. G. XXIII.

No. 101. Nimm von uns Herr, du treuer Gott.
- 102. Herr, deine Augen sehen nach dem Glauben.
- 103. Ihr werdet weinen und heulen.
- 104. Du Hirte Israel, höre.
- 105. Herr, gehe nicht ins Gericht.
- 106. Gottes Zeit ist die allerbeste Zeit.
- 107. Was willst du dich betrüben.
- 108. Es ist euch gut, dass ich hingehe.
- 109. Ich glaube, lieber Herr.
- 110. Unser Mund sei voll Lachens.

B. G. XXIV.

No. 111. Was mein Gott will, das g'scheh' allzeit.
- 112. Der Herr ist mein getreuer Hirt.
- 113. Herr Jesu Christ, du höchstes Gut.
- 114. Ach, lieben Christen, seid getrost.
- 115. Mache dich, mein Geist, bereit.
- 116. Du Friedensfürst, Herr Jesu Christ.
- 117. Sei Lob und Ehr' dem höchsten Gut.
- 118. O Jesu Christ, meins Lebens Licht.
- 119. Preise, Jerusalem, den Herrn.
- 120. Gott, man lobt dich in der Stille.

B. G. XXVI.

No. 121. Christum wir sollen loben schon.

No. 122. Das neugebor'ne Kindelein.
- 123. Liebster Immanuel, Herzog der Frommen.
- 124. Meinen Jesum lass' ich nicht.
- 125. Mit Fried' und Freud ich fahr' dahin.
- 126. Erhalt' uns, Herr, bei deinem Wort.
- 127. Herr Jesu Christ, wahr'r Mensch und Gott.
- 128. Auf Christi Himmelfahrt allein.
- 129. Gelobet sei der Herr, mein Gott.
- 130. Herr Gott, dich loben alle wir.

B. G. XXVIII.

No. 131. Aus der Tiefe rufe ich, Herr, zu dir.
- 132. Bereitet die Wege, bereitet die Bahn.
- 133. Ich freue mich in dir.
- 134. Ein Herz, das seinen Jesum lebend weiss.
- 135. Ach Herr, mich armen Sünder.
- 136 Erforsche mich, Gott, und erfahre mein Herz.
- 137. Lobe den Herren, den mächtigen König der Ehren.
- 138. Warum betrübst du dich, mein Herz.
- 139. Wohl dem, der sich auf seinen Gott.
- 140. Wachet auf, ruft uns die Stimme.

B. G. XXX.

No. 141. Das ist je gewisslich wahr.
- 142. Uns ist ein Kind geboren.
- 143. Lobe den Herrn, meine Seele.
- 144. Nimm, was dein ist.

No. 145. So du mit deinem Munde.
- 146. Wir müssen durch viel Trübsal.
- 147. Herz und Mund und Tat und Leben.
- 148. Bringet dem Herrn Ehre seines Namens.
- 149. Man singet mit Freuden vom Sieg.
- 150. Nach dir, Herr, verlanget mich.

B. G. XXXII.

No. 151. Süsser Trost, mein Jesus kommt.
- 152. Tritt auf die Glaubensbahn.
- 153. Schau, lieber Gott.
- 154. Mein liebster Jesus.
- 155. Mein Gott, wie lang.
- 156. Ich steh' mit einem Fuss.
- 157. Der Friede sei mit dir.
- 158. Ich lasse dich nicht.
- 159. Sehet, wir geh'n hinauf gen Jerusalem.
- 160. Ich weiss, dass mein Erlöser lebt.

B. G. XXXIII.

No. 161. Komm, du süsse Todesstunde.
- 162. Ach, ich sehe, jetzt da ich zur Hochzeit gehe.
- 163. Nur jedem das Seine.
- 164. Ihr, die ihr euch von Christo nennet.
- 165. O heil'ges Geist- und Wasserbad.
- 166. Wo gehest du hin.
- 167. Ihr Menschen, rühmet Gottes Liebe.
- 168. Tue Rechnung! Donnerwort.
- 169. Gott soll allein mein Herze haben.
- 170. Vergnügte Ruh', beliebte Seelenlust.

B. G. XXXV.

No. 171. Gott, wie dein Name, so ist auch dein Ruhm.
- 172. Erschallet, ihr Lieder.
- 173. Erhöhtes Fleisch und Blut.
- 174. Ich liebe den Höchsten von ganzem Gemüte.
- 175. Er rufet seinen Schafen mit Namen.
- 176. Es ist ein trotzig und verzagt Ding.
- 177. Ich ruf' zu dir, Herr Jesu Christ.
- 178. Wo Gott der Herr nicht bei uns hält.
- 179. Siehe zu, dass deine Gottesfurcht nicht Heuchelei sei.
- 180. Schmücke dich, o liebe Seele.

B. G. XXXVII.

No. 181. Leichtgesinnte Flattergeister.
- 182. Himmelskönig, sei willkommen.
- 183. Sie werden euch in den Bann tun. Second Composition.
No. 184. Erwünschtes Freudenlicht.
- 185. Barmherziges Herze der ewigen Liebe.
- 186. Ärgre dich, o Seele, nicht.
- 187. Es wartet alles auf dich.
- 188. Ich habe meine Zuversicht.
- 189. Meine Seele rühmt und preist.
- 190. Singet dem Herrn ein neues Lied. (Lobe Zion, deinen Gott.)

B. G. XLI. (Supplementary Volume.)

Incomplete Cantatas.

Nun danket alle Gott.
Ihr Pforten zu Zion.
Ehre sei Gott.
O ewiges Feuer (incomplete Wedding Cantata).
Herr Gott, Beherrscher (incomplete Wedding Cantata).

B. G. XIII[1]. Wedding Cantatas.

Dem Gerechten muss das Licht.
Der Herr denket an uns.
Gott ist unsre Zuversicht.

A CATALOG OF SELECTED DOVER BOOKS IN ALL FIELDS OF INTEREST

A CATALOG OF SELECTED DOVER BOOKS IN ALL FIELDS OF INTEREST

CONCERNING THE SPIRITUAL IN ART, Wassily Kandinsky. Pioneering work by father of abstract art. Thoughts on color theory, nature of art. Analysis of earlier masters. 12 illustrations. 80pp. of text. 5⅜ × 8½. 23411-8 Pa. $2.25

LEONARDO ON THE HUMAN BODY, Leonardo da Vinci. More than 1200 of Leonardo's anatomical drawings on 215 plates. Leonardo's text, which accompanies the drawings, has been translated into English. 506pp. 8⅜ × 11¾. 24483-0 Pa. $10.95

GOBLIN MARKET, Christina Rossetti. Best-known work by poet comparable to Emily Dickinson, Alfred Tennyson. With 46 delightfully grotesque illustrations by Laurence Housman. 64pp. 4 × 6¾. 24516-0 Pa. $2.50

THE HEART OF THOREAU'S JOURNALS, edited by Odell Shepard. Selections from *Journal*, ranging over full gamut of interests. 228pp. 5⅜ × 8½. 20741-2 Pa. $4.00

MR. LINCOLN'S CAMERA MAN: MATHEW B. BRADY, Roy Meredith. Over 300 Brady photos reproduced directly from original negatives, photos. Lively commentary. 368pp. 8⅜ × 11¼. 23021-X Pa. $11.95

PHOTOGRAPHIC VIEWS OF SHERMAN'S CAMPAIGN, George N. Barnard. Reprint of landmark 1866 volume with 61 plates: battlefield of New Hope Church, the Etawah Bridge, the capture of Atlanta, etc. 80pp. 9 × 12. 23445-2 Pa. $6.00

A SHORT HISTORY OF ANATOMY AND PHYSIOLOGY FROM THE GREEKS TO HARVEY, Dr. Charles Singer. Thoroughly engrossing non-technical survey. 270 illustrations. 211pp. 5⅜ × 8½. 20389-1 Pa. $4.50

REDOUTE ROSES IRON-ON TRANSFER PATTERNS, Barbara Christopher. Redouté was botanical painter to the Empress Josephine; transfer his famous roses onto fabric with these 24 transfer patterns. 80pp. 8¼ × 10⅞. 24292-7 Pa. $3.50

THE FIVE BOOKS OF ARCHITECTURE, Sebastiano Serlio. Architectural milestone, first (1611) English translation of Renaissance classic. Unabridged reproduction of original edition includes over 300 woodcut illustrations. 416pp. 9⅜ × 12¼. 24349-4 Pa. $14.95

CARLSON'S GUIDE TO LANDSCAPE PAINTING, John F. Carlson. Authoritative, comprehensive guide covers, every aspect of landscape painting. 34 reproductions of paintings by author; 58 explanatory diagrams. 144pp. 8⅜ × 11. 22927-0 Pa. $4.95

101 PUZZLES IN THOUGHT AND LOGIC, C.R. Wylie, Jr. Solve murders, robberies, see which fishermen are liars—purely by reasoning! 107pp. 5⅜ × 8½. 20367-0 Pa. $2.00

TEST YOUR LOGIC, George J. Summers. 50 more truly new puzzles with new turns of thought, new subtleties of inference. 100pp. 5⅜ × 8½. 22877-0 Pa. $2.25

THE MURDER BOOK OF J.G. REEDER, Edgar Wallace. Eight suspenseful stories by bestselling mystery writer of 20s and 30s. Features the donnish Mr. J.G. Reeder of Public Prosecutor's Office. 128pp. 5⅜ × 8½. (Available in U.S. only)
24374-5 Pa. $3.50

ANNE ORR'S CHARTED DESIGNS, Anne Orr. Best designs by premier needlework designer, all on charts: flowers, borders, birds, children, alphabets, etc. Over 100 charts, 10 in color. Total of 40pp. 8¼ × 11. 23704-4 Pa. $2.25

BASIC CONSTRUCTION TECHNIQUES FOR HOUSES AND SMALL BUILDINGS SIMPLY EXPLAINED, U.S. Bureau of Naval Personnel. Grading, masonry, woodworking, floor and wall framing, roof framing, plastering, tile setting, much more. Over 675 illustrations. 568pp. 6½ × 9¼. 20242-9 Pa. $8.95

MATISSE LINE DRAWINGS AND PRINTS, Henri Matisse. Representative collection of female nudes, faces, still lifes, experimental works, etc., from 1898 to 1948. 50 illustrations. 48pp. 8⅜ × 11¼. 23877-6 Pa. $2.50

HOW TO PLAY THE CHESS OPENINGS, Eugene Znosko-Borovsky. Clear, profound examinations of just what each opening is intended to do and how opponent can counter. Many sample games. 147pp. 5⅜ × 8½. 22795-2 Pa. $2.95

DUPLICATE BRIDGE, Alfred Sheinwold. Clear, thorough, easily followed account: rules, etiquette, scoring, strategy, bidding; Goren's point count system, Blackwood and Gerber conventions, etc. 158pp. 5⅜ × 8½. 22741-3 Pa. $3.00

SARGENT PORTRAIT DRAWINGS, J.S. Sargent. Collection of 42 portraits reveals technical skill and intuitive eye of noted American portrait painter, John Singer Sargent. 48pp. 8¼ × 11⅛. 24524-1 Pa. $2.95

ENTERTAINING SCIENCE EXPERIMENTS WITH EVERYDAY OBJECTS, Martin Gardner. Over 100 experiments for youngsters. Will amuse, astonish, teach, and entertain. Over 100 illustrations. 127pp. 5⅜ × 8½. 24201-3 Pa. $2.50

TEDDY BEAR PAPER DOLLS IN FULL COLOR: A Family of Four Bears and Their Costumes, Crystal Collins. A family of four Teddy Bear paper dolls and nearly 60 cut-out costumes. Full color, printed one side only. 32pp. 9¼ × 12¼.
24550-0 Pa. $3.50

NEW CALLIGRAPHIC ORNAMENTS AND FLOURISHES, Arthur Baker. Unusual, multi-useable material: arrows, pointing hands, brackets and frames, ovals, swirls, birds, etc. Nearly 700 illustrations. 80pp. 8⅜ × 11¼.
24095-9 Pa. $3.50

DINOSAUR DIORAMAS TO CUT & ASSEMBLE, M. Kalmenoff. Two complete three-dimensional scenes in full color, with 31 cut-out animals and plants. Excellent educational toy for youngsters. Instructions; 2 assembly diagrams. 32pp. 9¼ × 12¼. 24541-1 Pa. $3.95

SILHOUETTES: A PICTORIAL ARCHIVE OF VARIED ILLUSTRATIONS, edited by Carol Belanger Grafton. Over 600 silhouettes from the 18th to 20th centuries. Profiles and full figures of men, women, children, birds, animals, groups and scenes, nature, ships, an alphabet. 144pp. 8⅜ × 11¼. 23781-8 Pa. $4.50

25 KITES THAT FLY, Leslie Hunt. Full, easy-to-follow instructions for kites made from inexpensive materials. Many novelties. 70 illustrations. 110pp. 5⅜ × 8½. 22550-X Pa. $1.95

PIANO TUNING, J. Cree Fischer. Clearest, best book for beginner, amateur. Simple repairs, raising dropped notes, tuning by easy method of flattened fifths. No previous skills needed. 4 illustrations. 201pp. 5⅜ × 8½. 23267-0 Pa. $3.50

EARLY AMERICAN IRON-ON TRANSFER PATTERNS, edited by Rita Weiss. 75 designs, borders, alphabets, from traditional American sources. 48pp. 8¼ × 11. 23162-3 Pa. $1.95

CROCHETING EDGINGS, edited by Rita Weiss. Over 100 of the best designs for these lovely trims for a host of household items. Complete instructions, illustrations. 48pp. 8¼ × 11. 24031-2 Pa. $2.00

FINGER PLAYS FOR NURSERY AND KINDERGARTEN, Emilie Poulsson. 18 finger plays with music (voice and piano); entertaining, instructive. Counting, nature lore, etc. Victorian classic. 53 illustrations. 80pp. 6½ × 9¼. 22588-7 Pa. $1.95

BOSTON THEN AND NOW, Peter Vanderwarker. Here in 59 side-by-side views are photographic documentations of the city's past and present. 119 photographs. Full captions. 122pp. 8¼ × 11. 24312-5 Pa. $6.95

CROCHETING BEDSPREADS, edited by Rita Weiss. 22 patterns, originally published in three instruction books 1939-41. 39 photos, 8 charts. Instructions. 48pp. 8¼ × 11. 23610-2 Pa. $2.00

HAWTHORNE ON PAINTING, Charles W. Hawthorne. Collected from notes taken by students at famous Cape Cod School; hundreds of direct, personal *apercus*, ideas, suggestions. 91pp. 5⅜ × 8½. 20653-X Pa. $2.50

THERMODYNAMICS, Enrico Fermi. A classic of modern science. Clear, organized treatment of systems, first and second laws, entropy, thermodynamic potentials, etc. Calculus required. 160pp. 5⅜ × 8½. 60361-X Pa. $4.00

TEN BOOKS ON ARCHITECTURE, Vitruvius. The most important book ever written on architecture. Early Roman aesthetics, technology, classical orders, site selection, all other aspects. Morgan translation. 331pp. 5⅜ × 8½. 20645-9 Pa. $5.50

THE CORNELL BREAD BOOK, Clive M. McCay and Jeanette B. McCay. Famed high-protein recipe incorporated into breads, rolls, buns, coffee cakes, pizza, pie crusts, more. Nearly 50 illustrations. 48pp. 8¼ × 11. 23995-0 Pa. $2.00

THE CRAFTSMAN'S HANDBOOK, Cennino Cennini. 15th-century handbook, school of Giotto, explains applying gold, silver leaf; gesso; fresco painting, grinding pigments, etc. 142pp. 6⅛ × 9¼. 20054-X Pa. $3.50

FRANK LLOYD WRIGHT'S FALLINGWATER, Donald Hoffmann. Full story of Wright's masterwork at Bear Run, Pa. 100 photographs of site, construction, and details of completed structure. 112pp. 9¼ × 10. 23671-4 Pa. $6.50

OVAL STAINED GLASS PATTERN BOOK, C. Eaton. 60 new designs framed in shape of an oval. Greater complexity, challenge with sinuous cats, birds, mandalas framed in antique shape. 64pp. 8¼ × 11. 24519-5 Pa. $3.50

THE BOOK OF WOOD CARVING, Charles Marshall Sayers. Still finest book for beginning student. Fundamentals, technique; gives 34 designs, over 34 projects for panels, bookends, mirrors, etc. 33 photos. 118pp. 7¾ × 10⅝. 23654-4 Pa. $3.95

CARVING COUNTRY CHARACTERS, Bill Higginbotham. Expert advice for beginning, advanced carvers on materials, techniques for creating 18 projects—mirthful panorama of American characters. 105 illustrations. 80pp. 8⅜ × 11. 24135-1 Pa. $2.50

300 ART NOUVEAU DESIGNS AND MOTIFS IN FULL COLOR, C.B. Grafton. 44 full-page plates display swirling lines and muted colors typical of Art Nouveau. Borders, frames, panels, cartouches, dingbats, etc. 48pp. 9⅜ × 12¼. 24354-0 Pa. $6.00

SELF-WORKING CARD TRICKS, Karl Fulves. Editor of *Pallbearer* offers 72 tricks that work automatically through nature of card deck. No sleight of hand needed. Often spectacular. 42 illustrations. 113pp. 5⅜ × 8½. 23334-0 Pa. $2.25

CUT AND ASSEMBLE A WESTERN FRONTIER TOWN, Edmund V. Gillon, Jr. Ten authentic full-color buildings on heavy cardboard stock in H-O scale. Sheriff's Office and Jail, Saloon, Wells Fargo, Opera House, others. 48pp. 9¼ × 12¼. 23736-2 Pa. $3.95

CUT AND ASSEMBLE AN EARLY NEW ENGLAND VILLAGE, Edmund V. Gillon, Jr. Printed in full color on heavy cardboard stock. 12 authentic buildings in H-O scale: Adams home in Quincy, Mass., Oliver Wight house in Sturbridge, smithy, store, church, others. 48pp. 9¼ × 12¼. 23536-X Pa. $3.95

THE TALE OF TWO BAD MICE, Beatrix Potter. Tom Thumb and Hunca Munca squeeze out of their hole and go exploring. 27 full-color Potter illustrations. 59pp. 4¼ × 5½. (Available in U.S. only) 23065-1 Pa. $1.50

CARVING FIGURE CARICATURES IN THE OZARK STYLE, Harold L. Enlow. Instructions and illustrations for ten delightful projects, plus general carving instructions. 22 drawings and 47 photographs altogether. 39pp. 8⅜ × 11. 23151-8 Pa. $2.50

A TREASURY OF FLOWER DESIGNS FOR ARTISTS, EMBROIDERERS AND CRAFTSMEN, Susan Gaber. 100 garden favorites lushly rendered by artist for artists, craftsmen, needleworkers. Many form frames, borders. 80pp. 8¼ × 11. 24096-7 Pa. $3.50

CUT & ASSEMBLE A TOY THEATER/THE NUTCRACKER BALLET, Tom Tierney. Model of a complete, full-color production of Tchaikovsky's classic. 6 backdrops, dozens of characters, familiar dance sequences. 32pp. 9⅜ × 12¼. 24194-7 Pa. $4.50

ANIMALS: 1,419 COPYRIGHT-FREE ILLUSTRATIONS OF MAMMALS, BIRDS, FISH, INSECTS, ETC., edited by Jim Harter. Clear wood engravings present, in extremely lifelike poses, over 1,000 species of animals. 284pp. 9 × 12. 23766-4 Pa. $8.95

MORE HAND SHADOWS, Henry Bursill. For those at their 'finger ends,'' 16 more effects—Shakespeare, a hare, a squirrel, Mr. Punch, and twelve more—each explained by a full-page illustration. Considerable period charm. 30pp. 6½ × 9¼. 21384-6 Pa. $1.95

SURREAL STICKERS AND UNREAL STAMPS, William Rowe. 224 haunting, hilarious stamps on gummed, perforated stock, with images of elephants, geisha girls, George Washington, etc. 16pp. one side. 8¼ × 11. 24371-0 Pa. $3.50

GOURMET KITCHEN LABELS, Ed Sibbett, Jr. 112 full-color labels (4 copies each of 28 designs). Fruit, bread, other culinary motifs. Gummed and perforated. 16pp. 8¼ × 11. 24087-8 Pa. $2.95

PATTERNS AND INSTRUCTIONS FOR CARVING AUTHENTIC BIRDS, H.D. Green. Detailed instructions, 27 diagrams, 85 photographs for carving 15 species of birds so life-like, they'll seem ready to fly! 8¼ × 11. 24222-6 Pa. $2.75

FLATLAND, E.A. Abbott. Science-fiction classic explores life of 2-D being in 3-D world. 16 illustrations. 103pp. 5⅜ × 8. 20001-9 Pa. $2.00

DRIED FLOWERS, Sarah Whitlock and Martha Rankin. Concise, clear, practical guide to dehydration, glycerinizing, pressing plant material, and more. Covers use of silica gel. 12 drawings. 32pp. 5⅜ × 8½. 21802-3 Pa. $1.00

EASY-TO-MAKE CANDLES, Gary V. Guy. Learn how easy it is to make all kinds of decorative candles. Step-by-step instructions. 82 illustrations. 48pp. 8¼ × 11. 23881-4 Pa. $2.50

SUPER STICKERS FOR KIDS, Carolyn Bracken. 128 gummed and perforated full-color stickers: GIRL WANTED, KEEP OUT, BORED OF EDUCATION, X-RATED, COMBAT ZONE, many others. 16pp. 8¼ × 11. 24092-4 Pa. $2.50

CUT AND COLOR PAPER MASKS, Michael Grater. Clowns, animals, funny faces...simply color them in, cut them out, and put them together, and you have 9 paper masks to play with and enjoy. 32pp. 8¼ × 11. 23171-2 Pa. $2.25

A CHRISTMAS CAROL: THE ORIGINAL MANUSCRIPT, Charles Dickens. Clear facsimile of Dickens manuscript, on facing pages with final printed text. 8 illustrations by John Leech, 4 in color on covers. 144pp. 8⅜ × 11¼. 20980-6 Pa. $5.95

CARVING SHOREBIRDS, Harry V. Shourds & Anthony Hillman. 16 full-size patterns (all double-page spreads) for 19 North American shorebirds with step-by-step instructions. 72pp. 9¼ × 12¼. 24287-0 Pa. $4.95

THE GENTLE ART OF MATHEMATICS, Dan Pedoe. Mathematical games, probability, the question of infinity, topology, how the laws of algebra work, problems of irrational numbers, and more. 42 figures. 143pp. 5⅜ × 8½. (EBE) 22949-1 Pa. $3.00

READY-TO-USE DOLLHOUSE WALLPAPER, Katzenbach & Warren, Inc. Stripe, 2 floral stripes, 2 allover florals, polka dot; all in full color. 4 sheets (350 sq. in.) of each, enough for average room. 48pp. 8¼ × 11. 23495-9 Pa. $2.95

MINIATURE IRON-ON TRANSFER PATTERNS FOR DOLLHOUSES, DOLLS, AND SMALL PROJECTS, Rita Weiss and Frank Fontana. Over 100 miniature patterns: rugs, bedspreads, quilts, chair seats, etc. In standard dollhouse size. 48pp. 8¼ × 11. 23741-9 Pa. $1.95

THE DINOSAUR COLORING BOOK, Anthony Rao. 45 renderings of dinosaurs, fossil birds, turtles, other creatures of Mesozoic Era. Scientifically accurate. Captions. 48pp. 8¼ × 11. 24022-3 Pa. $2.25

JAPANESE DESIGN MOTIFS, Matsuya Co. Mon, or heraldic designs. Over 4000 typical, beautiful designs: birds, animals, flowers, swords, fans, geometrics; all beautifully stylized. 213pp. 11⅜ × 8¼. 22874-6 Pa. $6.95

THE TALE OF BENJAMIN BUNNY, Beatrix Potter. Peter Rabbit's cousin coaxes him back into Mr. McGregor's garden for a whole new set of adventures. All 27 full-color illustrations. 59pp. 4¼ × 5½. (Available in U.S. only) 21102-9 Pa. $1.50

THE TALE OF PETER RABBIT AND OTHER FAVORITE STORIES BOXED SET, Beatrix Potter. Seven of Beatrix Potter's best-loved tales including Peter Rabbit in a specially designed, durable boxed set. 4¼ × 5½. Total of 447pp. 158 color illustrations. (Available in U.S. only) 23903-9 Pa. $10.50

PRACTICAL MENTAL MAGIC, Theodore Annemann. Nearly 200 astonishing feats of mental magic revealed in step-by-step detail. Complete advice on staging, patter, etc. Illustrated. 320pp. 5⅜ × 8½. 24426-1 Pa. $5.95

CELEBRATED CASES OF JUDGE DEE (DEE GOONG AN), translated by Robert Van Gulik. Authentic 18th-century Chinese detective novel; Dee and associates solve three interlocked cases. Led to van Gulik's own stories with same characters. Extensive introduction. 9 illustrations. 237pp. 5⅜ × 8½. 23337-5 Pa. $4.50

CUT & FOLD EXTRATERRESTRIAL INVADERS THAT FLY, M. Grater. Stage your own lilliputian space battles.By following the step-by-step instructions and explanatory diagrams you can launch 22 full-color fliers into space. 36pp. 8¼ × 11. 24478-4 Pa. $2.95

CUT & ASSEMBLE VICTORIAN HOUSES, Edmund V. Gillon, Jr. Printed in full color on heavy cardboard stock, 4 authentic Victorian houses in H-O scale: Italian-style Villa, Octagon, Second Empire, Stick Style. 48pp. 9¼ × 12¼. 23849-0 Pa. $3.95

BEST SCIENCE FICTION STORIES OF H.G. WELLS, H.G. Wells. Full novel *The Invisible Man,* plus 17 short stories: "The Crystal Egg," "Aepyornis Island," "The Strange Orchid," etc. 303pp. 5⅜ × 8½. (Available in U.S. only) 21531-8 Pa. $3.95

TRADEMARK DESIGNS OF THE WORLD, Yusaku Kamekura. A lavish collection of nearly 700 trademarks, the work of Wright, Loewy, Klee, Binder, hundreds of others. 160pp. 8¾ × 8. (Available in U.S. only) 24191-2 Pa. $5.00

THE ARTIST'S AND CRAFTSMAN'S GUIDE TO REDUCING, ENLARGING AND TRANSFERRING DESIGNS, Rita Weiss. Discover, reduce, enlarge, transfer designs from any objects to any craft project. 12pp. plus 16 sheets special graph paper. 8¼ × 11. 24142-4 Pa. $3.25

TREASURY OF JAPANESE DESIGNS AND MOTIFS FOR ARTISTS AND CRAFTSMEN, edited by Carol Belanger Grafton. Indispensable collection of 360 traditional Japanese designs and motifs redrawn in clean, crisp black-and-white, copyright-free illustrations. 96pp. 8¼ × 11. 24435-0 Pa. $3.95

CHANCERY CURSIVE STROKE BY STROKE, Arthur Baker. Instructions and illustrations for each stroke of each letter (upper and lower case) and numerals. 54 full-page plates. 64pp. 8¼ × 11. 24278-1 Pa. $2.50

THE ENJOYMENT AND USE OF COLOR, Walter Sargent. Color relationships, values, intensities; complementary colors, illumination, similar topics. Color in nature and art. 7 color plates, 29 illustrations. 274pp. 5⅜ × 8½. 20944-X Pa. $4.50

SCULPTURE PRINCIPLES AND PRACTICE, Louis Slobodkin. Step-by-step approach to clay, plaster, metals, stone; classical and modern. 253 drawings, photos. 255pp. 8⅛ × 11. 22960-2 Pa. $7.00

VICTORIAN FASHION PAPER DOLLS FROM HARPER'S BAZAR, 1867-1898, Theodore Menten. Four female dolls with 28 elegant high fashion costumes, printed in full color. 32pp. 9¼ × 12¼. 23453-3 Pa. $3.50

FLOPSY, MOPSY AND COTTONTAIL: A Little Book of Paper Dolls in Full Color, Susan LaBelle. Three dolls and 21 costumes (7 for each doll) show Peter Rabbit's siblings dressed for holidays, gardening, hiking, etc. Charming borders, captions. 48pp. 4¼ × 5½. 24376-1 Pa. $2.00

NATIONAL LEAGUE BASEBALL CARD CLASSICS, Bert Randolph Sugar. 83 big-leaguers from 1909-69 on facsimile cards. Hubbell, Dean, Spahn, Brock plus advertising, info, no duplications. Perforated, detachable. 16pp. 8¼ × 11. 24308-7 Pa. $2.95

THE LOGICAL APPROACH TO CHESS, Dr. Max Euwe, et al. First-rate text of comprehensive strategy, tactics, theory for the amateur. No gambits to memorize, just a clear, logical approach. 224pp. 5⅜ × 8½. 24353-2 Pa. $4.50

MAGICK IN THEORY AND PRACTICE, Aleister Crowley. The summation of the thought and practice of the century's most famous necromancer, long hard to find. Crowley's best book. 436pp. 5⅜ × 8½. (Available in U.S. only) 23295-6 Pa. $6.50

THE HAUNTED HOTEL, Wilkie Collins. Collins' last great tale; doom and destiny in a Venetian palace. Praised by T.S. Eliot. 127pp. 5⅜ × 8½. 24333-8 Pa. $3.00

ART DECO DISPLAY ALPHABETS, Dan X. Solo. Wide variety of bold yet elegant lettering in handsome Art Deco styles. 100 complete fonts, with numerals, punctuation, more. 104pp. 8⅛ × 11. 24372-9 Pa. $4.00

CALLIGRAPHIC ALPHABETS, Arthur Baker. Nearly 150 complete alphabets by outstanding contemporary. Stimulating ideas; useful source for unique effects. 154 plates. 157pp. 8⅜ × 11¼. 21045-6 Pa. $4.95

ARTHUR BAKER'S HISTORIC CALLIGRAPHIC ALPHABETS, Arthur Baker. From monumental capitals of first-century Rome to humanistic cursive of 16th century, 33 alphabets in fresh interpretations. 88 plates. 96pp. 9 × 12. 24054-1 Pa. $3.95

LETTIE LANE PAPER DOLLS, Sheila Young. Genteel turn-of-the-century family very popular then and now. 24 paper dolls. 16 plates in full color. 32pp. 9¼ × 12¼. 24089-4 Pa. $3.50

KEYBOARD WORKS FOR SOLO INSTRUMENTS, G.F. Handel. 35 neglected works from Handel's vast oeuvre, originally jotted down as improvisations. Includes Eight Great Suites, others. New sequence. 174pp. 9⅜ × 12¼.
24338-9 Pa. $7.50

AMERICAN LEAGUE BASEBALL CARD CLASSICS, Bert Randolph Sugar. 82 stars from 1900s to 60s on facsimile cards. Ruth, Cobb, Mantle, Williams, plus advertising, info, no duplications. Perforated, detachable. 16pp. 8¼ × 11.
24286-2 Pa. $2.95

A TREASURY OF CHARTED DESIGNS FOR NEEDLEWORKERS, Georgia Gorham and Jeanne Warth. 141 charted designs: owl, cat with yarn, tulips, piano, spinning wheel, covered bridge, Victorian house and many others. 48pp. 8¼ × 11.
23558-0 Pa. $1.95

DANISH FLORAL CHARTED DESIGNS, Gerda Bengtsson. Exquisite collection of over 40 different florals: anemone, Iceland poppy, wild fruit, pansies, many others. 45 illustrations. 48pp. 8¼ × 11. 23957-8 Pa. $1.75

OLD PHILADELPHIA IN EARLY PHOTOGRAPHS 1839-1914, Robert F. Looney. 215 photographs: panoramas, street scenes, landmarks, President-elect Lincoln's visit, 1876 Centennial Exposition, much more. 230pp. 8⅜ × 11¼.
23345-6 Pa. $9.95

PRELUDE TO MATHEMATICS, W.W. Sawyer. Noted mathematician's lively, stimulating account of non-Euclidean geometry, matrices, determinants, group theory, other topics. Emphasis on novel, striking aspects. 224pp. 5⅜ × 8½.
24401-6 Pa. $4.50

ADVENTURES WITH A MICROSCOPE, Richard Headstrom. 59 adventures with clothing fibers, protozoa, ferns and lichens, roots and leaves, much more. 142 illustrations. 232pp. 5⅜ × 8½. 23471-1 Pa. $3.50

IDENTIFYING ANIMAL TRACKS: MAMMALS, BIRDS, AND OTHER ANIMALS OF THE EASTERN UNITED STATES, Richard Headstrom. For hunters, naturalists, scouts, nature-lovers. Diagrams of tracks, tips on identification. 128pp. 5⅜ × 8. 24442-3 Pa. $3.50

VICTORIAN FASHIONS AND COSTUMES FROM HARPER'S BAZAR, 1867-1898, edited by Stella Blum. Day costumes, evening wear, sports clothes, shoes, hats, other accessories in over 1,000 detailed engravings. 320pp. 9⅜ × 12¼.
22990-4 Pa. $9.95

EVERYDAY FASHIONS OF THE TWENTIES AS PICTURED IN SEARS AND OTHER CATALOGS, edited by Stella Blum. Actual dress of the Roaring Twenties, with text by Stella Blum. Over 750 illustrations, captions. 156pp. 9 × 12.
24134-3 Pa. $7.95

HALL OF FAME BASEBALL CARDS, edited by Bert Randolph Sugar. Cy Young, Ted Williams, Lou Gehrig, and many other Hall of Fame greats on 92 full-color, detachable reprints of early baseball cards. No duplication of cards with *Classic Baseball Cards*. 16pp. 8¼ × 11. 23624-2 Pa. $2.95

THE ART OF HAND LETTERING, Helm Wotzkow. Course in hand lettering, Roman, Gothic, Italic, Block, Script. Tools, proportions, optical aspects, individual variation. Very quality conscious. Hundreds of specimens. 320pp. 5⅜ × 8½.
21797-3 Pa. $4.95

THE RIME OF THE ANCIENT MARINER, Gustave Doré, S.T. Coleridge. Doré's finest work, 34 plates capture moods, subtleties of poem. Full text. 77pp. 9¼ × 12. 22305-1 Pa. $4.95

SONGS OF INNOCENCE, William Blake. The first and most popular of Blake's famous "Illuminated Books," in a facsimile edition reproducing all 31 brightly colored plates. Additional printed text of each poem. 64pp. 5¼ × 7. 22764-2 Pa. $3.00

AN INTRODUCTION TO INFORMATION THEORY, J.R. Pierce. Second (1980) edition of most impressive non-technical account available. Encoding, entropy, noisy channel, related areas, etc. 320pp. 5⅜ × 8½. 24061-4 Pa. $4.95

THE DIVINE PROPORTION: A STUDY IN MATHEMATICAL BEAUTY, H.E. Huntley. "Divine proportion" or "golden ratio" in poetry, Pascal's triangle, philosophy, psychology, music, mathematical figures, etc. Excellent bridge between science and art. 58 figures. 185pp. 5⅜ × 8½. 22254-3 Pa. $3.95

THE DOVER NEW YORK WALKING GUIDE: From the Battery to Wall Street, Mary J. Shapiro. Superb inexpensive guide to historic buildings and locales in lower Manhattan: Trinity Church, Bowling Green, more. Complete Text; maps. 36 illustrations. 48pp. 3⅞ × 9¼. 24225-0 Pa. $1.75

NEW YORK THEN AND NOW, Edward B. Watson, Edmund V. Gillon, Jr. 83 important Manhattan sites: on facing pages early photographs (1875-1925) and 1976 photos by Gillon. 172 illustrations. 171pp. 9¼ × 10. 23361-8 Pa. $7.95

HISTORIC COSTUME IN PICTURES, Braun & Schneider. Over 1450 costumed figures from dawn of civilization to end of 19th century. English captions. 125 plates. 256pp. 8⅜ × 11¼. 23150-X Pa. $7.50

VICTORIAN AND EDWARDIAN FASHION: A Photographic Survey, Alison Gernsheim. First fashion history completely illustrated by contemporary photographs. Full text plus 235 photos, 1840-1914, in which many celebrities appear. 240pp. 6½ × 9¼. 24205-6 Pa. $6.00

CHARTED CHRISTMAS DESIGNS FOR COUNTED CROSS-STITCH AND OTHER NEEDLECRAFTS, Lindberg Press. Charted designs for 45 beautiful needlecraft projects with many yuletide and wintertime motifs. 48pp. 8¼ × 11. 24356-7 Pa. $1.95

101 FOLK DESIGNS FOR COUNTED CROSS-STITCH AND OTHER NEEDLECRAFTS, Carter Houck. 101 authentic charted folk designs in a wide array of lovely representations with many suggestions for effective use. 48pp. 8¼ × 11. 24369-9 Pa. $1.95

FIVE ACRES AND INDEPENDENCE, Maurice G. Kains. Great back-to-the-land classic explains basics of self-sufficient farming. The one book to get. 95 illustrations. 397pp. 5⅜ × 8½. 20974-1 Pa. $4.95

A MODERN HERBAL, Margaret Grieve. Much the fullest, most exact, most useful compilation of herbal material. Gigantic alphabetical encyclopedia, from aconite to zedoary, gives botanical information, medical properties, folklore, economic uses, and much else. Indispensable to serious reader. 161 illustrations. 888pp. 6½ × 9¼. (Available in U.S. only) 22798-7, 22799-5 Pa., Two-vol. set $16.45

DECORATIVE NAPKIN FOLDING FOR BEGINNERS, Lillian Oppenheimer and Natalie Epstein. 22 different napkin folds in the shape of a heart, clown's hat, love knot, etc. 63 drawings. 48pp. 8¼ × 11. 23797-4 Pa. $1.95

DECORATIVE LABELS FOR HOME CANNING, PRESERVING, AND OTHER HOUSEHOLD AND GIFT USES, Theodore Menten. 128 gummed, perforated labels, beautifully printed in 2 colors. 12 versions. Adhere to metal, glass, wood, ceramics. 24pp. 8¼ × 11. 23219-0 Pa. $2.95

EARLY AMERICAN STENCILS ON WALLS AND FURNITURE, Janet Waring. Thorough coverage of 19th-century folk art: techniques, artifacts, surviving specimens. 166 illustrations, 7 in color. 147pp. of text. 7⅞ × 10¾. 21906-2 Pa. $8.95

AMERICAN ANTIQUE WEATHERVANES, A.B. & W.T. Westervelt. Extensively illustrated 1883 catalog exhibiting over 550 copper weathervanes and finials. Excellent primary source by one of the principal manufacturers. 104pp. 6⅛ × 9¼. 24396-6 Pa. $3.95

ART STUDENTS' ANATOMY, Edmond J. Farris. Long favorite in art schools. Basic elements, common positions, actions. Full text, 158 illustrations. 159pp. 5⅜ × 8½. 20744-7 Pa. $3.50

BRIDGMAN'S LIFE DRAWING, George B. Bridgman. More than 500 drawings and text teach you to abstract the body into its major masses. Also specific areas of anatomy. 192pp. 6½ × 9¼. (EA) 22710-3 Pa. $4.50

COMPLETE PRELUDES AND ETUDES FOR SOLO PIANO, Frederic Chopin. All 26 Preludes, all 27 Etudes by greatest composer of piano music. Authoritative Paderewski edition. 224pp. 9 × 12. (Available in U.S. only) 24052-5 Pa. $6.95

PIANO MUSIC 1888-1905, Claude Debussy. Deux Arabesques, Suite Bergamesque, Masques, 1st series of Images, etc. 9 others, in corrected editions. 175pp. 9⅜ × 12¼. (ECE) 22771-5 Pa. $5.95

TEDDY BEAR IRON-ON TRANSFER PATTERNS, Ted Menten. 80 iron-on transfer patterns of male and female Teddys in a wide variety of activities, poses, sizes. 48pp. 8¼ × 11. 24596-9 Pa. $2.00

A PICTURE HISTORY OF THE BROOKLYN BRIDGE, M.J. Shapiro. Profusely illustrated account of greatest engineering achievement of 19th century. 167 rare photos & engravings recall construction, human drama. Extensive, detailed text. 122pp. 8¼ × 11. 24403-2 Pa. $7.95

NEW YORK IN THE THIRTIES, Berenice Abbott. Noted photographer's fascinating study shows new buildings that have become famous and old sights that have disappeared forever. 97 photographs. 97pp. 11⅜ × 10. 22967-X Pa. $6.50

MATHEMATICAL TABLES AND FORMULAS, Robert D. Carmichael and Edwin R. Smith. Logarithms, sines, tangents, trig functions, powers, roots, reciprocals, exponential and hyperbolic functions, formulas and theorems. 269pp. 5⅜ × 8½. 60111-0 Pa. $3.75

HANDBOOK OF MATHEMATICAL FUNCTIONS WITH FORMULAS, GRAPHS, AND MATHEMATICAL TABLES, edited by Milton Abramowitz and Irene A. Stegun. Vast compendium: 29 sets of tables, some to as high as 20 places. 1,046pp. 8 × 10½. 61272-4 Pa. $19.95

REASON IN ART, George Santayana. Renowned philosopher's provocative, seminal treatment of basis of art in instinct and experience. Volume Four of *The Life of Reason*. 230pp. 5⅜ × 8. 24358-3 Pa. $4.50

LANGUAGE, TRUTH AND LOGIC, Alfred J. Ayer. Famous, clear introduction to Vienna, Cambridge schools of Logical Positivism. Role of philosophy, elimination of metaphysics, nature of analysis, etc. 160pp. 5⅜ × 8½. (USCO) 20010-8 Pa. $2.75

BASIC ELECTRONICS, U.S. Bureau of Naval Personnel. Electron tubes, circuits, antennas, AM, FM, and CW transmission and receiving, etc. 560 illustrations. 567pp. 6½ × 9¼. 21076-6 Pa. $8.95

THE ART DECO STYLE, edited by Theodore Menten. Furniture, jewelry, metalwork, ceramics, fabrics, lighting fixtures, interior decors, exteriors, graphics from pure French sources. Over 400 photographs. 183pp. 8⅜ × 11¼. 22824-X Pa. $6.95

THE FOUR BOOKS OF ARCHITECTURE, Andrea Palladio. 16th-century classic covers classical architectural remains, Renaissance revivals, classical orders, etc. 1738 Ware English edition. 216 plates. 110pp. of text. 9½ × 12¾. 21308-0 Pa. $10.00

THE WIT AND HUMOR OF OSCAR WILDE, edited by Alvin Redman. More than 1000 ripostes, paradoxes, wisecracks: Work is the curse of the drinking classes, I can resist everything except temptations, etc. 258pp. 5⅜ × 8½. (USCO) 20602-5 Pa. $3.50

THE DEVIL'S DICTIONARY, Ambrose Bierce. Barbed, bitter, brilliant witticisms in the form of a dictionary. Best, most ferocious satire America has produced. 145pp. 5⅜ × 8½. 20487-1 Pa. $2.50

ERTÉ'S FASHION DESIGNS, Erté. 210 black-and-white inventions from *Harper's Bazar*, 1918-32, plus 8pp. full-color covers. Captions. 88pp. 9 × 12. 24203-X Pa. $6.50

ERTÉ GRAPHICS, Erté. Collection of striking color graphics: *Seasons, Alphabet, Numerals, Aces* and *Precious Stones*. 50 plates, including 4 on covers. 48pp. 9⅜ × 12¼. 23580-7 Pa. $6.95

PAPER FOLDING FOR BEGINNERS, William D. Murray and Francis J. Rigney. Clearest book for making origami sail boats, roosters, frogs that move legs, etc. 40 projects. More than 275 illustrations. 94pp. 5⅜ × 8½. 20713-7 Pa. $1.95

ORIGAMI FOR THE ENTHUSIAST, John Montroll. Fish, ostrich, peacock, squirrel, rhinoceros, Pegasus, 19 other intricate subjects. Instructions. Diagrams. 128pp. 9 × 12. 23799-0 Pa. $4.95

CROCHETING NOVELTY POT HOLDERS, edited by Linda Macho. 64 useful, whimsical pot holders feature kitchen themes, animals, flowers, other novelties. Surprisingly easy to crochet. Complete instructions. 48pp. 8¼ × 11. 24296-X Pa. $1.95

CROCHETING DOILIES, edited by Rita Weiss. Irish Crochet, Jewel, Star Wheel, Vanity Fair and more. Also luncheon and console sets, runners and centerpieces. 51 illustrations. 48pp. 8¼ × 11. 23424-X Pa. $2.00

YUCATAN BEFORE AND AFTER THE CONQUEST, Diego de Landa. Only significant account of Yucatan written in the early post-Conquest era. Translated by William Gates. Over 120 illustrations. 162pp. 5⅜ × 8½. 23622-6 Pa. $3.50

ORNATE PICTORIAL CALLIGRAPHY, E.A. Lupfer. Complete instructions, over 150 examples help you create magnificent "flourishes" from which beautiful animals and objects gracefully emerge. 8⅛ × 11. 21957-7 Pa. $2.95

DOLLY DINGLE PAPER DOLLS, Grace Drayton. Cute chubby children by same artist who did Campbell Kids. Rare plates from 1910s. 30 paper dolls and over 100 outfits reproduced in full color. 32pp. 9¼ × 12¼. 23711-7 Pa. $2.95

CURIOUS GEORGE PAPER DOLLS IN FULL COLOR, H. A. Rey, Kathy Allert. Naughty little monkey-hero of children's books in two doll figures, plus 48 full-color costumes: pirate, Indian chief, fireman, more. 32pp. 9¼ × 12¼. 24386-9 Pa. $3.50

GERMAN: HOW TO SPEAK AND WRITE IT, Joseph Rosenberg. Like *French, How to Speak and Write It.* Very rich modern course, with a wealth of pictorial material. 330 illustrations. 384pp. 5⅜ × 8½. (USUKO) 20271-2 Pa. $4.75

CATS AND KITTENS: 24 Ready-to-Mail Color Photo Postcards, D. Holby. Handsome collection; feline in a variety of adorable poses. Identifications. 12pp. on postcard stock. 8¼ × 11. 24469-5 Pa. $2.95

MARILYN MONROE PAPER DOLLS, Tom Tierney. 31 full-color designs on heavy stock, from *The Asphalt Jungle, Gentlemen Prefer Blondes,* 22 others. 1 doll. 16 plates. 32pp. 9⅜ × 12¼. 23769-9 Pa. $3.50

FUNDAMENTALS OF LAYOUT, F.H. Wills. All phases of layout design discussed and illustrated in 121 illustrations. Indispensable as student's text or handbook for professional. 124pp. 8⅛. × 11. 21279-3 Pa. $4.50

FANTASTIC SUPER STICKERS, Ed Sibbett, Jr. 75 colorful pressure-sensitive stickers. Peel off and place for a touch of pizzazz: clowns, penguins, teddy bears, etc. Full color. 16pp. 8¼ × 11. 24471-7 Pa. $2.95

LABELS FOR ALL OCCASIONS, Ed Sibbett, Jr. 6 labels each of 16 different designs—baroque, art nouveau, art deco, Pennsylvania Dutch, etc.—in full color. 24pp. 8¼ × 11. 23688-9 Pa. $2.95

HOW TO CALCULATE QUICKLY: RAPID METHODS IN BASIC MATHEMATICS, Henry Sticker. Addition, subtraction, multiplication, division, checks, etc. More than 8000 problems, solutions. 185pp. 5 × 7¼. 20295-X Pa. $2.95

THE CAT COLORING BOOK, Karen Baldauski. Handsome, realistic renderings of 40 splendid felines, from American shorthair to exotic types. 44 plates. Captions. 48pp. 8¼ × 11. 24011-8 Pa. $2.25

THE TALE OF PETER RABBIT, Beatrix Potter. The inimitable Peter's terrifying adventure in Mr. McGregor's garden, with all 27 wonderful, full-color Potter illustrations. 55pp. 4¼ × 5½. (Available in U.S. only) 22827-4 Pa. $1.50

BASIC ELECTRICITY, U.S. Bureau of Naval Personnel. Batteries, circuits, conductors, AC and DC, inductance and capacitance, generators, motors, transformers, amplifiers, etc. 349 illustrations. 448pp. 6½ × 9¼. 20973-3 Pa. $7.95